SPATIAL COGNITION
BRAIN BASES AND DEVELOPMENT

D0732679

SPATIAL COGNITION
BRAIN BASES AND DEVELOPMENT

EDITED BY

JOAN STILES-DAVIS
UNIVERSITY OF CALIFORNIA, SAN DIEGO

MARK KRITCHEVSKY
V.A. MEDICAL CENTER, SAN DIEGO AND
UNIVERSITY OF CALIFORNIA, SAN DIEGO

URSULA BELLUGI
THE SALK INSTITUTE FOR BIOLOGICAL STUDIES

 LEA
LAWRENCE ERLBAUM ASSOCIATES, PUBLISHERS
1988 Hillsdale, New Jersey   Hove and London

Lawrence Erlbaum Associates, Inc., Publishers
365 Broadway
Hillsdale, New Jersey 07642

Library of Congress Cataloging in Publication Data

Spatial cognition : brain bases and development / edited by Joan
  Stiles-Davis, Ursula Bellugi, Mark Kritchevsky.
     p.   cm.
  Based on the Spatial Cognition Workshop held Apr. 1984 at the Salk
  Institute for Biological Studies.
  Bibliography: p.
  Includes index.
  ISBN 0-8058-0046-8.   ISBN 0-8058-0078-6 (pbk.)
  1. Space perception–Physiological aspects–Congresses. 2. Space
perception in children–Congresses. 3. Neuropsychology–Congresses.
I. Stiles-Davis, Joan. II. Bellugi, Ursula, 1931–   .
III. Kritchevsky, Mark. IV. Spatial Cognition Workshop (1984 : Salk
Institute for Biological Studies)
QP443.S63 1987
152.1′42–dc19   87-20154
                                                                 CIP

Printed in the United States of America
10 9 8 7 6 5 4 3 2 1

CONTENTS

LIST OF CONTRIBUTORS

LINDA ACREDOLO
University of California, Davis, CA

RICHARD ANDERSEN
The Salk Institute for Biological Studies, La Jolla, CA

URSULA BELLUGI
The Salk Institute for Biological Studies, La Jolla, CA

MARTHA FARAH
Carnegie Mellon University, Pittsburgh, PA

JUDITH JOHNSTON
University of Indiana, Bloomington, IN

MARK KRITCHEVSKY
V.A. Medical Center, San Diego and Department of Neurosciences,
UCSD School of Medicine

BARBARA LANDAU
Columbia University, New York, NY

LYNN S. LIBEN
The Pennsylvania State University, University Park, PA

DIANE LILLO-MARTIN
University of Connecticut, Storrs, CT

JEAN MANDLER
University of California, San Diego, CA

LISA MORROW
Western Psychiatric Institute and Clinic, Pittsburgh, PA

HELEN NEVILLE
The Salk Institute for Biological Studies, La Jolla, CA

AGELIKI NICOLOPOULOU
University of California, San Diego, CA

LAURA PETITTO
McGill University, Montreal, Canada

HERBERT PICK
University of Minnesota, Minneapolis, MI

GRAHAM RATCLIFF
Harmarville Rehabilitation Center, Pittsburgh, PA

HELENE SABO
Department of Neurology, Cornell University Medical College, New York, NY

ROGER SHEPARD
Stanford University, Stanford, CA

JOAN STILES-DAVIS
University of California, San Diego, CA

JANICE A. SWALLOW
Department of Psychology, McMaster University, Hamilton, Ontario, Canada

PAULA TALLAL
University of California, San Diego, CA

JYOTSNA VAID
Department of Psychology, Texas A&M University, College Station, TX

SANDRA F. WITELSON
McMaster University, Hamilton, Ontario, Canada

DENNIS WOLF
Harvard University, Cambridge, MA

STUART ZOLA-MORGAN
V.A. Medical Center, San Diego and Department of Psychiatry, UCSD School of Medicine

Preparation of this volume began in April 1984 with a workshop on *The Development of Spatial Cognition* held at the Neurosciences Conference Center of the Salk Institute. The workshop was sponsored by the San Diego Node of the John D. and Catherine T. MacArthur Foundation Network on "The Transition from Infancy to Childhood." The Infancy Network was established in 1982 with the intent of encouraging collaborative research efforts focused on the topic of early development. The Network is composed of five groups, or nodes, each located in a different region of the country. Within the San Diego Node the two principle areas of research emphasis have been cognitive development and the brain bases of behavior. Beginning with our early collaborations within the context of MacArthur, spatial cognition became an area of focus at San Diego.

Our motivation for holding the Workshop stemmed from a need to tie together some very different lines of research on spatial cognition that were developing. Ursula Bellugi was investigating spatial cognition in deaf children within the context of a spatially mediated language, American Sign Language. Joan Stiles-Davis was pursuing a line of evidence suggesting very early spatial cognitive deficits in young brain-damaged children. From the somewhat different perspective of adult behavioral neurology, Mark Kritchevsky was focused on spatial deficits in brain-damaged adults. The common theme that emerged from discussions centering around these very different research endeavors was the brain bases of spatial cognition, with special emphasis on the relation between cognitive and brain development. All the members of our node (Elizabeth Bates, Ursula Bellugi, Larry Fenson, Jean Mandler, Joan Stiles-Davis, and Paula Tallal) and several members of the network as a whole participated actively in the workshop.

The Spatial Cognition Workshop was organized around the major themes of development and brain bases. The questions we wanted to pursue were: First, how does spatial cognition develop within the first few years of life? That is, how do young children come to know about personal and extrapersonal space? Second, what is the relation between spatial cognition and the brain? What brain areas and processes mediate spatial understanding in the adult, and what are the biological bases of spatial cognition in the developing brain?

These themes cut across traditional research boundaries, and answers to our questions require a multidisciplinary approach.

Our aim in organizing the workshop was to bring together researchers with a common interest in spatial cognition, but who, like the research group that was organizing itself under the auspices of the MacArthur Foundation Network, represented diverse disciplines with very different perspectives and approaches. We asked scientists from disciplines as varied as cognitive, developmental, and neuropsychology, and behavioral neurology and neurobiology to meet in a single forum to discuss the early development of spatial cognition, and to exchange ideas about how findings from their own fields might be productively applied to issues of development.

The themes of the workshop are elaborated in the present volume. The discussions of the brain bases of spatial function focus principally on specifying brain areas and pathways responsible for carrying out particular spatial functions. They address the issue of whether spatial dysfunction resulting from localized brain lesions occurs in well-defined and circumscribed ways, or whether the patterns of deficit are less well defined. The discussions of this issue derive from a diverse research base, including studies of adults, children, and monkeys.

The early development of spatial cognition has begun recently to receive considerable attention within the literature on cognitive development. There is a growing body of data on the early development of a variety of spatial cognitive functions, but the literature is far from complete. We are beginning to know a lot about the early development of specific spatial skills and what we know coheres, but we do not know how to integrate the information in our accumulating data base. The discussions of spatial cognitive development in the present volume present different perspectives within the developmental literature, and offer views from researchers working with populations with various neurological and sensory disorders.

Preparation for the book actually began at the workshop. For each session scribes took extensive notes on presentations and discussions. In addition, all sessions were tape recorded, and the recordings later transcribed. Using the conference material as a basis, we then developed a plan for the book. The volume includes adapted and extended versions of papers presented at the conference, but it goes beyond those papers and includes contributions from other major figures in the various fields. To integrate the chapters, we went over each one with the contributors and suggested major revisions. The contributors have revised each of the chapters and in some cases re-revised them to unify the set of chapters into a cohesive whole for the purposes of the book.

The preparation for this book was funded by a special grant from the MacArthur Foundation Network on "The Transition from Infancy to Early Childhood." We are especially grateful to Robert Emde, Jerry Kagan and the Network Publications Committee for their support in helping us bring these diverse strands together. We would like to thank Jonas Salk for his enthusiastic support of this multidisciplinary effort. We are grateful for the participation of each contributor to this volume, and thank them for their patience and effort in the process. Finally we thank Angela Cohen and Brenda Hillier for their assistance in the typing and editing of this volume.

This book, *Spatial Cognition: Brain Bases and Development*, and the conference it reports are of great interest not only for the importance of the subject matter but also for the approach to understanding complex cognitive and brain functions. For understanding such phenomena we now recognize the need to integrate the perceptions from scientists in many related disciplines including neurobiology, psychobiology, psychoneurobiology, developmental neurobiology, linguistics, and psycholinguistics. The relationship between brain, mind, and behavior will be revealed only through creative integration of the knowledge and wisdom of those engaged in the study of such phenomena. This volume shows how the spiral of understanding grows to reveal the mysteries of the development of the human spatial cognition.

It is significant that the conference from which this book emerged was held at the Neuroscience Conference Center of The Salk Institute for Biological Studies, reflecting the trend in seeking the biological basis for understanding relationships between brain, mind and behavior. It is also encouraging to see the fruitfulness of the John D. and Catherine T. MacArthur Foundation support for creative collaboration among scientists in cross-disciplinary networks for developing a better understanding of ourselves in the natural scheme of things.

The organizer and contributors to this volume have added importantly to an elucidation of Spatial Cognition, and they have done so in a creative and effective way.

Jonas Salk

PART I

SPATIAL COGNITION IN ADULTS

Our knowledge of spatial cognition comes in large part from studying the spatial abilities of normal adults and the patterns of spatial dysfunction of adults with brain damage. The chapters in this section summarize much of these data so that they can be related to the development of spatial cognition in the normal child and in the child with a different early experience.

In the first chapter, Lisa Morrow and Graham Ratcliff provide an extensive discussion of the neuropsychological abnormalities of spatial cognition which are seen in brain damaged adults. They review recent literature on the effects of localized brain injury on spatial cognition. The emphasis of their discussion is on the dissociation of cognitive functions in the brain, and the specification of brain mechanisms that underlie different facets of spatial cognition.

In the next chapter, Martha Farah discusses the spatial cognitive process of mental image generation. Farah focuses on a componential analysis of imagery to investigate the neurological bases of image generation. She reviews data on patients with deficits of mental imagery and suggests that those cases with specific deficits of image generation have left posterior hemisphere lesions. Further studies, including a recent case report, experiments in split brain patients and tachistoscopic studies of normal adults support the view that the left hemisphere plays an important role in the process of mental image generation.

In the next chapter, Richard Andersen describes the anatomy and physiology of the parietal lobe and presents important new evidence concerning the role of the parietal lobe in spatial cognition. Andersen shows that there are multiple cortical areas within the inferior parietal lobule which appear to be specialized for the processing of different aspects of spatial perception. In particular, he discusses recent landmark data from single cell recordings of electrical activity in behaving monkeys that the inferior parietal lobule is involved in the transformation of retinal coordinates into true spatial egocentric/body centered coordinates. There is also evidence that the inferior parietal lobule is involved in attention.

In his chapter, Roger Shepard presents the role of transformations in spatial cognition. The position of a rigid object in space can be described by six parameters—the three rectangular coordinates of its center of gravity and three angular coordinates describing its orientation in space. The position of an object can then be represented by a point in a non-Euclidean six-dimensional manifold. He shows that in apparent motion and mental rotation experiments normal adults perform as though objects undergo rigid displacements along some shortest path of least action in this manifold. This implies that there are internalized constraints concerning motion of rigid objects. Shepard analyzes relevant data to determine just what these internalized constraints are. This is equivalent to determining the psychological metric of the six-dimensional manifold.

In the final chapter of this section, Mark Kritchevsky proposes a model of spatial cognition. In this model he outlines a set of modality independent elementary spatial functions which can be defined by the discrete patterns of spatial dysfunction seen in patients with brain damage. The elementary spatial functions described are (a) spatial perceptual functions of object localization, line orientation detection and spatial synthesis; (b) spatial short-term and long-term memory; (c) spatial attention to right and left hemispace; (d) spatial mental operations; and (e) spatial construction. The right parietal lobe is shown to be crucial for many of these functions, and the role of other brain structures in spatial cognition is elaborated. Examples are then given of how these elementary spatial functions can easily and effectively be used in the analysis of more complex behaviors.

In this section, spatial cognition in the normal and brain damaged adult is approached from neuropsychological, neurophysiological, psychological, and neurobehavioral perspectives. The chapters demonstrate that there is a well-defined neuroanatomic basis for the components of spatial behavior and that focal brain damage will cause very specific patterns of breakdown. There are internalized constraints concerning at least some of the components of spatial behavior as well. This data base and general scheme should prove helpful in the analysis of spatial behavior in the developing child and in children with different early experiences.

NEUROPSYCHOLOGY OF SPATIAL COGNITION: EVIDENCE FROM CEREBRAL LESIONS

1

LISA MORROW
Western Psychiatric Institute and Clinic

GRAHAM RATCLIFF
Harmarville Rehabilitation Center

INTRODUCTION

There is ample evidence that spatial knowledge is a separate component of human intelligence, distinct from verbal and analytic aspects (Thurstone, 1938). This "spatial factor" is not, however, a unidimensional concept, but includes the ability to represent and organize the surrounding environment into a coherent spatial framework, to integrate visual percepts, to attend to specific locations in space, and to manipulate objects, either visually or tactually. The skill, or skills, necessary to carry out these spatial tasks may vary across measures, as well as individuals (McGee, 1979; Lohman, 1979; Cooper, 1984). For example, reading a map or finding one's way around a new environment does not tap the same "spatial skills" as imagining how an object would look if it were rotated through 90 degrees.

Cognitive psychologists have usually investigated spatial processes in individuals with intact nervous systems, typically working within a developmental, psychometric, or information-processing framework. A very different approach has been taken by clinical neuropsychologists. Rather than looking at these processes as they occur normally, neuropsychologists examine spatial disorders resulting from cerebral damage. Until recently, the majority of research on spatial cognition in neuropsychology was descriptive and focused mainly on cerebral localization of function. However, neuropsychologists are now beginning to approach spatial disorders from a more

"cognitive" or "information-processing" position. Simply knowing
that left unilateral neglect follows posterior right hemisphere lesions
does not tell us anything about the specific mechanism(s) responsible, nor how these mechanisms operate to produce the symptom.
Thus, the goal today in neuropsychology is to identify the particular
processes which are disrupted after cerebral damage and determine
how these processes relate to specific neural substrates or neural systems. The purpose of this chapter is to provide an overview of previous work on visuospatial disorders that result from cerebral lesions
and to highlight the current research being carried out in this field.

EARLY WORK ON VISUOSPATIAL DISORDERS

One of the earliest accounts of visuospatial disorders following brain
damage was published by Hughlings Jackson in 1876. He described
a woman with a left hemiplegia who was suddenly unable to find her
way to a nearby park, a journey she had been making for over 30
years. In addition, she had difficulty dressing, recognizing objects,
and identifying familiar persons, disorders we would refer to today
as dressing apraxia, visual agnosia and prosopagnosia, respectively.
Jackson labeled this cluster of impairments "imperception, a defect
as special as aphasia" (p. 438).

Neurologists continued to document similar deficits in subsequent
case histories. Badal (1888) discussed a patient who had a cluster of
spatial deficits—dressing apraxia, errors in copying and drawing pictures from memory, failure to reach for and localize objects accurately, and problems with route finding. Cases were also reported in
which there was loss of only a single spatial ability. Forster (1890)
described a patient whose sole deficit seemed to be a disruption of
topographical orientation. Visual recognition, drawing, and
language functions were all intact but the learning and recall of spatial arrangement was impaired. The patient was unable to describe
or draw the spatial layout of his office or home, and could no longer
locate well-known city landmarks. New spatial learning was also
compromised: even after 3 weeks he was unable to demonstrate any
knowledge of the spatial layout of his hospital room, and became lost
going from his room to the washroom next door.

Visual disturbances were also reported to play an important role
in spatial disorders. Balint (1909) described a patient who tended to
fixate his gaze to the right half-field, with a corresponding inattention to stimuli situated in the left half-field. In addition, visually
guided movements with his right hand in both fields were particu-

larly impaired. Extraocular movements and visual fields were described as normal. Ten years later, Holmes (1919) gave a detailed description of similar disorders of visual orientation. Unlike Balint's case, Holmes's patients were found to have impaired ocular movements, as well as defective visual-guided reaching. They failed to maintain fixation and could not accurately move their eyes directly to a new target, although there was no actual paralysis of gaze. Holmes considered that these difficulties were due to a loss of "local sign" information—a disturbance of the ability to locate the position of the stimulus which was to be the target of the hand or eye movement.

Although reports of perceptual and spatial deficits resulting from brain lesions continued to appear during this time, inconsistencies in terminology from author to author make it difficult to compare their reports. Most researchers in the field recognized that the loss of spatial skills was distinct from aphasia, but the fact that the damage causing spatial disorders usually included the posterior half of the right hemisphere was rarely noted in the literature. This failure to appreciate the significance of right hemisphere involvement may have occurred because, unlike most other spatial deficits, a bilateral lesion is required to produce the florid symptoms of Balint's syndrome and visual disorientation as described by Holmes. However, it is interesting to note that Jackson hypothesized that the posterior lobes were the seat of visual ideation and that the "right posterior lobe is the 'leading' side, the left the more automatic" (Jackson, 1876, p. 438).

It was not until Zangwill and his colleagues published a series of papers on *groups* of patients with right hemisphere lesions that the crucial role of the right hemisphere in spatial disorders was emphasized (Ettlinger, Warrington & Zangwill, 1957; McFie, Piercy & Zangwill, 1950; Paterson & Zangwill, 1944). McFie et al. (1950) described eight patients who displayed a variety of spatial impairments: 3 had disturbances in right-left orientation, 4 were apraxic for dressing, 5 were impaired on topographical orientation, 6 failed to attend to the left half of space, 6 had oculomotor deficits, 7 had visual field impairments, and all had deficits in constructional apraxia (impaired drawings or block construction). The authors described this class of disorders as an "inability to apprehend or reproduce all but the simplest visual spatial relationships,...[as well as] a peculiar restriction and fragmentation of visual perception in its spatial aspects" (p. 186). This was particularly noticeable when one patient was asked to reproduce, from memory, the layout of his house (see Figure 1.1). The drawing produced lacked a

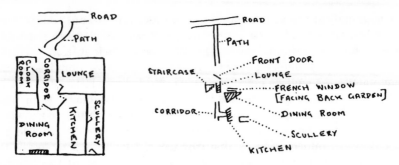

Figure 1.1. Drawing of a floor plan made by a patient with a right fronto-parietal tumor. The correct arrangement is shown on the left. The labels were added to the patient's drawing. (Redrawn from McFie et al., 1950).

coherent framework, and the various landmarks were placed randomly with no regard for their relative positions in space. This drawing is a particularly good example of the most salient feature in this group of patients: the inability to recognize or order the spatial relations of objects.

The clinical literature has continued to provide evidence that disruption of certain neural substrates in the right hemisphere can cause impairments in perceptual matching, drawing, dressing, attention to spatial coordinates, route finding, construction, spatial exploration, memory for spatial locations, and face and object recognition (cf. De Renzi, 1982). However, the very diversity of these deficits has tended to create problems with their interpretation. One of the major impediments has been the terminology employed to describe spatial disorders. As noted earlier, Jackson (1876) coined the term "imperception" to describe the symptoms he published. Neurologists following Jackson seemed to be most concerned with their patients' inability to identify objects by sight and adopted such terms as "asemia," "asymbolia," "mindblindness," and "visual agnosia" to describe these phenomena (Nielsen, 1937). The term "visual-spatial agnosia" was added to these in order to designate the independence of object agnosia from the spatial impairments frequently reported in these patients. Today visuospatial agnosia, besides losing the hyphen, has come to denote any or all of the following: unilateral neglect, constructional apraxia, topographical disorientation, impaired memory for spatial locations, and the inability to locate objects accurately. It does not, however, include the ability to *identify* objects, a distinct deficit for which the term visual agnosia has survived (see Ratcliff & Newcombe, 1982, for review).

Visuospatial agnosia, as it is used currently, is basically a grab bag term for the clinical manifestation of spatial disorders occurring after right hemisphere lesions (Ratcliff, 1982). However, it is becoming increasingly clear that the general category of "perceptual and spatial disorders" may be fractionated into distinct deficits. Furthermore, current research is providing clues as to the neural systems involved, as well as implicating specific cognitive processes which may limit performance on spatial tasks.

THE TWO CORTICAL VISUAL SYSTEMS

One major distinction which can be drawn from the clinical literature is the separation of "perceptual" disorders from those which are obviously "spatial." There is striking evidence from both animal and human studies for a behavioral and anatomical dissociation between perceptual recognition and spatial orientation. Mishkin and his colleagues have shown that in primates, lesions involving two separate cortical pathways, one occipito-temporal, the other occipito-parietal, result in distinct impairments on two behavioral measures (Mishkin, Ungerleider & Macko, 1983; Mishkin & Ungerleider, 1982; Ungerleider & Mishkin, 1982; Ungerleider, 1985). These two cortical pathways are now referred to as the "two cortical visual systems," and the research to date indicates that the temporal cortex is involved in recognizing *what* objects are, while the parietal cortex predominates in determining *where* they are located.

Converging studies in the clinical literature have found a similar dissociation in humans. Newcombe and Russell (1969) administered both a perceptual test (visual closure), and a spatial test (maze learning) to patients with penetrating missile wounds, and reported a double dissociation in performance. They found that patients with lesions involving the inferior temporal lobe were impaired on the facial recognition test but could easily learn the maze, whereas, those patients with lesions limited to the parietal cortex had no difficulty recognizing faces, but were significantly impaired on the maze test. A more recent study has also found that patients with lesions involving the right medial temporal lobe perform poorly when asked to identify perceptually degraded stimuli (Wasserstein, Zapulla, Rosen & Gerstman, 1984).

Similar findings have been reported with respect to a loss of imagery (Levine, Warach & Farah, 1985). These authors described two patients who showed a dissociation between visual-object imagery and visual-spatial imagery. Although both patients had bilateral posterior lesions, in one case the damage was more inferior and included the right temporal area, while the second case had more posterior parietal damage. The patient with the temporal lesion had difficulty recognizing objects and a corresponding deficit in object-color imagery, but showed no problems locating objects in space or finding his way around. His spatial imagery was also excellent; that is, he could give detailed descriptions of how to get from one place to another. On the other hand, the patient with the parietal lesion had no difficulty in recognizing objects shown to him and demonstrated an equally intact ability to imagine properties of animals or faces. He was, however, very impaired in locating objects, and could not accurately reach for an object or determine the relative position of two objects. In addition, he got lost in his own home and reported no spatial imagery. That is, he could not describe the route from his home to the corner store, a journey he had made for over 5 years prior to his illness. Based on these findings, the authors have suggested that just as object recognition and spatial orientation are behaviorally and anatomically distinct, disorders of visual-object imagery and spatial-imagery may be clinically and anatomically separate.

A case of agenesis of the corpus callosum has recently been reported which bears special relevance to the two visual systems and their contribution to the analysis of spatial information (Martin, 1985). In cases of agenesis of the corpus callosum interhemispheric communication is thought to occur via the anterior commissure. This structure transfers information between the two temporal lobes and is often overdeveloped in these patients. In a series of tachistoscopic tasks, Martin found that when words were flashed to the left hemisphere they were identified quicker than when those same words were flashed to the right hemisphere. An efficient transfer of visual information to the left hemisphere speech mechanisms was suggested, since the patient was able to name words which were only seen by the right hemisphere. However, when required to identify the *location* of letters, the left hemisphere was quite inaccurate when compared to the right hemisphere's performance. This would suggest that the "what" information was transferred more efficiently between the hemispheres than the "where" information. Martin interprets this as indicating that the anterior commissure was available to transfer information from a right temporal "what" system, whereas the right parietal "where" system was isolated by the absence of the posterior portion of the corpus callosum which normally connects these regions. Thus, his results provide support for the notion of two cortical visual systems subserving different aspects of vision.

THE NATURE OF SPATIAL IMPAIRMENT

The experimental evidence to date seems to suggest that the right parietal lobe deals with information about the spatial aspect of objects rather than identifying what they are. We next need to define more precisely the nature of this spatial dominance. Certainly, some restrictions do apply. First, the right parietal lobe seems to be more involved in disturbances of *extrapersonal space,* as opposed to *personal space.* Disorders of personal space are characterized by a confusion in right-left orientation, or by an inability to identify specific body parts (autotopagnosia), and are more common after left hemisphere damage (Butters, Soeldner & Fedio, 1972; Gerstmann, 1958; Sauguet, Benton & Hecaen, 1971; Semmes, Weinstein, Ghent & Teuber, 1963).

A second distinction is that the right hemisphere does not bear exclusive responsibility for the localization of single points in space with respect to the body, a function which Benton (1969) has described as "absolute localization" as opposed to "relative localization." Ratcliff and Davies-Jones (1972) demonstrated that parietal lesions of either hemisphere produce a corresponding deficit in localizing targets (via pointing) in the contralateral half-field. Moreover, they found this disorder to be equally common after right or left sided lesions. It is important to note that the patients who manifested this impairment didn't always have problems with other spatial tasks. This disorder, even though having a "spatial" component, seems to occur at relatively early stages of visual processing and may be unrelated to the difficulties these patients experience when solving more complex spatial tasks. It has also been hypothesized that certain low-level sensory analyses (e.g. brightness or contour) are carried out equally well by either hemisphere, and that it is only when the task requires a higher level, more complex analysis of the spatial components that the right hemisphere comes into play (Moscovitch, 1979; Young & Ratcliff, 1983).

A final point we would like to stress is that differences in task demands may play a crucial role in determining performance on spatial measures. That is, the spatial task itself is very likely to involve a number of cognitive processes (e.g., attention, or working memory), each of which may be differentially affected by various cerebral lesions. Furthermore, different tasks may involve these individual cognitive processes in varying degrees. Take, for example, constructional apraxia, defined as the inability to produce spatially coherent drawings or block arrangements. In order to correctly carry out such a complex task as copying a figure or drawing an object from memory, a number of component processes must all be functioning smoothly. An impairment in any number of operations (e.g., visual scanning, working memory, eye-hand coordination), can, in themselves, result in a less than perfect outcome.

Constructional apraxia was first thought to occur mainly after left hemisphere lesions (Kleist, 1934). Today, this disorder is usually assumed to be a sign of a right posterior lesion, and in most instances this assumption is correct. However, damage to either hemisphere can result in constructional apraxia, though qualitative differences in performance exist.

Figure 1.2 shows freehand drawings of a bicycle made by patients with lesions involving either the right or left hemisphere. Obviously, all are poorly drawn but performances are qualitatively different and probably not due to a deficit of the same underlying mechanism. Studies designed to analyze these qualitative differences have shown that drawings produced by patients with right hemisphere lesions tend to be piecemeal, unorganized, fragmented, and have parts missing on the left side, while patients with lesions confined to the left hemisphere produce drawings which preserve the actual spatial relationship but they are painstakingly executed, oversimplified, and have parts left out (cf. Warrington, 1969). Most authors speculate that the constructional difficulties manifested by patients with right hemisphere lesions are due either to a scanning or attentional deficit, or a failure to code the elements into a coherent spatial framework (Brain, 1941; Gainotti & Tiacci, 1970; Piercy, Hecaen & Ajuriaguerra, 1960), while the deficits displayed by patients with left hemisphere damage are due either to a general intellectual impairment, a deficiency in motor programming, or a practic deficit (Hecaen & Assal, 1970; LeDoux, Wilson & Gazzaniga, 1977; McFie & Zangwill, 1960; Warrington, James & Kinsbourne, 1966). There is, however, evidence which suggests that the practic component may not be the sole reason for the left hemisphere lesioned patient's failure on constructional tests. Several authors have noted that even when motor movements are controlled, left hemisphere patients may still perform poorly on certain perceptual tests (Arena & Gainotti, 1978; Dee, 1970; Kim, Morrow, Passafiume & Boller, 1984).

In his doctoral dissertation, John Green (Green, 1971) hypothesized that the qualitative performance differences found on constructional tasks between left and right hemisphere lesioned patients might be related to two basic perceptual factors which had been documented in the psychometric literature: perceptual integration and perceptual differentiation. Administering a series of visuoperceptual tests modified for tachistoscopic presentation, he found

Left-sided Lesions   Right-sided Lesions

Figure 1.2. Freehand drawings of bicycles made by patients with left and right hemisphere lesions. Drawings on the left are those done by left hemisphere cases and those on the right by right hemisphere cases. (Redrawn from McFie & Zangwill, 1960).

evidence of three factors, the two hypothesized, as well as a third factor labeled "visualization." Tests which loaded on the first factor, perceptual integration, required the determination of a complete figure from two fragmented pictures. Tests which loaded on perceptual differentiation required, for example, the identification of overlapping figures. The third factor, visualization, included tests which required parts to be mentally rearranged with respect to one another. Analysis of factor scores revealed that patients with right hemisphere lesions involving either the anterior or posterior cortex were impaired on tests which loaded on the integration factor. Anterior and posterior lesions of *both* hemispheres impaired performance on tests of perceptual differentiation, whereas right hemisphere lesions involving only the posterior cortex impaired performance on tests of visualization.

Green postulated that this between group difference reflected the differential cortical organization of these spatial components. The ability to differentiate perceptual stimuli into their component parts is a function of the entire cortex. Evidence for that is provided by the fact that both right and left lesioned groups performed comparably on tests which loaded on perceptual differentiation. The ability to integrate stimuli into wholes, and to manipulate or transform complex visual stimuli, is a function of the right hemisphere, signified by this group's lowered scores on tests of perceptual integration and visualization. Thus, the qualitative differences between left and right hemisphere lesioned patients on constructional tasks may be due to the differential cortical representation of these component processes, all of which operate to produce a coherent, spatially integrated design.

DISORDERS OF TOPOGRAPHICAL ORIENTATION

For the most part, neuropsychologists investigating spatial disorders confine themselves to research in small-scale space—asking the patient to sit down at a desk and draw a picture, learn a maze, or recall the spatial locations of objects. We know relatively little about the effects of spatial disorders in large-scale space—the space that surrounds the individual and cannot be viewed in its entirety from a single vantage point (for a more detailed review of small and large scale differences see Acredolo, 1981). It would seem especially crucial to investigate topographical impairments with respect to the large-scale environment, since in many instances the patients complain of getting lost in their home or city and this can be the first sign of cerebral dysfunction. Defective route finding refers to the inability to find one's way around a new environment (Benton, 1969), while topographical memory loss or topographical amnesia refers to an impairment in recalling previously familiar routes (De Renzi, Faglioni & Villa, 1977; Hecaen, Tzortzis & Rondot, 1980), and topographical disorientation is a term used to describe either or both (Paterson & Zangwill, 1945).

The inability to learn new routes is often associated with posterior *unilateral* lesions of the right hemisphere, and may be due to a faulty appreciation of spatial relations, inability to recognize and recall significant landmarks, or the result of a left side neglect or a confusion in making left and right turns (Brain, 1941; Hecaen et al., 1980; Pallis, 1955; Whiteley & Warrington, 1978). Patients who become lost in previously familiar surroundings typically have posterior *bilateral* lesions, and the deficit is likely to be related to a memory disorder, or as Benton (1969) defined it: "a failure to recall and describe familiar routes or...a failure to retrieve long established visual memories" (p. 219). A mislocalization of cities or states on a map has also been associated with a disturbance in topographical knowledge, though most errors of this sort are related to contralateral neglect or the patient's educational level (Benton, Levin & Van Allen, 1974).

The two procedures most frequently used to assess topographical orientation in the clinic are locomotor maze and stylus maze tests. The *locomotor maze test* (Semmes, Weinstein, Ghent & Teuber, 1955) is the only formal test used to investigate topographical orientation in a more or less large-scale environment. This test consists of giving the patient a map which corresponds to markers laid out on the floor and having the patient follow specific paths indicated on the map. *Visually guided stylus mazes* (Milner, 1965; Newcombe & Russell, 1969) are learning tests in which the patient sits in front of a square apparatus consisting of a matrix of raised blocks or bolt heads, and must either find a specific route through the matrix or retrace a path previously demonstrated by the examiner. An early study conducted by Semmes and her colleagues found that a lesion involving either the left or right parietal lobe impaired performance on the locomotor test (Semmes et al., 1955). The authors later reanalyzed the data according to whether the lesion was anterior or posterior, as opposed to the lobe involved, and demonstrated that both unilateral and bilateral posterior lesions resulted in lowered performance (Semmes et al., 1963). A similar study by Ratcliff and Newcombe (1973), using both the locomotor and stylus maze, found only patients with posterior bilateral lesions to be impaired on the locomotor maze, while their right posterior group was impaired on the stylus maze. They reported several patients who exemplified this dissociation: one patient with a right posterior lesion failed to learn the stylus maze in 25 trials, but made only one error on the locomotor maze test, while a patient with a posterior bilateral lesion was able to reach criterion on the stylus maze in only 5 trials, but made 40 errors on the locomotor maze test.

Those inconsistencies which do exist in the literature relating lesion site and locomotor performance may relate to the differences in groups studied (missile wound vs. strokes), as well as to the method of administering the task, since some authors have used idiosyncratic modifications. A number of other investigators who have administered variants of the stylus maze learning test have consistently found that the most impaired patients are those with right sided damage, typically in the posterior area (De Renzi et al., 1977; Corkin, 1965; Hecaen et al., 1980). The evidence so far suggests that a unilateral lesion on the right side impairs performance on a stylus maze while in most cases a bilateral lesion is necessary to hamper the ability to perform a locomotor maze. We would like to suggest, though, that the reason patients become lost in the real world may be due to a number of factors: neglect, failure to appreciate spatial relations, inability to orient using the body as a frame of reference, or simply a failure to employ the appropriate strategy. Strategies may be especially crucial. Hecaen et al. (1980) reported a patient who had great difficulty finding his way around, not recognizing streets and becoming confused at intersections, although he could give very good verbal descriptions of routes. In the clinic he was unable to learn the stylus maze and could only perform a variant of the locomotor maze when he was provided with verbally codable landmarks along the route. Whitty and Newcombe (1973) reported a patient who, 30 years after a right parietal lesion, had regained the ability to find his way from his home to his office by means of verbal mediation and memorization of detailed cues related to significant landmarks.

Thus far, we have emphasized the crucial role of the right hemisphere in spatial functions, and have argued that this dominance occurs for relatively complex tasks in extrapersonal space. Furthermore, lesions outside the right parietal area may produce deficits on spatial tasks but these are, for the most part, qualitatively distinct from those seen following damage to the right posterior cortex. Several other points should also be noted. First, spatial deficits are not limited to the visual modality, but can occur on tactile (Chedru, 1976; Corkin, 1965; De Renzi, Faglioni & Scotti, 1968, 1970;

Faglioni, Scotti & Spinnler, 1971; Teuber, 1963) as well as auditory tasks (Bisiach, Cornacchia, Sterzi & Vallar, 1984; Heilman & Valenstein, 1972a). Second, while it has been demonstrated that patients with right hemisphere lesions and visual field defects perform more poorly on spatial tasks than those without field defects, it is probably not the field defect per se which is primarily responsible for the deficit. Most lesions which are associated with spatial impairments tend to occur very near the optic radiation, and thus produce a high incidence of visual field defects. In support of this are associations between visual field defects and poor performance on tactile tasks (Chedru, 1976; De Renzi & Scotti, 1969; De Renzi et al., 1970). Such findings cannot then be explained by a visual failure.

Finally, just as there are lesions outside the right parietal area which result in impaired performance on spatial tasks, there are also tasks which are not entirely spatial but are frequently found to be impaired in these patients. These tasks usually employ stimuli which are perceptually difficult, such as overlapping drawings (Kimura, 1963; De Renzi & Spinnler, 1966), degraded figures (Lansdell, 1968; Warrington & James, 1967), or unusual views of objects (Warrington & Taylor, 1973). As we will see in the final section of this chapter, it may be the cognitive, rather than the perceptual level, which underlies the right hemisphere's involvement.

UNILATERAL NEGLECT

In many instances of posterior brain injury, patients confronted with stimuli presented to the side contralateral to their lesion behave as if they had not perceived that stimulus. This syndrome of unilateral neglect, or hemi-inattention, is a very common occurrence, and manifests itself in a variety of behavioral symptoms (cf. Heilman, 1979). Patients may deny the existence of the contralateral side of their body, orient away from their affected side, fail to move their contralateral arm even in the absence of motor deficits, or they may produce drawings that have one side missing, or have parts misplaced. A copy of the Rey-Osterrieth figure, made by one of our patients with left-side neglect, is shown in Figure 1.3. The patient's drawing has all of the features of the right side present but none from the left side.

There have been numerous reports of such cases in the literature. A case reported by Battersby, Bender, Pollack and Kahn (1956) gives some insight into the typical findings and clinical course of patients with neglect. This particular individual (Mr. B.) presented with a

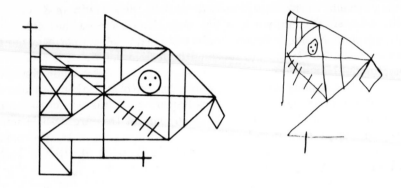

Figure 1.3. The Rey-Osterrieth Complex Figure and a copy attempted by a patient with left side neglect.

left homonymous hemianopsia, and failed to localize sounds to his left, or look to left on command. He ignored people when they spoke to him from his left side, and his drawings had features of the left side missing. He read only the right side of phrases, and his descriptions of objects were limited to the right side. During the course of recovery the patient's clinical signs of neglect rapidly cleared, but there remained a left-side visual field defect. The following protocol was reported after all clinical symptoms had cleared:

> The last time I read these things (phrases), I would start at the left and jump all the way over to the right. (Why did you do that Mr. B.?). I don't know, what with the left side being so bad and all, I just didn't want to look that way. You know my wife accused me of ignoring her, she was on my left talking to me and I didn't even answer her. (Why didn't you talk to her Mr. B.?) I don't know, it's just that that side was so bad (Battersby et al., p. 87).

The pervasive features of neglect are quite remarkable, and severe neglect is usually transient, appearing only in the acute phase. The responsible lesions are normally located in the posterior section of the right hemisphere, accounting for the predominance of left sided neglect.

It is also important to note that neglect can occur in the absence of sensory and motor deficits. Patients with dense hemianopia may exhibit no signs of neglect, while individuals with severe neglect may have no visual field cut (McFie et al, 1950; Rosenberger, 1974). Likewise, patients' failure to use their affected arm or turn their head to the neglected side cannot be due to a peripheral deficit, because in many instances they may have strength in both arms and full extraocular movements. It seems to be more of a "reluctance rather than an inability" (Friedland & Weinstein, 1977, p. 3).

Theories of Neglect

A number of theories have been postulated to explain the nature of the neglect syndrome. Early theorists thought neglect was primarily due to a failure of the sensory system (Battersby et al., 1956; Denny-Brown, Meyer & Horenstein, 1952; McFie et al., 1950). The interhemispheric transfer theory proposed by Kinsbourne (1970; 1977) suggests that patients are forced to direct attention to the ipsilateral side due to an alteration of inhibitory mechanisms. According to this theory, when a lesion occurs in one hemisphere there is a release of inhibition, allowing the opposite hemisphere to bias behavior toward the ipsilateral side. Consequently, neglect is brought about by excessive orienting toward the lesion side.

Heilman and his associates have advanced an attention-arousal hypothesis which suggests that neglect is due to a unilateral disruption of a corticolimbic-reticular loop (Heilman & Valenstein, 1979; Heilman & Watson, 1977; Heilman, 1979). This hypothesis proposes that the manifestations of neglect are due to decreased arousal, concomitant with a defect in the orienting response. In the intact hemisphere, when a novel or meaningful stimulus activates awareness there is an orienting reflex (Sokolov, 1963). This orienting reflex is controlled by the reticular formation which has projections to the cortex. Each hemisphere is proposed to have its own cortico-reticular loop, and any lesion disrupting this loop causes a unilateral deficit in the orienting responses by means of a reduction in arousal. A number of ablation studies in animals have supported this by demonstrating that lesions in the reticular formation produce unilateral neglect (Watson, Heilman, Cauthen & King, 1973; Watson, Heilman, Miller & King, 1974). In addition to animal studies, several cases of neglect following damage to the right frontal area have been reported, suggesting disruptions of connections to the limbic system (Heilman & Valenstein, 1972b; Van Der Linden, Seron, Gillet & Bredart 1980).

To explain the more prevalent findings of neglect following right hemisphere lesions, Heilman and Valenstein (1979) postulate that the mediation of arousal is *asymmetrical*. That is, the right hemisphere is able to attend to stimuli bilaterally, while the left hemisphere attends only to stimuli in the contralateral hemifield. Left hemisphere lesions are less likely to produce neglect because of the ability of the intact right hemisphere to mediate arousal to ipsilateral stimuli. Support for the notion of greater right hemisphere involvement in the mediation of arousal has been provided by a number of studies. Patients with right hemisphere lesions have been found to have arousal deficits, in the sense that they have virtually no galvanic skin response to either mild electric shock or affective stimuli (Heilman, Schwartz & Watson, 1978; Morrow, Vrtunski, Kim & Boller, 1981; Zoccolotti, Scabini & Violani, 1982). In addition, reaction time studies have found right hemisphere lesions produce greater slowing than left side lesions (De Renzi & Faglioni, 1965; Howes & Boller, 1975). Evidence for the dominance of the right hemisphere in mediating attention bilaterally has also been suggested in studies with nonlesioned subjects (Heilman & Van Den Abell, 1979; Verfaellie, Bowers, Williams & Heilman, 1985). However, this has not been replicated in younger subjects (see Shapiro & Hynd, 1985), and in a small sample of commissurotomy patients Plourde and Sperry (1984) found the left hemisphere *could* attend to the left half of space.

If neglect is an attention-arousal deficit, as proposed by Heilman (1979), this presupposes a differential hemispheric organization of attention, with the right hemisphere being the dominant side. However, if the right hemisphere is more involved in mediating arousal/ attention to both sides of space, why isn't there a subsequent bilateral neglect after right hemisphere damage? Conversely, if the causal mechanism of neglect is due to a release of inhibition, as suggested by Kinsbourne (1977), why don't left hemisphere lesions produce more cases of right sided neglect? One way to reconcile these differences might be a combination of the two theories. If we assume the right hemisphere plays a dominant role in mediating attention, and is specialized to deal with spatial information, we might conclude that the right hemisphere is better able to *represent* and attend to the entire spatial field. Neglect is necessarily an inattention to space and it may be the disruption of this spatial representation ability that underlies neglect. In addition, if there is also a release of inhibition after right hemisphere damage, as suggested by Kinsbourne (1970; 1977), the left hemisphere should be able to invoke its lowered, albeit adequate attentional mechanisms, therefore sustaining attention to the right hemifield.

A Cognitive Approach to Attentional Deficits

Recent research from Michael Posner's laboratory has begun to elucidate possible mechanisms which may play a role in the neglect syndrome. For a number of years Posner and his colleagues have been investigating the operations involved in the orienting of attention, which has both "overt" and "covert" components (cf. Posner, 1980). For example, when a signal in the environment alerts an organism, there is usually movement of the head and eyes in the direction of the stimulus—an overt alignment of attention. However, attention can be directed to the environmental stimulus without any physical movement—a covert alignment of attention. In order to measure covert attention, Posner and his associates have designed a reaction time task where subjects must detect the presence of a bright asterisk which occurs at various spatial locations within the visual field. Three boxes are displayed on a video display terminal, a central box and two peripheral boxes. On each trial one of the three boxes cues attention by brightening and is subsequently followed by a target stimulus plotted in one of the two peripheral boxes. Subjects are required to maintain fixation at center and to press a key as quickly as possible when the target appears.

Trials can be either valid, invalid or neutral. A valid trial, which occurs the majority of the time, consists of a cue occurring in one of the peripheral boxes followed by the target in the same box. An invalid trial is one in which the cue occurs in a peripheral box and the target appears in the box on the opposite side. On neutral trials, the center box is the cue and the target occurs with equal frequency in either the left or right box. Findings with normal subjects have shown a facilitation to targets which are preceded by cues in the same spatial location; that is, reaction times to expected targets are significantly shorter than reaction times to targets which are preceded by invalid or neutral cues, presumably because the cue has covertly drawn attention to the appropriate location (Posner, Nissen & Ogden, 1977). Using the same basic paradigm of target detection, Posner (1980) replaced the cued condition of brightening one of the three boxes with a cue which was a central arrow pointing either left or right (endogenous cue). On most trials the arrow correctly indicated which side would produce the target stimulus. When the arrow was followed by a target in the indicated direction, facilitation effects were found, thus demonstrating that endogenous stimuli are equally effective in summoning attention to various spatial locations.

Studies such as these with normals have led Posner and his colleagues to suggest that shifts of visual attention are composed of three successive mental operation, *disengage, move,* and *engage* (cf. Posner, Walker, Friedrich & Rafal, 1984). For example, when subjects are presented with a cue in a particular location which signifies an upcoming target in the same location, subjects, given sufficient time, need only engage attention once the target is introduced. If no cue is given as to the whereabouts of an upcoming target (neutral condition) the subject needs to first move attention to the location of the target and then engage attention there. When a cue is presented in one field and the target appears in the opposite field, subjects must disengage attention from the cue, move to the new location, and engage attention at the target.

Application of this model to patients with cerebral lesions has suggested a possible inefficiency in one of these mental operations which may have significant bearing on the neglect phenomenon. Using their reaction time paradigm, Posner and his colleagues found that patients with unilateral parietal lobe lesions exhibited near-normal reaction times except on trials when the target occurred on the side contralateral to the lesion *preceded* by a cue on the ipsilateral side (Posner et al., 1984). These results were most pronounced in right hemisphere lesioned patients. They found that when attention is engaged in any part of the visual field other than the contralateral side, by either a cue on the ipsilateral side or a neutral cue at center, patients with parietal lesions take significantly longer to disengage attention from their current focus. Thus, there seems to be a specific deficit in the disengage operation of covert attention. The move and engage operations appear to be functioning adequately, as patients react faster to both ipsilateral and contralateral targets with the presence of a valid cue. That is, a cue is equally effective in summoning attention to either field, and once attention is correctly oriented there the target can be quickly engaged. It is only when the required orientation is to the contralateral side, and attention has been drawn to a different location, that there is a profound disruption of performance. These same results were obtained even when there was an endogenous cue of an arrow pointing left or right, and suggests that the difficulty in disengaging occurs irrespective of whether attention is shifted by means of external or internal control.

An impairment of the disengage operation may not be the sole explanation for the predominantly left-side neglect syndrome, because *both* left and right hemisphere lesioned patients were found to have this operation disrupted. However, the available data from Posner's laboratory have succeeded in delineating a number of specific mental operations involved in covert orientating of attention, and further demonstrated the presence of a single component process which seems to be disrupted following parietal lesions.

Moreover, these operations are affected by lesions involving different neural systems, as patients with supranuclear palsy (lesions involving the midbrain) have been found to be impaired on the move operation (Posner, Cohen & Rafal, 1982), while patients with Parkinson's disease (lesions involving the basal ganglia) show no deficits on any of the three operations (Rafal, Posner, Walker & Friedrich, 1984).

This rather lengthy discussion of recent work from Posner's lab was undertaken in order to demonstrate how the experimental approach of the cognitive sciences can be successfully merged with clinical neuropsychology. Such crossovers between the two fields are noteworthy and, hopefully, will help us to better understand how different neural pathways may affect aspects of spatial cognition.

EVIDENCE FOR A REPRESENTATION DEFICIT

There is also evidence that neglect is not limited to stimuli in the external world, but can occur for internal representations as well. Studies by Bisiach and his colleagues have reported several neglect patients who, when asked to recall and describe a familiar scene from memory, neglected the left half in both views (Bisiach & Luzzatti, 1978). Two patients with neglect, both with lesions involving the right parietal cortex, recalled the location of buildings situated around the Piazza del Duomo, a well known square in the center of Milan, Italy. They were first asked to imagine that they were standing in the center of the square facing the Duomo and to report all of the buildings which would be seen from that perspective. Next they were asked to recall the scene a second time, but this time they were to imagine they had their back to the Duomo. In both orientations the patients failed to mention buildings which were situated to the left, even though in the second condition, with their back to the Duomo, the buildings they neglected to name had previously been named when they had imagined they were facing the Duomo.

These clinical observations were subsequently tested empirically on a group of patients with right hemisphere lesions who also had signs of unilateral neglect (Bisiach, Luzzatti & Perani, 1979). Patients and controls were presented with pairs of novel shapes which were either the same or varied in their configuration on the left or right side. The shapes were presented successively behind a narrow vertical opening in order to assure that all parts of the stimuli were exposed in the same spatial location. Unlike controls, patients were less likely to detect differences in shapes which were dissimilar on the left side, irrespective of the direction in which they were moving. The authors interpreted their findings as evidence that unilateral neglect affects the internal mental representations of reconstructed visual stimuli. Ogden (1985) has recently replicated these findings in both right and left hemisphere lesioned patients. That is, patients with right side lesions neglected the left half of reconstructed images, while patients with left side lesions neglected the right side of their images. In addition, she found that patients who demonstrated no neglect on paper and pencil tests still neglected the contralateral side of moving shapes. Other studies from Bisiach's lab have led them to suggest that there is indeed "an analog structure of space representation in the brain" (Bisiach, Berti & Vallar, 1985, p. 239).

In a similar vein, a pilot study from our laboratory (Morrow, 1987) has shown that patients with neglect manifest a neglect of internal representations of material which is stored in long-term memory. Patients with neglect and control subjects were asked to imagine a map of the United States, and then to name as many states as they could think of, using their mental image to aid in their naming. It was hypothesized that if subjects were accessing the map in an image form and using this image to recall states, then the western states, which are situated to the left, would be named less often by patients with neglect. Even though our subjects would be expected to name more states in the east, as they all live in the eastern section, we found that most of our controls named states scattered across the country, and all of the western states were named by at least half of the controls. However, very few patients with neglect named states in the western half. One might argue that these differences merely reflect a difference in our groups on travel or geographical experience. Informal questioning indicated comparable travel experience, and the conversation of one patient in particular suggests this not to be the case. After he had finished the state naming task, and had reported only states in the east, he was asked if he had done much traveling. He replied that he had traveled quite a bit, and when asked which states he had traveled to he immediately named Texas, California and Colorado—states he had neglected to name a few seconds earlier in the image condition. It seems that when relying on an imaginal strategy, this patient with neglect had a subsequent neglect of his reconstructed image; in contrast, utilizing a verbal strategy helped to elicit performance by a seemingly unimpaired route.

Explanations in terms of a defective internal representation have been extended to other disorders besides neglect. Ratcliff (1979) presented schematic drawings of human figures to control subjects and to patients with penetrating missile wounds whose lesions were located either in the anterior or posterior regions of either the right or left hemisphere. The schematic drawings were presented in one of four positions (facing front or back, inverted or upright) and in each of the conditions the patient had to determine which hand held a black disc. Patients with right posterior lesions were impaired when the figures were in the inverted position, but did not differ from controls or left posterior lesioned patients in the upright condition. The two conditions in this task were identical except for the orientation. If visual disorders, neglect, or a confusion in right-left orientation was a causal factor, one would have expected to find deficits in all conditions. Furthermore, there was no memory component, as the figures were present during the entire test, and the responses were entirely verbal, thereby eliminating motor involvement. While not specifically attributing the impairment to a faulty internal representation, Ratcliff did suggest the disorder may be due to a disruption of "spatial thought."

A recent study from our clinic, designed to control for those executive problems commonly seen after right hemisphere lesions (perceptual disorders, poor memory, neglect, constructional problems), suggests that spatial deficits following right hemisphere lesions may be due to a deficiency of the internal representation (Morrow, Ratcliff & Johnston, 1985). We asked patients to visualize a map of the United States and to make distance estimates between pairs of cities. Subsequently they were asked to locate the position of each city on an outline map. Finally, patients were asked to estimate distances between symbols on a page which were arranged in the same geographic location as the cities. The right hemisphere group performed significantly more poorly than controls only on the city estimation task. There were no differences in their ability to locate cities or estimate distances between the symbols. Thus, a spatial deficit could be demonstrated on a task that required no construction or visual scanning, and presumably relied on knowledge available in the subjects' repertoire before onset of their illness. We believe that this fundamental spatial deficit reflects a failure to establish and/or operate on an adequate internal representation, and may be a key limiting factor in these patients' performance on spatial tasks.

DIRECTIONS FOR FUTURE RESEARCH

In this chapter we have selectively reviewed the literature on disorders of spatial cognition. While valuable information can be gained from clinical studies of brain damaged individuals or small groups of patients, further progress in understanding the factors which limit spatial performance can only be achieved when the behavioral deficits, as well as the spatial tasks themselves, are more clearly defined. Until very recently, most neuropsychologists had been content with the knowledge that spatial disorders had some type of cognitive component; few had actually attempted to model the constellation of cognitive processes which underlie those deficits. Fortunately, there is now a movement amongst researchers in both cognitive psychology and neuropsychology to take this latter, process-oriented approach. Studies by Posner and Bisiach and their associates provide excellent examples of the usefulness of these procedures in patients with spatial disorders. Similarly, Farah (this volume) has successfully utilized this approach to analyze disturbances of visual imagery in brain damaged patients. This very elegant research demonstrates the effectiveness of these techniques in delineating the cognitive structures of spatial disorders.

REFERENCES

Acredolo, L. 1981. Small and large scale spatial concepts in infancy and childhood. In L. S. Liben, A. H. Patterson, & N. Newcombe (Eds.), *Spatial representation and behavior across the life span: Theory and application* (63-81). New York: Academic Press.

Arena, R. & Gainotti, G. 1978. Constructional apraxia and visuoperceptive disabilities in relation to laterality of cerebral lesion. *Cortex.* 14:463-473.

Badal, J. 1888. Contribution a l'etude des cecites psychique: alexia, agraphie, hemianopsie inferieure, trouble du sens de l'espace. *Archiv. Opthamologie.* 8:97-117.

Balint, R. 1909. Seelenlahmung des Schauens, optische Ataxie, raumliche Storung der Aufmerksamkeit. *Monatschrift fur Psychiatrie und Neurologie.* 25:51-81.

Battersby, W. S., Bender, M., Pollack, M., & Kahn, R. L. 1956. Unilateral 'spatial agnosia' (inattention) in patients with cerebral lesions. *Brain.* 79:68-93.

Benton, A. L. 1969. Disorders of spatial orientation. In P. J. Vinken & G. W. Bruyn (Eds.), *Handbook of clinical neurology.* Vol. 3:212-228. Amsterdam: North-Holland.

Benton, A. L., Levin, H. S., & Van Allen, M. W. 1974. Geographic orientation in patients with unilateral cerebral disease. *Neuropsychologia.* 12:183-191.

Bisiach, E., Berti, A., & Vallar, G. 1985. Analogical and logical disorders underlying unilateral neglect of space. In M. I. Posner & O. S. M. Marin (Eds.). *Attention and performance.* Vol. 11:239-249. Hillsdale, NJ: Lawrence Erlbaum Associates.

Bisiach, E., Cornacchia, L., Sterzi, R., & Vallar, G. 1984. Disorders of perceived auditory lateralization after lesions of the right hemisphere. *Brain.* 107:37-52.

Bisiach, E., & Luzzatti, C. 1978. Unilateral neglect of representational space. *Cortex.* 14:129-133.

Bisiach, E., Luzzatti, C., & Perani, D. 1979. Unilateral neglect, representational schema and consciousness. *Brain.* 102:609-618.

Brain, W. R. 1941. Visual disorientation with special reference to lesions of the right cerebral hemisphere. *Brain.* 64:244-272.

Butters, N., Soeldner, C., & Fedio, P. 1972. Comparison of parietal and frontal lobe spatial deficits in man: Extrapersonal vs. personal (egocentric) space. *Perceptual Motor Skills.* 34:27-34.

Chedru, F. 1976. Space representation in unilateral spatial neglect. *Journal of Neurology, Neurosurgery, and Psychiatry.* 39:1057-1061.

Cooper, L. A. 1984. Recent themes in visual information processing: A selected overview. In R. S. Nickerson (Ed.), *Attention and Performance.* Vol. 8. Hillsdale, NJ: Lawrence Erlbaum Associates.

Corkin, S. 1965. Tactually-guided maze learning in man: Effects of unilateral cortical excisions and bilateral hippocampal lesions. *Neuropsychologia.* 3:339-351.

Dee, H. L. 1970. Visuoconstructive and visuoperceptive deficits in patients with unilateral cerebral lesions. *Neuropsychologia.* 8:305-314.

Denny-Brown, D., Meyer, J. S., & Horenstein, S. 1952. The significance of perceptual rivalry resulting from parietal lesion. *Brain.* 75:433-471.

De Renzi, E. 1982. *Disorders of space exploration and cognition.* New York: Wiley.

De Renzi, E., & Faglioni, P. 1965. The comparative efficiency of intelligence and vigilance tests in detecting hemispheric cerebral damage. *Cortex.* 1:410-433.

De Renzi, E., Faglioni, P., & Scotti, G. 1968. Tactile spatial impairment and unilateral cerebral damage. *Journal of Nervous and Mental Disease.* 146:468-475.

De Renzi, E., Faglioni, P., & Scotti, G. 1970. Hemispheric contribution to exploration of space through the visual and tactile modality. *Cortex.* 6:191-203.

De Renzi, E., Faglioni, P., & Villa, P. 1977. Topographical amnesia. *Journal of Neurology, Neurosurgery, and Psychiatry.* 40:498-505.

De Renzi, E., & Scotti, G. 1969. The influence of spatial disorders in impairing tactual discrimination of shapes. *Cortex.* 5:53-62.

De Renzi, E., & Spinnler, H. 1966. Visual recognition in patients with unilateral cerebral disease. *Journal of Nervous and Mental Disease.* 142:515-525.

Ettlinger, G., Warrington, E., & Zangwill, O. L. 1957. A further study of visual-spatial agnosia. *Brain.* 80:335-361.

Faglioni, P., Scotti, G., & Spinnler, H. 1971. The performance of brain-damaged patients in spatial localization of visual and tactile stimuli. *Brain.* 92:443-454.

Forster, R. 1890. Ueber Rindenblindheit. *Graefe's Archiv. fur Opthamologie.* 36:94-108.
Friedland, R. P., & Weinstein, E. A. 1977. Hemi-inattention and hemisphere specialization: Introduction and historical review. In E. A. Weinstein & R. P. Friedland (Eds.), *Advances in Neurology.* Vol. 18:1-31. New York: Raven Press.
Gainotti, G., & Tiacci, C. 1970. Patterns of drawing disability in right and left hemispheric patients. *Neuropsychologia.* 8:379-384.
Gerstmann, J. 1958. Psychological and phenomenological aspects of disorders of the body image. *Journal of Nervous and Mental Disease.* 126:499-512.
Green, J. G. 1971. *A factorial study of perceptual function in patients with cerebral lesions..* Unpublished doctoral dissertation, University of Glasgow, Scotland.
Hecaen, H., & Assal, G. 1970. A comparison of constructive deficits following right and left hemispheric lesions. *Neuropsychologia.* 8:289-303.
Hecaen, H., Tzortzis, C., & Rondot, P. 1980. Loss of topographic memory with learning deficits. *Cortex.* 16:525-542.
Heilman, K. M. 1979. Neglect and related disorders. In K. M. Heilman & E. A. Weinstein (Eds.), *Clinical Neuropsycology.* 268-307. Oxford: Oxford University Press.
Heilman, K. M., Schwartz, H. D., & Watson, R. T. 1978. Hypoarousal in patients with the neglect syndrome and emotional indifference. *Neurology.* 28:229-232.
Heilman, K. M., & Valenstein, E. 1972a. Auditory neglect in man. *Archives of Neurology.* 26:32-35.
Heilman, K. M., & Valenstein, E. 1972b. Frontal lobe neglect in man. *Neurology.* 22:660-664.
Heilman, K. M., & Valenstein, E. 1979. Mechanisms underlying hemispatial neglect. *Annals of Neurology.* 5:166-170.
Heilman, K. M., & Van Den Abell, T. 1979. Right hemisphere dominance for mediating cerebral activation. *Neuropsychologia.* 17:315-321.
Heilman, K. M., & Watson, R. T. 1977. The neglect syndrome—A unilateral defect of the orienting response. In S. Harnad, R. W. Doty, C. Goldstein, J. Jaynes and G. Krauthamer (Eds.), *Lateralization in the nervous system.* 285-302. New York: Academic Press.
Holmes, G. 1919. Disturbances of visual space perception. *British Medical Journal.* 2:230-233.
Howes, D., & Boller, F. 1975. Simple reaction time: evidence for focal impairment from lesions of the right hemisphere. *Brain.* 98:317-332.
Jackson, J. H. 1876. Case of large cerebral tumour without optic neuritis and with left hemiplegia and imperception. *Royal London Opthamological Hospital Reports.* 8:434-444.
Kim, Y., Morrow, L., Passafiume, D., & Boller, F. 1984. Visuoperceptual and visuomotor abilities and locus of lesion. *Neuropsychologia.* 22:177-185.

Kimura, D. 1963. Right temporal lobe damage. *Archives of Neurology.* 8:264-271.

Kinsbourne, M. 1970. A model for the mechanism of unilateral neglect of space. *Trans. American Neurological Association.* 95:143-145.

Kinsbourne, M. 1977. Hemi-neglect and hemisphere rivalry. In R.P. Weinstein and E.A. Weinstein (Eds.), *Advances in Neurology.* Vol.18:41-49. New York: Raven Press.

Kleist, K. 1934. *Gehirn-Pathologie Vornehmlich auf Grund der Kriegser-fahrunger.* Leipzig: Barth.

Lansdell, H. 1968. Effect of extent of temporal lobe ablations on two lateralized deficits. *Physiology and Behavior.* 3:271-273.

LeDoux, J. E., Wilson, D. H., & Gazzaniga, M. S. 1977. Manipulo-spatial aspects of cerebral lateralization: Clues to the origin of lateralization. *Neuropsychologia.* 15:743-750.

Levine, D. N., Warach, J., & Farah, M. 1985. Two visual systems in mental imagery: Dissociation of "what" and "where" in imagery disorders due to bilateral posterior cerebral lesions. *Neurology.* 35:1010-1018.

Lohman, D. F. 1979. Spatial ability: A review and reanalysis of the correlational literature. Technical Report No. 8, Aptitude Research Project, School of Education, Stanford University.

Martin, A. 1985. A qualitative limitation on visual transfer via the anterior commissure. *Brain.* 108:43-63.

McFie, J., Piercy, M. F., & Zangwill, O. L. 1950. Visual-spatial agnosia associated with lesions of the right cerebral hemisphere. *Brain.* 73:167-190.

McFie, J., & Zangwill, O. L. 1960. Visual-constructive disabilities associated with lesions of the left cerebral hemisphere. *Brain.* 83:243-260.

McGee, M. G. 1979. Human spatial abilities: Psychometric studies and environmental, genetic, hormonal and neurological influences. *Psychological Bulletin.* 86:889-918.

Milner, B., 1965. Visually-guided maze learning in man: Effects of bilateral hippocampal, bilateral frontal, and unilateral cerebral lesions. *Neuropsychologia.* 3:317-338.

Mishkin, M., & Ungerleider, L. G. 1982. Contribution of striate inputs to the visuospatial functions of parieto-preoccipital cortex in monkeys. *Behavioral Brain Research.* 6:57-77.

Mishkin, M., Ungerleider, L. G., & Macko, K. A. 1983. Object vision and spatial vision: Two cortical pathways. *Trends in Neuroscience.* 6:414-417.

Morrow, L. 1987. Cerebral lesions and internal spatial representation. In P. Ellen & C. Thinus-Blanc (Eds.), *Cognitive processes and spatial orientation in animal and man.* 156-164. Dordrecht, Netherlands: Martinus Nijhoff.

Morrow, L., Ratcliff, G., & Johnston, C. S. 1985. Externalising spatial knowledge in patients with right hemisphere lesions. *Cognitive Neuropsychology.* 2:265-273.

Morrow, L., Vrtunski, P. B., Kim, Y., & Boller, F. 1981. Arousal responses to emotional stimuli and laterality of lesion. *Neuropsychologia.* 19:65-71.

Moscovitch, M. 1979. Information processing and the cerebral hemispheres. In M. S. Gazzaniga (Ed.), *Handbook of Behavioral Neurobiology: Vol. 2 Neuropsychology.* 379-446. New York: Plenum Press.

Newcombe, F., & Russell, W. R. 1969. Dissociated visual perceptual and spatial deficits in focal lesions of the right hemisphere. *Journal of Neurology, Neurosurgery, and Psychiatry.* 32:73-81.

Nielsen, J. M. 1937. Unilateral cerebral dominance as related to mind blindness: Minimal lesion capable of causing visual agnosia for objects. *Archives of Neurology and Psychiatry.* 38:108-135.

Ogden, J. A. 1985. Contralesional neglect of constructed visual images in right and left brain-damaged patients. *Neuropsychologia.* 23:273-277.

Pallis, C. A. 1955. Impaired identification for faces and places with agnosia for colours. *Journal of Neurology, Neurosurgery, and Psychiatry.* 18:218-224.

Paterson, A., & Zangwill, O. L. 1944. Disorders of visual space perception associated with lesions of the right cerebral hemisphere. *Brain.* 67:331-358.

Paterson, A., & Zangwill, O. L. 1945. A case of topographical disorientation associated with a unilateral cerebral lesion. *Brain.* 68:188-211

Piercy, M. F., Hecaen, H., & Ajuriaguerra, J. de. 1960. Constructional apraxia associated with unilateral cerebral lesions—left and right sided cases compared. *Brain.* 83:225-242.

Plourde, G., & Sperry, R. W. 1984. Left hemisphere involvement in left spatial neglect from right-sided lesions: A commissurotomy study. *Brain.* 107:95-106.

Posner, M. I. 1980. Orienting of attention. *Quarterly Journal of Experimental Psychology.* 32:3-25.

Posner, M. I., Cohen, Y., & Rafal, R. D. 1982. Neural systems control of spatial orienting. *Philosophical Transactions of the Royal Society of London B.* 298:187-198.

Posner, M. I., Nissen, M. J., & Ogden, W. C. 1977. Attended and unattended processing modes: The role of set for spatial location. In H. L. Pick & I. J. Saltzman (Eds.), *Modes of perceiving and processing information.* 137-157. Hillsdale, NJ: Lawrence Erlbaum Associates.

Posner, M. I., Walker, J. A., Friedrich, F. J., & Rafal, R. D. 1984. Effects of parietal injury on covert orienting of attention. *The Journal of Neuroscience.* 4:1863-1874.

Rafal, R. D., Posner, M. I., Walker, J. A., & Friedrich, F. J. 1984. Cognition and the basal ganglia: Separating mental and motor components of performance in Parkinsons's disease. *Brain, 107,* 1083-1094.

Ratcliff, G. 1979. Spatial thought, mental rotation and the right cerebral hemisphere. *Neuropsychologia.* 17:49-54.

Ratcliff, G. 1982. Disturbances of spatial orientation associated with cerebral lesions. In M. Potegal (Ed.), *Spatial abilities: development and physiological foundations.* 301-331. New York: Academic Press.

Ratcliff, G., & Davies-Jones, G. A. B. 1972. Defective visual localization in focal brain wounds. *Brain*. 95:49-60.

Ratcliff, G., & Newcombe, F. 1973. Spatial orientation in man: Effects of left, right, and bilateral posterior cerebral lesions. *Journal of Neurology, Neurosurgery, and Psychiatry*. 36:448-454.

Ratcliff, G., & Newcombe, F. 1982. Object recognition: Some deductions from the clinical evidence. In A. W. Ellis (Ed.), *Normality and Pathology in Cognitive Function*. 147-171. New York: Academic Press.

Rosenberger, P. 1974. Discriminative aspects of visual hemi-inattention. *Neurology*. 24:17-23.

Sauguet, J., Benton, A. L., & Hecaen, H. 1971. Disturbances of the body schema in relation to language impairment and locus of lesion. *Journal of Neurology, Neurosurgery, and Psychiatry*. 34:496-501.

Semmes, J., Weinstein, S., Ghent, L., & Teuber, H. L. 1955. Spatial orientation in man after cerebral injury: I. Analysis by locus of lesion. *Journal of Psychology*. 39:227-244.

Semmes, J., Weinstein, S., Ghent, L., & Teuber, H.L. 1963. Correlates of impaired orientation in personal and extrapersonl space. *Brain*. 86:747-772.

Shapiro, M. S., & Hynd, G. W. 1985. The development of functional lateralization of visual hemifield attention. *Developmental Neuropsychology*. 1:67-80.

Sokolov, Y. N. 1963. *Perception and the conditioned reflex*. Oxford: Pergamon Press.

Teuber, H. L. 1963. Space perception and its disturbances after brain injury in man. *Neuropsychologia*. 1:47-57.

Thurstone, L. L. 1938. Primary mental abilities. *Psychometric Monographs*. 1.

Ungerleider, L. G. 1985. The corticocortical pathways for object recognition and spatial perception. In C. Chagas, R. Gattass & C. Gross (Eds.), *Pattern recognition mechanisms*. 21-37. Vatican City: Pontificial Academy of Sciences.

Ungerleider, L. G., & Mishkin, M. 1982. Two cortical visual systems. In D. J. Ingle, M. A. Goodale & R. J. W. Mansfield (Eds.), *Analysis of Visual Behavior*. 549-586. Cambridge, MA.: MIT Press.

Van Der Linden, M., Seron, X., Gillet, J., & Bredart, S. 1980. Heminegligence par lesion frontale droite. *Acta Neurologica Belgica*. 80:298-310.

Verfaellie, D., Bowers, D., Williams, S., & Heilman, K. M. 1985, February. *Dissociation of attention and intention in normal subjects*. Paper presented at the 13th annual meeting of the International Neuropsychological Society, San Diego.

Warrington, E. K. 1969. Constructional apraxia. In P. J. Vinken & G. W. Bruyn (Eds.), *Handbook of clinical neurology*. Vol. 3:67-83. Amsterdam: North-Holland.

Warrington, E. K., & James, M. 1967. Disorders of visual perception in patients with unilateral cerebral lesions. *Neuropsychologia*. 5:253-266.

Warrington, E. K., James, M., & Kinsbourne, M. 1966. Drawing disability in relation to laterality of lesion. *Brain*. 89:53-82.

Warrington, E. K., & Taylor, A. M. 1973. The contribution of the right parietal lobe to object recognition. *Cortex.* 9:152-164.

Wasserstein, J., Zapulla, R., Rosen, J., & Gerstman, L. 1984. Evidence for differentiation of visual-perceptual functions. *Brain and Cognition.* 3:51-56.

Watson, R. T., Heilman, K. M., Cauthen, J. C., & King, F. A. 1973. Neglect after cingulectomy. *Neurology.* 23:1003-1007.

Watson, R. T., Heilman, K. M., Miller, B. D., & King, F. A. 1974. Neglect after mesencephalic reticular formation lesions. *Neurology.* 24:294-298.

Whiteley, A. M., & Warrington, E. K. 1978. Selective impairment of topographical memory: A single case study. *Journal of Neurology, Neurosurgery, and Psychiatry.* 41:575-578.

Whitty, C. W. M., & Newcombe, F. 1973. R. C. Oldfields's study of visual and topographic disturbances in a right occipito-parietal lesion of 30 years duration. *Neuropsychologia.* 11:471-475.

Young, A. W., & Ratcliff, G. 1983. Visuospatial abilities of the right hemisphere. In A. W. Young (Ed.), *Functions of the right cerebral hemisphere.* 1-32. London: Academic Press.

Zoccolotti, P., Scabini, D., & Violani, C. 1982. Electrodermal responses in patients with unilateral brain damage. *Journal of Clinical Neuropsychology.* 4:143-150.

THE NEUROPSYCHOLOGY OF MENTAL IMAGERY: CONVERGING EVIDENCE FROM BRAIN-DAMAGED AND NORMAL SUBJECTS

2

Martha J. Farah
Carnegie Mellon University

IMAGERY AND SPATIAL COGNITION

Is the front door to your house in the center or off to one side? If you were moving, and had to carry your dining room table out the front door, could you carry it upright, or would you need to angle it through some special path in space to make sure it clears the woodwork? In answering these questions, you probably formed a series of mental images of your door and of your dining room table at different orientations in the doorway. Although there are countless possible strategies for retrieving spatial information and solving problems concerning spatial relationships, most people spontaneously use mental imagery in these circumstances.

Certain intrinsic properties of imagery make this a good choice. First, images are rich in implicit spatial information. For example, you need never have explicitly noted the position of your front door in order for that information to be represented in an image of the front of your house. Images are stored representations from some level of perceptual processing prior to semantic categorization, and can therefore contain visual/spatial information that the person generating the image has never explicitly noticed (Finke, Pinker & Farah, 1986). Second, the isomorphism that exists between spatial relationships in images and in the physical world (Shepard & Chipman, 1970) allows us to mentally simulate and evaluate the effects of spatial transformations such as the repositioning of the dining room table in the doorway without explicit calculations or inferences; once you have imaged the two objects at their correct relative sizes, the amount of clearance is immediately available in the image.

Spatial cognition has traditionally been defined in relatively phenomenon-oriented ways, in terms of specific kinds of tasks failed after brain damage, or in terms of "what spatial abilities tests test," rather than in theory-oriented ways, in terms of the systems of internal processing, such as imagery, that could account for performance in spatial tasks. Attempts to understand the neural basis of spatial ability have been hindered by this dearth of theory, because the psychological entities that we would like to relate to the brain are not directly observable behaviors but the underlying cognitive systems, which theory has yet to characterize. Fortunately, the mental imagery system is one of the exceptions to this generalization. Two decades of cognitive psychology have taught us a lot about the functional characteristics of mental imagery as a system for retrieving and manipulating visual/spatial information. Thus, where neuropsychologists investigating other types of spatial cognition must engage in a kind of theoretical bootstrapping, to delineate and characterize the cognitive system whose neural properties they are studying, we can make things *relatively* easy on ourselves by beginning with a cognitive system that has already been modeled by cognitive psychologists.

Having selected at a functional, or information-processing, level the system to be studied, what are the goals of the research reported here? There are several questions that we can ask about mental imagery in the context of a neuropsychological investigation. Not surprisingly, some of these questions have to do with the neural hardware per se: what is the neural substrate of mental imagery ability? Is it localized to particular regions of the brain? Is it lateralized to one hemisphere or the other? These are all questions that are addressed in this chapter.

In addition, neurological data can be used to answer questions about a cognitive system at the functional level. Patterns of association and dissociation among abilities after brain damage can reveal relationships among different components of the *functional* architecture not readily apparent through the study of intact brains. We can use such associations and dissociations to address the following questions about imagery: Is image generation a separate "module" from other forms of memory recall, or do the same basic information retrieval processes underlie visualizing an object and recalling nonimagistic memory representations, for example, a telephone number? What is the internal functional structure of the imagery system, and in particular, are the subcomponents postulated by the

Kosslyn (1980) model psychologically real? What abilities rely upon the mental imagery system, and, in particular, what sorts of spatial abilities rely on imagery?

Plan of the Chapter

The research strategy taken here is to converge on the answers to the questions posed above using several different methodologies. Whereas any research method has weaknesses, leaving open some alternative explanations of a result, different methods usually have different weaknesses. One can exploit those differences by using the strengths of one method to "cover" the weaknesses of another; if the same result is obtained across methods, then it is unlikely to be due to particular methodological weaknesses.

Accordingly, the chapter will be broken down into a series of sections, presenting in logical (if not exactly historical) sequence a set of studies of the neurological basis of mental imagery. The outcome of the initial study, based on a retrospective analysis of neurological case reports of patients with imagery deficits, suggests some tentative answers to the questions raised above. The two firmest conclusions of this initial study, namely the dissociability and localizability of the image generation process, will then become the subjects of scrutiny, and a series of alternative explanations of these results will be considered and tested with different subject populations and experimental techniques: controlled experiments with a new case of loss of imagery, experiments with a split-brain patient, and an experiment with normal subjects.

INITIAL STUDY: RETROSPECTIVE ANALYSIS OF CASE REPORTS

A search of the English language neurological literature yielded 37 case reports of patients who, after brain damage, were no longer able to experience mental images (Farah, 1984). Evidence of the imagery deficit varied from case to case, but a composite picture of one such case would include spontaneous complaints to the physician that "picture memory" was gone, an inability to describe the appearance of familiar objects from memory, and an inability to draw from memory with preserved drawing from a model. Despite their common imagery deficit, there was little neuropathological consistency among these cases. Most of the brain lesions were posterior, but this is about as far as one can generalize; there were many cases of bilateral damage, some of unilateral left hemisphere damage, a few unilateral right hemisphere cases and, to the extent that more precise intrahemispheric localization was possible, there was no consistency of lesion location within the posterior lobes.

What are we to make of this lack of association between loss of imagery and lesion sites? Before we abandon the project of finding consistent relationships between mental imagery and particular brain areas, we should consider an analogy between that project and the project of mapping language functions in the brain. If one were to collect a number of patients with language deficits and examine their brains for a consistent lesion site, one would probably be disappointed by the heterogeneity of this group too. Severe disruptions of language can follow damage to various sites in the left frontal or temporal lobes (Goodglass & Kaplan, 1972), not to mention damage to thalamic structures (Brown, 1974), or even areas of the right hemisphere (Ross & Mesulam, 1979). This heterogeneity does not imply that language functions are nonlocalizable. Rather, it tells us about the brain's division of labor for the different components of language processing. The qualitative nature of the language deficit is related to the lesion location, and in many cases it has been possible to characterize the different deficits in terms of linguistically and psychologically motivated distinctions (Zurif, 1984).

The analogy between imagery and language deficits suggests that, like language, imagery may have an internal componential structure, and the different components of imagery may have different neural loci. If we could delineate subgroups of patients according to the component of imagery that has been damaged, we might then be able to find more consistency in their lesion sites, and thereby localize the components of imagery. To do this requires two things: A theory of imagery that specifies the different components of imagery ability, and a way of finding out, for each of the 37 cases, which component of imagery has been damaged.

Kosslyn (1980) has provided a comprehensive and well-supported theory of visual imagery in normal adults. For present purposes, only the highest level "parse" of the system will be used. At this very general level, we can distinguish among the following components of imagery: (1) the *long-term visual memories* of the appearances of objects, (2) the *visual buffer*, the short-term array-format medium in which images occur, (3) the *generation process*, which takes the information in long-term visual memory and creates the image by activating the appropriate patterns of activation in the visual buffer, and (4) the *inspection process*, which organizes and transmits the information displayed in the visual buffer to other cognitive systems.

According to this analysis of the imagery system, a patient would be expected to fail any task requiring imagery, and experience no imagery on introspection, if any of the four components above were destroyed. Image transformation processes, such as rotation, are not included here, as their loss would be expected to give rise to distinct deficits in visual/spatial thought, but not to the loss of imagery altogether.

The particular component of imagery that was impaired in each patient was inferred from descriptions of the patient's abilities and deficits by the following technique. For each of the 37 cases, task analyses were constructed for the cognitive and perceptual tasks that were described in the case reports. These tasks included describing the appearances of familiar objects and scenes from memory, drawing objects from memory, drawing visually presented objects, and recognizing visually presented objects. By comparing the components that occurred in successfully and unsuccessfully performed tasks, it was possible in most cases to infer the component of the mental imagery system that was damaged. To anticipate the results of these inferences, twenty-seven of the thirty-seven cases could be classified into three main groups, corresponding to deficits in different components of imagery: the image generation process, the long-term visual memories, and the inspect process. The remaining ten case reports merely asserted that the patient had lost imagery ability, without providing the behavioral evidence that brought the author to that conclusion.

The patients in the three groups had imagery deficits as evidenced by one or more of the following criteria: they could not draw from memory but could draw objects shown to them; they could not describe the appearance of objects from memory but were neither aphasic nor did they have a visual-verbal disconnection syndrome; they reported that they could no longer visualize objects from memory, but maintained that their vision was unchanged. In each case, they were unable to perform an imagery task but were able to perform the corresponding task without imagery. Note that only three patients were classified solely on the basis of the third, and most subjective, criterion, involving self-report.

Eight patients had imagery deficits but were able to recognize visually presented objects (i.e. they were not visual agnosics). For these patients, the underlying deficit was inferred to be in the *image generation process*, by the following logic. To explain the imagery deficit in nonagnosic patients we must postulate damage to some component of the imagery system that is not shared with visual recognition; that is, if visual recognition is intact, then the long-term visual memories must be intact and so must the visual buffer. (This inference rests on the assumptions that the same long-term visual memories are used in imagery and recognition, and that the visual buffer and inspect process in imagery is also shared with perception. Evidence for the first assumption will be presented shortly; evidence for the second comes from Finke & Kosslyn, 1980 and from Farah, 1985.) By a process of elimination, this leaves only the image generation process, which converts the long-term visual memory information into an image in the visual buffer, as the impaired component of imagery ability.

In these eight cases of inferred image generation process deficit, the predominant site of damage was the posterior left hemisphere. As can be seen in part A of Table 2.1, *most* of the patients had *most* of their damage in this quadrant of the brain. It should be pointed out that, in general, the localizing information in these cases was quite poor. For this reason it seemed worthwhile to examine some additional cases to see if they follow the same trend. This was done by returning to the set of ten cases for which no evidence of loss of imagery was given, and selecting the six nonagnosic cases. For these nonagnosic cases, *if* they are cases of imagery deficit, then they are cases of image generation process deficit, by the process of elimination just described. As can be seen in part B of Table 2.1, all six of these cases had left posterior lesions. It thus appears that image generation is a function of the posterior left hemisphere.

For 13 patients, the deficit appeared to be in the *long-term visual memories*, for the following reasons. These patients had both imagery deficits and recognition deficits. Furthermore, their recognition deficit, or agnosia, was of the "associative" type; that is, careful testing revealed that their perceptual abilities were good enough to permit recognition, implying that the deficit must lie somewhere in the process of associating the percept with memory representations. For patients in this group there are two possible accounts of their deficits: either the long-term visual memories that underlie both imagery and recognition are deficient, or both the image generation process and the process that matches the percept with the long-term visual memories are deficient. Parsimony favors the interpretation that one rather than two separate components are damaged. In addition, there are more substantive reasons for preferring this interpretation, based on the *content-specificity* of the imagery and recognition deficits in this group. Several of the patients were able to image some classes of stimuli and not others. This content-specificity implicates that damage has been done to a representational, or information-bearing, component of the system, that is to

Table 2.1.
(A) Cases inferred to have an image generation process deficit. For each case the
etiology and general cortical area of damage is listed.
(B) Nonagnosic cases lacking reported evidence for an imagery deficit. If these
cases do have imagery deficits, then they are cases of image generation process
deficit (see text for explanation). For each case the etiology and general cortical
area of damage is given.

	Case	Etiology	Lesion Site
A.	Brain (1954) Case 1	Head injury	Left posterior
	Brain (1954) Case 2	Head injury	?
	Brownell et al. (1983)	Cerebrovascular accident	Bilateral parietal (greater on right), left frontal
	Humphrey & Zangwill (1951) Case 3	Penetrating head wound	Right posterior (left handed & dysphasic subsequent to injury)
	Lyman et al. (1938)	Neoplasm	Left posterior
	Nielsen (1946) p. 200	Cerebrovascular accident	Left posterior
	Nielsen (1946) p.227	Neoplasm	Left posterior
	Spalding & Zangwill (1950)	Penetrating head wound	Bilateral (greatest in left posterior)
B.	Arbuse (1947)	Neoplasm	Left posterior
	Nielsen (1946) p. 203 (cited as loss of imagery, 1955)	Cerebrovascular accident	Left posterior
	Nielsen (1955) Case 7	Neoplasm	Left posterior
	Nielsen (1955) postscript Case 1	Neoplasm	Left posterior
	Nielsen (1955) postscript Case 2	Neoplasm	Left posterior
	Wilbrand (1887) described by Nielsen (1955)	Cerebrovascular accident	Left posterior

memories rather than to processes that access the memories. Furthermore, for the four cases in which both imagery and recognition were tested for a range of objects, the deficits paralleled each other: things that could be imaged could also be recognized and things that could not be imaged could not be recognized. This parallelism implies that the impaired component of imagery is the same as the impaired component of recognition, again favoring the inference that these patients have long-term visual memory deficits. In one additional case (i.e. not one of the 13 just described, nor one of the cases of image generation process deficit described earlier), the recognition abilities and content-specificity of the imagery deficit were described in ambiguous terms and it was therefore not clear whether the patient had an image generation process deficit or a long-term visual memory deficit.

The lesions causing the long-term visual memory deficits were generally bilateral and posterior, although there were two cases of left posterior damage (one of whom was left-handed) and one case of right posterior damage. Although this group of cases does not suggest a localization for long-term visual memory, it does present us with an interesting functional association between content-specific imagery and recognition deficits. This association suggests that imagery and recognition share long-term visual memories, and thereby vindicates the use of that assumption earlier, in the analysis of the image generation process group.

For five patients, the damaged component of imagery was inferred to be the *inspect process*, based on the failures of these patients on all perceptual and imagery tasks except for the simplest perceptual detection tasks. The one component occurring in all and only the failed tasks is the inspect process, so on the grounds of parsimony it is likely to be the damaged component. It should be noted that this inference is less certain than the previous two, in that it depends exclusively on parsimony. The neuropathology in these patients was the most extensive, involving large bilateral areas of damage in each case.

What has been learned about visual imagery from this analysis of imagery deficits following brain damage? Let us go through each of the questions raised in the introduction and see how the present data reflect on each. The neural substrate of the image generation process appears to be roughly localizable. Furthermore, even this coarse-grained localization in the posterior left hemisphere reveals a strong lateralization for image generation. The hemisphericity of this process is surprising, given the widespread assumption (discussed by Ehrlichman & Barrett, 1983) that imagery is a right hemisphere function. As Ehrlichman and Barrett pointed out, this assumption was based on the conflation of imagery with other forms of visual processing and spatial ability. This error highlights the importance of distinguishing between the different cognitive systems at the functional level before attempting to study their neural bases.

The present analysis also has implications for the nature of imagery at a functional, or information-processing, level. Most of the patients with image generation process deficits did not have difficulty with other forms of recall. The finding that the critical lesion site for the image generation process is unrelated to the known neuroanatomy for memory strengthens the argument for a functional dissociation of the recall of images (i.e. generation of images) from recall of nonimaginal information. This dissociation implies that imagery is a separate system from other forms of memory, in contrast to the claims of some authors (e.g. Pylyshyn, 1981) that the recall of an image, even when accompanied by the phenomenology of a "picture in the head," is accomplished by the same processes as the recall of nonimaginal information such as telephone numbers or historical facts. On the latter type of account, people could selectively lose imagery ability only if they lost the long-term visual memories from which images are generated. Cases of long-term visual memory deficit can be explained this way, but the cases of image generation process deficit, in which visual recognition is preserved, cannot.

We can also use the results of the present analysis as evidence for the four-component parse of the imagery system supplied by the Kosslyn model. It might at first seem circular to view the cases as supporting the model given that they were interpreted *using* the model. However, the case reports could have disconfirmed the model if there had been patients whose patterns of performance across tasks could not have been interpreted by the model. For example, content-specific imagery deficits with no recognition deficits would not be interpretable by the present model. Out of 37 cases, none resisted interpretation. This provides some measure of confirmation that the cognitive components postulated in the model are "neuro-logically real," and hence psychologically real.

No deficits in other areas of functioning were mentioned consistently in the case reports, so it appears that imagery is not critical for any of the everyday activities that patients were queried about. Unfortunately, this generalization is dependent on the areas of functioning that the original authors of the case reports decided to test, and this bias is compounded by the authors' decisions about what findings to report. Despite these limitations on the available information, some tentative conclusions can be drawn. First, in the realm of spatial functioning, one can assume that topographic orientation was usually investigated, as this is an ability of obvious functional significance to the patient and one about which neurologists are likely to inquire. Therefore, the finding that deficits in topographic orientation were not frequently reported, and were sometimes reported to be absent, suggests that "cognitive maps" do not consist just of mental images. This finding, however, does not imply that all of spatial cognition is independent of mental imagery. One case in particular, described by Brain (1954, case 1), indicates a role for imagery in the representation of three-dimensional architectural structures. The patient was a builder's manager, whose job it was to inspect buildings under construction for adherence to the architects' specifications. The patient complained that his imagery deficit was a handicap in his work, as he was no longer able to visualize a plan or elevation, and as a consequence was constantly referring to the specifications during inspections. This spatial deficit is especially significant given the general intellectual sparing in this patient.

Many of the patients in the case reports had been involved either vocationally or avocationally in "visual/spatial" activities such as building, architecture, carpentry, set design or painting and in several cases these patients were reported to be impaired in their visual/spatial activities as a result of their brain injury. One might speculate that these impairments were related to their imagery deficits.

Two additional associations found in the case reports are informative with respect to the nature of imagery at a functional level of description. First, the association between content-specific imagery and recognition deficits, already mentioned in the description of the long-term visual memory deficit group, implies that the imagery and recognition systems share long-term visual memories. Second, there was a strong association between waking imagery deficits and loss or severe alteration of dreaming. Of the 17 case reports mentioning dreaming, 14 stated that dreaming had either stopped, lost its visual component, or become extremely infrequent. Greenberg and Farah (1986) found that cases of cessation of dreaming often report a loss of waking imagery and never report that waking imagery is intact. Waking and dream imagery thus appear to share some common components, a proposition which makes enormous intuitive sense but which would be difficult to support objectively using traditional cognitive methodologies with normal subjects.

Having surveyed the ways in which this preliminary study of imagery deficits can illuminate the neural basis of the imagery system and certain aspects of its functional structure, let us now focus on one particular aspect of these results, the dissociability of the image generation process and its localization in the posterior left hemisphere, and attempt to strengthen the case for these conclusions. The following sections include further investigations of the neural basis of image generation, each one aimed at dispelling a particular alternative explanation of the results on image generation presented above.

A DISCONNECTION SYNDROME? STUDIES OF A NEW CASE

An alternative explanation of the left posterior lesion site in the cases of image generation process deficit is that these patients have a disconnection between the language comprehension areas of the posterior left hemisphere and intact image generation areas located elsewhere (see Geschwind, 1965). This would account for the observed deficits in these patients, because all of the imagery tasks, including drawing from memory, involved comprehending some verbal query or request. Furthermore, the left posterior location of the critical lesion site is particularly suggestive of such a disconnection. How can we distinguish between the possibility of a functional loss of image generation ability and a language-imagery disconnection? The critical data would be the performance of one of these patients on imagery tasks for which neither the instructions, the stimuli nor the patient's response are verbal. Although no such data exist in the case reports reviewed earlier, my colleagues and I recently examined a new patient with an image generation deficit and tested the disconnection hypothesis (Farah, Levine & Calvanio, in press).

R.M. is a college-educated man in his early-sixties who suffered a left posterior stroke. Aside from an imagery deficit, residual cognitive difficulties at the time of testing were minimal, involving some word-finding problems, a mild deficit in recent memory, and verbal alexia. In particular, he was not agnosic (i.e. he could recognize visually presented objects), and therefore his imagery deficit is attributable to the image generation process, the one component of imagery that is not shared with recognition. His imagery deficit became apparent in the course of my first conversation with him, from which the following exchanges have been excerpted:

Examiner: What does an elephant look like?
R.M.: It's a great huge mountainous animal with a big body but a tiny waist.

E: What about its face—its nose and ears, for example?

R.M.: Oh, I don't know. It's been a long time since I've seen one.

E: What does a pineapple look like?

R.M.: Oh, I don't bother with those in the stores.

E: Do you know where they're grown?

R.M.: Hawaii.

E: And what's the big brand name?

R.M.: Dole.

E: And do they have leaves?

R.M.: I don't know. They probably have leaves, yes.

E: And are the leaves rounded or pointy?

R.M.: Rounded.

E: And is there a stem?

R.M.: Sure, there must be a stem.

E: Is the stem long and thin or short and stubby or what?

R.M.: It's a long stem.

E: Can you tell me what the White House looks like?

R.M.: Well, I've been there, but it's been a long time.

E: Is it really white?

R.M.: I don't know, I haven't seen it in a long time.

E: Tell me which of the following you think it had, last time you were there: Columns, ivy-covered walls, a dome-shaped roof...

R.M.: (after each of the above, refused to guess)

In his ability to draw, as well as to describe appearances from memory, he resembled previous cases of imagery deficit from the literature; a look through his records revealed unrecognizable drawings of a clock and an elephant, done to command, and clumsy but vastly superior copies of drawings of the same objects. Further evidence of his imagery deficit comes from his performance on a task adapted from the work of Eddy and Glass (1981). Eddy and Glass devised two sets of sentences, one of which seemed introspectively to require imagery for verification (e.g. True or False: "A grapefruit is larger than a canteloupe") and the other of which did not (e.g. True or false: "Salt is used less often than pepper"). After equating the two sets for difficulty, Eddy and Glass used a visual interference paradigm (see Brooks, 1968) to demonstrate objectively that subjects did rely on imagery to verify the sentences that seemed to require imagery. Whereas subjects could verify the two sets of sentences equally quickly and accurately when presented auditorially, their performance on just the imagery sentences dropped significantly when presented visually. Therefore, the Eddy and Glass sentences comprise a validated test of imagery along with a non-imagery test of identical format, which normal subjects find equally difficult.

R.M. did virtually perfectly on the Eddy and Glass (1981) non-imagery control sentences (33 out of 34 correct) but made many errors on the imagery sentences (23 out of 34 correct), a highly significant difference. His performance on a validated test of imagery is thus consistent with his performance on the informal bedside tests of imagery that formed the basis of previous studies of imagery deficit reviewed earlier.

In order to distinguish between the "loss" and "disconnection" accounts of this patient's deficit, two new tasks were devised that tested the patient's imagery abilities nonverbally. The first was a coloring task. If you are asked "What color is a football?" you will probably generate an image in order to answer. We presented R.M. with the equivalent nonverbal task, by giving him black and white line drawings of common objects and a choice of three colored pencils with which to color each drawing. The objects were chosen to have characteristic colors that are nevertheless not verbally associated (as "grass" and "green" are). We expected that R.M. would need to generate an image of the depicted object in order to retrieve information about its color. In order to assess his long-term visual memories for color information without requiring image generation, we added a control condition in which three already-colored drawings of a given object were presented for him to choose among. R.M. performed well in the control condition (37/40 correct) and significantly worse in the imagery condition (26/40 correct). By this nonverbal test of imagery, R.M. still appeared to have an imagery deficit.

A second nonverbal imagery task involved completing drawings of common objects and scenes from which single components were missing, for example a fishbowl without fish. This task is effectively the same as a traditional drawing-from-memory task, except that the item to be drawn is communicated nonverbally, by the depicted context. To assess his long-term memories for the appearances of the items to be drawn, R.M. was asked to choose the correct picture completions from pairs of subtly different drawings. Finally, to assess his drawing ability per se, he was asked to copy correct completions. Performance in this task is difficult to quantify, and only five drawings were administered, but it can be said that his completions from memory were either poor or unrecognizable, whereas his copies were merely clumsy (attributable to cerebellar damage) and his discrimination of correctly from incorrectly drawn completions was perfect. In this second nonverbal test of image generation, R.M. still performed poorly. An example of his performance on this task is shown in Figure 2.1.

To summarize, R.M. performed poorly on a variety of tasks requiring image generation, including one in which normal subjects are known to rely on imagery. His good performance on the control tasks and his lack of an agnosia imply that the impaired component of imagery is the image generation process per se. His lesion site is consistent with the tentative localization inferred in the last section. For these reasons, his syndrome appears to be of a kind with that of the patients in the image generation process deficit group discussed in the last section. The results of two nonverbal imagery tasks indicate that his performance is not sensitive to the presence or absence of verbal processing. We therefore conclude that R.M. does not have a language-imagery disconnection, but rather an impairment in image generation per se.

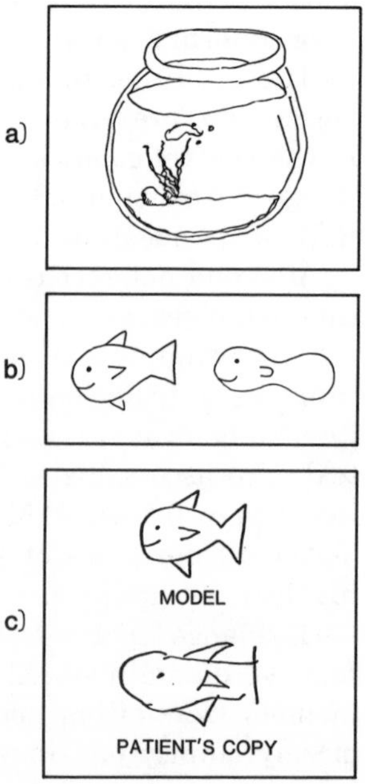

Figure 2.1. An example of R.M.'s performance in the drawing completion task.
(a) Imagery—R.M.'s fish drawn from memory.
(b) Recognition—correctly and incorrectly drawn fish, which R.M. was able to discriminate.
(c) Copying ability—simple model and R.M.'s copy.

A SAMPLING BIAS? STUDIES OF A SPLIT-BRAIN PATIENT

A second alternative explanation of the left posterior lesion site in cases of image generation process deficit is that the sample of case reports, which formed the data base for the initial study, was skewed to underrepresent right hemisphere-damaged patients. This explanation is not as ad hoc as it might at first appear; there are, in fact, two reasons to expect right hemisphere-damaged patients to be underrepresented in a sample of this kind. First, right hemisphere-damaged patients are initially less likely to come to the attention of a neurologist because their language abilities will not have been endangered. Second, right hemisphere-damaged patients often show a surprising tendency to deny their deficits, including deficits far more obvious and dysfunctional than a loss of imagery, such as paralysis or blindness (Hecaen & Albert, 1978) and many of the investigations of imagery deficits in the published case reports were initiated based on patients' self-reports. Perhaps both hemispheres play an essential role in image generation, and the apparent left-sided localization resulted from a sampling bias that excluded right hemisphere-damaged patients. One way to assess this proposal is to test the image generation ability of each of the hemispheres of a split-brain patient. Split-brain patients are epileptic patients who have had their two hemispheres disconnected by surgical transection of the corpus callosum in order to control their epilepsy (Wilson, Reeves & Gazzaniga, 1978). By testing the image generation capabilities of each of the disconnected hemispheres of a split-brain patient separately we can obtain information about hemispheric specialization that is unaffected by the sampling biases described above. If the image generation process is truly lateralized to the left hemisphere, then only the left hemisphere of a split-brain patient should be able to generate images. If the image generation process depends upon structures in both hemispheres, such that damage to either hemisphere could impair imagery ability, then neither hemisphere of split-brain patient, functioning independently, should be able to generate images. Two other possible outcomes of the split-brain study are that both hemispheres can perform an imagery task (in which case we would infer that the image generation process can be carried out by either hemisphere) and that only the right hemisphere can perform an imagery task (in which case we would infer that the image generation process is lateralized to the right hemisphere). The last two outcomes would be hard to square with the results of the first two studies, above, but are nevertheless possibilities in the following experimental paradigm.

In order to assess the image generation abilities of each hemisphere separately, my collaborators and I adapted a simple imagery
task from one already used in imagery studies, and devised a pair of
control tasks that required all of the cognitive components of the
imagery task except for the image generation process itself (Farah,
Gazzaniga, Holtzman & Kosslyn, 1985). The imagery task was a
letter classification task used by Weber and others (Weber & Castleman, 1970; Weber & Malmstrom, 1979). In the original version subjects went through the alphabet from memory classifying the lowercase forms of each letter from a to z as "ascending" (e.g. "d"), "descending" (e.g. "g"), or neither e.g. "a"). In the version we adapted
for use with the split-brain patient, a particular letter was cued by
the presentation of its upper case form. So, for example, if the
stimulus was "p," the correct response was "descending." In order
to cue just one hemisphere at a time with the letter to be imaged
and classified, we presented the uppercase forms at one and a half
degrees to the left or to the right of the patient's fixation. This mode
of presentation results in only the contralateral hemisphere
receiving the visual input, and thus only that hemisphere is in a
position to respond to the stimulus. An additional minor change in
the present task is that the ascending and descending response
categories were collapsed, resulting in "medium" (e.g. "a") and "not
medium" (e.g. "f, "g") response categories.

In order to infer that a failure in this task reflects an image generation deficit per se, additional control tasks were developed to
assess each hemisphere's ability to perform all other components of
the imagery task. A task analysis of the imagery task suggests that
the following processing steps are required: (1) The recognition of
the uppercase letter (i.e. matching the visual input with long-term
visual memory), (2) the retrieval of the associated lowercase form
with the uppercase stimulus, (3) the generation of an image of the
lowercase letter, (4) the classification of the lowercase letter into the
appropriate response category, and (5) the execution of a response (in
this case pressing one of two buttons). The following two control
tasks together require all of the above processes except for image
generation. In the *letter association* task, uppercase letters were
presented to a single hemisphere (one and a half degrees out from
fixation) and the patient's task was to select the corresponding lowercase form from a nonalphabetically arranged array of letters in free
vision. Successful performance of this task shows that the hemisphere receiving the uppercase letter is capable of recognizing the
uppercase and lowercase letters and associating them correctly. In
the *perceptual classification* task, lowercase letters were presented to

a single hemisphere and the patient's task was to classify the letter into the appropriate response category (medium or not medium) and respond. Unlike the imagery task, this task simply requires the patient to classify what he can actually see. Successful performance on this task shows that the hemisphere receiving the letter is capable of performing the letter height discrimination and responding. It follows that if a hemisphere can perform both control tasks, a failure in the imagery task cannot be attributed to a difficulty in perceptual encoding, letter recognition and association, height discrimination, or response production.

As hoped, both hemispheres were able to perform the control tasks. The right hemisphere made one error out of twenty-six trials in the the *letter association* task and the left hemisphere performed errorlessly for the same number of trials. As can be seen in Figure 2.2, in the *perceptual classification* task, the right hemisphere was able to correctly classify 90% of the lowercase letters presented to it

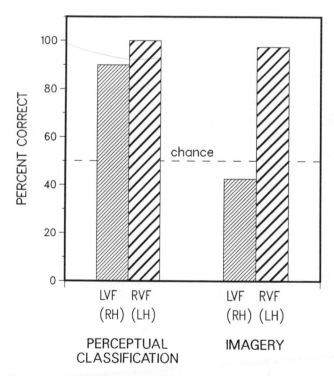

Figure 2.2. Accuracy of the two hemispheres of a split-brain patient on the Weber imagery task and a perceptual control task.

as "medium" or "not medium," and the left hemisphere correctly classified all of the lowercase letters presented to it. In contrast to the control tasks, the performance of the two hemispheres diverged sharply on the imagery task: the right hemisphere performed at chance level, 43% correct, whereas the left hemisphere continued to perform essentially perfectly, 97% correct. These results are consistent with the hypothesis that the left hemisphere contains all of the structures necessary for image generation, whereas the right hemisphere does not. They are inconsistent with the hypothesis that both hemispheres are required for image generation, which was the alternative hypothesis under consideration here, as well as with the hypotheses that both the right and left hemispheres have image generation capability or that only the right has image generation capability. The results of the letter association control task also confirm that the long-term visual memories are bilaterally represented.

OVERGENERALIZING FROM THE ABNORMAL? A LATERALITY MEASURE FROM NORMAL SUBJECTS

The results of the split-brain study support a dissociation and localization of the image generation process, separate from long-term visual memory and lateralized to the left hemisphere. Furthermore, these results are immune to the "case sampling bias" explanation of the left hemisphere localization inferred from the initial analysis of published case reports. Nevertheless, there are reasons for skepticism about the conclusions of the split-brain study. First, the presence of severe epilepsy implies that the patient's brain was abnormal before surgery, and may have developed an unusual pattern of lateralization of function as a result of early brain damage and/or compensation. Second, we cannot be sure that the right hemisphere's failure on the imagery task was not due to an inadequate understanding of the task, rather than an inability to generate images. Although one may point to other complex cognitive tasks that the right hemisphere of this patient has been able to perform (e.g. see Gazzaniga, Smylie, Bayns, Hirst & McCleary, 1984; Holtzman, 1984) to reduce the plausibility of such an alternative explanation, there is in general no way to ascertain that the right hemisphere has understood a task that it has failed.

The discovery of an asymmetry in the image generation performance of normal subjects would not be susceptible to the above alternative explanations, and would therefore strengthen the claim that image generation is a function of the left hemisphere. Toward that end, the following experiment with normal subjects was carried out (Farah, 1986). On each trial, subjects were briefly shown one of six forms, presented at two degrees to the left or right of fixation. As shown in Figure 2.3a, two of the forms were designated targets and the remaining four were nontargets. Figure 2.3b shows a schematic representation of the *baseline* condition, in which subjects were precued with the side on which the stimulus would occur, and their task was simply to respond (by button press) "target" or "nontarget" as quickly as possible. Just as for the split-brain patient, the lateralized stimulus presentations in this experiment ensure that the stimuli are received only by the contralateral half of the visual cortex. Unlike a split brain, however, a normal subject's brain can then transfer a representation of the stimulus to the unstimulated hemisphere. So, whereas access to a lateralized visual stimulus is all or none for the hemispheres of a split-brain patient, for a normal subject it is merely direct versus indirect (and, by being indirect, delayed and degraded). Therefore, if one hemisphere is superior at a particular function, then the subject will perform that function faster and more accurately on stimuli that are presented directly to that hemisphere.

In the *imagery* condition of the experiment, subjects imaged one of the targets on each trial. As in the baseline condition, they were cued with the side on which the stimulus would occur. In addition, they were also cued with a brief central presentation of the target to be imaged in the position of the up-coming stimulus. Except for

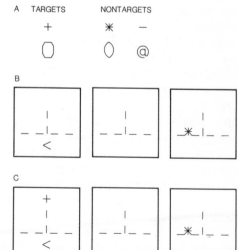

Figure 2.3. Image generation performance of normal subjects.
(a) The stimuli used.
(b) A typical trial sequence in the baseline condition.
(c) A typical trial sequence in the imagery condition.

imaging, their task was the same as in the baseline condition; they responded "target" to either of the two targets and "nontarget" to the four nontargets, regardless of the similarity or match between the stimulus and the image.

Cooper and Shepard (1973) and Posner, Boies, Eichelman and Taylor (1969) have shown that imaging a target can facilitate performance in visual discrimination tasks. In this task, we should therefore expect facilitation of the discrimination between targets and nontargets with imagery, particularly when the image and stimulus are visually similar (as, for example, "+" is to "+," "−," and "*"). Thus, there are two independent measures of the effectiveness of imagery in this experiment: the degree of facilitation with an image, relative to performance in the same visual discrimination task without an image, and degree of facilitation with an image that is visually similar to the stimulus being presented, relative to performance in the same visual discrimination task with an image that is visually different from the stimulus being presented. If the left hemisphere is specialized for image generation, then these two measures of image-mediated facilitation should be greatest when image-stimulus overlap occurs in the left hemisphere, where the image was generated.

Figure 2.4 shows the mean response latencies relevant to the two predictions stated above. As can be seen from part A, performance in the baseline condition did not depend on which hemisphere initially received the stimulus: mean response times for the left and right hemispheres were 815 milliseconds and 818 milliseconds respectively. In contrast, when the same task was performed using an image as a template, there was an overall left hemisphere superiority: the mean response times for the right and left hemispheres were 776 milliseconds and 754 milliseconds, respectively. Furthermore, these differences in response time cannot be attributed to hemispheric differences in speed-accuracy tradeoffs: The left hemisphere maintained the same error rate in the baseline and imagery conditions (20.5%) and the right hemisphere error rate was only 0.3 percentage points more in the baseline than in the imagery condition (23.4% and 23.1% respectively).

Part B of Figure 2.4 shows that the left hemisphere advantage in the imagery condition was greater when the images and stimuli were similar than when they were different: mean response times for the left and right hemispheres were 717 milliseconds and 755 milliseconds respectively with a similar image (with error rates of 18.5% and 24.4%, respectively) and were 790 milliseconds and 797 milliseconds respectively with a different image (with error rates of

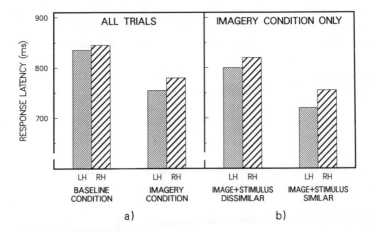

Figure 2.4. Response latencies to stimuli presented to each hemisphere of normal subjects in a visual discrimination task with and without imagery.
(a) Data from all trials: baseline condition (no imagery) and imagery condition.
(b) Data from imagery condition only: image and stimulus visually dissimilar and visually similar.

22.5% and 21.8%, respectively). Both of these predicted interactions were statistically significant.

To summarize, the effect of image generation on visual discrimination performance in normal subjects is asymmetrical in a direction consistent with a left hemisphere basis for image generation. This finding cannot be explained by any of the previously proposed alternative hypotheses. The one hypothesis that accounts naturally for the results of all four of the studies described here is that image generation is a specialized function of the left hemisphere.

CONCLUSIONS

Cognitive psychology has made enormous progress in last 20 years, largely within the theoretical confines of the information-processing paradigm, a basic tenet of which is that the neural substrate of cognition can be ignored. The idea of an autonomous information-processing level of explanation allowed us to theorize about such mentalistic things as imagery without having to give an account of their physiological bases. However, the fact that one *need* not attend to neural substrate does not imply that the properties of the neural substrate are not relevant or could not be helpful, even for theories cast at the information-processing level of description. On the contrary, they may provide a powerful new source of data for the cognitive psychologist. For example, finding of a brain area that is critical for image generation but not for other forms of recall is useful evidence bearing on the issue of the modularity of imagery as a system of memory representation. Similarly, associations like the ones between imagery and dreaming, or between the contents of long-term memory available to the imagery and perception systems, and dissociations like the one between imagery and topographic orientation, suggest relations among different information-processing systems that would probably not otherwise be uncovered.

The benefits of this approach are reciprocal for neuropsychology. In the realm of intelligent behavior, "brain-behavior mappings" probably do not exist; rather, the mappings will be between the cognitive processes that *underlie* behavior and regions or properties of the brain. This is where cognitive theories can play a crucial role. Neuropsychology has traditionally tried to localize, and in other ways generalize about, task-defined abilities and task-defined deficits. In the neuropsychology of spatial ability, one of the greatest challenges at present is simply to delineate the cognitive systems that underlie intelligent spatial behavior. The crucial role of cognitive theory in the present project is illustrated by the inference that the image generation process is dependent upon structures in the posterior left hemisphere. Cognitive theory made it possible to go beyond the task-defined deficits of inability to draw from memory and so on to the particular behavioral profile indicative of an underlying image generation process deficit, and its associated lesion site.

ACKNOWLEDGEMENTS

The writing of this chapter was supported by NIH fellowship F32 MHO8876-02, the Research Service of the Veterans Administration, NIH Program Project Grant NS06209-21 to the Aphasia Research Center of the Boston University School of Medicine, and the MIT Center for Cognitive Science under a grant from the H. P. Sloan Foundation. I thank Howard Gardner for his usual helpful comments and criticisms on an earlier draft of this chapter.

REFERENCES

Arbuse, D. I. 1947. The Gerstmann syndrome: Case report and review of the literature. *Journal of Nervous and Mental Diseases.* 105:359-371.

Brain, R. W. 1954. Loss of visualization. *Proceedings of the Royal Society of Medicine.* 47:288-290.

Brooks, L. R. 1968. Spatial and verbal components in the act of recall. *Canadian Journal of Psychology.* 22:349-368.

Brown, J. W. 1974. Language, cognition, and the thalamus. *Confin. Neurol.* 36:33-60.

Brownell, H. H., Farah, M. J., Harley, J. P. & Kosslyn, S. M. 1983. Distinguishing imagistic and linguistic thought: A case report. Paper presented to the 11th North American Meeting of the International Neuropsychology Society, Mexico City.

Cooper, L. A. & Shepard, R. N. 1973. Chronometric studies of the rotation of mental images. In W. G. Chase (Ed.), *Visual information processing.* New York: Academic Press.

Eddy, J. K. & Glass, A. L. 1981. Reading and listening to high and low imagery sentences. *Journal of Verbal Learning and Verbal Behavior.* 20:333-345.

Ehrlichman, H. & Barrett, J. 1983. Right hemisphere specialization for mental imagery: A review of the evidence. *Brain and Cognition.* 2:39-52.

Farah, M. J. 1984. The neurological basis of mental imagery: A componential analysis. *Cognition.* 18:245-272.

Farah, M. J. 1985. Psychophysical evidence for a shared representational medium for mental images and percepts. *Journal of Experimental Psychology: General.* 114:91-103.

Farah, M. J. 1986. The laterality of mental image generation: A test with normal subjects. *Neuropsychologia.* 24:541-551.

Farah, M. J., Gazzaniga, M. S., Holtzman, J. D. & Kosslyn, S. M. 1985. A left hemisphere basis for visual mental imagery? *Neuropsychologia.* 23:115-118.

Farah, M. J. Levine, D. N. & Calvanio, R. In press. A case study of image generation deficit. *Brain and Cognition.*

Finke, R. A. & Kosslyn, S. M. 1980. Mental imagery acuity in the peripheral visual field. *Journal of Experimental Psychology: Human Perception and Performance.* 6:126-139.

Finke, R. A., Pinker, S. & Farah, M. J. Reinterpreting patterns in visual images. Manuscript submitted for publication, 1986.

Gazzaniga, M. S., Smylie, C. S., Baynes, K., Hirst, W. & McCleary, C. 1984. Profiles of right hemisphere language and speech following brain bisection. *Brain and Language.* 22:206-220.

Geschwind, N. 1965. Disconnexion syndromes in animals and man. *Brain.* 88:237-294, 585-644.

Goodglass, H. & Kaplan, E. 1972. *The assessment of aphasia and related disorders.* Philadelphia: Lea & Febiger.

Greenberg, M. S. & Farah, M. J. 1986. The laterality of dreaming. *Brain and Cognition.* 5:307-321.

Hecaen, H. & Albert, M. L. 1978. *Human Neuropsychology.* New York: Wiley.

56   FARAH

Holtzman, J. D. 1984. Interactions between cortical and subcortical visual areas: evidence from human commisurotomy patients. *Vision Research.* 24:801-814.

Humphrey, M. E. & Zangwill, O. L. 1951. Cessation of dreaming after brain injury. *Journal of Neurology, Neurosurgery and Psychiatry.* 14:322-325.

Kosslyn, S. M. 1980. *Image and Mind.* Cambridge: Harvard University Press.

Lyman, R. S., Kwan, S. T. & Chao, W. H. 1938. Left parieto-occipital brain tumor with observations on alexia and agraphia in Chinese and English. *Chinese Medical Journal.* 54:491-516.

Nielsen, J. M. 1946. *Agnosia, apraxia, aphasia: Their value in cerebral localization.* New York: Paul B. Hoeber.

Nielsen, J. M. 1955. Occipital lobes, dreams and psychosis. *Journal of Nervous and Mental Disease.* 121:30-32.

Posner, M. I., Boies, S. J., Eichelman, W. H., & Taylor, R. L. 1969. Retention of visual and name codes of single letters. *Journal of Experimental Psychology Monograph.* 79:1, Pt. 2.

Pylyshyn, Z. W. 1981. The imagery debate: Analogue media versus tacit knowledge. *Psychological Review.* 87:16-45.

Ratcliff, G. 1982. Disturbances of spatial orientation associated with cerebral lesions. In M. Potegal (Ed.) *Spatial abilities: Development and physiological foundations.* New York: Academic Press.

Ross, E. D. & Mesulam, M. M. 1979. Dominant language functions of the right hemisphere? *Archives of Neurology.* 36:144-148.

Shepard, R. N. & Chipman, S. 1970. Second-order isomorphism of internal representations: Shapes of states. *Cognitive Psychology.* 1:1-17.

Spalding, J. M. K. & Zangwill, O. L. 1950. Disturbance of number-form in a case of brain injury. *Journal of Neurology, Neurosurgery & Psychiatry.* 13:24-29.

Weber, R. J. & Castleman, J. 1970. The time it takes to imagine. *Perception & Psychophysics.* 8:165-168.

Weber, R. J. & Malmstrom, F. V. 1979. Measuring the size of mental images. *Journal of Experimental Psychology: Human Perception and Performance.* 5:1-12.

Wilson, D. H., Reeves, A., & Gazzaniga, M. S. 1978. Division of the corpus callosum for uncontrollable epilepsy. *Neurology.* 28:649-653.

Zurif, E. 1984. Neurolinguistics: Some analyses of aphasic language. In M.S. Gazzaniga (Ed.), *Handbook of Cognitive Neuropsychology.* New York: Plenum.

THE NEUROBIOLOGICAL BASIS OF SPATIAL COGNITION: ROLE OF THE PARIETAL LOBE

3

Richard A. Andersen
Salk Institute for Biological Studies

The posterior parietal cortex has long been implicated in spatial aspects of perception and behavior in primates. Deficits after lesion to this area in humans indicate that this cortical region is essential for accurate visually guided motor activity, for appreciation of the orientation of self within the extrapersonal space, for normal spatial perception, and for the operation of spatial aspects of attention. Lesions to homologous areas in monkeys produce a similar set of signs and symptoms to those seen in humans, and the available psychophysical literature suggests that visual-spatial processing mechanisms are likely to be similar in the two species. Thus, neurophysiologists use the monkey as an animal model for understanding cortical spatial processes in humans.

An important issue in cortical physiology is how space might be represented in regions of the brain, such as the inferior parietal lobule, which are important for spatial aspects of behavior. Visual information is gathered in retinal coordinates as a result of the focusing of visual images on the retinae. The contralateral visual field is represented in several different areas of the central nervous system through an orderly retinotopic mapping of projections from retina to brain and between visual areas in the brain. However, a retinotopic coordinate frame for visual space is not useful for many aspects of motor behavior, particularly rapid eye and limb movements made without visual feedback. Such movements are made to locations in space referenced to the body rather than the retina. At some point in the nervous system visual information must be converted into an ego-centered coordinate frame using eye and head position signals so that these ballistic aspects of motor activity can be made with accuracy within the extrapersonal space. The perceptual apparatus also appears to transform visual inputs to non-retinal spatial representations since our perceptions of visual space remain quite stable regardless of the fact that we make on the average three eye movements a second. Many of the defects that are seen with lesions to the inferior parietal lobule could be accounted for by a disruption in the transformation of retinal coordinate frames to spatial coordinate frames.

In this chapter I will first review some of the spatial defects that are found in humans with lesions to the inferior parietal lobule. This review is meant to be selective and indicate some of the features that neurophysiologists use as clues to designing experiments in animals aimed at increasing our understanding of the functions of the human cortex. Next I will briefly review the defects caused by lesions to this area in the monkey. We will then cover the anatomy of the area in man and monkey with particular emphasis on its relation to the visual system. Last, we will examine what has been learned of the role of this area in spatial processing from single unit recording experiments in monkeys.

HUMAN LESIONS

Damage to the inferior parietal lobule in humans produces visual defects that can be divided into two general categories: those that affect visual attention and those that affect spatial perception. Sideness plays a role in the expression of this disorder in humans with right hemisphere lesions in right-handed individuals often causing more frequent and severe parietal lobe syndromes (Piercy, Hecaen & Ajuriaguerra, 1960; McFie & Zangwill, 1960; Critchley, 1953). However, some students of the parietal lobe believe that left-sided parietal lesions in the absence of aphasia and the agnosias can produce a syndrome similar to that seen with right-sided lesions (Denny-Brown & Banker, 1954; Paterson & Zangwill, 1944). Unilateral lesions can produce disturbances that are only contralateral, or particularly with right hemisphere lesions, bilateral.

Attentional defects. Patients with posterior parietal lesions can exhibit visual inattention or "neglect" which is often confined to the hemifield contralateral to the lesion. A vivid example of a contralateral neglect is shown in Figure 3.1. The patient was a painter who was asked to paint self-portraits at various times over several months during recovery from a stroke. As illustrated in Figure 3.1, in the early portraits he completely ignored the contralateral side of his face in the paintings and it was only after several months of recovery that the portraits appeared normal.

The neglect can also extend to the body with patients exhibiting aspontaneity of the contralateral body half, difficulty in dressing and lack of grooming of the contralateral side. In severe cases patients will deny that the contralateral body half is theirs or will have distortions of the body image such as perceived supernumerary limbs (Denny-Brown & Banker, 1954; Brain, 1941; Hecaen, Penfield, Bertrand & Malmo, 1956; Hecaen & Ajuriaguerra, 1954; De Renzi, Faglioni & Scotti, 1970; Critchley, 1953). It has been argued that the neglect of the body and neglect in the visual hemifield are signs of a common origin (Brain, 1941; Hecaen et al., 1956).

Spatial defects. Spatial defects with posterior parietal lesions are wide ranging and include visual disorientation, defects in visual localization, constructional apraxia, disturbances in topographical relationships, and loss of spatial memories.

The defective localization of objects in space in the absence of visual object agnosia has been termed visual disorientation. This deficit can occur with normal visual acuity and without visual field defects (Brain, 1941; Semmes, Weinstein, Ghent & Teuber, 1963). Patients report that their environments appear "confused" or "jumbled," and these spatial defects, when severe, can be more debilitating than blindness (Critchley, 1953). Such patients cannot judge the position of two objects in relation to one another (Holmes, 1919) and often are unable to notice two objects simultaneously (Holmes, 1919; Ettlinger, Warrington & Zangwill, 1957). Reports such as "when I look at one thing, the rest vanish" are common (Kinsbourne & Warrington, 1962). Patients are unable to attend to backgrounds (Semmes et al., 1963) or to apply uniform frames of reference (Paterson & Zangwill, 1944). They do not appreciate a figure as a spatially organized unit, and attention to any one part of it destroys the effect of the whole (Paterson & Zangwill, 1944).

Errors in visual localization following posterior parietal lesions are indicated by mistakes in pointing to visual targets (Paterson & Zangwill, 1944; Ratcliff & Davies-Jones, 1972; Holmes, 1919); these defects are strictly visuospatial and are not defects in reaching (Ratcliff & Davies-Jones, 1972). These deficits are generally confined

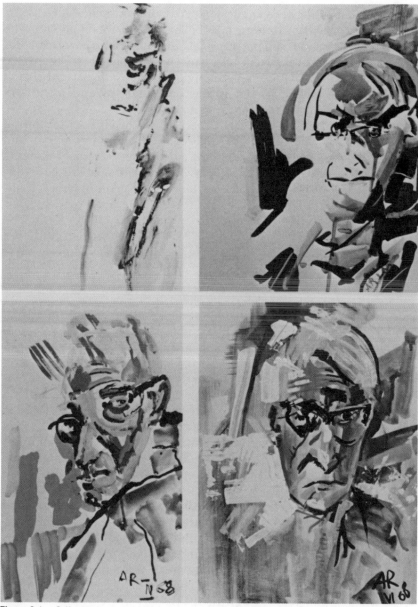

Figure 3.1. Self-portraits by German artist Anton Raderscheidt. These portraits were made at different times after a stroke that damaged the right parietal cortex. The portraits were made two months (upper left), three and a half months (upper right), six months (lower left) and nine months (lower right) after the lesion. Note that in the earlier portraits the side of the face contralateral to the lesion is profoundly neglected. The figure is reprinted from Wurtz, Goldberg & Robinson (1982); the self-portraits were originally published by Jung (1974).

to the contralateral space for reaching with either limb. Other spatial defects occur in distance estimation (Paterson & Zangwill, 1944; Holmes, 1919), appreciation of the relative lengths and sizes of objects (Holmes, 1919), and the occasional loss of stereopsis (Carmon & Bechtoldt, 1969; Critchley, 1953; Riddoch, 1917).

Constructional apraxia refers to an inability to reproduce spatial relations in a model, as for instance, in drawing (Benson & Barton, 1970; Piercy et al., 1960; Mcfie & Zangwill, 1960; Paterson & Zangwill, 1944; Hecaen et al., 1956; Hecaen & Ajuriaguerra, 1954). Constructional defects after posterior parietal cortex lesions are often global and include abnormal representations of perspective and depth, abnormalities of relative size and articulation, and a piecemeal approach whereby the patient wanders through a drawing going from detail to detail in no coherent spatial frame. Some authors consider constructional apraxia to be a secondary result of a visuospatial defect (Paterson & Zangwill, 1944; Butters & Barton, 1970; Hecaen et al., 1956). Figure 3.2 shows an example of constructional apraxia in which a patient has been asked to model with blocks the structure in the left panel with the poor results pictured in the right panel.

Following posterior parietal lobe lesions disturbances of topographical relationships, as in route-finding (Teuber, 1963; Brain, 1941; Semmes et al., 1963; Hecaen et al., 1956; Holmes, 1919), are also found. Investigators believe that visuospatial defects contribute to these signs although defects in spatial memories also appear to play a role. The first account in the literature of a topographic memory deficit comes from Charcot's description in 1883 of a patient who, in a town previously well known to the patient, could no longer recognize even commonplace landmarks. The patient claimed he felt as if he were at sea in what was at one time a familiar world. Wilbrand (1887) also described a patient who could not call up remem-

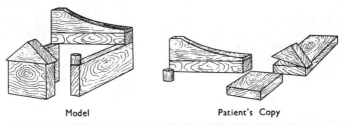

Model   Patient's Copy

Figure 3.2. Constructional apraxia. A patient with a left fronto-parietal metastatic tumor was asked to model the block construction on the left. The patient's copy on the right indicates a poor performance on this three-dimensional task. Figure from Critchley, 1953.

bered visual images of a topological or geographical nature. Those few topographic images the patient could generate from memory were profoundly spatially distorted. For instance, the patient imagined that the street lay just outside her parlor when actually a bedroom intervened and believed that articles of her furniture were in the street rather than in her home. Both of these patients had other visual memory defects as well (Charcot-Wilbrand syndrome); however, since that time many cases have been described in which the memory deficit is restricted to topographic-spatial memory (reviewed in De Renzi, 1982). Moreover, these memory deficits have been distinguished from perceptual deficits (Critchley, 1953).

Certain aspects of the hemi-neglect commonly found with parietal lesions seem to derive from the defect in spatial memory. In an illuminating experiment with parietal patients exhibiting contralateral neglect, Bisiach and Luzzatti (1978) asked these patients to describe from memory, landmarks bordering a square familiar to the patients, the Piazza del Duomo in Milan (Figure 3.3). They were first asked to imagine that they were standing on the steps of the cathedral at one end of the square; in this instance they described mostly those establishments on the side of the street ipsilateral to the lesion. Next they were asked to imagine that they were on the

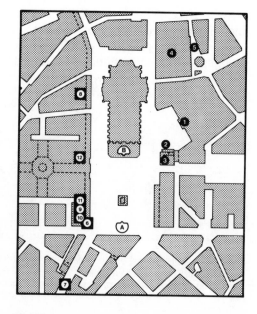

Figure 3.3. A map of the Piazza del Duomo in Milan. Contralateral neglect is demonstrated in patient I.G. who, after suffering a right hemisphere stroke, was asked to recall from memory landmarks on the square from the two perspectives indicated in the figure (A and B). The numbered dark circles indicate the positions of landmarks she recalled from perspective A and the numbered dark squares the landmarks recalled from perspective B. The figure is modified from Bisiach and Luzzatti (1978).

other side of the square facing the cathedral; they then described mostly establishments on the other side of the street. In interpreting these results the investigators reasoned that spatial memories are stored bilaterally with half of space represented contralaterally in each hemisphere.

Parietal lesions not only eliminate old and deeply rooted spatial memories as in the previous examples, but also interfere with the formation of new spatial memories. In clinical tests it has been found that such patients require significantly larger numbers of trials to learn spatial tasks such as memorizing a path through a maze or tapping a sequence of blocks based on their spatial position (De Renzi, Faglioni & Previdi, 1977; De Renzi, Faglioni & Villa, 1977).

Since parietal lobe lesions affect all spatial memories including both old memories recorded prior to the lesion and the formation of new memories after the lesion, it is likely that the posterior parietal area either contains the topological memory traces or is necessary for their recall. The dual nature of this amnesia distinguishes the posterior parietal area from certain other classical memory regions such as the hippocampal formation, which appear to be involved in the consolidation of memory since lesions to these regions primarily affect the acquisition of new memories. These observations are consistent with Mishkin's (1982) proposal that memories are stored in association cortex by way of a consolidating action of hippocampal and related structures on these cortices.

MONKEY LESION EXPERIMENTS

Posterior parietal lesions in monkeys produce many visual-spatial deficits similar to those recorded in humans. Unilateral lesions or cooling of posterior parietal cortex produce animals that exhibit contralateral disuse of the body, neglect in the contralateral visual field, and contralateral extinction for visual stimuli.

A most extensively studied defect is that of impaired spatial localization as indicated by inaccuracy in reaching with the contralateral limb under visual guidance following unilateral lesions (LaMotte & Acuna, 1978; Ettlinger & Kalsbeck, 1962; Hartje & Ettlinger, 1974; Moffet, Ettlinger, Morton & Piercy, 1967; Ratcliff, Ridley & Ettlinger, 1977; Faugier-Grimaud, Frenois & Stein, 1978). This defect is confined to the contralateral limb for reaching in either hemifield. The ipsilateral limb can reach accurately to objects in either hemifield. Thus, the defect manifests itself as if spatial vision had been severed from the one limb but not the other.

Bilateral ablations of posterior parietal cortex produce severe deficits in visual-spatial orientation. Such animals cannot discriminate the spatial relation of two or more objects in the visual field (Mendoza & Thomas, 1975; Brody & Pribram, 1978; Pohl, 1973; Ungerleider & Brody, 1977). Monkeys with bilateral posterior parietal lesions also have topographic deficits as measured by their performance on route-following tasks (Petrides & Iversen, 1979) and exhibit visual extinction (Lynch & McLaren, 1984). It can be seen, then, that the posterior parietal cortex of the monkey, as in man, is important in visual-spatial perception.

ANATOMY

The cerebral hemispheres are divided by large sulci into six major lobes. These lobes can be further subdivided into cortical fields which are areas of the cortex that differ in their connections, internal structure, and functional roles. Many cortical fields can be further subdivided into repeating functional modules; these modules are often referred to as cortical columns.

The anterior aspect of the parietal lobe contains Brodmann's areas 3, 1, and 2. These areas are often collectively referred to as primary somatosensory cortex, although they are functionally and anatomically distinct cortical areas.

The posterior parietal cortex is subdivided into superior and inferior parietal lobules. The superior parietal lobule consists of somatosensory association cortex and the inferior parietal lobule consists of high order visual and somatosensory cortical fields. Brodmann's area 5 encompasses the superior parietal lobule and his area 7 the inferior parietal lobule (see Figure 3.4a). Area 7 was further subdivided into a medial (7a) and lateral (7b) field by Vogt and Vogt (1919). Further confirmation for these cytoarchitectural subdivisions came from von Bonin and Bailey (1947) whose PE cortical area roughly corresponds to area 5 and whose PG and PF correspond to 7a and 7b (Figure 3.4b).

The exact homologies of these cortical areas in the monkey with those in the human are unclear. Brodmann believed that the cellular architecture of area 7 of the inferior parietal lobule of the monkey was identical to the posterior-most aspect of the human superior parietal lobule with area 5 in man located more anteriorly in the superior parietal lobule (Figure 3.4c). He recognized two cortical areas in the human inferior parietal lobule, corresponding to the angular (area 39) and marginal gyri (area 40), which he believed had

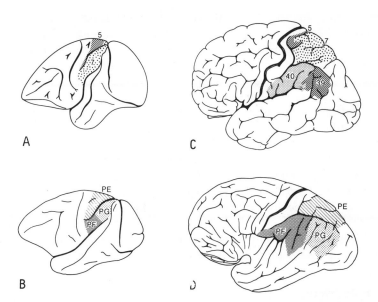

Figure 3.4. Cytoarchitectonics of the posterior parietal cortex. Lateral views of monkey and human cerebral cortices showing cytoarchitectural parcellations made by different anatomists of the posterior parietal cortex.

  (a) Brodmann's (1905) parcellation of the monkey cortex (Cercopithecus).
  (b) von Bonin and Bailey's (1947) parcellation of the monkey cortex (Macaca mulatta).
  (c) Brodmann's (1907) classification of the human cortex.
  (d) von Economo's (1929) map of the human posterior parietal cortex.

no homologies in the old world monkey. Von Bonin and Bailey criticized Brodmann's work in the monkey and asserted that their areas PG and PF of the monkey inferior parietal lobule were homologous to area PG and PF of the human (Von Economo, 1929) which encompass the inferior parietal lobule of man (Figure 3.4d). Support for von Bonin and Bailey's view comes from the observation that lesions of the inferior parietal lobule of monkeys produce visual-spatial defects and thus are more like the inferior parietal lesions in humans which also produce visual-spatial defects and less like superior parietal lesions in humans which tend to result in somatic disturbances.

In the past 15 years a great deal has been learned from anatomical and physiological experiments about the structure and function of the posterior parietal cortex in monkeys. I will emphasize the inferior parietal lobule and particularly the visual cortical fields within this brain area since the most progress has been made in these areas. The use of visual rather than somatosensory paradigms has proven to be most productive since visual stimuli are more easily controlled and a good deal more is known about the earlier stages of processing in the visual system.

The inferior parietal lobule receives visual inputs from visual association cortical fields (so called extrastriate cortical fields to distinguish them from striate or primary visual cortex) and somatosensory inputs from somatosensory association cortex. Its major thalamic input is from the pulvinar. The inferior parietal lobule is part of a net of reciprocal interconnections between cortical fields concerned with some of the highest order cortical functions including the prefrontal cortex, cingulate gyrus, parahippocampal gyrus, and cortex of the superior temporal sulcus. Recent studies reveal that the inferior parietal lobule is composed of not one or even two but probably several cortical fields that differ in their anatomical connections and in their functional roles in spatial processing.

Visual Pathways

The visual inputs to the inferior parietal lobule are derived primarily from other extrastriate visual cortical fields. Until recently the exact sources of these visual inputs were unknown. It is now clear that the inferior parietal lobule receives visual information from several converging cortical sources including visual areas in the prelunate gyrus (V4 and the dorsal prelunate area; Seltzer & Pandya, 1980; Andersen, Asanuma & Cowan 1985, Andersen, Siegel, Essick & Asanuma, 1985), the parieto-occipital visual area (Colby, Gattass, Olson & Gross, 1983; Andersen, Siegel, Essick & Asanuma, 1985), cortical areas within the superior temporal sulcus and visually responsive areas within the occipital-temporal sulcus (Mesulam, Van Hoesen, Pandya & Geschwind, 1977; Desimone & Gross, 1979; Andersen, Siegel, Essick & Asanuma, 1985). None of these areas receive direct projections from primary visual cortex (V1) but some of them do receive inputs from visual areas that receive V1 projections (Andersen, Siegel, Essick & Asanuma, 1985; Colby et al., 1983; Maunsell & Van Essen, 1983). Thus, although the inferior parietal lobule receives projections from several extrastriate visual areas, all of these parallel visual pathways are at least three steps removed from the primary visual cortex. The several visual projections have different patterns of termination within the inferior parietal lobule with the different cortical fields receiving different proportions of input from these pathways (Andersen, Siegel, Essick & Asanuma, 1985).

Ascending Thalamic Inputs

The major source of thalamic projection to the inferior parietal lobule is from the medial, lateral and oral divisions of the pulvinar (Trojanowski & Jacobson, 1976; Kasdon & Jacobson, 1978; Asanuma, Andersen & Cowan, 1982; Asanuma, Andersen & Cowan, 1985). These areas in turn receive ascending projections from the deep oculomotor layers of the superior colliculus and from the pretectum (Benevento & Standage, 1983). The areas of the pulvinar that project to the inferior parietal lobule receive feedback corticothalamic projections from the same cortical areas to which they project (Asanuma et al., 1985). The areas of the pulvinar that project to the visually responsive cortical fields of the inferior parietal lobule contain light-sensitive neurons (neurons that respond to visual stimuli) with large receptive fields and no clear retinotopic organization (Benevento & Miller, 1981; Bender, 1981; Petersen, Robinson & Keys, 1982). Many neurons in these areas of the pulvinar also have activity related to saccades (ballistic eye movements) which likely obtains from the projection of the deep layers of the superior colliculus (Perryman, Lindsley & Lindsley, 1980; Petersen et al., 1982). The visual inputs of these neurons probably are largely of cortical origin and are derived from descending corticothalamic projections (Bender, 1983; Ogren & Hendrickson, 1979). The oral pulvinar, which projects to area 7b, contains neurons with predominantly somatosensory properties (Acuna, Gonzalez & Dominguez, 1983).

Area 7a receives its pulvinar input almost exclusively from three disk-like arrays of neurons in the medial pulvinar (Asanuma et al. 1982, 1985). There is a topographic relationship in the reciprocal connections between 7a and these disks indicating that area 7a is represented three times in the medial pulvinar (Asanuma et al., 1982, 1985). The medial pulvinar also projects to other higher cortical areas such as the prefrontal cortex and cortex of the superior temporal sulcus in the form of disklike aggregates of neurons (Asanuma et al., 1982, 1985; Trojanowski & Jacobson, 1974; Siqueira, 1965, 1971). In double label experiments in which the arrays of neurons projecting to two different locations in the brain can be visualized on single sections of the brain, it has been found that for the prefrontal cortex and area 7a the disks in the pulvinar are partially overlapping with the frontal projecting disks located more medially (Asanuma et al., 1982, 1985). The cells in the overlapping regions of the projections are intermingled but single neurons almost never send axons to both cortical areas.

It is likely that all of the higher cortical areas that are reciprocally interconnected with 7a also receive projections from disks in
the medial pulvinar. These pulvinar projections terminate most
heavily in the lower aspect of cortical layer three (Trojanowski &
Jacobson, 1976). Interestingly this cortical layer is the major source
of cortico-cortical connections (Andersen, Essick & Siegel, 1984).
Thus the medial pulvinar may act as a regulator of transmission
between these cortical regions involved in the highest aspects of
cortical function. The partial overlapping of pulvinar projection
disks and the multiple representations of cortical areas across
several disks is a revealing structure in terms of the regulation of
cortico-cortical communication. This structure enables any locus in
the medial pulvinar to connect, in an anatomically precise fashion,
segregated areas within several widely separated cortical areas.
Therefore, one might predict that the pulvinar plays a role in attention by linking together processes that are occurring in different
cortical areas. Such a general attentional role for all of pulvinar
would explain why monkeys or humans with inferior or lateral pulvinar lesions do poorly in visual search (Ungerleider & Christensen,
1977, 1979; Ogren, Mateer & Wyler, 1984)-they are not able to con-
join features of an object for which they are searching since these
features are processed in different parts of the brain and are atten-
tionally linked by the pulvinar. This linking process in the pulvinar
may in turn be regulated by the reticular thalamic nucleus (Crick,
1984).

Many area 7a neurons receive eye position signals. These eye
position signals are probably derived from oculomotor structures in
the brainstem that send eye position information to the cortex via
the intralaminar thalamic nuclei (Schlag-Rey & Schlag, 1984).

In summary, the major thalamic input to the inferior parietal
lobule is from the pulvinar. The pulvinar in turn receives ascending
inputs from oculomotor structures in the midbrain. A likely role of
the pulvinar is the regulation of cortical processes involved in
directed attention.

Multiple Cortical Areas in the Inferior Parietal Lobule

In the early pioneering studies of Mountcastle and colleagues,
several classes of neurons having visual, oculomotor, or somatic properties were identified in the inferior parietal lobule (Mountcastle,
Lynch, Georgopoulos, Sakata & Acuna 1975; Lynch, Mountcastle,
Talbot & Yin, 1977). The properties of these neurons were determined by recording their activity with microelectrodes while the

animals performed various motor and oculomotor tasks. These investigators made the observation that neurons with similar properties tended to be clustered together. From reconstructions of the locations of recording sights, they found no clear segregation of these properties into cortical fields (Lynch et al., 1977). They reasoned that the inferior parietal lobule was one large cortical field with a columnar organization of functional properties. The different functional columns were assumed to be more or less evenly dispersed. However, their data were pooled from several animals and referenced to sulcal patterns; this practice can smear considerably any topographic organization since the sulcal patterns and the relations of cortical fields to sulcal patterns vary extensively from animal to animal. Hyvarinen and colleagues (Hyvarinen & Shelepin, 1979; Hyvarinen, 1981) mapped the inferior parietal lobule and found a gradient of localization with somatic properties located more laterally and visual properties more medially. However, the methods used for determining the classification of cells were not well controlled in their experiments. In recent years anatomical experiments have indicated that the inferior parietal lobule can be subdivided into a number of different areas on the basis of connections (Pandya & Seltzer, 1982; Andersen, Asanuma & Cowan, 1985; Andersen, Siegel, Essick & Asanuma, 1985). Recent functional mapping experiments (in which large numbers of microelectrode penetrations are made, and the locations of the recordings are reconstructed, in individual animals) indicate functionally segregated areas in the inferior parietal lobule that coincide with the anatomically (connectionally) defined subdivisions (Essick, Andersen & Siegel, 1984; Andersen, Asanuma & Cowan, 1985; Andersen, Siegel, Essick & Asanuma, 1985). The following is a brief list of these newly recognized cortical areas, whose locations are diagrammed in Figure 3.5.

Lateral intraparietal area. This area is unique in being the only region of the inferior parietal lobule that projects strongly to the frontal eyefields (Barbas & Mesulam, 1981; Andersen, Asanuma & Cowan, 1985) and the superior colliculus (Lynch & Graybiel, 1983; Andersen, Asanuma & Cowan, 1985); both are structures involved with the generation of saccadic eye movements. The neurons in this area respond to both visual stimuli and to saccadic eye movements (Essick et al., 1984). Also, electrical stimulation of the area produces saccadic eye movements (Shibutani, Sakata & Hyvarinen, 1984). However, it is unlikely that this area is involved in the generation of saccades since the saccade-related component of the cells' responses generally occurs at or just after the beginning of an eye

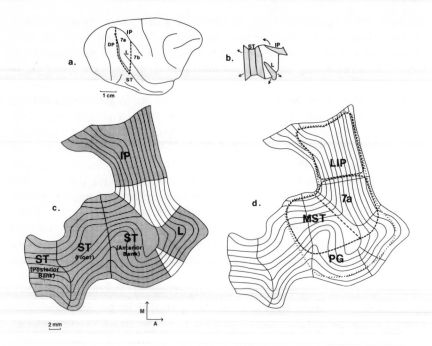

Figure 3.5. Flattened reconstructions of the inferior parietal lobule. Locations of different cortical areas in the inferior parietal and adjoining dorsal prelunate cortex.

(a) Dorsolateral view of the right hemisphere of a macaque monkey. The dotted line indicates a section of the inferior parietal lobule that has been diagrammatically flattened in the remaining panels.

(b) The method of flattening the inferior parietal lobule. The cortex is treated as a folded sheet centered on layer IV. The cortex buried in the superior temporal sulcus is pulled out to the left, the cortex of the intraparietal sulcus is flipped upward and the cortical walls of the lateral sulcus are pulled apart.

(c) Shading indicates flattened areas that lie within sulci.

(d) Locations of two cortical areas, the lateral intraparietal area and the medial superior temporal area, which lie buried within the sulci. Also indicated is the cytoarchitectural subdivision PG of von Bonin and Bailey (1947) which includes the dorsal prelunate area. Figure modified from Andersen, Siegel, Essick and Asanuma, 1985.

movement (Essick et al., 1984). Rather, this area appears to be receiving a corollary discharge from motor structures such as the frontal eye fields informing this perceptual region to be prepared for a change in sensory input due to an eye movement.

Area 7a. Nearly every cell in area 7a can be shown to respond to visual stimuli (Andersen, Asanuma & Cowan, 1985). The receptive fields of these neurons are large and quite often bilateral (Motter & Mountcastle, 1981). Many of these cells also get eye position inputs and the visual response is modified by this eye position signal (Andersen & Mountcastle, 1983; Andersen et al., 1984). This area has a heavy projection to area 46 of the dorsolateral prefrontal cortex (Andersen, Asanuma & Cowan, 1985).

Area 7b.   Area 7b contains neurons that respond to somatosensory stimuli and reaching behavior (Andersen, Asanuma & Cowan, 1985). This area projects to somatosensory association cortex (Andersen, Asanuma & Cowan, 1985).

Medial superior temporal area.   This area is located primarily in the anterior bank of the caudal aspect of the superior temporal sulcus. This region receives a prominent visual input from the parieto-occipital area, the dorsal prelunate area, and the middle temporal area in the superior temporal sulcus (Colby et al., 1983; Andersen, Siegel, Essick & Asanuma, 1985; Maunsell & Van Essen, 1983). The middle temporal area is specialized for processing visual motion. The medial superior temporal area also appears to be specialized for aspects of motion processing since it contains a preponderance of cells with visual pursuit activity and motion sensitivity (Sakata, Shibutani & Kawano, 1983).

Dorsal prelunate area.   This region is adjacent to the inferior parietal lobule and provides it with a major visual input (Andersen, Asanuma & Cowan, 1985). This cortical area is situated just dorsal to V4 on the dorsal-most tip of the prelunate gyrus and receives inputs from V4 and visual areas in the anecent gyrus (Andersen, Asanuma & Cowan, 1985).

The cortico-pontine projections and the patterns of thalamic input to the inferior parietal lobule are unique for each of the cortical areas outlined above (May & Andersen, 1984; Asanuma et al., 1985). The presence of these anatomically and functionally different subdivisions suggests that each of these sub-areas is specialized to process separate aspects of spatial perception.

PHYSIOLOGY

Most recent information on the processing role of the posterior parietal cortex for visual-spatial perception has come from single unit recordings made in behaving monkeys. In experiments of this type animals are trained to perform various motor and oculomotor tasks. Each trial of one of these tasks lasts 3 to 5 seconds. The animals do one to two thousand trials over a six hour recording period and, with the successful completion of each trial, they receive a drop of juice as reward. While performing these tasks the activity of single cortical neurons is recorded. The functional properties of a cortical area are determined by correlating the behavior of the animals with the activity of the neurons.

The response properties of posterior parietal neurons was first described by Hyvarinen and Poranen (1974) and Mountcastle and colleagues (1975). In their pioneering experiments Mountcastle and colleagues (Mountcastle et al., 1975; Lynch et al., 1977) described several classes of neurons in the inferior parietal lobule that were active with reaching, with fixation, and with saccade and tracking eye movements. These investigators proposed that the posterior parietal cortex integrated information on the internal state of the animal with events in the external environment, and generated general commands for motor operation in the extrapersonal space. This command hypothesis was challenged by Robinson and colleagues (Robinson, Goldberg & Stanton, 1978) who found large numbers of units in the posterior parietal cortex to be active to visual and somatosensory stimuli. They proposed that cell activity related to reaching was actually somatosensory in origin and that all presumed fixation, saccade and tracking activity was an artifact of visual stimulation by the laboratory environment as the animal moved his eyes or fixated different locations in space. They therefore assigned a sensory role to this area.

The issue of cell classification has recently been reexamined using paradigms that separate the visual and eye movement or eye position components of the neuronal responses (Sakata, Shibutani & Kawano, 1980; Sakata et al., 1983; Essick et al., 1984). These experiments show that these neurons generally receive a visual signal *and* have an eye movement or eye position component to their response. The saccade-related activity is consistent with a corollary discharge since the activity generally occurs at or just after the beginning of an eye movement. As elaborated in the next section, the interaction of visual and eye position signals may result in the mapping of visual space in head-centered coordinates (Andersen et al., 1984).

The Representation of Space in Area 7a

The observations that motor movements are made accurately to locations in space regardless of eye position and that the perception of visual space is constant in spite of eye movements suggest that the motor and perceptual systems have access to neural representations of visual space that are head-centered or ego-centered. A transformation from the retinal representations, which are the general feature of early cortical processing, to spatial representations requires interaction between retinal and eye position signals. This type of interaction has been shown to exist in the inferior parietal lobule (Andersen & Mountcastle, 1983; Andersen et al., 1984). Furthermore, given the profound spatial disturbances that result from parietal lobe lesions, the inferior parietal lobule is the most likely candidate for a cortical region that represents the visual scene in a head-centered or body-centered spatial frame.

The effect of the eyes' angle-of-gaze on light sensitive neurons in area 7a is to change the level of visual sensitivity dependent on eye position (Andersen et al., 1984). Thus, for the most preferred angle-of-gaze, the retinal receptive field will be extremely responsive to visual stimuli whereas at the least preferred angle-of-gaze the neuron will generally be completely unresponsive to visual stimuli. There is a smooth gradient in responsiveness with eye position between these two extremes. Thus, in its simplest form the activity of each of these cells can be described by a gain factor, which is a function of the angle-of-gaze, multiplied by the response profile of the retinal receptive field of the neuron. These cells are tuned to respond best to locations in head-centered coordinates which are defined by the best angle-of-gaze and the most sensitive part (center) of the receptive field. Cells are found tuned to every location in head-centered space in each hemisphere. Since the response is dependent on eye position, a spatially invariant response that is independent of eye position can only be found in the activity of groups of space-tuned neurons in area 7a.

Motion

Relative motion is the differential movement of elements of the visual field. This type of motion is important for spatial perception, indicating depth with motion parallax, movement in depth with expansions or contractions of the field, and the relative position of objects from occlusion and disocclusion during self-motion. Cells in the inferior parietal lobule show exquisite sensitivity for relative motion. Motter and Mountcastle (1981) described an opponent vector organization for motion sensitivity, finding cells with bilateral receptive fields which are active for stimuli moving either inward or outward from the fixation point. Such neurons would be maximally active for translation of the head forward or backward in the environment and could provide information about position by analyzing flow fields during motion. Sakata and colleagues (Sakata, Shibutani, Kawano & Harrington, 1985) have described different sets of cells in the inferior parietal lobule that appear to be selective for rotations in the sagittal, horizontal or frontal planes. Many of the relative-motion-sensitive neurons are located in the anterior bank of the superior temporal sulcus and may receive a convergence of directional information from the middle temporal cortical field.

Attention

Considering the profound defects in visual attention after lesions to this area, it is not surprising to find that the level of activity of these neurons is dependent on visual attention. Cells respond more vigorously to a visual stimulus if it is behaviorally relevant to the animal (Bushnell, Goldberg & Robinson, 1981). The responsiveness of the cells, even for stimuli that are not behaviorally significant, is greatly facilitated when the animal performs tasks requiring attentive fixations (Mountcastle et al., 1981). This facilitation is not a sensory effect since it is still present if the fixation target is removed as long as the animal maintains fixation. The facilitation of area 7 neurons is also not one of general arousal since it is not present in tasks requiring the animal's attention but without fixation. The spatial tuning of cells with angle-of-gaze effects is less pronounced without attentional fixations (Andersen & Mountcastle, 1983). This finding suggests a link between spatial and attentional processes in the parietal lobe.

CONCLUSION

The inferior parietal lobule plays a central role in spatial perception and visual attention. Lesions to this area in monkeys and humans profoundly disrupt spatial abilities. Many of the cells in this area appear to encode the position of visual objects in head- or ego-centered coordinates. The area also appears to play a role in extracting spatial information from relative motion. The visual activity of the cells is dependent on behavioral state and may provide clues for the role of this area in spatial aspects of attention. The inferior parietal lobule is not one cortical field but several, each of which appears to be specialized for certain aspects of spatial analysis.

In the future it will be important to know whether there is a topographic representation of space in head- or body-centered coordinates within this area or whether groups of cells encode locations of objects by learned connections within random networks. Do learned adjustments to spatial perceptions and motor guidance which accompany spatial distortions in visual inputs introduced, for instance, by prisms lead to long-term changes in the activity of space-tuned cells? What is the source of the eye-position signal-proprioception or efference copy? Much more needs to be known about the division of labor among the various cortical fields in the inferior parietal lobule and how they interact to provide spatial constancy.

ACKNOWLEDGMENTS

Supported by NIH Grant EY 05522. The author is recipient of a McKnight Foundation Scholars Award and a Sloan Foundation Scholarship, and is a Clayton Foundation Investigator.

REFERENCES

Acuna, C., Gonzalez, F. & Dominguez, R. 1983. Sensorimotor unit activity related to intention in the pulvinar of behaving Cebus Apella monkeys. *Experimental Brain Research.* 52:411-422.

Andersen, R. A., Asanuma, C., & Cowan, W. M. 1985. Callosal and prefrontal associational projecting cell populations in area 7a of the macaque monkey: a study using retrogradely transported fluorescent dyes. *Journal of Comparative Neurology.* 232:443-455.

Andersen, R. A., Essick, G. K., & Siegel, R. M. 1984. The role of eye position on the visual response of neurons in area 7a. *Society for Neuroscience Abstract,.* 10:934.

Andersen, R. A., & Mountcastle, V. B. 1983. The influence of the angle of gaze upon the excitability of the light-sensitive neurons of the posterior parietal cortex. *Journal of Neuroscience.* 3:532-548.

Andersen, R. A., Siegel, R. M., Essick, G. K., & Asanuma, C. 1985. Subdivision of the inferior parietal lobule and dorsal prelunate gyrus of macaque by connectional and functional criteria. *Investigative Ophthalmology and Visual Science Abstract.* 26(Suppl.):266.

Asanuma, C., Andersen, R. A., & Cowan, W. M. 1982. Divergent cortical projections of the medial pulvinar nucleus: a retrograde fluorescent tracer study in the monkey. *Society for Neuroscience Abstract.* 8:210.

Asanuma, C., Andersen, R. A., & Cowan, W. M. 1985. The thalamic relations of the caudal inferior parietal lobule and the lateral prefrontal cortex in monkeys: divergent cortical projections from cell clusters in the medial pulvinar nucleus. *Journal of Comparative Neurology.* 241:357-381.

Barbas, H., & Mesulam, M-M. 1981. Organization of afferent inputs to subdivisions of area 8 in rhesus monkeys. *Journal of Comparative Neurology.* 200:407-431.

Bender, D. B. 1981. Retinotopic organization of macaque pulvinar. *Journal of Neurophysiology.* 46:672-693.

Bender, D. B. 1983. Visual activation of neurons in the primate pulvinar depends on cortex but not colliculus. *Brain Research.* 279:258-261.

Benevento, L. A., & Miller, J. 1981. Visual responses of single neurons in the caudal lateral pulvinar of the macaque monkey. *Journal of Neuroscience.* 11:1268-1278.

Benevento, L. A., & Standage, G. P. 1983. The organization of projections of the retinorecipient and nonretinorecipient nuclei of the pretectal complex and layers of the superior colliculus to the lateral pulvinar and medial pulvinar in the macaque monkey. *Journal of Comparative Neurology.* 217:307-336.

Benson, D. F., & Barton, M. I. 1970. Disturbances in constructional ability. *Cortex.* 6:19-46.

Bisiach, E., & Luzzatti, C. 1978. Unilateral neglect of representational space. *Cortex.* 14:129-133.

Brain, W. R. 1941. Visual disorientation with special reference to lesions of the right cerebral hemisphere. *Brain.* 64:244-272.

Brodmann, K. 1905. Beitrage zur histologischen Lokalisation der Grosshirnrinde. Dritte Mitteilung: Die Rindenfelder, der niederen Affen. *Journal fur Psychologie und Neurologie.* 4:177-226.

Brodmann, K. 1907. Beitrage zur histologischen Lokalisation der Grosshirnrinde. Sechste Mitteilung: Die Cortex gliederung des Menschen. *Journal fur Psychologie und Neurologie.* 10:231-246.

Brody, B. A., & Pribram, K. H. 1978. The role of frontal and parietal cortex in cognitive processing: tests of spatial and sequential functions. *Brain.* 101:607-633.

Bushnell, M. C., Goldberg, M. E., & Robinson, D. L. 1981. Behavioral enhancement of visual responses in monkey cerebral cortex. I. Modulation in posterior parietal cortex related to selective visual attention. *Journal of Neurophysiology.* 46:755-772.

Butters, N., & Barton, M. 1970. Effect of parietal lobe damage on the performance of reversible operations in space. *Neuropsychologia,* 8:205-214.

Carmon, A., & Bechtoldt, H. P. 1969. Dominance of the right cerebral hemisphere for stereopsis. *Neurospychologia.* 7:29-39.

Colby, C. L, Gattass, R. Olson, C. R., & Gross, C. G. 1983. Cortical afferents to visual areas in the macaque. *Society for Neuroscience Abstract.* 9:152.

Crick, F. 1984. Function of the thalamic reticular complex: the searchlight hypothesis. *Proceedings of the National Academy of Science, U.S.A.* 81:4586-4590.

Critchley, M. 1953. *The Parietal Lobes,* New York: Hafner Press.

Denny-Brown, D., & Banker, B. 1954. Amorphosynthesis from left parietal lesion. *A.M.A. Archives of Neurology and Psychiatry.* 71:302-313.

De Renzi, E. 1982. Memory disorders following focal neocortical damage. *Philosophical Transactions of the Royal Society of London B.* 298:73-83.

De Renzi, E., Faglioni, P., & Previdi, P. 1977. Spatial memory and hemispheric locus of lesion. *Cortex.* 13:424-433.

De Renzi, E., Faglioni, P., & Scotti, G. 1970. Hemispheric contribution to exploration of space through the visual and tactile modality. *Cortex.* 6:191-203.

De Renzi, E., Faglioni, P., & Villa, P. 1977. Topographical amnesia. *Journal of Neurology, Neurosurgery and Psychiatry.* 40:498-505.

Desimone, R. & Gross, C. G. 1979. Visual areas in the temporal cortex of the macaque. *Brain Research.* 178:363-380.

Essick, G. K., Andersen, R. A., & Siegel, R. M. 1984. Fixation and saccade-related area 7a neurons receive visual inputs. *Society for Neuroscience Abstracts.* 10:476.

Ettlinger, G., & Kalsbeck, J. E. 1962. Changes in tactile discrimination and in visual reaching after successive and simultaneous bilateral posterior parietal ablations in the monkey. *Journal of Neurology, Neurosurgery and Psychiatry.* 25:256-268.

Ettlinger, G., Warrington, E., & Zangwill, O. L. 1957. A further study of visual-spatial agnosia. *Brain.* 80:335-361.

Faugier-Grimaud, S., Frenois, C., & Stein, D. G. 1978. Effects of posterior parietal lesions on visually guided behavior in monkeys. *Neuropsychologia.* 16:151-168.

Hartje, W., & Ettlinger, G. 1974. Reaching in light and dark after unilateral posterior parietal ablations in the monkey. *Cortex.* 9:346-354.

Hecaen, H., & Ajuriaguerra, de J. 1954. Balint's syndrome (psychic paralysis of visual fixation) and its minor forms. *Brain.* 77:373-400.

Hecaen, H., Penfield, W., Bertrand, C., Malmo, R. 1956. The syndrome of apractognosia due to lesions of the minor cerebral hemisphere. *A.M.A. Archives of Neurology and Psychiatry.* 75:400-434.

Holmes, G. 1919. Disturbances of visual space perception. *British Medical Journal.* 2:230-233.

Hyvarinen, J. 1981. Regional distribution of functions in parietal association area 7 of the monkey. *Brain Research.* 206:287-303.

Hyvarinen, J., & Poranen, A. 1974. Function of the parietal associative area 7 as revealed from cellular discharges in alert monkeys. *Brain.* 97:673-692.

Hyvarinen, J., & Shelepin, Y. 1979. Distribution of visual and somatic functions in the parietal associative area 7 of the monkey. *Brain Research.* 169:561-564.

Jung, R. 1974. Neuropsychologie under Neurophysiologie des Kontar-und Formsehens in Zeichnung und Mulerei. In Wieck H. H. (ed.) *Psychopathologie Musischer Gestaltungen.* Schattauer Verlag, Stuttgart, 29-88.

Kasdon, D. L., & Jacobson, S. 1978. The thalamic afferents to the inferior parietal lobule of the Rhesus monkey. *Journal of Comparative Neurology.* 177:685-706.

Kinsbourne, M., & Warrington, E. K. 1962. A disorder of simultaneous form perception. *Brain.* 45:461-486.

LaMotte, R. H., & Acuna, C. 1978. Defects in accuracy of reaching after removal of posterior parietal cortex in monkeys. *Brain Research.* 139:309-326.

Lynch, J. C., & Graybiel, A. M. 1983. Comparison of afferents traced to the superior colliculus from the frontal eye fields and from two sub-regions of area 7 of the rhesus monkey. *Society for Neuroscience Abstract.* 9:750.

Lynch, J. C., & McLaren, J. W. 1984. A quantitative study of contralateral inattention in monkey following lesions of posterior parietal, prestriate, and prefrontal cortex. *Society for Neuroscience Abstract.* 10:59.

Lynch, J. C., Mountcastle, V. B., Talbot, W. H., & Yin, T. C. T. 1977. Parietal lobe mechanisms for directed visual attention. *Journal of Neurophysiology.* 40:362-389.

Maunsell, J. H. R., & Van Essen, D. C. 1983. The connections of the middle temporal visual area (MT) and their relationship to a cortical hierarchy in the macaque monkey. *Journal of Neuroscience.* 3:2563-2586.

May, J. G., & Andersen, R. A. 1984. Different patterns of cortico-pontine projections from different cortical regions within the inferior parietal lobule and dorsal prelunate gyrus of the monkey. *Society for Neuroscience Abstract.* 10:577.

McFie, J., & Zangwill, O. L. 1960. Visual-constructive disabilities associated with lesions of the left cerebral hemisphere. *Brain.* 83:243-260.

Mendoza, J. E., & Thomas, R. K. 1975. Effects of posterior parietal and frontal neocortical lesions in the squirrel monkey. *Journal of Comparative and Physiological Psychology.* 89:170-182.

Mesulam, M. -M., Van Hoesen, G. W., Pandya, D. N., & Geschwind, N. 1977. Limbic and sensory connections of the inferior parietal lobule (area PG) in the rhesus monkey: a study with a new method for horseradish peroxidase histochemistry. *Brain Research.* 136:393-414.

Mishkin, M. 1982. A memory system in the monkey. *Philosophical Transactions of the Royal Society of London B.* 298:85-95.

Moffett, A., Ettlinger, G., Morton, H. B., & Piercy, M. F. 1967. Tactile discrimination performance in the monkey: the effects of ablation of various subdivision of the posterior parietal cortex. *Cortex.* 3:59-96.

Motter, B. C., & Mountcastle, V. B. 1981. The functional properties of the light sensitive neurons of the posterior parietal cortex studied in waking monkeys: foveal sparing and opponent vector organization. *Journal of Neuroscience.* 1:3-26.

Mountcastle, V. B., Andersen, R. A., & Motter, B. C. 1981. The influence of attentive fixation upon the excitability of the light-sensitive neurons of the posterior parietal cortex. *Journal of Neuroscience.* 1:1218-1235.

Mountcastle, V. B., Lynch, J. C., Georgopoulos, A., Sakata, H., & Acuna, C. 1975. Posterior parietal association cortex of the monkey: command functions for operations within extrapersonal space. *Journal of Neurophysiology.* 38:871-908.

Ogren, M. P., & Hendrickson, A. E. 1979. The morphology and distribution of striate cortex terminals in the inferior and lateral subdivisions of the

Macaca monkey pulvinar. *Journal of Comparative Neurology.* 188:197-200.

Ogren, M. P., Mateer, C. A., & Wyler, A. R. 1984. Alterations in visually related eye movements following left pulvinar damage in man. *Neuropsychologia.* 22:187-196.

Pandya, D. N., & Seltzer, B. 1982. Intrinsic connections and architectonics of posterior parietal cortex in the rhesus monkey. *Journal of Comparative Neurology.* 204:196-210.

Paterson, A., & Zangwill, O. L. 1944. Disorders of visual space perception associated with lesions of the right hemisphere. *Brain.* 67:331-358.

Perryman, K. M., Lindsley, D. F., & Lindsley, D. B. 1980. Pulvinar neuron responses to spontaneous and trained eye movements and to light flashes in squirrel monkeys. *Electroencephalography and Clinical Neurophysiology.* 49:152-161.

Petersen, S. E., Robinson, D. L., & Keys, W. 1982. A physiological comparison of the lateral pulvinar and area 7 in the behaving macaque. *Society for Neuroscience Abstract.* 8:681.

Petrides, M., & Iversen, S. E. 1979. Restricted posterior parietal lesions in the rhesus monkey and peformance on visuospatial tasks. *Brain Research.* 161:63-77.

Piercy, M., Hecaen, H., & Ajuriaguerra, J. 1960. Constructional apraxia associated with unilateral cerebral lesions—left and right sided cases compared. *Brain.* 83:225-242.

Pohl, W. 1973. Dissociation of spatial discrimination deficits following frontal and parietal lesions in monkeys. *Journal of Comparative and Physiological Psychology.* 82:227-239.

Ratcliff, G., & Davies-Jones, G. A. B. 1972. Defective visual localization in focal brain wounds. *Brain.* 95:49-60.

Ratcliff, G., Ridley, R. M., & Ettlinger, G. 1977. Spatial disorientation in the monkey. *Cortex.* 13:62-65.

Riddoch, G. 1917. On the relative perceptions of movement and a stationary object in certain visual disturbances due to occipital injuries. *Proceedings of the Royal Society of Medicine.* 10:13-34.

Robinson, D. L., Goldberg, M. E., & Stanton, G. B. 1978. Parietal association cortex in the primate: sensory mechanisms and behavioral modulations. *Journal of Neurophysiology.* 41:910-932.

Sakata, H., Shibutani, H., & Kawano, K. 1980. Spatial properties of visual fixation neurons in posterior parietal association cortex of the monkey. *Journal of Neurophysiology.* 43:1654-1672.

Sakata, H. Shibutani, H., & Kawano, K. 1983. Functional properties of visual tracking neurons in posterior parietal association cortex of the monkey. *Journal of Neurophysiology.* 49:1364-1380.

Sakata, H., Shibutani, H., Kawano, K., Harrington, T. L. 1985. Neural mechanism of space vision in the parietal association cortex of the monkey. *Vision Research.* 25:453-463.

Schlag-Rey, M., & Schlag, J. 1984. Visuomotor functions of central thalamus in monkey. I. Unit activity related to spontaneous eye movements. *Journal of Neurophysiology.* 6:1149-1174.

Seltzer, B., & Pandya, D. N. 1980. Converging visual and somatic sensory cortical input to the intraparietal sulcus of the rhesus monkey. *Brain Research.* 192:339-351.

Semmes, J., Weinstein, S., Ghent, L., & Teuber, H. L. 1963. Correlates of impaired orientation in personal and extrapersonal space. *Brain.* 86:747-772.

Shibutani, H., Sakata, H., & Hyvarinen, J. 1984. Saccade and blinking evoked by microstimulation of the posterior parietal association cortex of the monkey. *Experimental Brain Research.* 55:1-8.

Siqueira, E. B. 1965. The temporo-pulvinar connections in the rhesus monkey. *Archives of Neurology.* 13:321-330.

Siqueira, E. B. 1971. The cortical connections of the nucleus pulvinaris of the dorsal thalamus in rhesus monkey. *International Journal of Neurology.* 8:139-154.

Teuber, H. L. 1963. Space perception and its disturbances after brain injury in man. *Neuropsychologia.* 1:47-57.

Trojanowski, J. Q., & Jacobson, S. 1974. Medial pulvinar afferents to frontal eye fields in rhesus monkey demonstrated by horseradish peroxidase. *Brain Research.* 80:395-411.

Trojanowski, J. Q., & Jacobson, S. 1976. Areal and laminar distribution of some pulvinar cortical efferents in rhesus monkey. *Journal of Comparative Neurology.* 169:371-392.

Ungerleider, L. G., & Brody, B. A. 1977. Extrapersonal spatial orientation: the role of posterior parietal, anterior frontal and inferotemporal cortex. *Experimental Neurology.* 56:265-280.

Ungerleider, L. G., & Christensen, C. A. 1977. Pulvinar lesions in monkeys produce abnormal eye movements during visual discrimination training. *Brain Research.* 136:189-196.

Ungerleider, L. G., & Christensen, C. A. 1979. Pulvinar lesions in monkeys produce abnormal scanning of a complex visual array. *Neuropsychologia.* 17:493-501.

Vogt, C., & Vogt, O. 1919. Allgemeine Ergebuisse unserer Hirnforschung. *Journal fur Psychologie und Neurologie.* 25:279-462.

von Bonin, G., & Bailey, P. 1947. *The Neocortex of Macaca Mulatta.* Urbana: University of Illinois Press.

von Economo, C. 1929. *The Cytoarchitectonics of the Human Cerebral Cortex.* London: Oxford University Press.

Wilbrand, H. 1887. *Die Seelenblindheit als Herderscheinung.* Wiesbaden: Bergmann.

Wurtz, R. H., Goldberg, M. E., & Robinson, D. L. 1982. Brain mechanisms of visual attention. *Scientific American.* 246:124-135.

THE ROLE OF TRANSFORMATIONS IN SPATIAL COGNITION

4

ROGER N. SHEPARD
Stanford University

INTRODUCTION

One thing that we all have in common with each other, and with most highly mobile animals (including other mammals, birds, fish, and insects), is that we have to find our ways about in a three-dimensional world populated with other significant objects that, like ourselves, are often mobile and always constrained to this same three-dimensional space. Moreover, we all confront this challenge as soon as we begin to move about or to manipulate other objects. Although my own experiments on spatial perception and cognition have been confined to normal human adults, I have come to attach increasing significance to the following circumstances: (1) The constraints on mobility imposed by three-dimensional space are physical invariants that have prevailed throughout biological evolution. (2) These constraints should therefore have become internalized in "higher" animals—accounting both for the widespread manifestation of such internalized constraints in diverse species and their early emergence (that is, development) in the young. (3) Fundamental among such constraints must be the kinematic constraints that govern the relative motions or spatial transformations between objects, and between objects and ourselves.

One might suppose that an experimental psychologist investigating spatial cognition should begin with the mental representation—whether in perception, memory, or imagination—of stationary objects or spatial layouts. Then, having gained an understanding of the

81

representation of spatial structures in this simplest, static case, such a researcher might go on to investigate the more complex, dynamic case of the representation of the possible motions or spatial transformations of such structures. However, there are a number of reasons to question the advisability of setting aside, even at the outset, the representation of transformations. I list ten:

Parametric simplicity. The representation of certain transformations, rigid motions, may in fact be simpler than the representation of static objects or layouts. A rigid displacement of an object in three-dimensional space, or a repositioning of the self with respect to an environmental layout, each requires only six parameters for its specification—three for the translational components (e.g., locational shifts along up-down, left-right, and forward-backward dimensions) and three for the rotational components (e.g., angular shifts of attitude, pitch, and yaw, in aeronautical parlance). In contrast, characterization of an arbitrary shape or layout in space requires an indefinite number of parameters.

Invariance throughout evolution. The objects (foods, predators, competitors, weapons, or tools) and the habitats (caves, trees, jungles, plains, mountains, or seas) that have been significant for our variously remote ancestors have shifted over evolutionary history. But spatial transformations of these objects or of our individual ancestors relative to these habitats have always been characterizable in terms of the same six degrees of freedom.

Primacy in development. The ability of humans to discriminate between rigid and nonrigid transformations of unfamiliar visual objects has been demonstrated to emerge in early infancy (Gibson, Owsley, & Johnston, 1978; Gibson & Spelke, 1983; Gibson & Walker, 1984; Spelke, 1982), suggesting that the neural mechanisms underlying this ability may be at least partly innate.

Automaticity. As adults, we have an immediate sense of how any presented real object might move or be moved, turn or be turned, this way or that, in our common three-dimensional space, even when the object is (in color, texture, and shape) unlike any we have previously encountered. And we are able to grasp, to deflect, to turn about, or to right a suddenly approaching or falling object even before we have time to recognize what that object is. Further, we automatically perceive the rigid (translational, rotational, or combined, i.e., helical) motion of a spatial structure (Shepard, 1984) even when the configuration is itself entirely random, and even when all that is available is merely a two-dimensional projection or shadow of the rigidly moving three-dimensional structure (as in the early computer-generated film produced by Green, 1961), or is merely the beginning and end projections, omitting the intervening motion (as in the phenomenon of rotational apparent motion investigated by Shepard & Judd, 1976).

Dependence of structural interpretation on orientation. The recognition of the shape and, hence, the identification of the object can critically depend on the interpretation of how the object is oriented in space—for example, in the two-dimensional case, the interpretation of what is the part of the object that (in the object's canonical orientation) would constitute its top (Rock, 1973; also see Palmer & Hemenway, 1978). Thus, the letters b, d, p, q can be identified only if we know whether, and if so how, the orientations in which they appear depart from their canonical orientations. As a consequence, the determination of the identity of a misoriented object (e.g., the classification of it as standard or reflected) or the accurate comparison of the shapes of two objects in different orientations can require imagining an object rotated into its canonical orientation, or into the orientation of the comparison object (Cooper & Shepard, 1984; Shepard & Cooper, 1982; Shepard & Metzler, 1971). Similarly, the determination of whether something is on another person's left or right may be achieved by imagining oneself in the position of that other person—which, in the case of the face-to-face or "canonical" encounter (Clark, 1973), requires imagining a 180 degree rotation (Shepard & Hurwitz, 1984). Such mental reorientations are also required in interpreting left and right turns in road maps, when the line representing the road leading into the turn is not heading upward on the map (Shepard & Hurwitz, 1984), and in interpreting the "you-are-here" maps erected in parks, campuses, shopping malls, and the like when, as so often is the case (Levine, 1981), upward on the map does not correspond to straight ahead in the environment of the person looking at the map (Levine, Jankovic, & Palij, 1982).

Dependence of structural interpretation on motion. In the case in which we have access only to the two-dimensional projection or shadow of a random configuration of points, it is only by virtue of the spatial transformation of the underlying three-dimensional structure that we are able to perceive the true three-dimensional shape of that structure—the striking phenomenon known as the kinetic depth effect (Wallach & O'Connell, 1953; also see Braunstein, 1976). And a similar dependence of the perception of structure on motion occurs when the motion is confined to the plane of the picture (e.g., see Cutting & Proffitt, 1982; Dunker, 1929/1967; Johansson, 1973; Proffitt & Cutting, 1979; Wallach, 1965/1976). Indeed, the perceptual segregation of a subset of points merely as *figure*, against a *ground* of random points, can depend on a correlated motion of the figural points in relation to the ground—an example of the Gestalt principle of "common fate" or "uniform destiny" (Wertheimer, 1923/1967).

Dynamic interpretation of static displays. Even when an object or event is visually presented as a purely stationary or frozen image, the perceptual or memory representation to which that image gives rise may be systematically influenced by knowledge of implicit dynamics—for example, in the case of pictures of familiar physical processes (falling objects, breaking waves, etc.), knowledge of the direction in which the transformation naturally evolves in time (Freyd, 1983a, 1983c; also see Freyd, 1983b; Freyd & Finke, 1984) or, in the case of handwritten letters or characters, knowledge of the order and direction in which the component strokes are usually executed in forming each character (Freyd, 1983d; Freyd & Babcock, 1984; also see Zimmer, 1982).

Psychological resonance to symmetries. Our internalization of the basic spatial transformations of translation, rotation, reflection, and change of scale may underlie our marked predisposition toward detecting, appreciating, constructing, and spontaneously experiencing symmetrical, regular, or periodic patterns. Certainly, such patterns are characterized by the fact that they are similar to themselves under these spatial transformations (Weyl, 1952). Perhaps for this reason, regular tessellations composed of square, rhombic, triangular, or hexagonal elements, circularly symmetric (mandala like) patterns, and spiral or vortical schemes are ubiquitous not only in contemporary "op art" but, long before, in the decorations of pottery, baskets, blankets, and rugs by primitive artisans throughout the world; in repeating architectural ornamentations, such as the fluted columns of ancient Greece, the carved architraves and leaded windows of Gothic cathedrals, the tessellated ceilings of Roman vaults and domes, and, especially, the intricate arabesques and filigrees of Islamic mosques; in the designs of commercially manufactured wallpapers, floor coverings, fabrics, and dishes; and in the "design phase" of young children's drawings (Kellogg & O'Dell, 1967). Indeed, these same geometrically regular "form constants" (Klüver, 1966) spontaneously emerge as purely visual phenomena during transitional (hypnagogic or hypnopompic) states between sleep and waking (Herschel, 1867; Shepard, 1978b, 1983; Shepard, Downing, & Putnam, 1985), under the influence of fever, sleep deprivation, or hallucinogenic drugs (Klüver, 1966; Siegel, 1977; West, 1962), or simply as a result of undifferentiated electrical, mechanical, or flickering optical stimulation of the visual system (Oster, 1966; Small & Anderson, 1976; Tyler, 1978; Younge, Cole, Gamble, & Rayner, 1975). Further, as Garner and his associates have demonstrated, the "figural goodness" of a pattern—as measured by how quickly and accurately it can be perceived, classified, or remembered—is determined by the size of the class of patterns that are equivalent to the given pattern under spatial transformations of rotation, reflection, and translation. Specifically, patterns that are more symmetrical, and that belong to a smaller equivalence class because their symmetry ensures that more transformations will leave them unchanged, have greater figural goodness in this sense (Garner, 1974; Garner & Clement, 1963; also see Palmer, 1983).

Possible transformational basis of shape perception. The very shape necessary for our identification of an object or habitat may be determined on the basis of the similarity that it bears to itself (its autocorrelation—cf. Uttal, 1975) under its possible spatial transformations (Palmer, 1982; Shepard, 1981; also see Weyl, 1952). Thus, self-similarity under reflections about a medial plane implies bilateral symmetry (as in a leaf, a fish, a human face, a ravine, a ridge), self-similarity under all rotations about a center implies a round or spherical shape (an orange, a berry, a drop of dew, the moon), self-similarity under rotations about only one axis implies a surface of revolution (a pear, a mushroom, an igloo, a volcanic crater or cone), self-similarity under rotations about and translations along the same axis implies a cylindrical shape (a stem, a tree trunk, an arm, a well), self-similarity under correlated rotations and changes of scale implies a spiral shape (a snail's shell, a sunflower's head, a vortex), and self-similarity under both rotations about any vertical axis and translations along any horizontal axis implies a horizontal plane (a table top, a flat terrain, the surface of a pond, lake, or sea). Further, self-similarity under transformations of only certain magnitudes implies a repeating pattern-as in the various cases of rotations (petals of a flower, grooves on a pumpkin, points of a snowflake), translations (peas in a pod, ducklings in a row, hairs of an eyelash, bones of a fish, stripes on a zebra, waves on a lake), and combinations of rotations, translations or changes of scale (cells of a honeycomb, scales on a pinecone or reptile, strands of a spiderweb).

Indeed, by allowing for varying degrees of self-similarity under different transformations, any shape may be specifiable in this way (Shepard, 1981; Shepard & Farrell, 1985). Thus the shape of a rectangle is defined by the fact that in addition to being identical to itself under 180 degree rotations and reflections about its vertical and horizontal axes, that shape is more or less similar to itself (according as it is more or less square) under 90 degree rotations and is also somewhat similar to itself under vertical and horizontal translations. And the shape of a pumpkin is largely defined by the facts that it is roughly preserved under all rotations about its center point, but is more fully preserved under rotations about one particular (vertical) axis through that center, and is still more fully preserved under rotations about that axis through multiples of one particular angle (the angle separating its vertically oriented, meridional grooves or depressions).

Inextricable entanglement of shape and orientation. There is, in any case, a geometrically determined mutual dependency between the representation of the shape of an object or layout and of its orientation in space (Farrell & Shepard, 1981; Shepard, 1981; Shepard & Farrell, 1985) such that the very same difference in shape may sometimes be represented either as a change in shape, with orientation held constant, or as a change in orientation, with shape held constant. For example, a vertically elongated rectangle can be changed into a horizontally elongated one either by decreasing its height and increasing its width, or by rigidly rotating the rectangle through 90 degrees in its own two-dimensional plane. Or, as is illustrated in Appendix A, continuous changes in the shape of a triangle necessarily produce shapes that are identical to the shape of the original triangle, but rigidly rotated in the plane.

Now those facts about the world that have been invariant throughout biological evolution are presumably the ones most likely to remain invariant in the future. To the extent that they do remain invariant, a species that has genetically internalized those constraints can only benefit. As I have previously suggested (e.g., Shepard, 1984), each individual organism of that species then does not have to learn each constraint, de novo, by trial and (possibly fatal) error. Moreover, by virtue of being the most enduring, these constraints are just the ones that will have had the longest time to be genetically internalized. In this way even the highly abstract constraints of kinematic geometry, which govern the six degrees of freedom of rigid motion in three-dimensional space might have become deeply incorporated into our neural representational systems of perception, cognition, and motor control (Shepard, 1981, 1984). In the following sections, I review some of the ways in which my associates and I have been attempting to discover and to formulate the internalized constraints on spatial transformations that underlie our spatial perception and cognition.

APPARENT MOTION AND IMAGINED TRANSFORMATION

The internalized constraints governing the mental representation of transformations of objects in space are perhaps most directly revealed under conditions in which only the starting and ending positions of the object are externally presented. If a mental representation of a passage over a connecting path arises under these conditions, that path must be a construction of the brain. The characteristics of its construction and traversal—for example, the particular path instantiated and the minimum time needed for its instantiation and traversal—can be inferred from objective measurements of the latency and accuracy of certain classificatory responses that the person makes, including responses to a probe stimulus that is presented at various delays and in various positions during the course of the mental process. In these ways, we have investigated internalized constraints on the representation of spatial transformations for two principal types of phenomena, apparent motion and imagined transformations (see Shepard & Cooper, 1982).

In the phenomenon of *apparent motion* temporally alternating presentations of two different views of an object give rise to the perceptual experience of a single object rigidly moving back and forth between those two positions. The spontaneous impletion of a connecting path presumably reflects an internalized principle of object conservation: Eschewing the hypothesis that one object went out of existence and another, identically shaped object immediately came into existence in a different location and/or orientation, the brain in effect adopts the hypothesis that one object continued to exist throughout and simply underwent a sudden rigid displacement. Moreover, on any one occasion the brain evidently tends to instantiate that continued existence in the perceptually concrete form of a motion over a particular path, out of the infinite set of possible paths through which the object could have moved from the one position to the other. The fact that the paths actually experienced tend to be the simplest or shortest possible paths of rigid motion presumably reflects a second internalized principle, which I have called a principle of least action (Shepard, 1981, 1984). In addition to determining the particular path of the experienced motion in our experiments, we generally determine the minimum onset-to-onset time (the stimulus onset asynchrony) required for the experience of rigid motion over that path. (For stimulus onset asynchronies shorter than this critical time, the experienced rigid motion breaks down to a nonrigid motion over some other, shorter path of nonrigid motion and, ultimately, to a flickering superposition of the two views, without any experienced motion between them.)

In the phenomenon of *imagined transformation* (mental rotation being perhaps the best known example), there is no temporal alternation of external stimuli and, accordingly, no involuntary, effortless experience of motion over some path. Instead, one voluntarily and effortfully imagines one object (whether visually presented, previously learned, or only imagined on the basis of a verbal description) rigidly transformed into the position of another object (whether presented, remembered, or imagined), in order to compare the two objects for identity or difference in their intrinsic shapes. Nevertheless, as in the case of apparent motion, experimental determinations can be made of the particular paths over which the transformation is represented and, particularly, of the minimum times needed to complete the imagined transformation over such paths. Although these critical times are much longer for imagined transformation than for the corresponding, externally driven and more automatic apparent motion, pervasive similarities in the transformational paths and in the patterns of the critical times suggest that the same internalized constraints may govern both apparent motion and imagined transformations.

Here, I give no more than a brief review of the evidence from the studies that my associates and I have carried out on mental rotation and apparent rotational motion. For pairs of asymmetrical objects such as the pairs of computer-generated perspective views of three-dimensional objects reproduced in Figure 4.1, a variety of different kinds of evidence has furnished converging support for the idea that the representational process actually passes through a series of internal states corresponding one-to-one to the ordered series of intermediate orientations along a path of transformation of the external object. Among the central findings are the following:

Transformation Time Depends on the Extent of the Transformation

As shown in Figure 4.2A, the time required to determine that two such views are of objects of identical shape (rather than being enan-

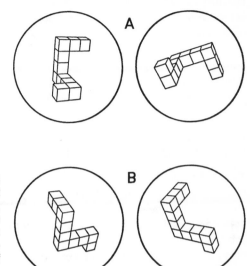

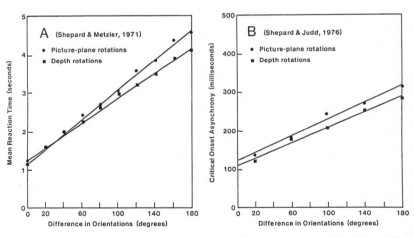

Figure 4.1. Pairs of perspective views of three-dimensional objects, of the sort used by Shepard and Metzler (1971), differing by a rigid rotation in the picture plane (A) and in depth (B). (From Shepard & Judd, 1976. Copyright, American Association for the Advancement of Science.)

Figure 4.2. For subjects presented with perspective views of three-dimensional objects like those shown in Figure 4.1, (A) shows time to determine that two simultaneously presented views portray objects of the same intrinsic shape (from Shepard & Metzler, 1971), and (B) shows the minimum stimulus onset asynchrony between two alternately presented views yielding rigid apparent rotational motion (from Shepard & Judd, 1976). In both cases, the times are plotted as a function of the angular difference in the two portrayed orientations—for differences that correspond to a rotation in the picture plane or in depth. (Copyright, in both cases, American Association for the Advancement of Science.)

tiomorphic or mirror-image objects) increases linearly with the angular difference between the orientations portrayed (Metzler & Shepard, 1974; Shepard & Metzler, 1971). Likewise, as shown in Figure 4.2B, the minimum stimulus onset asynchrony for the illusion of rigid apparent rotational motion, when the two views are alternately presented in the same spatial location, increases linearly with their angular difference (Shepard & Judd, 1976).

The Transformation is Represented as if Three-dimensional Space

The rates of apparent or mental rotation implied by the slopes of these linear functions are essentially independent of the orientation in three-dimensional space of the axis of the rotational difference between the two objects (although rotations about a natural axis of the object itself are generally easier and faster). Indeed, pairs of objects differing by a rotation about the line of sight (Figure 4.1A), which yield retinal images differing only by a rigid rotation, are classified no more quickly than pairs of objects differing by a rotation in depth (Figure 4.1B), which yield retinal images differing by a non-rigid and often discontinuous transformation (Metzler & Shepard, 1974; Shepard & Judd, 1976; Shepard & Metzler, 1971; also see Shepard, 1984).

The Transformation is Represented over a Particular Connecting Path

For pairs differing by large angles, subjects can be either unknowingly primed or explicitly instructed to carry out the apparent or mental rotation the long or the short way around the circle. Accordingly, the obtained function relating time to angular difference either continues to increase as a linear extrapolation beyond 180 degrees or else reverses and decreases with a negative slope of equal magnitude beyond 180 degrees (Cooper, 1975; Farrell & Shepard, 1981; Metzler & Shepard, 1974; Shepard, 1981; also see Shepard & Zare, 1983).

Successive Portions of the Path are Mentally Traversed at Successive Times

During the course of apparent or mental rotation, subjects respond most rapidly and accurately to test probes that are in further rotated orientations at later times, demonstrating that the internal process is an analog process in the sense that it passes through a succession of states corresponding one-to-one to successively more rotated orientations in external three-dimensional space (Cooper, 1976; Cooper & Shepard, 1973; Metzler & Shepard, 1974; Robins & Shepard, 1977).

These findings concerning the representation of rotational transformations, together with similar findings concerning the representation of such other spatial transformations as translation, size scaling, reflection, and folding and adjoining of individual rigid parts (e.g., Bundesen, Larsen, & Farrell, 1981, 1983; Farrell, 1983; Shepard, 1984; Shepard & Cooper, 1982; Shepard & Feng, 1972), support the following conclusions: First, our representation of a three-dimensional object captures something of the three-dimensional structure of the object as it exists in isotropic three-dimensional space, and is relatively unrelated to its two-dimensional retinal projection. Second, the representation is not, however, of the inherent three-dimensional shape of the object considered purely in itself; it is always of that object as viewed in a particular orientation. Third, in successfully interpreting two such views as being of the same object, the brain constructs a representational path of rigid transformation between them. And fourth, the path that is thus constructed and mentally traversed tends to be one, out of the infinite set of possible alternatives, that is in some sense the simplest or shortest. But in what sense?

FORMALIZATION OF A LEAST-ACTION THEORY

It will not do either to define a path of transformation as a one-dimensional curve or line in ordinary three-dimensional Euclidean space or to use the ordinary Euclidean metric to define distance along such a path. These are at least two reasons: First, because the objects themselves reside and have physical extension in that space, the choice of which two points are to be connected by the path to be measured appears arbitrary. Second, even if some particular points are chosen (such as the centroid of an object in each of its two positions), a path between those points, while it may reflect the translational component, does not discriminate between motions that include various amounts of rotation (around, say, the moving centroid).

Fundamentally, the problem is that ordinary Euclidean space, being only three-dimensional, cannot itself represent the six degrees of freedom of rigid displacement in that space, which include, as I already noted, three degrees of freedom of rotation in addition to the three degrees of freedom of translation. What we need is a more abstract, six-dimensional space in which each point has a unique one-to-one correspondence to the position (both locational and orientational) of an object, whatever its intrinsic shape. In order to achieve a satisfactory formalization, we must follow the lead of theoretical physics where laws take on their simplest and most general form when stated in terms of the appropriate abstract space—to give three examples, the four-dimensional Riemannian space of general relativity; the 6n-dimensional phase space of statistical mechanics; or the infinite-dimensional Hilbert space of quantum mechanics.

In our more modest case, we need a six-dimensional space endowed with sufficient structure that paths within it can be compared with respect to length or simplicity. Moreover, because three of these six dimensions—the dimensions corresponding to orientations—are circular, the space we seek is necessarily curved, that is, non-Euclidean. The required space is in fact a six-dimensional differentiable manifold (a smooth hypersurface) that can be embedded in a Euclidean space of no fewer than seven dimensions (much as the two-dimensional non-Euclidean surface of a sphere can be embedded in a Euclidean space of no fewer than three dimensions).

Any rigid motion of the object between two positions is then represented by a one-dimensional curve, lying in this curved six-dimensional manifold and connecting the two points representing the beginning and end positions of the object. Formally, this manifold corresponds to the *proper Euclidean group*, E^+ of rigid motions of three-dimensional Euclidean space into itself—a group that is expressible as the semidirect product of the translation group R^3 and the rotation group SO(3) (Cartan, 1927; O'Neill, 1966):

$$E^+ = R^3 \text{ s } SO(3)$$

Thus, somewhat as the two-dimensional surface of a cylinder can be factored into a one-dimensional straight line and a one-dimensional circular curve, the six-dimensional space of possible positions of an object can be factored into a three dimensional space (corresponding to R^3) of locations, which is equivalent to ordinary Euclidean space, and a three-dimensional closed manifold of orientations (corresponding to SO(3)), which is topologically equivalent to a quite different, projective space. With respect to a particular reference orientation, any possible orientation of an object can be specified in terms of the direction of an axis of rotation through the center of the object (a direction that we can represent by the direction of a vector issuing from the origin in a three-dimensional space), and in terms of the angle of the rotation about that axis (an angle that we can represent by the length of that vector). Because rotations exceeding 180 degrees by an angle ⊖ are identical to rotations around the oppositely directed vector falling short of 180 degrees by that same angle ⊖, the manifold of possible orientations corresponds to the interior and surface of a sphere (of radius 180 degrees), with diametrically opposite points on the surface identified (that is, regarded as the same point).

Using, as the object, a cube (with faces labeled F for "front," T for "top," etc.), Figure 4.3 portrays one two-dimensional section through this three-dimensional closed manifold of orientations. Notice that diametrically opposite points correspond, as claimed, to identical orientations of the cube. Of course, this one section does not include all orientations; there are infinitely many other sections. Moreover, this flat representation of the section is valid only topologically. For the natural metric induced by the orthogonal group SO(3), these sections are more appropriately regarded as hemispheres with, again, opposite points around their perimeters identified. Rotations of the object about any fixed axis then correspond to locally shortest paths, that is, the arcs of the great circles, on this hemispherical surface; and arc length corresponds to the angle of the corresponding rotation. A complete 360 degree rotation of the object corresponds to a complete circle in the manifold, where such completion is ensured by the facts that any great circle in a subspace like that portrayed in Figure 4.3 must intersect its perimeter and that opposite points on that perimeter are, again, regarded as the same point.

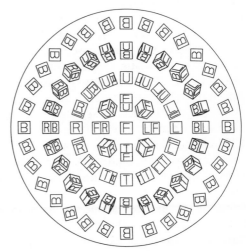

Figure 4.3. Topological representation of a two-dimensional section through the closed manifold of possible orientations of a three-dimensional object—portrayed here as a cube with labeled faces. (Diametrically opposite points around the perimeter of the disk represent the same orientation and, hence, should be regarded as the same point.) (From Shepard & Farrell, 1985. Copyright Elsevier Science Publishers.)

With the collaboration of Eloise Carlton, who is exploring the relevant mathematics of differentiable manifolds and Lie groups, and Susan Zare, who is collecting data on paths of apparent motion in the laboratory, I am currently seeking the appropriate psychological structure for the six-dimensional manifold of positions. By "the appropriate psychological structure," I mean the group-theoretic structure for which the *geodesics* (the analogues of great circles on a globe) correspond to the paths that are actually experienced in apparent motion or are mentally traversed in imagined transformation. A question remains as to whether, to what extent, or under what conditions the appropriate structure more fully reflects the highly abstract constraints of kinematic geometry or the more concrete ones of physical dynamics (cf. Freyd & Finke, 1984; Foster, 1975; Shepard, 1984). Possibly, in order to achieve a fully satisfactory account, we may have to follow the lead of relativity theory further and go over to a still higher-dimensional manifold that explicitly incorporates the time dimension, t (cf. Caelli, Hoffman, & Lindman, 1978; Jones, 1976; Shepard, 1981).

FORMALIZATION OF THE CONNECTION
BETWEEN SHAPES AND THEIR TRANSFORMATIONS

In introducing the six-dimensional manifold of possible positions of a three-dimensional object, I proceeded as if the object were completely asymmetric and, hence, as if there were no axis and angle of rotation short of 360 degrees for which the object manifested a local increase in similarity to itself. In fact, however, except for the uniquely symmetrical case of the sphere, which realizes the limit of exact self-identity under every rotation about its center, objects of interest more or less approximate self-similarity at particular special angles of rotation about particular axes. Thus if the cube that I used for purposes of illustration had not had distinctively marked faces, it would have become identical to itself under 90 degree rotations about any of the three axes through opposite faces, under 180 degree rotations about any of the six axes through opposite edges, or under 120 degree rotations about any of the four axes through opposite vertexes (see Appendix B). Likewise, any elongated or flattened object, including a rectangular solid, will become, if not strictly identical, at least locally more similar to itself under rotation through 180 degrees about any axis orthogonal to the natural axis of the object, that is, the axis coinciding with the elongated object or normal to the flattened object. And a triangle will generally resemble itself under those rotations that bring each vertex into closer proximity to some other vertex of its unrotated counterpart (see Appendix A).

The three-dimensional submanifold of possible orientations (Figure 4.3) does not, as it was described, provide for the representation of augmented self-similarities at angles short of 360 degrees. For example, distance in that space was always greatest between orientations differing by 180 degrees, regardless of possible approximations to symmetry in the object. Increased self-similarity of the object at certain angles could however be accommodated by deforming the three-dimensional manifold of orientations in such a way as to bring previously remote points of the manifold closer together in a higher-dimensional embedding space. The fact that a given object resembles itself under a certain rotation would then be represented by the shortened distances, through the embedding space, between all pairs of points separated by a certain distance along a particular closed geodesic within the curved manifold of possible orientations.

If the object is, as the unmarked cube, exactly identical to itself under such particular rotations, previously remote points in the manifold would become coincident, changing even the topological structure of that manifold (as indicated in Appendix B). Indeed, for objects possessing an axis of rotational symmetry such that a rotation of any angle about that axis leaves the object unchanged, the identification of points in the manifold leads to a reduction of the dimensionality of the manifold. Thus, for an elongated or a flattened object that is identical to itself under every rotation about its axis of symmetry, the originally three-dimensional space collapses into a one-dimensional circle; and for a perfectly spherical object, it collapses further into a zero-dimensional point.

For intermediate cases, such symmetries are only approached to some degree. Such cases are of wide significance because, as I have already implied, these degrees of approach to these symmetries define the very shape of the object itself (Shepard, 1981). In such cases, because originally remote points in the manifold of possible positions must be brought closer together in the embedding space, though not into complete coincidence, the resulting manifold can become quite contorted and difficult to visualize. However, the situation is not hopeless. These contortions affect only the distances cutting directly through the embedding space; they are not expected to affect the intrinsic group structure of the manifold itself or, hence, to alter the paths within that manifold that are the geodesics. The psychologically relevant consequence is that as long as a rigid motion is experienced or imagined, it should be the same motion regardless of the degree of approximation to symmetry in the object (short of complete symmetry—i.e., identity under rotation through some angle less than 360 degrees). The effect of the shortened paths cutting through the embedding space is, rather, to alter only the probabilities and latencies of traversing the different, fixed paths falling within the curved manifold and, hence, representing rigid transformations (see Farrell & Shepard, 1981; Shepard, 1984; Shepard & Zare, 1983). Nevertheless, to the extent that we wish to account for such probabilities and latencies, we must take cognizance of the deformations of the manifold of positions that are induced by approximations to symmetry in the object.

As consideration of such simple figures as triangles (Appendix A), cubes (Appendix B), and rectangular solids reveals, the deformed manifold of perceptually distinguishable orientations of a particular object generally possesses a complex and not readily visualizable structure. We can achieve a simplification by considering, rather than any one particular object, an ensemble of objects having in common only one particular type of symmetry such, for example, as symmetry under 180 degree rotation. Although the space of perceptually distinguishable orientations for any one of the objects will still possess convolutions dictated by the structural features unique to that object, the whole ensemble of objects can be approximately represented by a kind of average manifold with a simpler structure dictated only by the shared feature of, say 180 degree rotational symmetry.

Two Experiments on the Connection
Between Shapes and Their Transformation

Adopting the strategy of simplification just mentioned, Joyce Farrell and I carried out two studies in which on each trial two planar polygons were presented that differed only in their orientations within the two-dimensional plane. We thus reduced the dimensionality of the manifold of possible orientations from three to one—corresponding to the single degree of freedom of angular position within that plane. Further, by systematically varying the point of interpolation between a randomly generated polygon and a corresponding derived polygon with perfect 180 degree symmetry, we experimentally manipulated the degree of symmetry of just this particular sort. (This variation in symmetry is illustrated for one such polygon across the top of Figure 4.4, which is reproduced from Shepard, 1981.) Although each individual polygon, by virtue of its unique shape, necessarily approximated various sorts of symmetries,

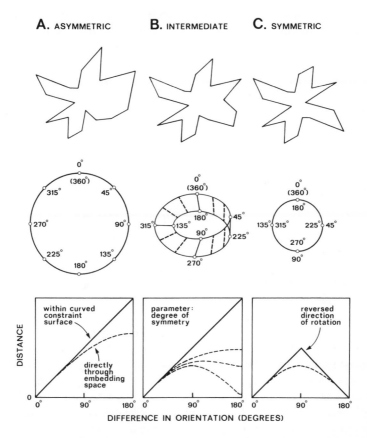

Figure 4.4. Representation of the set of orientations of a polygon that is asymmetric (A), symmetric under 180 degree rotation (C), or intermediate between these (B). The closed curves across the middle illustrate the one-dimensional manifold of orientations, and the plots at the bottom show how distance of transformation depends on angular difference for transformations that are rigid (solid lines) or nonrigid (dashed curves). (Reproduced from Shepard, 1981. Copyright Lawrence Erlbaum Associates.)

over the whole ensemble of polygons, approximations to all symmetries except the experimentally introduced 180 degree symmetry tended to average out.

Mathematical analysis (Shepard, 1981) revealed that the one-dimensional manifold corresponding to the internal representation of possible planar orientations for this ensemble of polygons is a particular closed curve that is isometrically embeddable in four-dimensional Euclidean space. Corresponding to the fact that all orientations of a polygon separated by a given angle are equally similar regardless of the absolute orientations, all points separated by a given distance along this closed curve are also separated by the same (shorter) distance directly through the four-dimensional embedding space. And corresponding to the fact that a close approximation to 180 degree rotational symmetry renders orientations differing by 180 degrees perceptually similar, such approximation to symmetry deforms the curve representing the orientations so that points that are mutually farthest from each other around the closed curve can be brought arbitrarily close together in the embedding space. The curve shown in the center of Figure 4.4, though necessarily projected down into a two-dimensional plane for pictorial representation, provides an approximate indication of the shape of this curve for an intermediate degree of symmetry of the object.

This curve, which can be regarded as falling on the two-dimensional surface of a torus in four-dimensional space, has the required property that all points corresponding to orientations differing by 180 degrees have been brought into the same, adjustable degree of proximity in the Euclidean embedding space. The straight dashed line segments represent the direct distances through that embedding space between the points in such pairs. (These connecting straight segments sweep out a nonorientable or "one-sided" Mobius strip in the four-dimensional space.) As the 180 degree rotational symmetry imposed on the ensemble of polygons is reduced to zero, the curve opens up and flattens out into a simple circle embeddable in a two-dimensional subspace, as illustrated on the left of the middle row in Figure 4.4. (This circle corresponds to a great circle in the manifold of orientations previously illustrated in Figure 4.3.) As the symmetry of the object is increased to 100%, the curve collapses down onto itself to form a smaller, double-wound circle, as illustrated on the right. In this latter case, each polygon is identical to itself under 180 degree rotation and, as a consequence, as such a polygon makes a complete 360 degree rotation, the corresponding point on the curve representing its perceived orientations makes two complete circuits around the circle shown on the right.

At the bottom of Figure 4.4, I have plotted, as a function of the angular difference between orientations of these polygons, both distance between points around the curve (solid lines) and the shorter distance between points directly through the embedding space (dashed lines), as these latter distances are averaged over all polygons in the ensemble. The distances around the curve, which is a geodesic path of rigid transformations, correspond, in this case, to angles of rigid rotation of a polygon. The straight distances through the embedding space (again, represented by the dashed curves at the bottom of the figure) correspond to the shorter, nonrigid transformations in which each part of the object deforms into the corresponding similar, but not identical, opposite part of the partially symmetric object while the object as a whole undergoes a reduced global rotation in the opposite direction. Farrell and I have shown that these two kinds of distances in the four-dimensional geometrical model actually predict the results that we empirically obtained in our two experiments.

On each trial of our first experiment (Farrell & Shepard, 1981), a polygon with some approximation to 180 degree rotational symmetry (such as one of the polygons illustrated at the top of Figure 4.4) would be presented alternately in two different orientations. The subject, by operating one of two keys, increased or decreased the rate of alternation in order to obtain the fastest rate of alternation at which the experience of rigid apparent rotational motion between the two orientations could be maintained. In agreement with the earlier results of Shepard and Judd (1976; reproduced here in Figure 4.2B), for asymmetric shapes (such as the one shown on the top left of Figure 4.4), the average critical stimulus onset asynchrony for rigid apparent motion increased linearly with angular difference between the two alternately presented views. However, for shapes that achieved as much as a 75% approximation to complete 180 degree rotational symmetry, the average critical stimulus onset asynchrony for rigid motion increased more rapidly and nonlinearly as the orientational difference approached 180 degrees, and the motion tended to "short circuit" into nonrigidity (also see Shepard, 1982). We argued that in this case, the strong "pull" of the much shorter path of nonrigid transformation (the path cutting directly through the embedding space) made the completion of the more circuitous but rigid transformation more difficult to achieve and, when it was achieved, slower. That is, we argued that when the direct distance (plotted as dashed lines at the bottom of Figure 4.4) became much shorter than the distance within the curve or manifold of orientations (plotted as solid lines), the existence of the much shorter nonrigid alternative inhibited the representation of the rigid motion. (This principle of path competition was subsequently corroborated with quite different stimuli by Shepard & Zare, 1983.)

In our second experiment (Shepard & Farrell, 1985), we collected a different type of chronometric data that we thought should be determined by the direct distances through the embedding space. Then, by applying multidimensional scaling (see Shepard, 1980) to these data, we sought to recover the four-dimensional structure of the manifold from the data themselves. On each trial in this experiment, we presented one of the polygons in two orientations, side-by-side, and measured the time the subject required to determine whether the two orientations were the same or different. On the basis of the pervasive finding that discriminative reaction time increases nonlinearly with the similarity between the two things to be discriminated, we reasoned that reaction time in our task would provide a measure of direct proximity between points in the embedding space (cf. Shepard, 1978a). Thus, polygons that are nearly symmetric would closely resemble each other when they differed by close to 180 degrees and, hence, would yield relatively long latencies of the response indicating "different orientation." Our results were in close conformity with this expectation. Moreover, application of multidimensional scaling—specifically INDSCAL (Carroll & Chang, 1970), with the different degrees of symmetry treated as "individuals"—yielded a closed curve embedded in four-dimensional space, exactly like that schematized in the middle of Figure 4.4 (Shepard & Farrell, 1985).

CONCLUSION

There are ample grounds for believing that we cannot attain a full understanding of the perception and cognition even of stationary objects and environmental layouts without an adequate characterization of the alternative positions that such objects or layouts can assume, relative to the self, in three-dimensional space or of the possible transformations between such positions in space. My attempt to work toward a psychologically adequate characterization has led me to rather abstract and complex geometrical structures, such as curved six-dimensional manifolds in still higher-dimensional embedding spaces. Although the psychological relevance of such exotic structures might seem nonintuitive, these structures have so far provided a close account of empirical data of quite different types, including the transformational paths and times determined in experiments on imagined transformations and apparent motion, and the discriminative reaction times in comparing the positions of objects in space. Moreover, these structures show promise of elucidating the intimate interconnection between the psychological representations of shapes and of their orientations. Finally, application of multidimensional scaling is indicating that these structures are actually implied by the empirical data that we have been collecting in the psychological laboratory.

As I have recently argued (Shepard, 1981, 1984), our long continued evolution in this three-dimensional world seems to have endowed us with a deeply internalized, if largely unarticulated, wisdom concerning the ways in which objects transform in the world—a wisdom that calls for a richer and more elegant characterization than we might have supposed.

ACKNOWLEDGMENTS

This work was supported by grants GS 2283, GB 3197X, BNS 75-02806, and BNS 80-05517 from the National Science Foundation. For helpful comments on the manuscript, I am indebted to James Cutting and to Jennifer Freyd.

REFERENCES

Braunstein, M. L. 1976. *Depth perception through motion.* New York: Academic Press.

Bundesen, C., Larsen, A., & Farrell, J. E. 1981. Mental transformations of size and orientation. In A. D. Baddeley & J. B. Long (Eds.), *Attention and performance IX* 279-294. Hillsdale, NJ: Lawrence Erlbaum Associates.

Bundesen, C., Larsen, A., & Farrell, J. E. 1983. Visual apparent movement: transformations of size and orientation. *Perception.* 12:549-558.

Caelli, T., Hoffman, W. C., & Lindman, H. 1978. Subjective Lorentz transformations and the perception of motion. *Journal of the Optical Society of America.* 68:402-411.

Carroll, J. D., & Chang, J. J. 1970. Analysis of individual differences in multidimensional scaling via an N-way generalization of "Eckart-Young" decomposition. *Psychometrika.* 35:283-319.

Cartan, E. 1927. La geometrie des groups de transformations. *Journal de Mathematique.* 6:1-119.

Clark, H. H. 1973. Space, time, semantics, and the child. In T. E. Moore (Ed.), *Cognitive development and the acquisition of language.* New York: Academic Press.

Cooper, L. A. 1975. Mental rotation of random two-dimensional shapes. *Cognitive Psychology.* 7:20-43.

Cooper, L. A. 1976. Demonstration of a mental analog of an external rotation. *Perception & Psychophysics.* 19:296-302.

Cooper, L. A., & Shepard, R. N. 1973. Chronometric studies of the rotation of mental images. In W. G. Chase (Ed.), *Visual information processing.* 75-176. New York: Academic Press.

Cooper, L. A., & Shepard, R. N. 1975. Mental transformations in the identification of left and right hands. *Journal of Experimental Psychology: Human Perception and performance.* 104:48-56.

Cooper, L. A., & Shepard, R. N. 1984. Turning something over in the mind. *Scientific American.* 251(6):106-114.

Cutting, J. E., & Proffitt, D. R. 1982. The minimum principle and the perception of absolute, common, and relative motions. *Cognitive Psychology.* 14:211-246.

Dunker, K. 1967. Induced motion. In W. D. Ellis (Ed.), *A source book of Gestalt psychology.* 161-172. New York: Humanities Press. (Original work published in 1929.)

Farrell, J. E. 1983. Visual transformations underlying apparent movement. *Perception & Psychophysics.* 33:85-92.

Farrell, J. E., & Shepard, R. N. 1981. Shape, orientation, and apparent rotational motion. *Journal of Experimental Psychology: Human Perception and Performance.* 7:477-486.

Foster, D. H. 1975. Visual apparent motion of some preferred paths in the rotation group SO(3). *Biological Cybernetics.* 18:81-89.

Freyd, J. J. 1983a. *Dynamic mental representations and apparent accelerated motion.* Ph.D. dissertation, Stanford University.

Freyd, J. J. 1983b. The mental representation of action. *The Behavioral and Brain Science.* 6:145-146.

Freyd, J. J. 1983c. The mental representation of movement when viewing static stimuli. *Perception & Psychophysics.* 33:575-581.

Freyd, J. J. 1983d. Representing the dynamics of a static form. *Memory & Cognition.* 11:342-346.

Freyd, J. J., & Babcock, M. K. 1984. *Sensitivity to dynamic information during perception of static handwritten patterns.* Paper presented at the twenty-fifth annual meeting of the Psychonomic Society, San Antonio, TX, November 8.

Freyd, J. J., & Finke, R. A. 1984. Representational momentum. *Journal of Experimental Psychology: Learning, Memory, and Cognition.* 10:126-132.

Garner, W. R. 1974. *The processing of information and structure.* Hillsdale, NJ: Lawrence Erlbaum Associates.

Garner, W. R., & Clement, D. E. 1963. Goodness of pattern and pattern uncertainty. *Journal of Verbal Learning and Verbal Behavior.* 2:446-452.

Gibson, E. J., Owsley, C. J., & Johnston, J. 1978. Perception of invariants by five-month-old infants: Differentiation of two types of motion. *Developmental Psychology.* 14:407-415.

Gibson, E. J., & Spelke, E. S. 1983. The development of perception. In J. H. Flavell & E. M. Marman (Eds.), *Handbook of child psychology: Vol. 3. Cognitive development.* 1-76. New York: Wiley.

Gibson, E. J., & Walker, A. S. 1984. Development of knowledge of visual-tactual affordances of substance. *Child development.* 55:453-460.

Green, B. F., Jr. 1961. Figure coherence in the kinetic depth effect. *Journal of Experimental Psychology.* 62:272-282.

Herschel, Sir J. F. W. 1867. *Familiar lectures on scientific subjects.* London: Strahan.

Johansson, G. 1973. Visual perception of biological motion and a model for its analysis. *Perception & Psychophysics.* 14:201-211.

Jones, M. R. 1976. Time, our lost dimension: Toward a new theory of perception, attention, and memory. *Psychological Review.* 83:323-355.

Kellogg, R., & O'Dell, S. 1967. *The psychology of children's art.* San Diego, CA: CRM Books. (Distributed by Random House.)

Klüver, H. 1966. *Mescal and mechanisms of hallucinations* Chicago: University of Chicago Press.

Levine, M. 1981. *Cognitive maps and you-are-here maps.* Invited address presented at the annual meeting of the American Psychological Association, Los Angeles, CA, August.

Levine, M., Jankovic, I. N., & Palij, M. 1982. Principles of spatial problem solving. *Journal of Experimental Psychology: General.* 111:157-175.

Metzler, J., & Shepard, R. N. 1974. Transformational studies of the internal representation of three-dimensional objects. In R. Solso (Ed.), *Theories in cognitive psychology: The Loyola Symposium.* 147-201. Potomac, MD: Lawrence Erlbaum Associates.

O'Neill, B. 1966. *Elementary differential geometry.* New York: Academic Press.

Oster, G. 1966. Phosphenes. *Art International.* 10(5):36-46.

Palmer, S. 1982. Symmetry, transformation, and the structure of perceptual systems. In J. Beck (Ed.), *Organization and representation in perception.* Hillsdale, NJ: Lawrence Erlbaum Associates.

Palmer, S. E. 1983. *On goodness, Gestalt, groups, and Garner.* Paper presented at the twenty-fourth annual meeting of the Psychonomic Society, San Diego, CA, November 18.

Palmer, S. E., & Hemenway, K. 1978. Orientation and symmetry: Effects of multiple, rotational, and near symmetries. *Journal of Experimental Psychology: Human Perception and Performance.* 4:691-702.

Proffitt, D. R., & Cutting, J. E. 1979. Perceiving the centroid of configurations on a rolling wheel. *Perception & Psychophysics.* 25:389-398.

Robins, C., & Shepard, R. N. 1977. Spatio-temporal probing of apparent rotational movement. *Perception & Psychophysics.* 22:12-18.

Rock, I. 1973. *Orientation and form.* New York: Academic Press.

Shepard, R. N. 1978a. The circumplex and related topological manifolds in the study of perception. In S. Shye (Ed.), *Theory construction and data analysis in the behavioral sciences.* 29-80. San Francisco: Jossey-Bass.

Shepard, R. N. 1978b. Externalization of mental images and the act of creation. In B. S. Randhawa & W. E. Coffman (Eds.), *Visual learning, thinking, and communication.* 139-189. New York: Academic Press.

Shepard, R. N. 1980. Multidimensional scaling, tree-fitting, and clustering. *Science.* 210:390-398.

Shepard, R. N. 1981. Psychophysical complementarity. In M. Kubovy & J. Pomerantz (Eds.), *Perceptual organization.* 279-341. Hillsdale, NJ: Lawrence Erlbaum Associates.

Shepard, R. N. 1982. Perceptual and analogical bases of cognition. In J. Mehler, M. Garrett, E. Walker (Eds.), *Perspectives in mental representation.* 49-67. Hillsdale, NJ: Lawrence Erlbaum Associates.

Shepard, R. N. 1983. The kaleidoscopic brain. *Psychology Today.* June, 62-68.

Shepard, R. N. 1984. Ecological constraints on internal representation: Resonant kinematics of perceiving, imagining, thinking, and dreaming. *Psychological Review.* 91:417-447.

Shepard, R. N., & Cooper, L. A. 1982 *Mental images and their transformations.* Cambridge, MA: MIT Press/Bradford Books.

Shepard, R. N., Downing, C., & Putnam, T. 1985. Inner vision. *Psychology Today.* February, 66-69.

Shepard, R. N., & Farrell, J. E. 1985. Representation of the orientations of shapes. *Acta Psychologica.* 59:103-121.

Shepard, R. N., & Feng, C. A. 1972. A chronometric study of mental paper folding. *Cognitive Psychology.* 3:228-243.

Shepard, R. N., & Hurwitz, S. 1984. Upward direction, mental rotation, and discrimination of left and right turns in maps. *Cognition.* 18:161-193.

Shepard, R. N., & Judd, S. A. 1976. Perceptual illusion of rotation of three-dimensional objects. *Science.* 191:952-954.

Shepard, R. N., & Metzler, J. 1971. Mental rotation of three-dimensional objects. *Science.* 171:701-703.

Shepard, R. N., & Zare, S. 1983. Path-guided apparent motion. *Science.* 220:632-634.

Siegel, R. K. 1977. Hallucinations. *Scientific American.* 237(4):132-140.

Small, E. S., & Anderson, J. 1976. What's in a flicker film? *Communication Monographs.* 43:29-34.

Spelke, E. S. 1982. Perceptual knowledge of objects in infancy. In J. Mehler, E. C. T. Walker, & M. Garrett (Eds.), *Perspectives on mental representation.* 409-430. Hillsdale, NJ: Lawrence Erlbaum Associates.

Tyler, C. W. 1978. Some new entoptic phenomena. *Vision Research.* 18:1633-1639.

Uttal, W. R. 1975. *An autocorrelation theory of form detection.* Hillsdale, NJ: Lawrence Erlbaum Associates.

Wallach, H. 1965. Visual perception of motion. In G. Keyes (Ed.), *The nature of the art of motion.* New York: Braziller. (Also in H. Wallach. *On perception.* New York: Quadrangle, 1976.)

Wallach, H., & O'Connell, D. N. 1953. The kinetic depth effect. *Journal of Experimental Psychology.* 45:205-217.

Wertheimer, M. 1967. Laws of organization in perceptual forms. In W. D. Ellis (Ed.), *A source book of Gestalt psychology.* 71-88. New York: Humanities Press. (Original work published 1923 in German.)

West, L. J. 1962. *Hallucinations.* New York: Grune & Stratton.

Weyl, H. 1952. *Symmetry.* Princeton, NJ: Princeton University Press.

Younge, R. S. L., Cole, R. E., Gamble, M., & Rayner, M. D. 1975. Subjective patterns elicited by light flicker. *Vision Research.* 15:1291-1293.

Zimmer, A. 1982. Do we see what makes our script characteristic or do we only feel it? Modes of sensory control in handwriting. *Psychological Research.* 44:165-174.

APPENDICES

Appendix A. The Space of Possible Triangles

I use the case of a triangle in the two-dimensional plane to illustrate that the representation of shape cannot be treated in a complete and satisfactory way without taking into account the possible transformations of that shape. Although the complete specification of a triangle requires six numbers (two coordinates for each of the three vertexes), two of the degrees of freedom specify the position of the triangle in the plane and one its orientation. Of the remaining three degrees of freedom, moreover, one can be associated with the size of the triangle. If we consider the triangle as rigidly fixed in size (or, equivalently, as viewed from a fixed distance), we are left with just two degrees of freedom to specify its intrinsic shape.

If, as a convenient normalization for position, orientation, and size, we fix the base, ab, of the triangle, then the two remaining degrees of freedom of shape will correspond to the two coordinates for the third vertex, c, as illustrated in Figure 4.5. The two-dimensional subregions of the plane into which that third vertex can fall are then of two types: those (labeled A) that correspond to acute triangles, and those (labeled B) that correspond to obtuse triangles. The one-dimensional boundaries between these two-dimensional regions then correspond to the special cases of the various right triangles, isosceles triangles, and degenerate triangles (in which one vertex falls on the line connecting the other two). Finally, the zero-dimensional intersections of these one-dimensional boundaries correspond to the singular cases of the equilateral triangle, the isosceles right triangle, and the two degenerate triangles in which one vertex falls either directly on one of the two other vertexes or exactly halfway between them.

Notice, however, that although the third vertex, c, can fall anywhere within the infinite plane containing the segment ab, all possible intrinsic shapes of a triangle (that is, shapes without regard to size, position, and orientation) are realized within just four adjacent regions, such as the central regions, A^L, A^R, B^L, B^R, enclosed in heavier lines in the figure. A point in any other region A^L_1, A^L_2, A^L_3, etc. corresponds to a triangle that is identical to one whose point falls in the corresponding unsubscripted region A^L, except that rela-

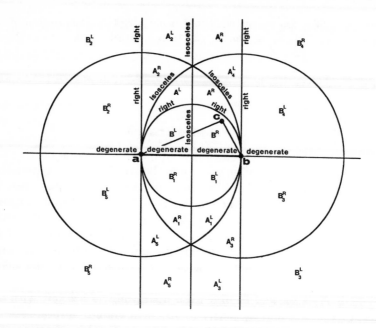

Figure 4.5. Two-dimensional space of possible shapes of a triangle with a fixed base, ab. (Points falling in different subregions can correspond to triangles of the same intrinsic shape, but rotated, reflected, expanded or contracted.)

tive to the latter triangle, the former has been expanded, translated, rotated, and/or permuted with respect to the labels, a, b, c, of its three vertexes. Moreover, points within any pair of regions that differ only in their superscripts (such as A^L and A^R, or B^L and B^R) correspond to triangles that are identical except for a reflection.

In the context of three-dimensional perception, such mirror-image triangles would be regarded as possessing the same intrinsic shape, but as differing by a rigid rotation in three-dimensional space. For the purposes of this illustration, however, I am treating the problem as a two-dimensional analogue of the three-dimensional case and, so, I am regarding left- and right-handed mirror images as intrinsically different in shape since they cannot (except in the degenerate case) be transformed into each other by a rigid transformation within the two-dimensional plane. This is consistent with the requirement that the participants in our experiments on mental rotation of both two-dimensional objects (Cooper & Shepard, 1973; Cooper, 1975), and three-dimensional objects (Cooper & Shepard, 1975; Metzler & Shepard, 1974; Shepard & Metzler, 1971), treat such enantiomorphic objects as distinct regardless of their orientations in the two- or three-dimensional spaces within which they lie.

The example of the triangle illustrates both the complexity of the problem of representing the possible shapes of even a trivially simple object and, also, the intimate connection between the problem of representing those shapes and the problem of representing their possible transformations. Ideally, we should like to factor the six-dimensional space of all possible triangles (differing in shape, size, and position) into two primary subspaces, one corresponding to the set of intrinsic shapes; the other corresponding to the alternative positions and sizes of each shape. (Positions and sizes might also be factored, further, into secondary subspaces for rotations, translations, and changes of scale—with, perhaps, changes of scale interpreted as resulting from translations in depth.) This can be done only by relinquishing a simple, flat Euclidean space like the two-dimensional plane exhibited in Figure 4.5 in favor of topologically more complex, curved space that is not isometrically embeddable in three-dimensional Euclidean space.

It is in fact orientation that is most inextricably entangled with shape; the remaining degrees of freedom of translational position and of size are more independent of shape and orientation and, so, can more nearly be factored out as orthogonal dimensions. The advantage of considering the simple case of a planar figure first is that orientation in the plane has only one degree of freedom. Thus, in the case of the triangle, if we suppose that the space of possible triangles has been properly transformed so that we can factor out the dimensions of location and size, we are left with a three-dimensional space for the representation of all possible shapes and orientations of triangles normalized, now, with respect to size and location.

The two degrees of freedom associated with intrinsic shape of the triangle correspond to possible motions within a triangular cross section of the space, like that formed by the group of four adjacent regions A^L, A^R, B^L, B^R in Figure 4.5. The third degree of freedom, associated with rotational orientation of the triangle, corresponds to possible motions orthogonal to the triangular cross section around a closed trajectory. The triangular cross section twists through 360 degrees in passing around this trajectory as roughly illustrated in Figure 4.6. Actually, this trajectory passes through each of the corresponding triangular subregions indicated in Figure 4.5. Thus, the true perceptual structures of the spaces schematically illustrated in Figure 4.5 and 4.6 are highly convoluted. Indeed, points on the bounding two-dimensional toroidal surface of the resulting twisted

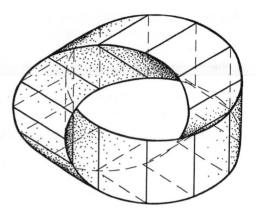

Figure 4.6. Schematic representation of the three-dimensional manifolds in which points represent either triangles differing in shape and orientation or else parallel projections of a cube with unlabeled faces in different orientations. (In both cases, separated points on the toroidal two-dimensional surface of this twisted structure are identified in such a way that the manifold is closed and unbounded.)

structure of triangular cross section are identified with each other in such a way that the resulting space becomes unbounded, though finite. In fact, points on one of the three edges twisting around the structure are identified with points 180 degrees away along that same edge. The space of possible figures as simple even as the triangle confined to a two-dimensional plane is remarkably complex.

Appendix B. The Space of Distinguishable Orientations of an Unmarked Cube

In describing the three-dimensional manifold of possible orientations of an object (and in illustrating one two-dimensional section of that manifold in Figure 4.3), I assumed that the object was asymmetrical and, hence, that any two different orientations of the object would be perceptually distinguishable. The cube illustrated in Figure 4.3 was rendered asymmetrical for this purpose by inscribing a different mark ("F," "T," "R," etc.) on each of its six faces. For an unmarked cube, of course, views that were distinguishable in Figure 4.3 would become indistinguishable. For example, the orientation shown in the center and displaying only one square face (originally marked "F") would become indistinguishable from the other orientations displaying only one square face (namely, those originally marked "L," "R," and "B" along the horizontal row passing through the center, and those originally marked "U," "T," and again, but upside down, "B" along the vertical column passing through the center). Because these orientations would then be perceptually identical, the manifold representing the set of perceptually distinguishable orientations of the unmarked cube could be obtained from the original manifold only by a deformation that brings all points corresponding to a set of such indistinguishable orientations of the cube into the same point.

As a consequence of the symmetries of a cube, the three-dimensional manifold of its possible orientations consists of 48 identically structured three-dimensional subregions, each bounded by a closed two-dimensional surface having the form of a circularly closed, twisted structure with a triangular cross section (similar to that already illustrated in Figure 4.6). Each such subregion corresponds to the set of orientations for which only the three faces meeting at a particular one of the eight vertexes of the cube are visible, and for which those three faces have one of their six possible orders with respect to the areas of their projections onto the two-dimensional plane.

The three corners of any triangular section through the toroidal subregion then correspond to the three limiting cases (a) in which only the face with the largest projection is visible (as a square), (b) in which only the two faces with the largest projections are visible, and equally so (as two adjacent rectangles in the projection), and (c) in which all three faces are equally visible (as three rhombs forming a regular hexagon in the projection). Two of the three degrees of freedom of the orientation of the cube thus correspond, locally, to motions within this triangular subregion and, hence, to changes in intrinsic shape of the planar (or retinal) projection. The third degree of freedom then corresponds to rotation of the object about the line of sight and, hence, to rigid rotation of the projection. It is the cyclic character of rotation that determines the globally circular form of each of these 48 subregions (as indicated in Figure 4.6).

Now, as all of the faces of the cube become indistinguishable (unmarked), 24 of the identical toroidal subregions become identified with each other as just one such subregion, while the remaining 24 subregions become identified with each other as a second such subregion. Moreover, because of the 180, 120, and 90 degree symmetries of a cube about axes through opposite edges, vertexes, or faces, respectively, points on the boundaries of each of these two subregions become further identified with each other. In particular, along the closed curve described by each of the three corners of the triangular cross section under 360 degree rotation of the cube, there is an identification of all pairs of points formerly separated by 180 degrees on one closed curve, of all triples of points formerly separated by 120 degrees on a second closed curve, and of all quadruples of points formerly separated by 90 degrees on the third closed curve. Finally, these two remaining subregions, which correspond to views of the cube differing only in whether the order from largest to smallest projection of the three visible faces has a clockwise or counterclockwise sense in the projection, have their bounding surfaces identified with each other so that each point on the boundary of one corresponds (under some rotation) to some point on the boundary of the other. After identifying appropriate points, we are left with an unbounded, inherently closed three-dimensional manifold, consisting of two complementary subspaces, for the representation of the set of perceptually distinct orientations of a cube.

THE ELEMENTARY SPATIAL FUNCTIONS OF THE BRAIN

5

MARK KRITCHEVSKY
V.A. Medical Center and University of California, San Diego

INTRODUCTION

Spatial cognition, in the broadest sense, refers to any aspect of an organism's behavior which involves space and is mediated by cerebral activity. How space is mediated by the brain has been a difficult question to answer experimentally. One major reason for this is that spatial behavior is often complex and often intimately associated with nonspatial behavior. In this chapter I propose that there is a set of elementary spatial functions which permit a clearer understanding of spatial behavior and which might aid in understanding the development of spatial cognition. The chapter will begin with a statement of premises upon which it is based. Then, the categories of elementary spatial function will be introduced and the specific elementary spatial functions will be presented and discussed in detail. The neuroanatomic correlates of each elementary spatial function will be reviewed and the relationship of this elementary spatial function to the other functions will be discussed. Some of the more complex spatial behaviors that are frequently studied in the literature will then be analyzed in terms of elementary spatial functions. Finally, the utility of these elementary spatial functions in understanding spatial behavior in the brain damaged and normal adult and in the developing infant and child will be discussed.

Spatial cognition is understood in terms of behavior. The first premise of this chapter is that at the present time spatial cognition is best understood in terms of behavior. Although this behavior may be spontaneous, it is more often a response to a well-defined experimental task. Behavior is particularly amenable to study because it can be easily and reliably tested in subjects with brain damage. It also seems to break down in well-defined ways in these subjects. In contrast, a person's verbal report of his mental process may be unobtainable or inaccurate in the presence of brain damage. Electrophysiologic, cerebral blood flow and cerebral metabolism studies may complement the behavioral data. Spatial cognition will, therefore, be best understood by an analysis of behavioral data from studies of normal humans, normal and experimentally lesioned animals, and especially brain damaged adult human subjects (see Chapters 1-4). The elementary spatial functions proposed in this chapter are based on these data.

Behavior must be divided into spatial and nonspatial components. It is the second premise of this chapter that when a behavior is studied, it must be carefully divided into spatial and nonspatial components. Thus, the perception of the location of an object relative to the observer is a spatial behavior (Benton, 1985b), whereas the perception of the color of an object is a nonspatial behavior. A more typical human behavior would be the perception of an object such as an orange. This task would include the spatial components of perception of location, size, shape and texture as well as the nonspatial components of perception of color and odor. In a study of spatial perception, then, it must be demonstrated that abnormal performance is due to difficulty with the spatial component or components of the perceptual task being used.

The spatial component of behavior is understood in terms of elementary spatial functions. The third premise of this chapter is that any given spatial component of behavior is best understood in terms of a set of elementary spatial functions. This type of approach was invaluable in the initial understanding of the language functions of the brain (Lichtheim, 1885) and has remained the basis of both the bedside behavioral neurologic language examination (Benson, 1979) and of the neuropsychologic language examination (Goodglass & Kaplan, 1983). Thus, the analysis of language behavior in terms of the elementary language functions of output, comprehension, repetition and naming has permitted the classification of the aphasias and the establishment of reliable clinical and neuroanatomic correlations. For example, language output has been found to be particularly dependent on the Broca's area of the left frontal lobe. A lesion

in Broca's area produces a well-defined aphasia syndrome characterized by poor output, repetition and naming with relatively preserved
comprehension. It will be demonstrated in this chapter that any spatial behavior can similarly be analyzed in terms of a set of elementary spatial functions.

The importance of the second and third premises is illustrated by
a consideration of topographical memory. This complex behavior
must be analyzed in terms of a nonspatial component (recognition of
landmarks) and two elementary spatial subcomponents (spatial
attention and spatial memory which are discussed fully later in this
chapter). Thus, a patient who is either "lost" in a previously familiar environment or cannot learn his way about a new one despite
what should be adequate experience has topographical amnesia (De
Renzi, 1982, Chapter 8). A patient with topographical amnesia who
is lost because of an inability to recognize landmarks despite normal
abilities to describe spatial layouts and draw maps (Whiteley & Warrington, 1978) illustrates the second premise. He has topographical
amnesia because of visual object agnosia. This is a nonspatial
disorder of recognition of familiar objects in a patient with normal
perception (Rubens & Benson, 1971). The third premise is demonstrated by the comparison of two further patients. One patient cannot find his way because of a deficit of spatial attention to left hemispace (Brain, 1941, Cases 4-6). He has an abnormal tendency to
make right turns and is likely to be lost when attempting to find a
spatial location to the left of where he starts. He will also draw a
map without the left side and will describe a recollected spatial layout with omission of features on the left (Bisiach & Luzzatti, 1978).
A second patient perceives landmarks and attends to space properly
but is lost because of a deficit of spatial memory. As part of more
general impairment of the ability to remember nonverbal or spatial
information, he cannot recall or learn the spatial locations of familiar landmarks relative to one another or to some point of reference.
These latter two patients have topographical amnesia due to dysfunction of two different elementary spatial functions—spatial attention and spatial memory.

A true spatial function is modality independent. The fourth and
final premise of this chapter is that a true spatial function is
independent of any particular sensory modality (Ratcliff, 1982). For
example, the location of an object relative to an observer may be perceived by visual (Ratcliff & Davies-Jones, 1972; Hannay, Varney &
Benton, 1976), auditory (Ruff, Hersh, & Pribram, 1981), tactile or
perhaps olfactory means. If the object is a body part, then it may

also be located by proprioception. Regardless of the sensory modality employed, the percept of object location becomes an abstract spatial quantity located in some mental coordinate system. The percept may be better refined if further information from a more accurate sensory modality becomes available. An object may be mislocalized because of a disorder of a primary sensory modality and this is not an impairment of a spatial function. Thus, a strabismus can cause a mislocalization of an object that is seen with the misaligned eye. Yet the object is properly localized when it is heard, felt or seen with the good eye. Similarly, a lesion of the occipital visual association area might produce a mislocalization of visual stimuli despite normal localization of auditory or tactile stimuli. In both of these cases, spatial localization is normal except when based on erroneous information from the visual system. True spatial mislocalization, on the other hand, is caused not by damage to a specific sensory system but presumably by periparietal or parietal lobe lesions. These have been reported to produce errors in localization when stimuli are perceived by visual (Ratcliff & Davies-Jones, 1972; Hannay et al., 1976), or auditory (Ruff et al., 1981) modalities. This syndrome is discussed further in the following section.

The elementary spatial function spatial attention also illustrates this final premise. It will be shown later that when dysfunction of this elementary spatial function is carefully studied, it typically involves multiple sensory modalities (Heilman & Valenstein, 1972a). Thus, spatial attention is also a modality independent function. Due to the dominant effect of the visual system on sensory input, the term "visuospatial" (Benton, 1985b) is often used with reference to true spatial function. Because true spatial function is independent of sensory modality, this use of the term is misleading. "Visuospatial" would best be used to refer to higher order visual function.

Categories of elementary spatial functions.. Brain damaged adults demonstrate a small number of well-defined syndromes of spatial dysfunction. From these syndromes may be inferred a set of elementary spatial functions and their brain bases. The fact that these proposed elementary spatial functions are commonly disrupted by brain lesions and that they may sometimes be affected in isolation suggest that the elementary spatial functions are of fundamental importance to the understanding of spatial behavior and spatial cognition.

The elementary spatial functions presented in this chapter are grouped into broad categories and are listed in Table 5.1. Similar categories have been used in recent reviews of spatial cognition (De Renzi, 1982; Ratcliff, 1982). The category of spatial perception

Table 5.1.
The Elementary Spatial Functions (ESFs)

Category	ESF	Major brain region implicated (see text for references)
Spatial Perception	Obect localization	Right, Left occipital, parietal
	Line orientation detection	Right parietal
	Spatial synthesis	Right temporal, parietal
Spatial Memory	Short-term spatial memory	Right hippocampus, medial thalamus
	Long-term spatial memory	Not known
Spatial Attention	Attention to Left hemispace	Right parietal
	Attention to Right hemispace	Left parietal
Spatial Mental Operations	Mental rotation	Right parietal
Spatial Construction	Spatial construction	Right, Left parietal

includes the elementary spatial functions of object localization, line orientation detection, and spatial synthesis. Spatial memory includes short-term and long-term spatial memory. Spatial attention is composed of spatial attention to right hemispace and spatial attention to left hemispace. The spatial mental operation discussed is mental rotation. The final category consists of the elementary spatial function of spatial construction. These elementary spatial functions will now be discussed in detail.

SPATIAL PERCEPTION

Object Localization

Although the simplest perceived spatial characteristic of an object is its location in space, it remains unclear whether object localization is an elementary spatial function. As discussed earlier, the location of an object is perceived by means of a particular sensory system but then becomes an abstract spatial quantity located in a mental coordinate system. This system may be egocentric, with location described relative to the position of the observer, or exocentric, with location described relative to the position of some fixed external object. Studies of object localization have focused on tasks wherein location is determined by only one sensory modality. For this reason true spatial object localization independent of sensory modality has not actually been demonstrated. In the absence of evidence to the contrary, this chapter will assume that there is an elementary spatial function of object localization. In an attempt to characterize this presumed elementary spatial function, studies of object localization by visual and auditory sensory modalities will be reviewed.

Visual localization. There is neuroanatomic and neurophysiologic evidence that occipital and parietal lobe neurons are involved in visual spatial perception (Hubel & Wiesel, 1959; Andersen & Mountcastle, 1983). There are also neuropsychologic data that brain damage in these regions can cause a specific defect of the ability to visually localize an object in space. Specifically, the following studies suggest that simple egocentric localization is dependent on the parietal lobe contralateral to the space in which the stimulus occurs whereas more complex exocentric localization is dependent on the function of the right posterior hemisphere (Benton, 1985b). Ratcliff and Davies-Jones (1972) required subjects to visually fixate in a central direction and then point to a brief peripheral stimulus without visual feedback of arm position. Both right and left brain damaged patients with posterior (mostly including parietal) lesions did poorly with stimuli located in the visual field contralateral to their brain injury. Patients with anterior lesions did as well as controls. This task required the egocentric localization of a single stimulus relative to the observer (and a pointing response). The egocentric task of perception of the distance from the observer to an object has also been shown to be mildly impaired in right brain damaged and left brain damaged patients (De Renzi, 1982, Chapter 5). Exocentric tasks have also been studied. Warrington and Rabin (1970) demonstrated that only patients with right parietal lesions had difficulty with a relatively easy visual task of point localization in which pairs of cards were to be matched based on the position of a dot in a vertical array. Hannay and colleagues (1976) designed a more difficult test of object localization which required the identification of the location of a pair of dots or a single dot which were briefly presented on a card. Again, patients with right posterior and right peri-Rolandic lesions did worse than the left brain damaged and control groups. This task required the exocentric localization of an object (the dot) relative to a reference object (the edge of the card or another dot). Stereoscopic vision for depth has also been shown to be abnormal in patients with right but not left posterior damage (Carmon & Bechtoldt, 1969; Benton & Hecaen, 1970). This task can be considered to be dependent on exocentric object localization in which depth is perceived by a comparison of the location of parts within the object.

Auditory localization. Simple object localization by means of the auditory modality has also been studied. Klingon and Bontecou (1966) performed a bedside auditory localization test to finger snapping. They found a mild deficit of sound localization in contralateral space for right and left brain damaged subjects. More technically elaborate studies (Sanchez-Longo, Forster, & Auth, 1957; Sanchez-Longo & Forster, 1958) have shown abnormal sound localization particularly with right or left temporal and parietal lobe lesions. Finally, Ruff and colleagues (1981) found defective auditory localization only in their group of patients with right posterior lesions. The different findings in these studies have not yet been reconciled.

Because the above data characterize the effects of brain damage on spatial localization only by individual visual or auditory sensory modalities, there is at the present time no evidence to prove that spatial object localization is in fact an elementary spatial function. Pending experimental confirmation, it is proposed that spatial object localization may be considered to be an elementary spatial function which is characterized by the more extensive data available on visual localization. Thus, egocentric localization of a single object is probably a function of the contralateral parietal and perhaps occipital lobe. Exocentric object localization is probably more dependent on right parietal function.

Line Orientation Detection

Although line orientation could be inferred from the object location of any two or more points on a line, there seems to be an independent elementary spatial function involved in the determination of line orientation. Thus, there is good neurophysiologic evidence that the human visual cortex has detectors of line orientation (Hubel & Wiesel, 1959). Neuropsychologic data have also shown that line orientation detection for visual (Warrington & Rabin, 1970; De Renzi, Faglioni, & Scotti, 1971; Benton, Hannay, & Varney, 1975; Bisiach, Nichelli, & Spinnler, 1976; Benton, Varney, & Hamsher, 1978; Meerwaldt & Van Harskamp, 1982) or tactile (De Renzi et al., 1971; Meerwaldt & Van Harskamp, 1982) stimuli can be disrupted by brain damage. For example, Benton and colleagues (1975) presented patients with brief visual stimuli consisting of one or two lines at various angles from the horizontal. A response card was then presented with standardized lines in eleven different directions and the patient was asked to indicate the line or lines which had been presented. Right brain damaged patients did significantly worse on this test than did patients with left brain lesions. Line orientation was tested by De Renzi and colleagues (1971) employing both tactile and visual stimuli. A metal rod with one fixed end could be oriented in any direction. The subject either felt or saw the rod then attempted to reproduce that orientation with a second rod. The patients with right brain damage and associated visual field defects did poorly on both tests. Similarly, Meerwaldt and Van Harskamp (1982) found a correlation of poor performance on both tasks with right posterior lesions. These studies suggest that a single brain lesion can disrupt the detection of line orientation regardless of the sensory modality with which that orientation is perceived. This suggests that there is an elementary spatial function of line orientation detection which may be specifically disrupted by right posterior brain damage.

Spatial Synthesis

The perception of an object depends in part on a spatial component involving the creation of a "spatial synthesis" from the perceived external spatial features of the object. For an object devoid of color, odor, sound and context, spatial synthesis could be identical to perception of the object. Spatial synthesis is best tested by matching test in which a subject must match a spatially complex test object to a number of similar models, one of which is identical. Perception of an unfamiliar face is one example of a task that is heavily dependent on spatial synthesis. Right hemisphere, especially posterior, lesions have been shown to cause abnormal performance in this task (De Renzi & Spinnler, 1966; Benton & Van Allen, 1968). Left hemisphere lesions that cause loss of language comprehension have also been shown to interfere with perception of an unfamiliar face (Hamsher, Levin & Benton, 1979). This suggests that there is a left hemisphere linguistic component in addition to the predominant right posterior spatial synthesis component in facial perception. A second task dependent on spatial synthesis, the identification of complex meaningless shapes by tactile perception, has been studied in patients with surgical section of the corpus callosum (Franco & Sperry, 1977). An increasing superiority of the left hand/right brain for the identification of increasingly difficult geometric figures of increasingly abstract geometry has been demonstrated. In summary, spatial synthesis may be considered the final and most complex of the spatial perceptual elementary spatial functions. It is probably particularly dependent on right temporal and parietal lobe function.

Personal space is not an elementary spatial function. The three spatial perceptual functions discussed all clearly refer to external or extrapersonal space. Regardless of whether an object is located egocentrically relative to the observer or exocentrically relative to another object, it is located outside of, or external to, the observer. A possible complementary function described in the neuropsychological literature is that of personal space, which refers to the "body schema" or "body image" (Frederiks, 1969; Benton, 1985a). It is likely, however, that personal "space" is in fact composed of two components, only one of which is spatial. The perception of the location of a body part in space is a special case of object localization which usually relies primarily on proprioceptive input. The actual recognition and identification of a body part as right arm or left ear probably depends mostly on nonspatial factors. Thus "body image" may be thought of as a combination of a spatial and a predominantly nonspatial function. This chapter will not refer to personal space as an elementary spatial function.

SPATIAL MEMORY

The second category of elementary spatial functions is that of spatial memory. The spatial information recalled includes that which has been perceived as spatial object localization, line orientation and spatial synthesis. Spatial memory, like memory in general, may be classified as immediate, short-term and long-term (Strub & Black, 1977). Immediate memory is the ability to repeat the data to be learned without an interval delay. It is dependent on adequate attention and repetition ability and it is a prerequisite for short-term memory. It is, however, not a true memory function and does not depend on the integrity of brain structures which when damaged produce amnesia. Short-term memory is the ability to recall information after a brief distraction or delay, often several minutes. A deficit of short-term memory is called anterograde amnesia. Long-term memory is the ability to recall information after a much longer interval. A deficit of long-term memory—particularly for information dating before the onset of amnesia—is called retrograde amnesia.

Short-Term Spatial Memory

Two areas of the brain whose damage has been thought to cause anterograde amnesia are the medial temporal lobe, in particular the hippocampus (Scoville & Milner, 1957; Victor, Angevine, Mancall, & Fisher, 1961; Woods, Schoene, & Kneisley, 1982; Cummings, Tomiyasu, Read, & Benson, 1984), and the diencephalon, in particular the mediodorsal nucleus of the thalamus (Victor, Adams, & Collins, 1971; McEntee, Biber, Perl, & Benson, 1976; Mills & Swanson, 1978; Castaigne, Lhermitte, Buge, Escourolle, Hauw, & Lyon-Caen, 1981; Guberman & Stuss, 1983). Bilateral damage to these areas produces amnesia that is characterized as global, affecting both verbal and nonverbal material. When damage occurs on only one side the deficit can be characterized as material specific. For example, there is good evidence that isolated lesions in right hippocampus or right thalamic mediodorsal nucleus may cause a syndrome of amnesia for predominantly nonverbal, including spatial, material. This occurs despite relative preservation of spatial perception in many cases. Thus, severe epileptic patients who have had a therapeutic excision of the right hippocampal formation as part of a right temporal lobectomy have been shown to have abnormal incidental recall of object location (Smith & Milner, 1981), impaired recall for recurring spatial figures (Kimura, 1963) and abnormal recall of unfamiliar faces (Milner, 1968). They have also been shown to be impaired on tests of visually guided and tactually guided maze learning (Corkin, 1965; Milner, 1965) although these are actually complex spatial tasks which test more than one elementary spatial function. The memory impairment may be mild and is often not apparent in the patient's daily life. Some associated spatial perceptual deficits have been noted (Kimura, 1963; Milner, 1968) but these are too mild to account for the amnesia seen. Speedie and Heilman (1983) have reported a patient with spatial anterograde amnesia after an infarction of the right mediodorsal thalamus. The patient was noted by his wife to be forgetful of daily events, although formal tests of verbal short-term and long-term memory were normal. He had significant anterograde amnesia for spatial material including drawings, unfamiliar faces and recurring figures. He was noted to have some mild associated spatial perceptual difficulties and some difficulty with drawing three-dimensional objects. He also performed abnormally on several tests which generally are sensitive to frontal lobe dysfunction— Wisconsin Card sorting, serial hand positions and design fluency. A further patient with right thalamic infarction was reported by Graff-Radford, Eslinger, Damasio, & Yamada (1984). Again, spatial but not verbal memory was significantly impaired. There were associated deficits of spatial perception and construction. In all these patients with thalamic lesions, the perceptual problems were mild and could not account for the deficit of short-term spatial memory.

Long-Term Spatial Memory

Spatial long-term memory has been difficult to assess. Tests where a patient is asked to place cities on a map of his country have been proposed but deficits on this sort of examination seem to be related primarily to decreased intellect and spatial inattention (Benton, Levin, & Van Allen, 1974).

Topographical memory is not an elementary spatial function. Topographical memory has been shown to be a complex spatial behavior which is dependent on a nonspatial component and on two elementary spatial functions (spatial memory and spatial attention).

The data presented here suggest that spatial short-term and perhaps long-term memory should be useful elementary spatial functions in the analysis of spatial behavior. Amnesia for spatial material is a well-defined syndrome which occurs secondary to damage to specific brain structures. It often occurs in the absence of significant disruption of other elementary spatial functions when it is caused by a right hippocampal lesion. It also may be caused by a right mediodorsal thalamic lesion, though in this case there are more frequently associated deficits of other elementary spatial functions.

SPATIAL ATTENTION

Spatial attention is the next category of elementary spatial functions. The well-defined behavioral disorders seen in patients with neglect and related syndromes (Heilman, Watson, & Valenstein, 1985) suggest that attention paid to left hemispace can be considered to be an elementary spatial function that is dependent on the right hemisphere, particularly the parietal lobe. Similarly, attention to right hemispace is an elementary spatial function dependent on the left hemisphere, particularly the parietal lobe. There are a number of behavioral manifestations of spatial inattention or neglect (Heilman et al., 1985). A patient may fail to report perceived sensory stimuli in the inattended hemispace (hemi-inattention). He may fail to report these stimuli only if there is a simultaneous stimulus in the normally attended hemispace (extinction to double simultaneous stimulation). Motor output of body parts in inattended "personal space" may be decreased or absent despite normal strength (hemiakinesia). Thus a patient who appears to have a paralyzed side in daily activities can be shown to have good strength on formal testing. In addition, one hemispace may be neglected in the performance of behavioral tasks (hemispatial neglect). For example, a patient with a right parietal lesion may neglect food on the inattended left side of a plate and fail to copy the parts of a drawing that are on its left side. When asked to describe and interpret a picture, he may fail to report the details present on the left side. Similarly, the left half of a sentence or word may also be neglected, making him unable to read for comprehension. Moreover, when asked to bisect a visually perceived line, he may place his mark far to the right because he has not attended to the left side (see Fig. 5.1a). This abnormal behavior often persists when the patient is asked to report a letter at the far left side of the line before the bisection (Heilman & Valenstein, 1979). Spatial inattention may also affect the body image so that body parts in inattended "personal space" are either totally ignored or felt to be foreign (Cutting, 1978). Finally, spatial inattention may affect the reporting of spatial memories. Bisiach and Luzzatti (1978) and Bisiach, Capitani, Luzzatti and Perani (1981) asked patients with right posterior hemisphere lesions to describe a recalled scene of a familiar city square. When patients imagined they were standing at one end of the

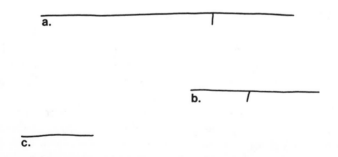

Figure 5.1. Left spatial inattention demonstrated by a line detection and bisection task. A man with a right parietal stroke was asked to mark the exact center of every line on the paper: (a) In the top line, the placement of his mark to the right indicated he had neglected some of the left side of the line. (b) The middle line was accurately bisected, demonstrating that there was less neglect when the line was located in the observer's attended space. (c) The bottom line lay farthest into inattended space and was not detected.

square, they tended to not report details on the left of the square. Yet when they imagined themselves at the other end of the square, facing their original position, they tended to omit details on the new left side. These authors proposed that each hemisphere was required for storage and recall of topographic information from contralateral space. A simpler interpretation is that patients first recall the entire scene but then only report details present in the attended space (Heilman et al., 1985). Each patient with spatial inattention may exhibit one or more of these related manifestations of the neglect syndrome.

Object-centered feature of spatial inattention.   The center or midline which divides left from right hemispace is determined partly by the object employed in the test of spatial attention. Thus, previously stated examples of hemispatial neglect demonstrated inattention for the left side of a meal, a picture or a word. This neglect generally persists whether the object itself is in the observer's attended or inattended hemispace. Moreover, a patient with spatial inattention who is asked to copy three figures in a row may omit half of the central figure but properly copy the figure lying farther out in the supposedly inattended space (Gainotti, Messerli, & Tissot, 1972).

Observer-centered feature of spatial inattention.   Behavioral data also show that the spatial midline is partly determined by the location of the attended object relative to the orientation of the observer. If the observer's eyes, head and trunk are aligned, then moving a visually or tactilely perceived object from attended to inattended space will often increase the degree of spatial inattention (Heilman & Valenstein, 1979; Bisiach, Capitani, & Porta, 1985). This is demonstrated by the line identification and bisection task in Figure 5.1. In addition, it can be shown that the degree of inattention is dependent on the location of the perceived object relative to the separate orientation of eyes, head and trunk (Coslett, Bowers, Haws, & Heilman, 1985).

Disorders of spatial attention are generally caused by contralateral parietal lobe lesions (McFie, Piercy, & Zangwill, 1950; Battersby, Bender, Pollack, & Kahn, 1956; Critchley, 1953) but may also be caused by contralateral dorsolateral frontal (Heilman & Valenstein, 1972b; Stein & Volpe, 1983), thalamic (Watson & Heilman, 1979; Watson, Valenstein, & Heilman 1981; Vilkki, 1984), striatal and white matter (Healton, Navarro, Bressman, & Brust, 1982) and perhaps midbrain (Villardita et al., 1983) lesions.

Although the salient behavioral findings suggest that attention for a given hemispace is primarily dependent on the contralateral hemisphere, particularly the parietal lobe, the two hemispheres do not have symmetric roles in spatial attention. The left spatial inattention seen with right parietal lobe lesions is more frequent and more severe than the right spatial inattention seen with left parietal lesions (Gainotti et al., 1972; Albert, 1973). Moreover, Gainotti and colleagues (1972) found that the phenomena of neglect of half of one figure with normal reporting of another figure lying farther into inattended space was seen only in patients with left spatial neglect This phenomenon has also been observed by the present author with the right spatial neglect of a left parietal lesion, but does appear to be uncommon in these cases. Another difference between right and left spatial inattention is that the former often improves or resolves in tasks with more strict demands for spatial exploration (Colombo, De Renzi, & Faglioni, 1976). All these studies are felt to indicate that the right hemisphere has a relative but not absolute dominance for spatial attention (Heilman & Van Den Abell, 1980; Mesulam, 1981).

Although spatial inattention may be an isolated finding, it is often associated with disorders of one or more of the other elementary spatial functions presented here (Critchley, 1953; Battersby et al., 1956; Oxbury, Campbell, & Oxbury, 1974; Hier, Mondlock, & Caplan, 1983). In some instances, these disorders are secondary to the inattention. For example spatial localization will often be abnormal for an object in inattended space and spatial synthesis will be difficult if half the object is relatively inattended. In other instances, the degree of spatial inattention present will not explain the quality or degree of dysfunction of the other elementary spatial function. A primary disorder of the other elementary spatial function is then present. Further examples of the effect of spatial inattention on other elementary spatial functions will be given in the next two sections.

SPATIAL MENTAL OPERATIONS

Spatial operations constitute a category of elementary spatial functions for which there is little neurobehavioral data. These mental operations may be performed on directly perceived, mentally recalled or mentally visualized objects. Operations such as mental translation (imagining what an object would look like if it were displaced along a line) and mental reflection (imagining what an object would look like reflected in a mirror) are included in this category. Mental rotation is the one spatial operation for which there are sufficient data to characterize it as an elementary spatial function. For example, mental rotation of complex geometric figures composed of small cubes was studied in normal subjects by Shepard and Metzler (1971). It was found that mental rotations were performed at a uniform rate. Thus, the time it took for a subject to identify whether a presented object was the same or different from a similar sample was directly proportional to the angle it took to rotate the object onto the sample. Ratcliff (1979) studied the ability of brain damaged patients to perform a task partly dependent on mental rotation. The subject was presented with a series of schematic drawings of a human figure (see Figure 5.2). Each figure could be seen to be facing toward or away from the subject and to be oriented in an upright or inverted fashion. The subject was then asked to report whether a black dot was on the figure's right or left hand. The patients with right posterior lesions were unable to perform the task when the stick figure was inverted. This was felt to be due to an inability to perform a mental rotation caused by the right parietal lesion. It was demonstrated that the patients had adequate spatial perception and attention to have performed this test. A related task was studied by Sauget, Benton and Hécaen (1971). Brain damaged patients were asked to identify left and right body parts of the confronting examiner. Performance was defective in about one quarter of the left brain damaged patients, but was related to aphasia and to inability to correctly identify their own left and right. In contrast, 13 percent of right brain damaged patients had difficulty with the task despite having normal language

Figure 5.2. Mental rotation task of Ratcliff (1979) with simpler stick figures. Each subject was shown a series of individual figures and asked to say if the black dot was on the figure's right or left hand. Patients with right parietal lesions had particular difficulty with the inverted figures, presumably due to a difficulty with performing a mental rotation.

comprehension and normal ability to identify their own left and right body parts. This could again be explained by an inability of certain right brain damaged patients to perform a spatial mental rotation.

These data suggest that spatial mental rotation is a useful elementary spatial function which may be affected by brain damage, particularly that of the right posterior hemisphere. Ratcliff (1979) demonstrated primary dysfunction of the elementary spatial function and it must be presumed that patients with severe disorders of spatial perception or attention might have a secondary inability to perform mental rotations. Dysfunction of this elementary spatial function may therefore be primary or secondary but in either case is generally associated with a right posterior hemisphere, particularly parietal, lesion.

SPATIAL CONSTRUCTION

Spatial construction, generally termed constructional praxis, is the final elementary spatial function. It consists of manually putting the parts of an object together into a whole (Warrington, 1969; De Renzi, 1982, Chapter 9). It is reflected in tasks like drawing, putting together sticks or assembling blocks according to a mental or perceived model. Common bedside constructional tasks include drawing or copying sketches of a flower, a house, a face or a person. Neuropsychological tests of spatial construction include the block design task of the revised Wechsler Adult Intelligence Scale (Lezak, 1983) and the three-dimensional block test of Benton (Benton & Fogel, 1962) in which the patient assembles blocks according to two- or three-dimensional models respectively. Although it has been suggested (Benton & Fogel, 1962; Benton, 1967) that drawing tasks may be testing a different ability than assembly tasks, other investigators have found good correlation between performance on these two types of constructional tasks in both right and left brain damaged patients (Arrigoni & De Renzi, 1964; Dee, 1970).

A disorder of spatial construction is called constructional apraxia (Warrington, 1969; De Renzi, 1982, Chapter 9). Constructional apraxia is seen with right or left hemispheric brain damage and is more likely to be caused by posterior, especially parietal, lesions than by other cortical or subcortical lesions. The early studies of constructional apraxia suggested that it was more common in right than in left brain damaged patients (Piercy, Hécaen, & Ajuriaguerra, 1960; Benton & Fogel, 1962; Arrigoni & De Renzi, 1964).

However, severely aphasic patients were probably excluded from these studies and it has subsequently been found that constructional apraxia in left brain damaged patients often is associated with receptive aphasia (Benton, 1973; Arena & Gainotti, 1978). The reports which have included aphasic patients have noted an incidence of 30-40% regardless of side of lesion (Benton, 1973; Colombo et al., 1976; Arena & Gainotti, 1978). Also, despite some early suggestion to the contrary, most studies employing copying of drawings or assembling blocks have demonstrated a similar degree of severity of constructional apraxia in left and right brain damaged patients (Arrigoni & De Renzi, 1964; Warrington et al., 1966). With right hemisphere lesions, constructional apraxia is most frequently seen with posterior, especially parietal, lesions (Warrington et al., 1966; Black & Strub, 1976; Hier et al., 1983). It may also be seen with anterior (Warrington et al., 1966; Black & Strub, 1976; Hier et al., 1983) or even subcortical (Hier et al., 1983; Speedie & Heilman, 1983; Graff-Radford et al., 1984) lesions. The constructional apraxia of left hemisphere lesions may also be seen with posterior (Warrington, James, & Kinsbourne, 1966; Black & Strub, 1976), anterior (Warrington et al., 1966) or subcortical (Graff-Radford et al., 1984) lesions.

Although the abnormalities of spatial construction of an individual patient often do not aid in lesion localization, distinct patterns of abnormality are seen which distinguish the constructional apraxia of groups of patients with left or right brain damage from each other (De Renzi, 1982, Chapter 9). It was noted in the early literature that the constructional apraxia of right brain damage (Paterson & Zangwill, 1944; McFie et al., 1950) was marked by disorganized spatial relationships of the parts copied. In contrast, the constructional apraxia of left brain damage (Mcfie & Zangwill, 1960) was characterized by a relative preservation of accurate spatial relationships with an oversimplified reproduction due to a decreased number of details. The performance on constructional tasks of right brain damaged patients was energetic in contrast to the slow, deliberate performance of left brain damaged patients. Warrington and colleagues (1966) noted that only the left brain damaged patients improved their performance on drawing a cube after practice sessions in which elements of the cube were copied. Additionally, although the two groups copied figures with or without inner detail or "structure" equally well, only the right brain damaged group used this structure to aid them in the task. Gainotti and Tiacci (1970) also found that the constructional apraxia of right brain damaged patients more frequently showed severe spatial disorganization characterized by altered spatial relations of parts of drawings. Additionally, a piecemeal approach was frequently taken in which the model was copied line after line without regard to the overall structure. There was also a tendency to overscore lines and add irrelevant writing or drawing. They found that the constructional apraxia of left brain damaged patients was characterized by a tendency to oversimplify. This included difficulty drawing angles. In summary, there are clear distinctions between the constructional apraxia of groups of right and left brain damaged patients. This suggests that the two hemispheres play different roles in the spatial construction process.

It has been proposed that one further distinctive characteristic of the constructional apraxia of left brain damage is that it is improved in some cases by what is termed programmation (Hécaen & Assal, 1970). In this paradigm a patient is asked to copy a drawing. On the test sheet cues such as one or more of the components of the object to be copied have already been drawn for him. With a related task, Pillon (1981) found the contradictory result that patients with both left and right posterior lesions improved with visual cues, as opposed to patients with constructional apraxia from frontal lesions. Additionally, Gainotti, Miceli and Caltagirone (1977) found that the only difference between left and right brain damaged groups was that due to a tendency for right brain damaged patients to ignore cues in left space. Hadano (1984) studied a similar effect with a block design task. Although left and right brain damaged patients both improved their performances, statistical analysis suggested that the left brain damage group had adopted a different strategy when cues were present. The role of programmation in spatial construction remains uncertain.

A heuristic consideration of the process of spatial construction suggests that it is best divided into secondary and primary components. Thus, a tangible model for a constructional task must be spatially perceived and adequate attention must be paid to the left and right components of the object. If the model is imagined, then spatial attention is still required. In either case, forming a spatial synthesis of the model may be helpful. This initial component of spatial construction is therefore dependent on other elementary spatial functions. Next, the subject must actually draw or assemble his copy of the model as he has perceived it. This may be regarded as the primary component of constructional praxis. Constructional apraxia is best thought of in terms of a secondary constructional apraxia due to a deficit of spatial perception (see Figure 5.3) or spatial attention (see Figure 5.4b) and a primary constructional apraxia which affects the actual constructional output (see Figure 5.4a).

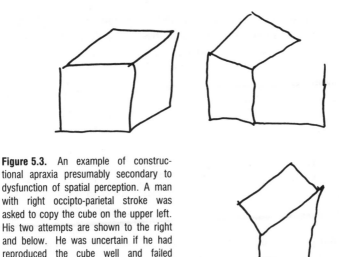

Figure 5.3. An example of constructional apraxia presumably secondary to dysfunction of spatial perception. A man with right occipto-parietal stroke was asked to copy the cube on the upper left. His two attempts are shown to the right and below. He was uncertain if he had reproduced the cube well and failed matching tests of comparable drawings.

When a patient is found to have constructional apraxia, a matching test with items comparable to the model to be constructed will identify whether the constructional apraxia is secondary to a spatial perceptual problem. An analysis of the errors made in the construction will then generally indicate whether spatial inattention is causing the constructional apraxia. In the absence of these two underlying deficits, a primary constructional apraxia may be diagnosed.

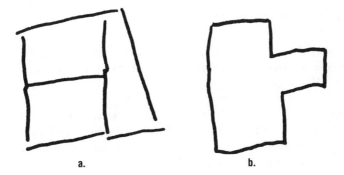

a.   b.

Figure 5.4. Examples of primary and secondary constructional apraxia. The same patient as in Figure 5.1 was asked to copy drawings of a three dimensional cube and of a cross: (a) The cube copy was poor with a complete loss of perspective, yet he demonstrated adequate perception on matching tests of comparable items and attended to all surfaces. (b) The cross copy was accurate except for the omission of the left arm due to left spatial inattention.

Experimental studies have confirmed that constructional apraxia may be primary or secondary and have shown that in both cases it is often associated with dysfunction of other elementary spatial functions. Thus, the constructional apraxia of right brain disease is frequently associated with, and is often actually due to, defective visual spatial perception (Belleza, Rappaport, Hopkins, & Hall, 1979; Dee, 1970; Dee & Benton, 1970; Mack & Levine, 1981) or left spatial inattention (Warrington et al., 1966; Gainotti & Tiacci, 1970; Oxbury et al., 1974; Colombo et al., 1976). However, in many cases this constructional apraxia cannot be completely accounted for by these other deficits (Warrington et al., 1966; Dee, 1970) demonstrating that primary as well as secondary constructional apraxia is seen in patients with right brain damage. The constructional apraxia of left brain disease is less frequently associated with spatial inattention (McFie & Zangwill, 1960; Warrington et al., 1966). Additionally, these patients have generally been shown not to have the spatial perceptual problems of comparable right brain damaged patients (Belleza et al., 1979; Mack & Levine, 1981) although some perceptual deficits may be seen (Dee, 1970; Dee & Benton, 1970). Thus, patients with left brain damage can also have primary or secondary constructional apraxia.

To conclude, the well-defined, albeit complex, manner in which primary constructional praxis may be disrupted by brain damage suggests that it is an elementary spatial function. Moreover, the right and left parietal lobes have important and separate roles in this spatial function.

COMPLEX SPATIAL BEHAVIORS

A number of complex "spatial" tasks are dependent on a combination of one or more elementary spatial functions, and sometimes on nonspatial functions as well.

Topographical memory. It was noted in the introduction that what has been called topographical memory is dependent on landmark recognition, spatial attention and spatial memory. Where sufficient data are available, published cases of patients with topographical amnesia are indeed seen to have this disorder secondary to deficits of one or more of these three functions (Brain, 1941; De Renzi, Faglioni, & Villa, 1977; Whitely & Warrington, 1978).

Stylus maze task. A stylus maze task requires that a path be learned by trial and error on a small maze which remains directly in front of the subject. Movements through the maze can be guided by somasthetic (Corkin, 1965) or visual perception (Milner, 1965; Newcombe & Russell, 1969; Ratcliff & Newcombe, 1973). The task is clearly dependent on spatial perception, spatial memory and spatial attention. Right hemisphere, particularly posterior, lesions (Newcombe & Russell, 1969; Ratcliff & Newcombe, 1973) have been shown to cause poor performance on the visually guided task. Additionally, right temporal lesions which include the hippocampus cause poor performance, presumably by means of a deficit of spatial memory (Milner, 1965). Insufficient information is available in the literature to determine whether abnormal performance on this task can always be explained by dysfunction of the elementary spatial functions upon which it appears to be dependent.

Locomotor maze task. A locomotor maze task also requires that the subject follow a path (Semmes, Weinstein, Ghent, & Teuber, 1963; Ratcliff & Newcombe, 1973). The subject holds a map which is always oriented with "north" in the direction he is facing. He must then walk the path designated by the map on a series of dots which have been placed on the floor in the exam room. It has been contended that the main difference between a stylus maze task and a comparable locomotor maze task is one of the "scale" of space—the former is a small-scale and the latter a large-scale spatial task. However, an analysis of the elementary spatial functions involved in a locomotor maze task shows that it is dependent on a spatial mental operation in addition to spatial perception and attention. Thus, once the subject has turned so that he no longer faces north, the map and room are "misaligned." A spatial mental rotation must then be performed to determine the next step in the locomotor maze which is required by the handheld map. Additionally, as the two tests have been presented here, only the stylus maze is dependent on spatial memory. Ratcliff and Newcombe (1973) found that patients with right or left posterior lesions did well on the locomotor maze task but that patients with bilateral posterior lesions did poorly. This is not a result that would have been predicted based on the earlier analysis of mental rotation. It is, however, consistent with the possibility that the task could have been performed either by a right parietal function of mental rotation or by a left hemisphere dependent verbal strategy. It has also been demonstrated that patients with frontal lobe lesions fail locomotor maze tasks (Semmes et al., 1963). Unfortunately, associated deficits were not reported. Perseveration (persistence in making an old, now incorrect response) is commonly seen in patients with frontal lesions and could have produced poor performance on this task. The locomotor maze task is therefore seen to be dependent on a number of elementary spatial functions as well as on nonspatial components of behavior. Available data suggest that abnormalities of these underlying elementary spatial functions or nonspatial components can account for abnormal maze performance.

Road-Map Test. The Road-Map Test of Money (Lezak, 1983) employs small-scale space but also asks the subject to perform mental rotations. A map sits in front of the subject and the examiner draws a path made of a series of straight lines on the map. At each turn the subject is asked whether a right or left turn is being made. The task is dependent on spatial perception, attention and spatial mental rotation. For this reason patients who fail this test might be expected to also fail the locomotor maze test. Butters, Soeldner, & Fedio (1972) found that left frontal lesions caused a very poor performance, and that right parietal lesions were also associated with some difficulty on this task. Temporal lobe lesions did not cause an abnormal performance and unfortunately right frontal and left parietal patients were not tested. Associated deficits were not reported but the poor performance of patients with frontal lesions might again be explained by perseveration. Right parietal damaged patients might have done poorly because of deficits of any of the elementary spatial functions upon which this more complex task was dependent.

CONCLUSIONS

It has been shown that spatial cognition is best understood in terms of behavior. Behavior in turn must be divided into spatial and nonspatial components. The spatial component of behavior is then best analyzed in terms of a set of modality independent elementary spatial functions. These elementary spatial functions, listed in Table 5.1, are defined by a small number of well-defined and circumscribed clinical syndromes of spatial dysfunction which are produced in adults with damage of specific brain structures.

The perceptual elementary spatial functions include object localization, line orientation detection and spatial synthesis. There is at present no definite evidence that object localization is in fact a modality independent or true spatial function. If it is, then the egocentric location of a single object to the right or left of the observer is probably dependent on contralateral parieto-occipital function. In contrast, the exocentric localization of an object relative to another is probably dependent on right parietal function. There is good evidence that line orientation detection and spatial synthesis are elementary spatial functions and that they are particularly disrupted by lesions of the right parietal and the temporal lobes, respectively.

Memory functions include short-term and long-term spatial memory. The patterns of abnormal spatial behavior seen in brain damaged adults suggest that at least the former is an elementary spatial function. Short-term spatial memory is dependent on the right medial temporal region, especially the hippocampus, and on right diencephalic structures, especially the mediodorsal nucleus of the thalamus. The neuroanatomic substrate of long-term spatial memory is unknown.

The elementary spatial functions of spatial attention to right and left hemispace are characterized by the neglect syndrome and are dependent particularly on the function of the left and right parietal lobes, respectively.

Mental rotation is the only spatial mental operation which has been well studied in brain-damaged adults. It is disrupted particularly by lesions of the right parietal lobe.

The final elementary spatial function is spatial construction. A lesion of either parietal region will generally produce an abnormality of constructional praxis.

It has been shown that all the proposed elementary spatial functions may be disrupted on a primary basis—independent of significant dysfunction of any other elementary spatial function. Additionally, an apparent dysfunction of some of the elementary spatial functions, particularly spatial construction and mental rotation, may in fact be secondary to a deficit of another elementary spatial function such as spatial perception or attention. Despite the need to clarify some disorders of elementary spatial functions as primary or secondary, the elementary spatial functions remain a very useful means for analyzing spatial behavior.

The author uses, in his neurobehavioral examination of brain damaged adult patients, a simple battery of spatial tests which are based on the elementary spatial functions presented in this chapter. Spatial perception is tested in a general sense by tasks where the subject is asked to match visually perceived drawings to a number of similar choices. Spatial short-term memory is examined by asking the patient to copy three simple "nonsense" drawings and then reproduce them from memory five minutes later. Spatial attention is checked by tasks of double simultaneous visual, auditory, and tactile stimulation, line bisection, picture interpretation and by the constructional tests described below. Mental rotation is examined by using the stick figure task described by Ratcliff (1979) and by asking the patient to identify the examiner's right and left sides. Finally, constructional praxis is tested by requesting the patient to spontaneously draw a house and then to copy a complex diagram. This set of tests allows the author to identify primary and secondary dysfunction of all the elementary spatial functions. The pattern of dysfunction demonstrated then gives valuable information about neuroanatomic localization of the underlying brain lesion and explains any dysfunction of more complex spatial behaviors which are found by history, examination or formal neuropsychological testing.

Because the elementary spatial functions are based on the specific patterns of abnormality seen in brain damaged adults, they are of great value in analyzing the abnormalities of spatial behavior seen in this population. Moreover, at least some of the elementary spatial functions have been shown to be useful in understanding spatial cognition in the normal adult. It is hoped that this set of elementary spatial functions will additionally help clarify the development of spatial cognition and the disorders of spatial cognition seen in the developing infant and child. For this purpose, the elementary spatial functions presented and discussed in this chapter are offered as potentially useful to those who are studying the development of spatial cognition.

ACKNOWLEDGMENTS

The author wishes to thank Dr. Stuart Zola-Morgan for critically reviewing the manuscript and Mrs. Georgiana Mau and Ms. Barbara Reader for technical assistance with the preparation of the manuscript.

REFERENCES

Albert, M. L. 1973. A simple test of visual neglect. *Neurology.* 23:658-664.
Andersen, R. A., & Mountcastle, V. B. 1983. The influence of the angle of gaze upon the excitability of the light-sensitive neurons of the posterior parietal cortex. *Journal of Neuroscience.* 3:532-548.
Arena, R., & Gainotti, G. 1978. Constructional apraxia and visuoperceptive disabilities in relation to laterality of cerebral lesions. *Cortex.* 14:463-473.
Arrigoni, G., & De Renzi, E. 1964. Constructional apraxia and hemispheric locus of lesion. *Cortex.* 1:170-197.

Battersby, W. S., Bender, M. B., Pollack, M., & Kahn, R. L. 1956. Unilateral "spatial agnosia" ("inattention") in patients with cerebral lesions. *Brain.* 79:68-93.

Belleza, T., Rappaport, M. Hopkins, H. K., & Hall, K. 1979. Visual scanning and matching dysfunction in brain-damaged patients with drawing impairment. *Cortex.* 15:19-36.

Benson, D. F. 1979. *Aphasia, alexia, and agraphia.* New York: Churchill Livingstone.

Benton, A. L. 1967. Constructional apraxia and the minor hemisphere. *Confinia Neurologica.* 29:1-16.

Benton, A. L. 1973. Visuoconstructive disability in patients with cerebral disease: its relationship to side of lesion and aphasic disorder. *Documenta Ophthalmologica.* 34:67-76.

Benton, A. 1985a. Body schema disturbances: finger agnosia and right-left disorientation. In K. M. Heilman & E. Valenstein (Eds.), *Clinical Neuropsychology* (2nd ed.) 115-129. New York: Oxford University Press.

Benton, A. 1985b. Visuoperceptual, visuospatial, and visuoconstructive disorders. In K. M. Heilman & E. Valenstein (Eds.), *Clinical Neuropsychology* (2nd ed.) 151-185. New York: Oxford University Press.

Benton, A. L., & Fogel, M. L. 1962. Three-dimensional constructional praxis. *Archives of Neurology.* 7:347-354.

Benton, A., Hannay, H. J., & Varney, N. R. 1975. Visual perception of line direction in patients with unilateral brain disease. *Neurology.* 25:907-910.

Benton, A. L., & Hécaen, H. 1970. Stereoscopic vision in patients with unilateral cerebral disease. *Neurology.* 20:1084-1088.

Benton, A. L., Levin, H. S., & Van Allen, M. W. 1974. Geographic orientation in patients with unilateral cerebral disease. *Neuropsychologia.* 12:183-191.

Benton, A. L., & Van Allen, M. W. 1968. Impairment in facial recognition in patients with cerebral disease. *Cortex.* 4:344-358.

Benton, A. L., Varney, N. R., & Hamsher, K. deS. 1978. Visuospatial judgement: a clinical test. *Archives of Neurology.* 35:364-367.

Bisiach, E., Capitani, E., Luzzatti, C., & Perani, D. 1981. Brain and conscious representation of outside reality. *Neuropsychologia.* 19:543-51.

Bisiach, E., Capitani, E., & Porta, E. 1985. Two basic properties of space representation in the brain: evidence from unilateral neglect. *Journal of Neurology, Neurosurgery, and Psychiatry.* 48:141-144.

Bisiach, E., & Luzzatti, C. 1978. Unilateral neglect of representational space. *Cortex.* 14:129-133.

Bisiach, E., Nichelli, P., & Spinnler, H. 1976. Hemispheric functional asymmetry in visual discrimination between univariate stimuli: an analysis of sensitivity and response criterion. *Neuropsychologia.* 14:335-342.

Black, F. W., & Strub, R. L. 1976. Constructional apraxia in patients with discrete missile wounds of the brain. *Cortex.* 12:212-220.

Brain, W. R. 1941. Visual disorientation with special reference to lesions of the right cerebral hemisphere. *Brain.* 64:244-272.

Butters, N., Soeldner, C., & Fedio, P. 1972. Comparison of parietal and frontal lobe spatial deficits in man: extrapersonal vs personal (egocentric) space. *Perceptual and Motor Skills.* 34:27-34.

Carmon, A., & Bechtoldt, H. P. 1969. Dominance of the right cerebral hemisphere for stereopsis. *Neuropsychologia.* 7:29-39.

Castaigne, P., Lhermitte, F. Buge, A., Escourolle, R., Hauw, J. J., & Lyon-Caen, O. 1981. Paramedian thalamic and midbrain infarcts; clinical and neuropathological study. *Annals of Neurology.* 10:127-148.

Colombo, A., De Renzi, E., & Faglioni, P. 1976. The occurrence of visual neglect in patients with unilateral cerebral disease. *Cortex.* 12:221-231.

Corkin, S. 1965. Tactually-guided maze learning in man: effects of unilateral cortical excisions and bilateral hippocampal lesions. *Neuropsychologia.* 3:339-351.

Coslett, H. B., Bowers, D., Haws, B., & Heilman, K. 1985. An analysis of the determinants of hemispatial performance. *INS Bulletin.* Nov. 1984:11 (Abstract).

Critchley, M. 1953. *The parietal lobes.* New York: Hafner Press.

Cummings, J. L., Tomiyasu, U., Read, S., & Benson, D. F. 1984. Amnesia with hippocampal lesions after cardiopulmonary arrest. *Neurology.* 34:679-81.

Cutting, J. 1978. Study of anosognosia. *Journal of Neurology, Neurosurgery and Psychiatry.* 41:548-555.

Dee, H. L. 1970. Visuoconstructive and visuoperceptive deficit in patients with unilateral cerebral lesions. *Neuropsychologia.* 8:305-314.

Dee, H. L., & Benton, A. L. 1970. A cross-modal investigation of spatial performances in patients with unilateral cerebral disease. *Cortex.* 6:261-272.

De Renzi, E. 1982. *Disorders of space exploration and cognition.* Chichester: Wiley.

De Renzi, E., Faglioni, P., & Scotti, G. 1971. Judgement of spatial orientation in patients with focal brain damage. *Journal of Neurology, Neurosurgery and Psychiatry.* 34:489-495.

De Renzi, E., Faglioni, P., & Villa, P. 1977. Topographical amnesia. *Journal of Neurology, Neurosurgery and Psychiatry.* 40:498-505.

De Renzi, E., & Spinnler, H. 1966. Facial recognition in brain-damaged patients: an experimental approach. *Neurology.* 16:145-152.

Franco, L., & Sperry, R. W. 1977. Hemisphere lateralization for cognitive processing of geometry. *Neuropsychologia.* 15:107-114.

Frederiks, J. A. M. 1969. Disorders of the body schema. In P. J. Vinken & G. W. Bruyn (Eds.), *Handbook of clinical neurology: Vol. 4. Disorders of speech, perception, and symbolic behavior,* 207-240. Amsterdam: North-Holland Publishing Company.

Gainotti, G., Messerli, P., & Tissot, R., 1972. Qualitative analysis of unilateral spatial neglect in relation to laterality of cerebral lesions. *Journal of Neurology, Neurosurgery and Psychiatry.* 35:545-550.

Gainotti, G., Miceli, G., & Caltagirone, C. 1977. Constructional apraxia in left brain-damaged patients: a planning disorder? *Cortex.* 13:109-118.

Gainotti, G., & Tiacci, C. 1970. Patterns of drawing disability in right and left hemispheric patients. *Neuropsychologia.* 8:379-384.

Goodglass, H., & Kaplan, E. 1983. *The assessment of aphasia and related disorders* (2nd ed.). Philadelphia: Lea & Febiger.

Graff-Radford, N. R., Eslinger, P. J., Damasio, A. R., & Yamada, T. 1984. Nonhemorrhagic infarction of the thalamus: behavioral, anatomic, and physiologic correlates. *Neurology.* 34:14-23.

Guberman, A., & Stuss, D. 1983. The syndrome of bilateral paramedian thalamic infarction. *Neurology.* 33:540-6.

Hadano, K. 1984. On block design constructional disability in right and left hemisphere brain-damaged patients. *Cortex.* 20:391-401.

Hamsher, K. deS., Levin, H. S., & Benton, A. L. 1979. Facial recognition in patients with focal brain lesions. *Archives of Neurology.* 36:837-839.

Hannay, H. J., Varney, N. R., & Benton, A. L. 1976. Visual localization in patients with unilateral brain disease. *Journal of Neurology, Neurosurgery and Psychiatry.* 39:307-313.

Healton, E. B., Navarro, C., Bressman, S., & Brust, J. C. M. 1982. Subcortical neglect. *Neurology.* 32:776-778.

Hécaen, H., & Assal, G. 1970. A comparison of constructive deficits following right and left hemispheric lesions. *Neuropsychologia.* 8:289-303.

Heilman, K. M., & Valenstein, E. 1972a. Auditory neglect in man. *Archives of Neurology.* 26:32-35.

Heilman, K. M., & Valenstein, E. 1972b. Frontal lobe neglect in man. *Neurology.* 22:660-664.

Heilman, K. M., & Valenstein, E. 1979. Mechanisms underlying hemispatial neglect. *Annals of Neurology.* 5:166-170.

Heilman, K. M., & Van Den Abell, T. 1980. Right hemisphere dominance for attention; the mechanism underlying hemispheric asymmetries of inattention (neglect). *Neurology.* 30:327-330.

Heilman, K. M., Watson, R. T., & Valenstein, E. 1985. Neglect and related disorders. In K. M. Heilman & E. Valenstein (Eds.), *Clinical Neuropsychology* (2nd ed.) 243-293. New York: Oxford University Press.

Hier, D. B., Mondlock, J., & Caplan, L. R. 1983. Behavioral abnormalities after right hemisphere stroke. *Neurology.* 33:337-44.

Hubel, D. H., & Wiesel, T. N. 1959. Receptive fields of single neurones in the cat's striate cortex. *Journal of Physiology.* 148:574-591.

Kimura, D. 1963. Right temporal lobe damage: perception of unfamiliar stimuli after damage. *Archives of Neurology.* 8:264-271.

Klingon, G. H., & Bontecou, D. C. 1966. Localization in auditory space. *Neurology.* 16:879-886.

Lezak, M. D. 1983. *Neuropsychological assessment* (2nd ed.). New York: Oxford University Press.

Lichtheim, L. 1885. On aphasia. *Brain.* 7:433-484.

Mack, J. L., & Levine, R. N. 1981. The basis of visual constructional disability in patients with unilateral cerebral lesions. *Cortex.* 17:515-532.

McEntee, W. J., Biber, M. P., Perl, D. P., & Benson D. F. 1976. Diencephalic amnesia: a reappraisal. *Journal of Neurology, Neurosurgery and Psychiatry.* 39:436-41.

McFie, J., Piercy, M. F., & Zangwill, O. L. 1950. Visual-spatial agnosia associated with lesions of the right cerebral hemisphere. *Brain.* 73:167-190.

McFie, J., & Zangwill, O. L. 1960. Visual-constructive disabilities associated with lesions of the left cerebral hemisphere. *Brain.* 83:243-260.

Meerwaldt, J. D., & Van Harskamp, F. 1982. Spatial disorientation in right-hemisphere infarction. *Journal of Neurology, Neurosurgery and Psychiatry.* 45:586-590.

Mesulam, M. M. 1981. A cortical network for directed attention and unilateral neglect. *Annals of Neurology.* 10:309-325.

Mills, R. P., & Swanson, P. D. 1978. Vertical oculomotor apraxia and memory loss. *Annals of Neurology.* 4:149-153.

Milner, B. 1965. Visually-guided maze learning in man: effects of bilateral hippocampal, bilateral frontal, and unilateral cerebral lesions. *Neuropsychologia.* 3:317-338.

Milner, B. 1968. Visual recognition and recall after right temporal-lobe excision in man. *Neuropsychologia.* 6:191-209.

Newcombe, F., & Russell, W. R. 1969. Dissociated visual perceptual and spatial deficits in focal lesions of the right hemisphere. *Journal of Neurology, Neurosurgery and Psychiatry.* 32:73-81.

Oxbury, J. M., Campbell, D. C., & Oxbury, S. M. 1974. Unilateral spatial neglect and impairments of spatial analysis and visual perception. *Brain.* 97:551-564.

Paterson, A., & Zangwill, O. L. 1944. Disorders of visual space perception associated with lesions of the right cerebral hemisphere. *Brain.* 67:331-358.

Piercy, M., Hécaen, H., & Ajuriaguerra, J.de. 1960. Constructional apraxia associated with unilateral cerebral lesions—left and right sided cases compared. *Brain.* 83:225-242.

Pillon, B. 1981. Troubles visuo-constructifs et méthodes de compensation: résultats de 85 patients atteints de lésions cérébrales. *Neuropsychologia.* 19:375-383.

Ratcliff, G. 1979. Spatial thought, mental rotation and the right cerebral hemisphere. *Neuropsychologia.* 17:49-54.

Ratcliff, G. 1982. Disturbances of spatial orientation associated with cerebral lesions. In M. Potegal (Ed.), *Spatial abilities: development and physiological foundations* (pp 301-331). New York: Academic Press.

Ratcliff, G., & Davies-Jones, G. A. B. 1972. Defective visual localization in focal brain wounds. *Brain.* 95:49-60.

Ratcliff, G., & Newcombe, F. 1973. Spatial orientation in man: effects of left, right, and bilateral posterior cerebral lesions. *Journal of Neurology, Neurosurgery and Psychiatry.* 36:448-454.

Rubens, A. B., & Benson, D. F. 1971. Associative visual agnosia. *Archives of Neurology.* 24:305-316.

Ruff, R. M., Hersh, N. A., & Pribram, K. H. 1981. Auditory spatial deficits in the personal and extrapersonal frames of reference due to cortical lesions. *Neuropsychologia.* 19:435-443.

Sanchez-Longo, L. P., & Forster, F. M. 1958. Clinical significance of impairment of sound localization. *Neurology.* 8:119-125.

Sanchez-Longo, L. P., Forster, F. M., & Auth, T. L. 1957. A clinical test for sound localization and its applications. *Neurology.* 7:655-663.

Sauguet, J., Benton, A. L., & Hécaen, H. 1971. Disturbances of the body schema in relation to language impairment and hemispheric locus of lesion. *Journal of Neurology, Neurosurgery and Psychiatry.* 34:496-501.

Scoville, W. B., & Milner, B. 1957. Loss of recent memory after bilateral hippocampal lesions. *Journal of Neurology, Neurosurgery and Psychiatry.* 20:11-21.

Semmes, J., Weinstein, S., Ghent, L., & Teuber, H. L. 1963. Correlates of impaired orientation in personal and extrapersonal space. *Brain.* 86:747-772.

Shepard, R. N., & Metzler, J. 1971. Mental rotation of three-dimensional objects. *Science.* 171:701-703.

Smith, M. L., & Milner, B. 1981. The role of the right hippocampus in the recall of spatial location. *Neuropsychologia.* 19:781-793.

Speedie, L. J., & Heilman, K. M. 1983. Anterograde memory deficits for visuospatial material after infarction of the right thalamus. *Archives of Neurology.* 40:183-186.

Stein, S., & Volpe, B. T. 1983. Classical "parietal" neglect syndrome after subcortical right frontal lobe infarction. *Neurology.* 33:797-799.

Strub, R. L., & Black, F. W. 1977. *The mental status examination in neurology.* Philadelphia: F. A. Davis.

Victor, M., Adams, R. D., & Collins, G. H. 1971. *The Wernicke-Korsakoff syndrome.* Philadelphia: F. A. Davis.

Victor, M., Angevine, J. B., Mancall, E. L., & Fisher, C. M. 1961. Memory loss with lesions of hippocampal formation. *Archives of Neurology.* 5:244-263.

Vilkki, J. 1984. Visual hemi-inattention after ventrolateral thalamotomy. *Neuropsychologia.* 22:399-408.

Villardita, C., Smirni, P. & Zappalá, G. 1983. Visual neglect in Parkinson's disease. *Archives of Neurology.* 40:737-739.

Warrington, E. K. 1969. Constructional apraxia. In P. J. Vinken & G. W. Bruyn (Eds.), *Handbook of clinical neurology: Vol. 4. Disorders of speech, perception, and symbolic behavior,* 67-83. Amsterdam: North-Holland Publishing Company.

Warrington, E. K., James, M., & Kinsbourne, M. 1966. Drawing disability in relation to laterality of cerebral lesion. *Brain.* 89:53-82.

Warrington, E. K., & Rabin, P. 1970. Perceptual matching in patients with cerebral lesions. *Neuropsychologia.* 8:475-487.

Watson, R. T., & Heilman, K. M. 1979. Thalamic neglet. *Neurology.* 29:690-694.

Watson, R. T., Valenstein, E., & Heilman, K. M. 1981. Thalamic neglect:

possible role of the medial thalamus and nucleus reticularis in behavior. *Archives of Neurology.* 38:501-506.

Whiteley, A. M., & Warrington, E. K. 1978. Selective impairment of topographical memory: a single case study. *Journal of Neurology, Neurosurgery and Psychiatry.* 41:575-578.

Woods, B. T., Schoene, W., & Kneisley, L. 1982. Are hippocampal lesions sufficient to cause lasting amnesia? *Journal of Neurology, Neurosurgery and Psychiatry.* 45:243-247.

PART II

THE DEVELOPMENT OF SPATIAL COGNITION

INTRODUCTION

The first section focused on spatial cognition in normal and brain damaged adults. This section focuses on the development of spatial cognition in young normal children, providing a state-of-the-art overview of current research issues. Topics range from the perception of space to cognitive issues such as the relation between language and space, and the logic of spatial construction.

Herbert Pick's chapter introduces the topic of spatial development with a focus on perceptual development. He first discusses the kinds of spatial perceptual information that are available to the child, and possible frames of reference for organizing that information. He then reviews the relation between perceptual input and conceptual knowledge. From this he concludes that perceptual and cognitive information about spatial layout do not conflict and that both contribute to the child's knowledge of space.

In her chapter, Linda Acredolo explores the relation between motor and cognitive development, focusing on self-locomotion and the mental frame of spatial reference. She demonstrates that there is a direct relation between the onset of the child's ability to move about in space unassisted and the ability to keep track of the position of a hidden object. Moreover she suggests that the influence of motor development on spatial cognition is most apparent when the child is first achieving a motor milestone.

Lynn Liben's chapter considers three specific issues in the study of spatial cognition: definitional issues, methodological issues and developmental issues. A variety of environmental and representational factors are summarized which must be considered in any definition of spatial cognition. In the methodological discussion, Liben argues that actions in a spatial context may or may not reflect children's representation of space. For that reason, spatial cognition should be assessed by multiple tasks designed to distinguish unambiguously between different forms of spatial knowledge. Liben focuses on two issues related to development. The first concerns the bidirectional nature of the information exchange between studies of spatial cognition in adults and children. The second issue is the normal variation of spatial abilities in any group of individuals.

In the next chapter, Judith Johnston examines the temporal relation between the child's understanding of spatial concepts such as "in" "on" or "behind" and the development of verbal representations for those concepts. The literatures on the acquisition of spatial terms in various languages and on the production of spatial relations in nonverbal play contexts are reviewed. It is shown that the order in which children acquire spatial terms is consistent across languages and that the understanding of spatial words follows the generation of the corresponding spatial relations.

Ageliki Nicolopoulou compares the development of children's understanding of spatial relations and a particular kind of logical relation, class relations. She shows that early in development these two domains of knowledge are linked. In tasks where children are given sets of toys to group, they consistently place similar objects near one another, while dissimilar objects are separated. Later in development, this systematic relation between class and spatial location disappears.

In the final chapter, Dennis Wolf's paper examines the very early development of children's drawing. Her paper focuses on developmental change in the two to four year age range, where these drawings had been viewed previously as scribbling. She reports that there are in fact distinct patterns of change in children's drawings during this period, and shows how these changes parallel development in other spatial cognitive domains.

The chapters in this section provide a multifaceted and cohesive overview of the development of children's understanding of space. A range of perspectives on the development of spatial cognition is presented which converge on the common themes of what the young child knows about space and how that knowledge develops in the first few years of life. The data presented in this section also form the basis for understanding spatial cognition in children with different early experiences.

PERCEPTUAL ASPECTS OF SPATIAL COGNITIVE DEVELOPMENT

6

HERBERT L. PICK, JR.
University of Minnesota

With few exceptions investigators of *perceptual* development have tended to ignore development of spatial cognition. The topic of spatial cognition, perhaps, as its name implies was seen by perception researchers to be a clearly cognitive area, concerned with knowledge, memory, the nature of representation, etc. On the other hand cognitive researchers interested in spatial cognitive development went on about their business studying relevant phenomena whether they seemed to fall in the domain of perception or more clearly in the pure cognitive realm. In fact, it may not be possible to define a sharp line between perception and cognition in this area, if indeed it is possible to do anywhere.

It is not uncommon to consider perception as being primarily concerned with the acquisition of information about the world from environmental sources and cognition as being primarily concerned with the further processing and transformation of that information. But these two processes become inexorably intertwined when it becomes evident that how one transforms information depends on what information was acquired in the first place and how it was acquired. At one level this interdependence is involved in what a person attends to in maintaining spatial orientation, that is the frames of reference which a person uses for maintaining orientation. At a more subtle level this interdependence arises in an analysis of the information available for solving certain kinds of spatial prob-

lems. From a traditional cognitive point of view rather impover-
ished spatial information is available in the form of certain cues
which then are evaluated and integrated to solve the problem. If
the information is richer to start with the cognitive load may be
reduced and/or transformed. And finally the kinds of *perceptual*
experience one has had through life may modify how one acquires
and transforms new information. In the present discussion an
attempt will be made to analyze how perception and perceptual
development impinges on spatial cognitive development in each of
the three ways noted above.

WHAT INFORMATION IS ATTENDED TO?

In many of the studies of spatial cognitive development children are
provided controlled experience with a spatial layout and then their
knowledge of this layout is evaluated. What they have attended to
during the controlled experience is critical. While potentially they
have available a great deal of information about the layout, in fact,
the task that they were involved in during their exposure to the layout may not (implicitly or explicitly) have been conducive to attending to layout information.

In particular, in a novel spatial environment children particularly
may be expending a great deal of attention on guidance of behavior
as opposed to acquiring a global spatial awareness. Sometimes these
two aims may coincide but they often are quite different. An
interesting experimental example may be drawn from Festinger,
Burnham, Ono, and Bamber (1967). Subjects in an experiment on
adaptation to wedge prisms were asked either to move a stylus along
a track paying particular attention to minimizing contact with the
sides or to move along the track in broad sweeping movements.
Subjects in the first group showed very little or no adaptation while
those in the second group did adapt. The point is that the kind of
local control required in moving along a track minimizing contact
errors calls attention to the momentary deviations from the track
and not its overall layout. (Evidence like this calls into question
some teaching practices where children are asked to trace letters in
learning to print or write. It may be that such exercise provides
practice in motor control but it may not help so much in teaching the
form of letters.)

More directly relevant to spatial cognition is the fact that there
are normally various kinds of spatial information simultaneously
available for maintaining spatial orientation. This has been investi-

gated in the many studies of the frames of reference used by children and adults to guide their spatial behavior. In the typical study a distinction is made between egocentric and non-egocentric frames of reference. One common paradigm has been to teach a subject some kind of spatial response in the presence of both egocentric and non-egocentric spatial information. Then in a test of spatial knowledge the egocentric and non-egocentric spatial information are put in conflict to ascertain which determines the response. A simple example of this can be taken from Acredolo (1978) who conditioned infants to turn their head to a window either to the left or the right, upon presentation of a tone, using the appearance of the experimenter's face as reinforcement. After conditioning reached a criterion the baby was moved to the other side of the room and turned back toward the center of the room. The tone was then presented again. The baby could respond with the same egocentric response and a different geographic response or the same geographic response but a different egocentric response. (The well-known results were that between 6 and 16 months of age there was a shift from egocentric responding to geographic responding.)

It has been common to distinguish primarily between egocentric and non-egocentric frames of reference. Non-egocentric frames of reference have often been signified by the term geographic as above or by geocentric or sometimes by the term allocentric. Strictly speaking the term allocentric implies reference to another person although it seems to have been used more generally than that to mean non-egocentric. This possibility of designating allocentric as a particular kind of non-egocentric reference system leads to a more general consideration that the binary distinction between egocentric and non-egocentric frames of reference is too crude. With the present example non-egocentric frames of reference can be geographic or allocentric. But geographic frames of reference can be further broken down, perhaps in terms of proximity to the location of consequence in some task or in the nature of the geographic markers comprising the reference system.

This analysis is all at a very abstract level; does it have any functional consequence? There has not been a lot of study of fine grain distinctions among reference systems. However, there are a few hints. One comes from another study by Acredolo (1976). In this study she distinguished between an egocentric and two geographic frames of reference. A child was taken into a relatively bare room which had a door at one end, a window at the other end and a table along one side. The child was taken to a corner of the table and blind-folded. Under blind-fold the child was taken on a short wind-

ing and disorienting walk back to the door or to the window end.
The blind-fold was removed and the child was asked to go back to
the place where the blind-folded walk had started. Unbeknownst to
the child on some trials the table was moved to the other side of the
room during the blind-folded walk. These various conditions gave
the possibility of distinguishing between use of an egocentric frame
of reference and a geographic reference system based on furniture or
one based on the walls of the room. Thus, suppose the blind-folded
walk was ended back at the door but the table had been moved to
the other side of the room. Use of an egocentric frame of reference
(e.g. turning toward the right hand wall again) or a geographic
frame defined by the walls of the room would both lead to the child
going back to the same side of the room as where it had been blind-
folded. On the other hand, use of furniture (i.e. the table) as a frame
of reference would lead to going to the opposite side. Suppose, now
that the child ended its walk near the window and the table was not
moved during the walk. An egocentric response (e.g. turning to the
right hand wall) would lead to going to the opposite side of the room
from where the walk started while use of either or both geographical
reference systems would lead to going back to the same side of the
room. Continuing, in this manner it is possible to pit each frame of
reference against the other two and determine relative dominance.
In Acredolo's situation she found that there was a shift in relative
dependence between three and seven years of age from egocentric to
geographic (furniture) to geographic (walls) reference systems. The
progression of reference systems seems to go from proximal to distal,
but in this situation it also goes toward decreasing mobility of reference objects. We don't know which of these factors is more important.

There are, of course, other ways of distinguishing among geographic reference systems. They can become increasingly abstract
and remote. They can be divided into man-made and natural reference systems, and so on. It is similarly possible to distinguish
different egocentric reference systems. For example, is egocentric
direction defined in terms of viewing direction or body direction?
Normally we think of these as identical. However, it is possible to
separate them as well. Suppose in a homogeneous environment
where there is no environmental reference system available, a person sits with their head turned 90 degrees to the right. They learn
to expect an event presented directly in front of their eyes. Now
they turn their heads back to facing front. Where will they expect
the event? To the right side of their body where it originally

occurred or straight in front of their eyes?[1] The use of different ego-centric reference systems might be relevant to the way space is used in signing for indexing and pronominal reference and for other semantic purposes. (See discussion by Petitto & Bellugi later in this volume).

Very little is known about the determiners of choice of frame of reference. It has been found possible to facilitate shifting from ego-centric to geocentric reference systems by making the geographic markers more salient (Acredolo & Evans, 1980) and by using a more familiar space (Acredolo, 1979). The effects of salience seem obvious although a priori the determiners of salience are not always obvious. Why familiarity aids a transition to geographic frames of reference is not clear. It may be because a familiar environment is more differentiated and hence has more spatial information available or it may be because the children who showed this effect were more secure in a familiar environment. The latter possibility makes the tacit assumption that use of geographic frames is more sophisticated or mature. This may be sometimes true but is not generally the case. Certainly very sophisticated people learn to type using an ego-centric frame of reference. It is probably the case that adaptive flexibility in the use of reference systems is the more mature behavior.

THE RELATION BETWEEN PERCEPTUAL AND COGNITIVE KNOWLEDGE

Adaptive flexibility in the use of reference systems would seem to imply cognitive strategies. While conscious voluntary strategies are certainly possible in choice of reference system it is probably the case that in many instances our choice of reference system is done unconsciously and automatically. A particular task in an appropri-ate environment may automatically put us into some sort of percep-tual processing mode.

In trying to decide what role perception as opposed to cognition plays in maintaining spatial orientation we must first of all decide when perceptual information is not sufficient and requires supple-

---

[1] There are at least two possible ways a person might arrive at responding to this situation by looking to the same side of their body. One is by initially encoding the event in terms of a body reference system. The other is by encoding the initial event in terms of visual direction from the eyes and then updating this direction in relation to the changed position of the eyes.

mentation by some constructive cognitive process. Normally cognitive processes, representations, etc. are invoked only when we don't have perceptual information available. Thus we don't pose an orientation or way-finding problem when the goal is in sight. We don't ask how one knows how to get to the table across the room.

James Gibson (1979) has proposed the most radical position with regard to the use of perception instead of cognition in maintaining spatial orientation. He has argued that finding one's way around does not normally depend on the use of representations such as cognitive maps but is done perceptually. He has rather convincingly argued that there is perceptual information available for the continued existence of an object as it goes out of sight. The way objects disappear provides information for their constancy. Thus the occlusion of objects by other objects is an event which is specified by very different information than the evaporation of an object. The disappearance of an object as it goes off into the distance is an event specified by very different information than the fragmentation of an object in an explosion.

Gibson would like to extend this type of explanation to the perception of the location of objects when they are out of sight. If we have perceptual information that something exists when it is out of view perhaps there is also perceptual information for where it is. At first hearing that idea is difficult to grasp. However it is really no more mysterious than perception of the future position of an object when it is in sight. For example, there is information available for the perception of the time of impact of approaching objects (Lee, 1974). That is, the present optical flow pattern projected by an approaching object specifies when it will reach an observer. In a somewhat similar vein Hofsten (1983) has shown that even infants' reaching may be perceptually guided to the future position of an object passing in front of them. If future positions of objects in view can be specified by present perceptual information it is not such a big step to propose that the future position of objects going out of sight can also be specified. If this is true then the burden carried by *representations* of spatial information can be reduced. Such a possibility may help explain the surprising sophistication of some animals in solving detour problems. For example certain species of birds have been found to be very good at tracking and intercepting targets that have moved behind screens. Krushinskii (1960) has termed this an extrapolation reflex and it may in fact be based on perceptual information. Thus in the same way that the future position of an object in view is specified by perceptual information the future position of an object out of view may have been specified by perceptual information. That information may be guiding our action just as it would if the object were in view. In this sense our awareness of the position of objects out of view does not necessarily have to be based on "map-like" representations of spatial layout. This argument can be equally well applied to objects going out of view due to observer movement as those disappearing due to their own movement. If our knowledge of the position of any out-of-sight objects can be so based on perceptual information it becomes very problematic how and where to draw the line between remembered and perceived spatial layout.

Nevertheless at some point it seems reasonable to distinguish between knowledge and perception of spatial layout. In such cases one can ask how those two kinds of information interact. Part of a study by Smith, Haake, and Pick (in preparation) illustrates the problem. Children were brought into a large room with their parent. Inside the room facing them was a smaller room with four identical doors, one in the center of each wall. Each child left their parent by the nearest door and was led three quarters of the way around the outside of the smaller room out of view of the parent and into the center of the smaller room. The child was then asked to find the parent. The majority of sixteen-month-old children simply reversed their route and went out the door they entered, and then walked all the way back around the entire small room. Only 10% of the children took the direct shortcut through the door by which they had left their parent. However immediate perceptual information of the parent's location was provided in other conditions. In one case the parent called to the child just before it started to return. This direct information resulted in 50% of the children taking the most efficient short-cut. In these cases the direct auditory information overruled the route knowledge the children presumably had. A sizeable pro-portion of 10-month-olds, however, still relied on their route knowledge and went all the way back around. In some of these cases the direct perceptual information seemed to play a rather different role, a motivating rather than guiding function. When the child heard the parent's voice it just lit up and took off turning around and reversing the route. (By the time children reach 24 months of age they do not in general need direct perceptual information to take the short-cut.)

In general, perceptual information and conceptual knowledge about spatial layout are not in conflict; either they are congruent or one or the other is absent. But the above example is not unique and one thing the developing child has to do is learn when one or the other is reliable. In the above example the children who continued to reverse their route seemed to rely on their conceptual knowledge of the route rather than the immediate information of the parent's voice. Another example can be taken from the studies of development of detour behavior by Lockman (1984). Infants were shown objects behind transparent barriers. At an age of about 10 months the babies tried to attain the objects by a direct attack, i.e. by trying to reach through the barrier. The very same babies were able to solve this detour problem when the barrier was opaque. Here they seemed to be relying on perceptual information rather than conceptual knowledge.

RELATION OF EARLY PERCEPTUAL EXPERIENCE TO SPATIAL COGNITION

Another way perceptual information and conceptual knowledge interacts involves the role of early experience on later spatial orientation. This has been studied by examining the spatial behavior of persons deprived of various amounts of visual experience by virtue of blindness. There has been a research tradition comparing the performance of blind persons with that of blind-folded sighted and partially sighted subjects on a variety of perceptual and orientation tasks. Although there have been some results showing superiority of the blind in some tasks and no differences in others, in more of the studies sighted subjects have performed better than blind subjects. However, typically the differences are not great and it has been difficult to understand the nature of any deficit due to blindness. Recently, in connection with studies of spatial orientation, there may be some progress toward such understanding.

Anecdotal reports of blind orientation and mobility instructors have suggested that many blind clients often have particular difficulty in coping with deviations from standard routes, for example, in making detours. They seem to know specific routes from place to place but not the general layout of the area and their own place in that layout.

As a first step in exploring this observation Rieser, Lockman, and Pick (1980) tried to compare the structure of the knowledge of a very familiar space by congenitally blind and sighted subjects. The space was one floor of a building in which both groups had had considerable experience. The subjects were asked to make comparative distance judgements of all pairs of 15 locations. When asked to make these judgements under neutral instructions the responses of the groups made a very reasonable fit with the functional (walking) distance between the various locations. In particular, the fit between their judgements and the functional distances was closer than the fit with the straight-line (or euclidean) distances between the various locations. Subsequently when specifically asked to respond in terms of the euclidean distance the sighted subjects were able to shift their responses so that they were more closely related to those straight-line distances. However the blind subjects were not able to bring their judgements into accord with the euclidean distances. These results may indicate that both sighted and blind subjects normally think about distances in a familiar space in terms of getting from place to place. In addition sighted subjects have available knowledge of the layout that would be useful in making detours, planning alternate routes, etc.

What is it about the lack of early visual experience that might cause difficulty for the blind in developing such spatial layout knowledge from their ordinary experience with a space? The implications of a study by Rieser, Guth, and Hill (1982) are relevant. Blind and blind-folded sighted subjects were taught a subset of the spatial relations of a simple spatial layout within a room. In essence they were taught to point quickly and accurately from a home base to each of locations A, B, and C. After reaching criterion performance in doing this, they were walked to one or another of the labeled locations and asked to point at the others. They were also asked while at home base to imagine that they were at one of the labeled locations and to point at the others. The sighted subjects after walking to the labeled locations pointed just as quickly and accurately as from home base, whereas the blind subjects were relatively slow and inaccurate. Both blind and blind-folded sighted subjects were slow and inaccurate when they tried to point while imagining themselves at a new location.

The subjects were asked how they performed these pointing tasks. The sighted subjects after walking to a new location almost didn't understand the question—the task was so obvious. They reported they simply knew where they were in relation to the locations in their environment. On the other hand, when pointing from an imagined location they reported going through an elaborate pseudogeometric or trigonometric procedure. They reported they imagined the direction to point from their actual present position, then how that direction would have to be transformed after moving to a new location. The blind subjects reported such a procedure in pointing both after walking to the new location and in the condition of imagining they were in the new location.

It may not be so surprising that it is more difficult to point at locations from an imagined position where one has little actual experience. But if that is so then it is somewhat surprising that walking to that position without any additional information about the spatial relations of locations with respect to the new position facilitates the pointing for the sighted subjects. Apparently actually moving to a new position somehow helps the sighted subjects keep track of where they are in relation to the surrounding space. Why is it that sighted subjects do this and blind subjects do not?

What is it about prior visual experience which would facilitate updating one's own position in space? One possibility is the pervasive presence of optical flow patterns during visually guided movement. For all their lives sighted subjects are bombarded by transformations of the optical array with every movement of their head and eyes, no matter how small. In Gibson's (1979) analysis this perspective structure in the optic array provides information about where the perceiver is and how she is moving about. There is much less perspective structure available for the blind person restricted to tactual and auditory information. The stimulation from both these modalities has some but limited perspective structure. In the case of auditory stimulation blind persons, in fact, may come to avoid searching for the perspective structure since so many of the sources of sound are themselves moving objects. These would pose the problem for perceivers of distinguishing between transformations due to one's own movement and transformations due to object movement or combinations of object and self movement. The hypothesis being suggested is that the constant exposure of sighted persons during their lives to perspective transformations as they move provides a background of sensitivity to how the relative positions of locations to themselves change. This sensitivity remains even when visual information is eliminated by blind-fold or by darkness (or by adventitious blindness[2]).

If this hypothesis is correct it might be possible to increase blind persons' sensitivity to perspective structure by providing them with intensive experience with stable auditory landmarks. However, there is little information to suggest what a good training regime might be or how flexible this system is after a prolonged period of visual deprivation.

---

[2] In the study by Rieser, Guth, and Hill a group of adventitiously blind subjects performed at a level intermediate between the sighted and congenitally blind subjects.

CONCLUSION

The present hypothesis can be related to the analysis of reference systems at the beginning of this chapter. There it was suggested that the spatial environment provides a variety of possible frames of reference for maintaining orientation. These variations are probably more subtle than many investigators have paused to realize. Particularly where the same stimulation carries information for guidance of different aspects of behavior the particular task may give some information an attentional advantage. In the case of perspective structure, its pervasiveness for sighted persons may cause them to habitually use a mode of guiding their movement through the world that blind persons do not ordinarily have.

The first part of the present discussion stressed the richness of spatial information in terms of the variety of frames of reference available for maintaining orientation. In the second part of the discussion it was pointed out that stimulation was possibly richer than ordinarily believed for providing spatial information. That is, some spatial problems could be solved perceptually rather than conceptually.

The presence of rich sources of perceptual information poses two theoretical problems for our understanding of spatial orientation. One is the problem of selection among these sources. How, when, and why is this done? The other is how perceptual information and conceptual knowledge interact when they are not congruent. Some illustrations of this were provided in the second part of the present discussion. The third part of the discussion concerned another way perception can interact with cognitive aspects of spatial orientation. In this case, if the suggested hypothesis is correct, prolonged exposure to perceptual information results in the development of a mode of processing information that goes on even in the absence of that information.

ACKNOWLEDGMENTS

The preparation of this manuscript was partially supported by Program Project Grant HD05027 from NICHHD to the Institute of Child Development of the University of Minnesota and by the Center for Research in Human Learning of the University of Minnesota.

REFERENCES

Acredolo, L. P. 1976. Frames of reference used by children for orientation in unfamiliar spaces. In G. T. Moore & R. G. Gollege (Eds.), *Environmental Knowing*. Stroudsburg, PA: Dowden, Hutchinson, & Ross.

Acredolo, L. P. 1978. Development of spatial orientation in infancy. *Developmental Psychology.* 14:224-234.

Acredolo, L. P. 1979. Laboratory versus home: The effect of environment on the nine-month-old infant's choice of spatial reference system. *Developmental Psychology.* 15:666-667.

Acredolo, L. P., & Evans, D. 1980. Developmental changes in the effects of landmarks on infant spatial behavior. *Developmental Psychology.* 16:312-318.

Festinger, L., Burnham, C. A., Ono, H., & Bamber, D. 1967. Efference and the conscious experience of perception. *Journal of Experimental Psychology Monograph.* 74(4), Whole No., 637.

Gibson, J. J. 1979. *The ecological approach to visual perception.* Boston: Houghton Mifflin.

Hofsten, C. von. 1983. Catching skills in infancy. *Journal of Experimental Psychology: Human Perception and Performance.* 9:75-85.

Krushinskii, A. V. 1960. *Formirovanie povedeniya zhivotnikh v norme i patologii.* (The formation of behavior of animals normally and in pathology). Moscow: Moscow University Press.

Lee, D. N. 1974. Visual information during locomotion. In R. B. MacLeod & H. L. Pick, Jr. (Eds.), *Perception: Essays in honor of James J. Gibson.* Ithaca, NY: Cornell University Press.

Lockman, J. J. 1984. Development of detour abilities in infants. *Child Development.* 55:482-491.

Rieser, J. J., Guth, D., & Hill, E. 1982. Mental processes mediating independent travel: Implications for orientation and mobility. *Journal of Visual Impairment and Blindness.* 76:213-218.

Rieser, J. J., Lockman, J. J., & Pick, H. L., Jr. 1980. The role of visual experience in knowledge of spatial layout. *Perception and Psychophysics.* 28:185-190.

INFANT MOBILITY AND SPATIAL DEVELOPMENT

7

LINDA ACREDOLO
University of California, Davis

HISTORICAL PERSPECTIVES

> The great event in the child's life is his new ability to move freely
> and to control his movements...Some children at this period for a
> while disregard all toys and show little interest in companions; they
> behave as if they were drunk with the idea of space and even of
> speed; they crawl, walk, march and run, and revert from one
> method of locomotion to the other with the greatest of pleasure. (A.
> Freud & Burlingham, 1944, p. 14-15)

Attention to the role of locomotor development in the psychological life of the child is hardly new. As the quotation above suggests,
the onset of self-produced and self-controlled movement in development has long been recognized as an event of great significance.
Indeed, psychoanalysts of the time were so impressed with the great
zest for movement shown by the children they studied that some
were even moved to speak of a "motor urge" or "instinct" on a par
with the oral, anal, and genital urges already fundamental to their
descriptions of development (Mittelmann, 1954).

However, the recognition that locomotion is a source of pleasure
for the child is hardly enough. Common sense alone provides clear
evidence that pleasure is but one by-product of this new-found skill.
Of equal, if not greater importance is the fact that, once mobile, the
child's whole mode of experiencing the world is forever changed. No
longer must the child be content to enjoy the items at his or her
fingertips; no longer need the child sit and wait for things to happen,

for people to come, for objects to be delivered. Once mobile, the child achieves for the first time a real measure of independence. Experiences begin to be chosen and structured by the child to a greater degree than ever before possible. The world opens up, horizons expand, and one-by-one the child encounters items, events, and vistas never before experienced. It is hardly surprising that children find joy in this fundamental change in their way of life. But what, if any, are the ramifications of these new experiences for the child's development?

It is not a trivial observation that the arena in which all this takes place is space. "Drunk with the idea of space" was the phrase suggested by Freud and Burlingham (1944) and one which rings true to even the most casual observer of infant behavior. In fact, one might even characterize the child's day during this period of new-found freedom as one long series of small exercises in spatial problem-solving, filled with such unspoken questions as "Where AM I?" "Now that I'm here, how do I get there?" "Where did the ball go and how can I reach it?" etc. Each one of these challenges, when met, will yield the child a richer understanding of his or her physical environment. Moreover, this understanding will be both at the concrete level of what route leads to what place, *and* at the more abstract level of expecting routes to be reversible and anticipating changes in perspective as one moves. Clearly, then, one should expect gains in spatial cognition to accompany the onset of self-produced locomotion. The storyline sounds convincing; now let's see if it fits the facts.

In truth, the search for correlations between motor development and cognitive development has had a long and fairly disappointing history. As Kopp (1979) points out in her review of this literature, there was a strong conviction among developmental psychologists in the 1930s and 1940s that motor precocity *should* predict intellectual abilities but very little data to support the claim. The speed with which one learned to crawl or walk simply did not predict longterm intellectual functioning. Faith in a motor-mind link was renewed in the 1960s with the sudden discovery of Piaget by American psychology. Afterall, for Piaget the roots of cognition lay solidly in the sensorimotor achievements of infancy. Given this, it seemed reasonable to expect correlations between these achievements and later cognitive functioning. Again, however, the search in the main proved futile.

Why? Where were these researchers going wrong? Are we really to believe that so radical a change in the child's life as the onset of self-produced movement has no effect on cognitive development? No.

The links were there, but just not uncovered by these early research-ers. The problem seems in part to be due to a failure to tailor their definitions of cognitive change to those specific aspects most likely to be affected by motor development. In other words, they were looking at broad measures of intellectual functioning, such as scores on the Bayley Scales of Infant Development, rather than at specific phenomena, like spatial orientation, for which a stronger theoretical case could be made. Second, many of the early pioneers were guilty of overlooking the importance of short-term influences in their quest for explanations of long-term individual differences in intelligence. What is being missed in this focus on long-term predictions is the possibility that achievement in the motor domain may have extremely significant effects on cognitive skills, but that positive correlations between the two domains may exist *only* during that time when not all children have manifested the gain in motor behavior. Once the skill is acquired by all, the correlations disappear (Blank, 1964; Kopp, 1979). This disappearance, of course, in no way diminishes the importance of the initial impact of the one skill on the other; it merely means that we have to narrow our focus to find evidence of its existence. In fact, as Kopp (1979) points out, some of Bayley's early data (Bayley, 1935) relating motor and mental development scores support this idea. Of all the ages tested (i.e., 4-6 months, 10-12 months, 18-24 months, and 33-36 months), by far the highest correlation ($r = +.42$) were found at 10-12 months, the period during which the most profound changes in motor skill are occurring, but occurring at different rates for different children.

CONTEMPORARY VIEWS

Having identified where research in the past has gone wrong, let us now look at more recent efforts. One set of studies relevant to this issue was designed by Gustafson (1984) to document precisely how the ability to locomote changes the way a child interacts with his or her environment. In these studies three groups of 6½ to 10-month-old infants were compared as they explored a laboratory space con-taining toys and their mother. The first two groups included infants who could not crawl but who had had extensive experience using a walker. Half of these infants were placed in a walker in the experi-mental space and half were placed on the floor at one end of the room. The third group of infants consisted of infants of the same age who were already proficient at crawling. Like the second subgroup of their non-crawling peers, these infants were simply placed on the floor. The infants were free to explore the room at their own pace while a variety of behaviors was recorded. The results showed quite clearly that the capacity for self-movement, whether in the walker or out, altered the infants' experiences in dramatic ways. The mobile infants compared to the non-mobile infants covered more distance, played with more toys, and attended to a wider variety of environmental stimuli, such as posters, doors, and tape on the floor. Thus, the assumption that mobility widens the child's experience of spatial features and perspectives was born-out. In addition, the mobile infants spent more time approaching, looking at, smiling at, and vocalizing to the people in the room. In fact, Gustafson concludes that a major impact of self-produced locomotion on infants lies in the more active role it allows them in patterning their social interactions.

Although the research by Gustafson provides clear evidence that mobility changes the infant's experience of the environment, it does not prove that these new experiences benefit the infant's spatial orientation skills. Fortunately such evidence is available elsewhere. As part of a multi-faceted investigation of the role of self-produced locomotion in infant development, Bertenthal, Campos, and Barrett (1984) report the results of a study in which three groups of 8-month-old infants were tested in a spatial orientation task designed originally by Acredolo and Evans (1980). The three groups included infants who could crawl, infants who could not crawl but who had had extensive locomotor experience in a walker, and infants who could not crawl and also had had no walker experience. Each infant was tested individually in a small room (10 × 10 ft.) made of green plastic curtains. Two identical small windows, themselves covered with white curtains, were cut in the center of two opposing walls. To differentiate these windows, one was surrounded by a string of tiny flashing lights. In addition, the wall containing this window was covered with vertical orange stripes.

Each infant began the procedure in a wheeled chair positioned in the middle of one of the non-windowed walls. Thus, the infant had to turn to the right to see one window and to the left to see the other. During a series of training trials, the infant was trained to anticipate the appearance of an experimenter at the lighted window following a buzzer which sounded in the center of the room. Once this anticipation had been established, the infant was rotated to the opposite side of the room, the buzzer was sounded, and the researchers noted toward which window the infant looked. Since the infant's view of the room was the reverse of that experienced during training, a look in the same direction relative to the infant's body would now be a look to the non-lighted window, the one through which the experimenter had never appeared. Such responses were labeled "egocentric." In contrast, a look from the new position to the lighted window was called a "landmark" response, based on the supposition that infants looking back at this window were at least in part showing sensitivity to the role of the lights and stripes as landmarks in the otherwise undifferentiated space. The results indicated a clear advantage of the two groups of locomotor infants (i.e., Crawling and Non-crawling + Walker) over the non-locomotor infants, the former showing much lower proportions of egocentric responses than the latter. Thus, infants with a history of self-produced movement were more readily able to compensate for a change in position and relocate the correct window than were their non-mobile age-mates.

The same testing procedure was also reported by Bertenthal, Campos, and Barrett (1984) to have been useful in delineating the development of spatial orientation skills in an orthopedically handicapped child. The child, born with two dislocated hips, wore a full body cast for 7½ months, and a lighter cast and harness for an additional month. Thus, it was not until she was about 8½ months old that she was given the freedom to try to crawl, a skill which she proceeded quite quickly to master. Based on the results of the study with normal infants just described, one would expect this new mobility to coincide with improved performance in the spatial orientation task, and this is exactly what Bertenthal et al. found. The child was tested once a month from the age of 6 months through 10 months, and during the first three visits showed high levels of egocentric responding (i.e., 100%, 60%, and 60% respectively). However, at the 9 month visit, the first visit following the onset of crawling, the level of egocentric responding dropped dramatically to 20%. Thus, once again we have evidence suggesting that the enriched experience provided by self-produced movement promotes the development of spatial orientation skills.

To this point the question of the role of self-produced locomotion in spatial development has been framed in terms of the shift from the non-locomotor to the locomotor stage as marked by the onset of crawling. The argument is that this milestone brings about fundamental changes in the ways the infant views space and the strategies available to the infant for solving spatial problems. Perhaps among the most important of these, as suggested by the data Bertenthal et al. report, are a growing disenchantment with an egocentric frame of reference and a growing appreciation for the role of landmarks. However, the role of self-produced movement in the spatial life of the infant can be viewed from another, somewhat more narrow, perspective. In addition to fostering fundamental, long-term changes, it also seems quite likely that self-produced movement could facilitate behavior in the context of an individual spatial problem at a given point in time. The idea here is that self-produced movement, specifically when compared to passive movement, will result in more sophisticated performance. We have ample evidence that this is true for adults (e.g., Appleyard, 1970) and older children (e.g., Feldman & Acredolo, 1979; Poag, Cohen, & Weatherford, 1983), but its demonstration for the infant takes on special significance since it would strengthen considerably our argument that the achievement of locomotion is causally related to improved spatial skills. If we can show that an infant allowed to move him or herself about an environment has a better grasp of its spatial features than one moved by others, we will have even more confidence in our assertion that the onset of locomotion is instrumental in improving spatial abilities.

Evidence supporting the facilitative effects of active over passive movement in infancy comes in part from research of my own. My colleagues and I (Acredolo, Adams, & Goodwyn, 1984) recently reported the results of two longitudinal studies with 12-month-old infants. In both experiments infants were tested first at 12 months and later at 18 months in a paradigm somewhat analogous to that originated by Acredolo and Evans (1980) and described by Bertenthal et al. (1984). Infants were presented with a .96 × .63 m (38 × 25 in.) plexiglass box containing two identical cloth-covered wells. The box was placed on the floor and constructed so that one of the walls (A) was broken in the middle by an opening through which the wells could be reached. (See Figure 7.1.) After becoming acquainted with the box, each infant was seated in the center of the wall opposite the one with the opening, wall C. During this phase of the experiment, wall C was removed so that the infant could directly retrieve a toy from the one well of the two in which it was hidden in each of a series of training trials. Once the infant had successfully retrieved the toy five times from the same well, wall C was replaced, the object was hidden again in the well, and the infant was either encouraged to move on its own around to the permanent opening in side A to retrieve the toy (active condition) or was carried to the opening by its parent (passive condition). In this latter case the infant was held under the arms and moved along with its feet skimming the floor on the same pathway experienced by the infants in the active condition.

The dependent variable of primary interest, of course, was the well chosen by the infant from the new vantage point. The question

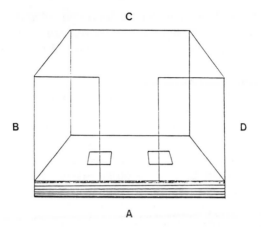

Figure 7.1. Experimental Box: Wall A = Front; Wall C = Back.

was whether or not the infants would compensate for their change in position and recognize that the correct well was the one which required a reach in the opposite direction relative to their midline that had been necessary during training. For example, if the target well had been to their right during training, it was now to their left.

The second behavior assessed was visual attention during transit. The question of interest here was whether self-produced movement would be associated with a different type of attentional behavior than passive movement. To answer this question we rated on a 4-point scale the degree to which infants tracked the target site as they moved.

The results of the first experiment showed a clear superiority at 12 months of the active condition over the passive. Infants in the former condition were significantly more likely than infants in the latter to search in the correct well on the test trial from the new position. Of equal interest, however, was the fact that the infants in the active condition were also significantly more likely than the passive infants to keep their eyes on the target as they moved themselves from one side to the other. In other words, at 12 months self-produced movement and visual tracking were strongly related to each other and to correct search. By 18 months, in contrast, these relationships had disappeared. Instead, correct search predominated for both active and passive conditions, and intense visual tracking was quite rare. By this age infants were capable of compensating for their change in position, at least in this task, no matter how it had been achieved and without dependence on visual tracking. Any work involved was being done mentally instead.

The second longitudinal study was designed to determine the precise nature of the relations discovered at 12 months among active movement, visual tracking, and correct search. One obvious possibility is that active movement promotes attention and that it is the attention rather than the active movement per se that enables the infant to choose correctly. However, it is also possible that the visual tracking at 12 months was actually secondary in importance to the information provided by the locomotion itself. In order to discriminate between these two possibilities, the two side walls of the box (B and D) were changed from transparent to opaque, and a group of 12-month-olds were run through the active condition. The purpose of this change was to disrupt any attempts by the infants to keep their eyes on the target as they moved themselves around the box. If the infants, despite this disruption, are still able to find the object, then the results would suggest that active movement per se, and not visual tracking, is the crucial element. However, if the number of infants searching correctly after active movement declines under these conditions, then it would seem likely that visual tracking is the more direct facilitator in this task.

The results supported the latter interpretation: There were significantly fewer correct searches among these 12-month-old infants allowed active movement than among their age-mates tested in the active condition in the first experiment. However, as one might anticipate from the 18-month data in Experiment 1, when these same infants were tested 6 months later, they searched correctly despite the opaque walls. Visual tracking was simply superfluous to this task by 18 months.

How do these results bear on the question at hand, namely, the impact of locomotion on infant spatial skills? There are several implications. First, it is clear from the results of Experiment 1 that self-produced locomotion is indeed associated with better spatial performance at the level of the individual task. The lesson here is that even in comparatively simple spatial tasks, infants benefit from being allowed to move on their own. Thus, the hypothesis that the onset of locomotion in the life of the infant will benefit the development of spatial skills receives additional support, albeit indirect.

Perhaps of even greater interest, however, is the clue these studies provide concerning at least one mechanism through which locomotion probably exerts its impact. The clue to which I refer, of course, lies in the relationship uncovered between self-produced locomotion and visual attention. The results of these two studies suggest that it was the latter rather than the former that was really responsible for more sophisticated spatial performance at 12 months. Although it has often been suggested that attention is an important by-product of self-produced locomotion, it has seldom been so clearly documented, particularly during infancy. As these infants moved around the space, they kept their eyes on the target, just as, I would argue, they do when faced with the multitude of spatial puzzles they encounter on a daily basis in their own environments. In fact, I would suggest that as infants explore the boundaries of their new-found freedom of movement, they replace useless egocentric information with a very useful strategy based on the rule, "If you want to find it again, keep your eyes on it." Such a strategy probably pays off well, both in the short run to solve individual problems, and in the long run to provide the raw material from which coordinated views of space are abstracted. In other words, by watching objects as he or she moves, the infant acquires first-hand knowledge about space as a container and self as but one object in relation to others. Views are coordinated, distances are calibrated, and landmarks achieve significance. Moreover, as the data from these little, daily experiments accumulate, and as the infant's capacity for mental representation improves, the stage is set for more and more sophisticated spatial behavior with less and less reliance on visual tracking. As we saw with the 18-month-olds in our studies, visual tracking becomes unnecessary once the layout of a space is mentally represented in a way that allows perspectives to be coordinated.

Of course, set any infant, or adult for that matter, down in an environment whose complexity taxes that individual's limits, and both visual tracking and the advantage of active over passive movement will return. Thus, the argument is not that self-produced movement is important to spatial behavior *only* during the early stages of its development. On the contrary, its importance appears to be one of the continuities across age. However, I do believe that the research cited here provides convincing evidence that self-produced movement has a role of particular significance to play during the period of its initial appearance in the repertoire of the infant. Through its link with attentional strategies, self-produced movement motivates infants to solve spatial problems on a daily basis, and by doing so moves them through an ever-expanding world and down the path toward increased understanding of underlying spatial principles. In other words, although infants may indeed be "drunk with space" as Freud and Burlingham (1944) suggested, they are not so drunk that they don't at times stop to notice where they are, where they have been, and how one turned into the other.

REFERENCES

Acredolo, L. P., Adams, A., & Goodwyn, S. W. 1984. The role of self-produced movement and visual tracking in infant spatial orientation. *Journal of Experimental Child Psychology.* 38:312-327.

Acredolo, L. P., & Evans, D. 1980. Developmental changes in the effects of landmarks on infant spatial behavior. *Developmental Psychology.* 16:312-318.

Appleyard, D. 1970. Styles and methods of structuring a city. *Environment and Behavior.* 2:100-116.

Bayley, N. 1935. The development of motor abilities during the first three years. *Monographs of the Society for Research in Child Development.* 1:1-26.

Bertenthal, B. I., Campos, J. J., & Barrett, K. C. 1984. Self-produced locomotion: An organizer of emotional, cognitive, and social development in infancy. In R. Emde and R. Harmon (Eds.), *Continuities and discontinuities in development.* 175-210. New York: Plenum.

Blank, M. 1964. A focal periods hypothesis in sensorimotor development. *Child Development.* 35:817-829.

Feldman, A., & Acredolo, L. P. 1979. The effect of active versus passive exploration on memory for spatial location in children. *Child Development.* 50:698-704.

Freud, A., & Burlingham, D. T. 1944. *Infants without families.* New York: International Universities Press.

Gustafson, G. E. 1984. Effects of the ability to locomote on infants' social and exploratory behaviors: An experimental study. *Developmental Psychology.* 20:397-405.

Kopp, C. B. 1979. Perspectives on infant motor system development. In M. H. Bornstein & W. Kessen (Eds.), *Psychological development from infancy: Image to intention.* 9-35. New York: Wiley.

Mittelmann, B. 1954. Mobility in infants, children, and adults: Patterning and psychodynamics. *Psychoanalytic Study of the Child.* 9:142-177.

Poag, C., Cohen, R., & Weatherford, D. L. 1983. Spatial representations of young children: The role of self- versus adult-directed movement and viewing. *Journal of Experimental Child Psychology.* 35:172-179.

CONCEPTUAL ISSUES IN THE DEVELOPMENT OF SPATIAL COGNITION

8

LYNN S. LIBEN
Pennsylvania State University

SPATIAL COGNITIVE DEVELOPMENT: CONCLUSIONS OR CONFUSIONS?

In reviewing and evaluating what is known about the development of spatial cognition, it is helpful to recall the proverbial three blind men examining the elephant. Their conclusions about the beast differ markedly depending upon whether they happen upon the legs, tail, or trunk. So, too, investigators' conclusions about spatial cognition differ radically, depending upon the particular piece of behavior they sample. The three blind men, at least, have the advantage that they all use similar tactile methodologies to study the elephant, and thus that their data may ultimately be combined to form a coherent picture of the animal. Furthermore, because any one of the blind men may be presumed to encounter a particular part of the elephant at random, repeated observations made by the same blind man should eventually yield a diversified data base, also capable of being integrated into a coherent whole.

Psychologists, in contrast, typically approach their subject with particular theoretical and methodological biases. This means that individual investigators are likely to gather highly restricted (if reliable) data sets, not readily integrated with one another. Of course, just as the elephant truly *has* legs, a tail, and trunk, humans may equally well "have" many varieties of spatial cognition. And, while it is no more legitimate to study one part of the physical or psychological anatomy than another, confusions do arise when observations of one part are used to draw conclusions about another part, or even about the beast in its entirety.

The argument developed in this chapter is that a variety of confusions about the development of spatial cognition have arisen because of insufficient attention to what is being studied, and correlatively, to what methodologies are appropriate to investigate the selected constructs. Furthermore, it is argued that these confusions are exacerbated by failing to evaluate and integrate isolated empirical findings in relation to broader theories of cognitive development.

More specifically, the first section of the chapter, "Definitional Issues," contains the argument that investigators interpret the term "spatial cognition" in fundamentally different ways, and that unless these differences are explicitly acknowledged, researchers will inevitably draw conflicting conclusions about phenomena that share a label, but little else. In the second section, "Measurement and Inferential Issues," it is argued that investigators often pay insufficient attention to the selection of tasks, dependent measures, and analytic techniques. Several classic studies in the literature on spatial cognitive development are examined to illustrate the ways in which inappropriate methodologies have led to unjustified conclusions. In the third and final section of the chapter, "Developmental Contributions," the value of approaching the study of spatial cognition from a developmental perspective is considered. It is argued that a developmental approach is valuable not only because it provides theories for evaluating and integrating a wide range of otherwise isolated empirical findings, but also because it provides insights into prerequisite and component spatial skills, leads to the identification of important individual differences in adult functioning, and permits the study of selected mechanisms that may be responsible for spatial development.

DEFINITIONAL ISSUES

One might legitimately argue that many of the apparently contradictory conclusions about human spatial cognition can actually be traced to differences in what is meant by "spatial cognition." Both aspects of the term—space and cognition—have varied interpretations. In discussing some of these definitional alternatives below, the goal is not to attempt to find consensual definitions of the terms, but rather to argue that greater attention to definitional issues would aid communication among investigators, and might well help to organize existing programs of research into complementary, rather than conflicting efforts.

Space

The multiple meanings of the term "spatial cognition" are attributed, in part, to the multiple interpretations of the concept of space itself. A number of fundamental distinctions are implicit or explicit in discussions of space. One such distinction, for example, is whether space is viewed as a particular space versus as a conceptual abstraction. This distinction was drawn at least as far back as Leibnitz (1717, cited in Jammer, 1954, p. 115):

> I will here show how Men come to form to themselves the Notion of Space. They consider that many things exist at once, and they observe in them a certain Order of Co-existence, according to which the relation of one thing to another is more or less simple. This Order is their Situation or Distance. When it happens that one of those Co-existent Things changes its Relation to a Multitude of others, which do not change their Relation among themselves; and that another Thing, newly come, acquires the same Relation to the others, as the former had; we then say it is come into the Place of the former...then we may say, that Those which have such a Relation to those fixed Existents, as Others had to them before, have now the same Place which those others had. And That which comprehends all those Places, is called Space.

This is an example of a distinction embedded, but often unrecognized, in contemporary work. That is, some investigators are interested in identifying individuals' knowledge about *particular* places, whereas others are interested in learning about individuals' understanding of space in the *abstract*.

That their goals differ may be obscured not only by the fact that both content domains can be referred to as "spatial," but also by the fact that the same empirical tasks may be used to explore either. For example, subjects may be asked about their neighborhood to find out what they know about the contents of their hometown, perhaps to determine if such knowledge relates to mode of locomotion through the environment (e.g., Appleyard, 1976) or to their exploration of it (Hart, 1981), or to the affective meaning of various places within it (Downs & Stea, 1977). But equally well, questions about neighborhood may be posed as a means of learning about individuals' abstract spatial concepts, such as the ability to use reference systems, conserve distances, comprehend projective relationships, and so on (e.g., as in Piaget, Inhelder, & Szeminska, 1960). Whereas children may well demonstrate that they possess considerable information about their environments, that information need not be structured in ways that imply mastery of abstract spatial concepts such as those mentioned above. It would be inappropriate to draw conclusions about children's abstract spatial competence only on the basis of their competence in knowing about a particular place.

Other fundamental definitional distinctions in the concept of space include the contrasts between relative versus absolute space; Euclidean versus non-Euclidean space; psychological versus physical space; and those drawn by Cassirer (1944) among the trichotomy of expressive, representative, and conceptual space. Discussion of these distinctions, and of their relevance for work on spatial cognition, has been presented elsewhere and thus will not be repeated here (see Liben, 1981; O'Keefe & Nadel, 1978).

The overarching conclusion from a close examination of philosophical, psychological, physical, and mathematical concepts of space is that communication among individuals may be impeded by failing to recognize and understand the kinds of definitional distinctions mentioned above. Ironically, communication may be simultaneously hampered by drawing unnecessary distinctions. An illustration of this problem is the by now classic distinction between "large-scale" and "small-scale" space, which was drawn largely as part of the initial emergence of the field of "environmental psychology." In distinguishing the subject matter of that discipline from more traditional psychological approaches to space (e.g., in the traditions of perception), Ittelson (1973) suggested that what characterizes large-scale space is "The quality of surrounding— the first, most obvious, and defining property—[that] forces the observer to become a participant. One does not, indeed cannot, observe the environment: one explores it" (p.13). Because large-scale space *surrounds* the individual, it is necessary to have multiple vantage points to view it, and correlatively, to integrate information obtained across these multiple encounters. In contrast, small-scale space is said to be viewable from outside the space in a single glance.

Although this distinction has, perhaps, served investigators well in defining and defending their scholarly turf, it may be wise in the context of raising definitional issues to re-examine the conceptual bases of this distinction. From several perspectives, the contrasts between large- and small-scale space blur upon closer examination. First, except in highly contrived circumstances, one cannot really argue for the irrelevance of large-scale space for small-scale spatial tasks, because small-scale spaces are inevitably *embedded within* large-scale spaces. This point has been demonstrated empirically (sometimes serendipitously) by a variety of investigators (e.g., Acredolo, 1979, 1981; Herman & Siegel, 1978; Huttenlocher & Presson, 1979; Huttenlocher & Newcombe, 1984). Experimenters may not intend subjects to use cues external to the table top (or its equivalent) but human subjects—like Tolman's rats—have the uncooperative habit of doing so anyway.

Even if one did screen off the external space satisfactorily (recognizing, of course, the trade-off between experimental control and ecological validity), one must still ask what would really differ between tasks devised to tap small- versus large-scale processes. As noted above, key features of large-scale space are that it surrounds the individual, and that it cannot be encompassed in a single view. What is critical about these features is that it creates first, the need to locate oneself in relation to the space, and second, the need to integrate across multiple views. These needs are, however, also evident in small spaces. For example, if one is to conceptualize relationships of objects in an array (as in the Piagetian three-mountains tasks, described later in this chapter), it is necessary to recognize the viewer's location relative to the array. That is, an understanding of projective spatial relationships includes the comprehension of relativity of viewpoint, regardless of whether the space is town-sized, room-sized, or table-sized. Similarly, just as one cannot encompass all views of a large-scale space in a single glance, one cannot encompass all views of even small spaces or objects in a single fixation. The task of integrating various aspects of an object or an array of objects also progresses with development at a perceptual level (e.g., see Girgus, 1973; Girgus & Hochberg, 1970) and may well require many of the same kinds of integrative processing skills that are required for integrating multiple views of large environments.

In short, most of the interesting issues of large-scale space (e.g., need to establish a self-space relationship; integration across multiple views) appear to have relevance for small-scale spaces as well. As a consequence, it is probably counterproductive to separate theoretical and empirical literatures on large- and small-scale space.

Cognition

The alert reader has undoubtedly recognized that the individual has been slipped into the discussion of "space." The concept of "surroundingness" for example, or of the viewer-array relationship, assumes an individual in the space. But we are not concerned simply with that individual's *presence* in a space; we are concerned with the individual's *cognition* of the space. Unfortunately, fundamental definitional differences in the interpretation of what is meant by this term have often gone unrecognized, thus leading to considerable confusion.

Within the developmental literature, Piaget (1954; Piaget & Inhelder, 1956) has distinguished between the *practical space* of infancy—the ability to negotiate one's way through the environment—and the *representational* or *conceptual space* of early childhood and beyond—the ability to re-present spatial relations to oneself, to manipulate them cognitively, to think about them. One would presumably like to restrict the term *cognition* to the latter. However, even having limited the definition to representation, there is a further issue of whether or not one insists upon some form of *cognizance* (awareness) in the individual. Individuals have large amounts of information about space contained "in the head" in some way, perhaps represented as truth propositions, pure relations, stimulus-response bonds, or in any other format, isolated or integrated. This knowledge has been referred to as *spatial storage*. The individual need not, however, be consciously aware of this information, and thus it should be distinguished from what has been called *spatial thought*. The latter refers to thinking that concerns or makes use of space in some way; information that individuals reflect upon, or manipulate, in short, information of which the individual *is* cognizant (Liben, 1981). This emphasis on phenomenological knowing is by no means unique. Comparable concepts are conscious access (Rozin, 1976), reflective access (Pylyshyn, 1978), and reflection (Gardner, 1978).

Importantly, a particular behavior may be motivated by a variety of mechanisms. For example, consider a case in which an infant crawls five feet and stops before bumping into a wall. If the child stops crawling before hitting the wall on the basis of looming perceptual cues, one need only implicate practical space. If the infant stops on the basis of past learning about the wall's location, one might well argue that the infant has stored information about that space in some form, although the infant might or might not be cognizant of that information. Again, the point is *not* to suggest that only one or another of these is a legitimate area for investigation. Rather, the point is to emphasize the importance of specifying which is being studied.

Summary

It has been argued that several aspects of the definition of spatial cognition may contribute to confusions within the literature to date. First, it is relevant to consider definitions of space itself. The distinction between space as place, versus space as an abstract system, illustrates this issue. If one defines competence in spatial cognition as place (environmental) knowledge, a different picture of developmental milestones and progress may well appear than if one defines competence in spatial cognition as mastery of abstract spatial concepts. Other distinctions in definitions of space such as Euclidean versus non-Euclidean space, or absolute versus relative space, have similar implications for psychological work. Second, it is critical to consider the meaning of "cognition" in the term spatial cognition. A fundamental distinction may be made between "doing" and "knowing." The former concerns activities in space that may be accounted for on the basis of perceptual cues, the latter those that must be attributed to some kind of internal spatial knowledge, of which the individual may be unaware (spatial storage), or aware and able to manipulate (spatial thought).

Unfortunately, the recognition of these definitional distinctions does not alone solve the problems of studying spatial cognition, since there is still the problem of determining what behavioral indices are appropriate for drawing inferences about particular aspects of spatial cognition. The legitimacy of various empirical approaches and inferences is discussed in this light in the next section.

MEASUREMENT AND INFERENTIAL ISSUES

The issue just raised concerning the need to distinguish between behaviors in space controlled by representational processes versus activities in space controlled by perceptual feedback, comprises the first problem discussed in this section. Even tasks that unquestionably tap spatial cognition, however, are not without their methodological problems. Some of the problems associated with inferring subjects' integrated spatial knowledge on the basis of their isolated responses are discussed next. The section concludes with a brief discussion of the necessity for more careful establishment of baseline performance on a variety of spatial tasks.

Spatial Activity versus Spatial Cognition

As noted in the discussion of definitional issues, behaviors may occur in space that do not necessarily demonstrate spatial cognition. Perhaps one of the more dramatic statements of this position was made by Piaget and Inhelder (1956) in describing the gradual mastery of a conceptual system of horizontal and vertical coordinate axes.

It will be said that as a result of lying flat on his back the child is aware of the horizontal right from the cradle, and that he discovers the vertical as soon as he attempts to raise himself. The postural system would thus appear to provide a ready-made co-ordinate space, the organs of equilibrium with their only too-well-known semicircular canals solving the entire problem.

Here we touch on one of the worst misconceptions which has plagued the theory of geometrical concepts. From the fact that the child breathes, digests and possesses a heart that beats we do not conclude that he has any idea of alimentary metabolism or the circulatory system.... Similarly, from the fact that he can stand up or lie flat, the child at first derives only a strictly empirical awareness of the two postures and nothing more (p. 378).

The core of the argument is that "doing" cannot be taken as evidence for "knowing." Again, "doing" does not preclude "knowing" and indeed, *some* "doing" tasks may well assess "knowing." But great caution must be exercised in designing such tasks. Such caution has not always been exercised, and as a consequence, some existing conclusions about spatial cognition are, at best, premature, and at worst, wrong.

One illustration of the doing versus knowing issue may be found in a study by Landau, Gleitman, and Spelke (1981). In this study, Kelli, a 2 1/2-year-old child who had been blinded shortly after birth, was first trained to travel between one landmark (her mother seated in a chair, M) and each of three other landmarks (a stack of pillows, P; a table, T; and a basket containing toys, B). She was then tested by asking her to go from T to P and back, from T to B and back, and from P to B and back. Because she succeeded in reaching these targets, despite the fact that none of these test routes had actually been traversed during training, Kelli was said to have been "guided by knowledge of the Euclidean properties of a spatial layout and by principles for making inferences based on those properties" (p. 1275).

The need to discriminate between perceptual solutions and cognitive solutions is, however, critical here. First, because the target objects were continually present, they provide potential distal cues.[1]

---

[1] Landau, Spelke, and Gleitman (1984) have since collected additional data concerning the possible role of distal cues (see Liben & Newcombe, 1981), and conclude that neither sound cues, nor experimenter bias, nor echolocation can account for Kelli's ability to reach the targets in the studies described in the text. These data must, however, be treated cautiously, given the repetitious testing of the same single child.

Thus, the fact that Kelli eventually reaches the targets does not permit the inference that she knows the angular and distance relationships among the starting points, since she could successfully reach the targets even by trial and error through continual perceptual feedback.[2] Her knowledge of angular relationships among landmarks would more reasonably be inferred from the *directness* of the route between initial position and target. The routes traveled by Kelli, however, are *not* consistently direct (see Landau et al., Figure 2 and Liben & Newcombe, 1981). Of course, because Kelli was not specifically instructed or trained to use direct paths, her failure to take direct paths data cannot be taken as evidence that she would have been *unable* to take direct paths. But her failure to follow straight-line paths surely does not support the conclusion that Kelli has understood angular relationships.

Similarly, the finding that Kelli ultimately arrives at the target cannot demonstrate distance knowledge. Suppose that Kelli's angular knowledge is actually accurate and she moves along the correct (i.e., direct) path. She may think that the object is close, but, not encountering it where expected, continue on. Or, alternatively, she might think the object is further on, but encountering it before anticipated, terminate her search. Or, of course, she may have no expectations about distance at all. To draw conclusions about distance knowledge, it would be necessary to test Kelli with the landmarks removed.

A landmark-absent condition was used in a later study (Experiment II) by Landau, Spelke, and Gleitman (1984). As in the initial study, Kelli's mother (M) was seated in a chair positioned like that in the first study. A second landmark was Kelli's table (T), occupying the same position as the pillow in the earlier study. After walking back and forth between mother and table twice, Kelli was told that in order to play a game, she and the experimenter were to have special places to sit. Kelli was walked twice from her mother to the experimenter's place (E) and back again, and similarly to her own place (S) and back. Positions E and S were those occupied by the toys and basket in the earlier study.

Following this training, Kelli was tested by asking her to go from particular starting locations to particular targets, specifically, from T to E, from T to S, and from E to S, and the inverse of each. To mark

---

[2] Even if one *were* to regard Kelli's final destination as a meaningful assessment of some kind of spatial knowledge, the particular measure of endpoint accuracy used by Landau et al. (1981) is also problematic in a number of ways (Liben, in preparation).

the positions for the places which did not have landmarks (i.e., E and S) she was given an object (rattle or pillow) and asked to put it at the appropriate place ("your place"/"my place").

To evaluate Kelli's knowledge of the distances between targets, trials in which she traveled to a location with no landmarks (i.e., E or S) were examined. The distance Kelli traveled before placing the objects was compared to the actual straight-line distance between the starting point and the true location. Distance errors on the six critical trials ranged from 0% to 70% error, with an average error of 27%. (In actuality there was a seventh relevant trial, but "There was a gross error in direction on that trial, which was therefore excluded from this analysis" [p. 238].)

It should be noted that these errors emerged despite the fact that Kelli was now a full year older than in the original study (43 rather than 31 months), and she had already participated in a minimum of three prior studies (i.e., three additional studies were described in Landau et al., 1984; it is unknown whether there were additional unpublished studies or pilot tests). These prior studies provided not only general experience with tasks of this kind, but also provided Kelli with experience with virtually the identical spatial layout: while the room size was increased from 8′ × 10′ in Experiment I to 10′ × 10′ in Experiment II, the configuration of the landmarks remained the same.

In discussing Kelli's errors in distance noted above, Landau et al. (1984) raise the possibility that—for some unspecified reason—"her sensitivity to distance [may be] underestimated by the present task" ending their discussion of this experiment with: "While she did not estimate distances perfectly, she was not grossly inaccurate: she never moved only 1 foot towards the target, nor did she ever insist on walking 20 feet to get to a target" (p. 238). However, one might well take the opposite stance and argue that her performance was actually overestimated because the exceedingly small room size of 10′ × 10′ and the location of two of the targets directly against the wall limit the range of errors that could reasonably be expected to occur. (Thus adding what might be called a "wall effect" to the ceiling and basement effects already well-known in psychological research.)

Importantly, it appears to be the stronger inferences that are emphasized in subsequent descriptions of this work, both by the investigators themselves, and by others citing their work. In a chapter on perceptual development in the recent *Handbook of Child Psychology*, for example, Gibson and Spelke (1983) write:

A child who is sensitive to Euclidean spatial relationships, such as distance and angle, should be able to develop knowledge of a unified layout of objects at definite distances from each other and to use that knowledge to direct locomotion along new paths through that layout. We have already referred to evidence that young children have this ability (p. 47).

Elsewhere, Landau argues that these experiments (and others not mentioned here, see Landau et al., 1984; Landau, this volume) provide:

definitive evidence for the existence of a spatial knowledge system by the age of about 2 years. That is, given sequential haptic-kinesthetic or visual information about a set of routes connecting objects in space, the child tends naturally to assemble this information in accordance with a geometric mental map that indicates the spatial relationships among objects in a layout (this volume).

Similarly, others citing this work echo the initial conclusions, although in some cases, appropriately attributing the Euclidean geometry to a model of what the child might know rather than to the child herself:

[Kelli] made some mistakes on the way, only sometimes self-corrected, but in general one must attribute to the child a spatial representation that included both angle and distance information, concepts most easily described in terms of Euclidean geometry (Mandler, 1983, p. 447).

In concluding the discussion of this series of studies, it should be noted that the argument being presented here is *not* that Landau and her colleagues are necessarily wrong about Kelli's inferential spatial achievements, but rather that their methodologies do not yet allow such strong conclusions to be drawn.

A second empirical illustration of the need to differentiate between perceptual and conceptual solutions to spatial problems comes from a study by Siegel and Schadler (1977). Arguing that the usual paper and pencil measures such as sketch maps underestimate young children's knowledge of their spatial environments, Siegel and Schadler asked kindergarten subjects to arrange a scale model to show the location of furniture in their highly familiar classroom. Consistent with the hypothesis that even young children have fairly well-developed cognitive maps of familiar environments, most children performed reasonably well on this model task. There were, however, exceptions including one now famous girl, Buffy, who simply clustered all model furniture together in the center of the model room. Although Buffy performed poorly on the task, Siegel (1981) noted that she was never "seen bumping into walls in her classroom," and suggested therefore that the "source of Buffy's poor performance is not in her internal representation of the classroom, but rather in the technique used to externalize the children's spatial knowledge" (p. 172).

While Siegel (1981) thereby implies that Buffy's ability to negotiate through the environment reflects her internalized knowledge of the classroom, it must be recognized again that her behavior need not necessarily imply "knowing." It is just as reasonable (and more conservative) to attribute Buffy's ability to get around her classroom to the perceptual information that is continually available to her, rather than to an underlying internal representation.

The findings reported by Siegel and Schadler do, however, raise an interesting question: Do children like Buffy actually *have* knowledge of the layouts of their familiar environments even though they fail to perform well on the model task? Although scale model tasks are less abstract than sketch map tasks, a scale model still lacks many of the cues present in the actual classroom (lighting, noises, smells, and details of the objects, walls, etc.). In addition, of course, the model task requires an ability to deal with the scale reduction, which incorporates at least some understanding of proportionality.

In a study designed to evaluate whether children's difficulties could be accounted for by these representational demands, Liben, Moore, and Golbeck (1982) designed a task that would assess preschoolers' knowledge of their classroom layout without any of the abstraction, scale reduction, or stimulus impoverishment necessarily found in representational tasks. All but a few pieces of furniture were moved out of the child's classroom (the exceptions were pieces of furniture that defined teacher areas to which children had no access, or were simply too heavy to be moved!), and the child was asked to help the experimenter put back each piece of furniture so that it would be "exactly where it is when you come to school in the morning." Each child was also given a scale model task much like that used by Siegel and Schadler. (For a description of several other tasks and measures, see Liben et al., 1982). It was expected that children would perform significantly better on the classroom task than on the model task. Of far greater interest, however, was whether Buffy-like performance would be found in the classroom task.

Consistent with the view that children have difficulty in meeting the demands of representational tasks even when the materials are highly iconic, the preschoolers did, indeed, perform significantly better on the classroom task than they did on the model task. For some children, the difference could be interpreted simply as a quantitative (e.g., a few items that were grossly misplaced on the model were correctly placed in the classroom), whereas for others, the difference was qualitative (e.g., placing all model furniture around the perimeter of the model, but placing most of the real furniture in the correct areas in the classroom). Even more critical, however, was the finding that there *were* still some children who performed extremely poorly even in the classroom task, placing furniture without apparent regard for conceptual groupings (e.g., not grouping the toy stove, sink, and refrigerator together; not grouping the music materials together, see also Golbeck, 1983), and without regard for spatial organization (e.g., abutting several pieces of furniture together, thereby making passage through the space difficult in the extreme).

Assuming that these individuals' poor performance cannot be attributed to their failure to understand the task, or to their lack of motivation to complete it (neither of which seemed to be the case, although this impression cannot be proven), it does appear that some children are strikingly incapable of reconstructing their highly familiar environments. This incapacity is evident even without changes in scale, materials, or loss of any other cues (light, noise, etc.) that might be imagined to be relevant. These data suggest that children like Buffy probably avoid walls because they are receiving perceptual feedback, not because they are carrying around good cognitive maps. This hypothesis might be evaluated by comparing children who perform well versus poorly on the model tasks under blindfolded conditions in the actual classroom, or on other cognitive measures. As in the discussion of Kelli's performance, the argument made here is *not* that children like Buffy definitely *lack* certain kinds of spatial cognition, but rather that their ability to negotiate through a perceptually rich environment should not be taken as evidence that they *have* this cognizance.

Isolated Representational Measures

In the preceding section, the argument was made that "doing" measures cannot be used to infer "knowing." Unfortunately, the inferential problem cannot be solved simply by using measures that are uncontroversially cognitive rather than perceptual in nature. The problem with any one representational measure is that it simultaneously draws upon spatial storage (as noted earlier, a term used to refer to information that is stored in some manner—S-R connections, truth propositions—in the individual, but of which the individual is not cognizant) as well as spatial thought (the subject's extraction and/or manipulation of that information). As a consequence, individual or developmental differences in performance on a particular spatial task might arise from differences in what the subject has stored about that space, and/or in how the subject goes about using that stored information under the demands of a particular task.

This issue may be illustrated by reference to a program of research initiated by Kosslyn, Pick, and Fariello (1974). These investigators were interested in whether children's and adults' knowledge of a spatial layout would be differentially affected by opportunities to travel between points in that space. Kosslyn et al. first trained kindergartners and adults to place each of 10 toys on its correct spot in a 16′-square room. The room had been divided into quadrants by opaque barriers along one axis and by transparent barriers along the other. The toys had been arranged within this space so that critical toy pairs were separated by either 3′ or 5′ and had either an opaque barrier between them, a transparent barrier between them, or no barrier between them (i.e., the no-barrier toy pairs were within the same quadrant). If functional (traveled) distance affects subjects' representations of the distance between objects, then toys separated by either kind of barrier (both of which prevent direct travel) should be thought of as further apart than toys *not* separated by a barrier. If, however, only *visual* distance is important, then cognitive distances could be expected to be exaggerated for toy pairs separated by the opaque barrier only, because neither the transparent nor the no barrier cases provide visual obstructions. If neither traveled distance nor visual integration is important, no barrier effects should be evident.

To assess knowledge of the relationships among the toys in the room, subjects were asked to make a series of rank-order judgments. Specifically, the subject was given one toy to hold in his or her lap, and then asked which of the remaining 9 toys was closest to it, next closest, next closest, and so on, until all 9 toys had been named. Each toy served once as the referent toy, yielding 90 judgments in all. The dependent measure was the number of "intervening items" named between critical pairs, averaged across all 10 positions, and across two exemplars of the relevant pair type. (Details and illustrations of this measure may be found in Kosslyn et al., 1974, and in Newcombe & Liben, 1982).

In comparison with the actual number of intervening items, kindergartners were found to exaggerate distance (i.e., name more intervening items) across transparent and opaque barriers, whereas adults exaggerated across opaque barriers only. A similar conclusion was reached through a multidimensional scaling analysis of the rank-order judgments. These findings could be interpreted as suggesting the greater importance of functional (traveled) distance for children than adults. Alternatively, these data might be attributed to differences in processing capacity of children and adults. Under the latter interpretation, the rank-ordering task is assumed to carry a heavy processing demand, hence leading the subject to chunk the space into more manageable units. Children might need to break the space into smaller units, hence using both types of barriers to organize the space. Adults might process larger units, and hence use only the (presumably more salient) opaque barriers.

What is critical for the discussion on methodological considerations here is that the former interpretation—functional distance—implies that the subject has encoded pairs separated by barriers as further apart than pairs not separated by barriers. In contrast, the latter interpretation—processing capacity—implies that the subject has stored the location of toys accurately, but outputs a distorted picture of the information in making the rank-order judgments. (It is recognized, of course, that these need not be mutually exclusive.) If the distortions are in the "knowledge" of the spatial layout itself, one should expect to find evidence of those distortions across a range of tasks. If, however, the distortions are in the manipulation of that knowledge required by the rank-ordering task, one should expect to find those distortions eliminated when other representational tasks are substituted.

In a study based on this logic, Newcombe and Liben (1982) followed the paradigm used by Kosslyn et al. However, only half the first grade and college students tested received the rank-ordering task. The remaining subjects were asked to make direct distance estimates between critical (and filler) pairs. One toy was placed at one end of an inverted tape measure. The experimenter then moved the second toy slowly away from the first until the subject thought that the toys were separated by the same distance as they had been in the room. Because these direct distance estimates require that the individual keep only two toys in mind simultaneously, this task was presumed to be within both children's and adults' processing capacities.

The data from the rank-ordering task replicated the findings of Kosslyn et al. Specifically, the intervening item measure showed that children exaggerated distance across both transparent and opaque barriers, whereas adults exaggerated across the opaque barriers only. Importantly, however, the direct distance measure did *not* yield a comparable age by barrier type interaction, suggesting that the processing demands of the rank-ordering task, rather than differential distortion of the spatial layout, may be responsible for the developmental differences in barrier effects observed earlier.

To investigate this possibility further, Liben and Newcombe (in preparation) had first-graders and adults learn the location of toys in a comparable layout, except that the physical barriers were replaced by masking tape lines which maintain the organizational divisions without travel restrictions. This study, like the earlier one (Newcombe & Liben, 1982), was also designed to investigate the extent to which children and adults may be differentially affected by the processing demands of the rank-ordering task, quite apart from any differences in what they learned about the spatial layout. Thus, in addition to eliciting rank-order judgments as in earlier research, subjects were asked to produce a map of the space. The mapping task required positioning line drawings of the 10 toys on a $3' \times 3'$ paper on which the quadrants had been marked. Because the continually available external map eliminates the need to hold the location of all toys in working memory, the mapping task was presumed to have far lower processing demands than the rank-ordering task.

To examine the accuracy of individual subjects' rank orders at each target position, the correct rank orders from each position were correlated with the rank orders actually given by each subject. In addition, rank orders were *derived* from subjects' maps. That is, from each toy (drawing) on the map, the closest toy on the map, the next closest toy, and so on were read off the map. These map-derived ranks were then correlated with the correct rank orders. Low correlations between the correct order and subjects' actual ranks could be due either to distortions in the underlying knowledge of the spatial layout and/or to difficulty in processing this knowledge to compute the rank orders. Low correlations between the correct order and the map-derived ranks would suggest inaccuracies in the underlying knowledge of the spatial layout itself, apart from processing difficulty. (This conclusion rests, of course, in the assumption that the mapping task does indeed have only minimal processing demands.) If, as hypothesized, children are especially troubled by meeting the processing demands of the rank-ordering task, they should show far lower correlations with their actual ranks than with their map-derived ranks. If the ranking task itself does not present difficulty for adults, both sets of correlations should be roughly equivalent.

Consistent with these hypotheses and earlier conclusions from Newcombe and Liben (1982), adults' correlations were high and significant both for actual and map-derived correlations (mean $r' =$ .79 and .86, respectively). The absolute levels of children's correlations for the map-derived ranks were lower than adults', but still significant ($r = .62$). Even more striking, however, was the large deficit in children's actual ranks ($r = .32$) when compared to their map-derived ranks. This pattern of results is consistent with the interpretation that the rank-ordering task represents a cognitively taxing task for young children, and that difficulty in performing accurately on it largely reflects problems in meeting the demands of the ranking task per se rather than fundamental distortions in knowledge of the spatial layout. It should also be noted that a subject by subject comparison of the actual and map-derived rankings at each target position highlights the large individual differences in meeting the rank-ordering processing demands in that not all children show striking contrasts between actual and map-derived ranks.

To determine whether the observed contrast between adults and children can be attributed simply to differences in the quantity of information to be processed, an additional study was run with adults using the identical paradigm, but including 20 toys in the space rather than 10. Again, adults were asked to complete the rank-ordering task and to produce a map of the space. Under these circumstances, the contrast between the rank-order judgments and the map-derived ranks was greater than in the 10-item space used earlier.[3] However, overall, the levels of accuracies were still high, far surpassing levels shown by children on the 10-item space.

Taken together, the data from these various studies suggest that the developmental changes in barrier effects reported by Kosslyn et al. are evident because the tasks they used required the manipulation of spatial knowledge in a way that exceeded children's, but not adults' processing capacity. This conclusion is consistent with the general point made at the beginning of this section on methodologi-

---

[3] The mean correlations were .87 and .95, respectively. The fact that the absolute size of these correlations is higher than for the 10-item space is attributable to the additional data points, since any one perturbation from the correct order has a larger effect with a 10-item ranking than with a 20-item ranking. The contrasts between the two sets of correlations may more readily be seen by looking at the distributions of correlations. For the map derived ranks, all correlations were extremely high for *all* subjects from *all* target positions (100% surpassed .85, and 94% surpassed .90). While virtually all (98%) correlations based on actual rank judgments were also significant, their absolute levels were strikingly lower (only 71% surpassed .85, and only 53% surpassed .90), with two subjects even producing extremely low, insignificant correlations (in the .30s and .40s) from some target positions.

cal issues. Just as one cannot simply replace a particular representational task with a task that may be solved on the basis of perceptual feedback, one cannot simply replace one representational task with some other representational task to reveal "true" underlying spatial knowledge (see also Newcombe, 1985). All measures cannot be assumed to reveal the same underlying spatial knowledge, because an individual's performance on a particular spatial task reflects not only that individual's knowledge of the space, but also that individual's manipulation of that knowledge. It is especially critical to appreciate this point for developmental research, because differences among age groups in task performance might be attributable to either (or both) of these components.

Establishing Baseline Performance

The third methodological issue raised here concerns the need to be more careful in establishing baseline performance on a variety of tasks. Investigators often assess some relatively complex spatial function without first making certain that the prerequisite component skills are present. This point may be illustrated from the perspective-taking literature. In this work, the fundamental question has been whether children understand projective spatial relations, that is, appreciate and compute spatial relations (e.g., left/right) that are relative to the observer's point of view. The classic assessment of projective understanding is the three-mountains task (Piaget & Inhelder, 1956) in which the child is seated on one side of an array of three paper-maché mountains, and is asked to select from a number of photographs or drawings the one that shows how the mountains look to an observer seated at another position (e.g., opposite the child). When subjects fail these tasks, their difficulty has been attributed to their failure to appreciate that different positions have different views, and/or to an inability to calculate what those differences will be. But these conclusions rest on the assumption that the child has no difficulty in selecting the correct representation of his or her *own* view.

In an empirical test of this assumption (Liben, 1978a), 3- to 7-year-old children were given perspective-taking tasks and systematically asked about their own view as well as about another's view. Strikingly, it was not until the age of 6 that errors on the child's own view became extremely rare. Subsequent research (e.g., Liben & Belknap, 1981; Light & Nix, 1983) has shown that children's errors on questions about their own view are at least in part attributable to their reluctance to select any representation that fails to include all components of a display that are known to be there, even if they are not all in immediate view (i.e., intellectual realism).

These results suggest the need for comparable research on many of the other paradigms used to study spatial cognition. For example, the Kosslyn et al. paradigm discussed above assumes that subjects had learned the toys' positions in the actual room. But because markers remained in the room during training, subjects need only to have linked each toy to its appropriate marker. In none of the research using this paradigm (including our own) have subjects been asked to replace toys in the room without such aids. Nor has anyone established a baseline performance for subjects' abilities to make distance estimates or rank-order judgments with visually accessible toys. In short, more careful consideration must be given to whether subjects have mastered the demands of prerequisite skills before drawing conclusions about their mastery of more complex functions. Without attention to these baseline skills, subjects' difficulties on particular tasks may be incorrectly attributed to higher level processing problems (e.g., as in perspective-taking) rather than to skills not directly of interest in the particular investigation (e.g., the child's ability to select correct two-dimensional representations of a three-dimensional display). Again, the argument made here is *not* that only the former is an interesting research question, but rather that *if* one is interested in the former, one must ascertain that tasks used do, indeed, assess the former rather than some other skill.

Summary

Three issues have been discussed in this section, each concerned with the appropriate way to assess spatial cognition. First it was argued that if one is interested in measuring spatial cognition, it is not appropriate to use tasks that may be solved on the basis of continual perceptual feedback. Second, it was argued that any one representational task cannot externalize the subjects' spatial knowledge. Tasks tap not only subjects' knowledge of a space, but also their ability to manipulate that knowledge. Caution must be exercised in drawing conclusions about developmental or individual differences in spatial knowledge on the basis of findings from any particular representational task. Finally, the importance of empirically testing, rather than blindly assuming the adequacy of prerequisite skills was discussed.

All three of these issues may be understood as admonishments to choose appropriate tasks—tasks that measure knowing rather than doing; tasks that can tap differentially the contributions of not only what is known about space (spatial storage) but also how that knowledge is manipulated (spatial thought); and tasks that assess component skills.

In addition to exercising caution in deciding what the subject is asked to do, however, it is also important to measure performance on the selected tasks appropriately. Suppose, for example, in the studies described earlier, Kelli *had* been asked to walk directly to a particular target rather than simply asking her to get there. The dependent measure appropriate for assessing her knowledge of angular relationships would be one that evaluated the directness of the route, not one that evaluated the accuracy with which she ultimately reached the target. Similarly, techniques of data reduction must be thoughtfully chosen. The analysis of performance on the barrier studies serves as a good illustration of this point. As explained earlier, the original measure used to demonstrate barrier effects, developed by Kosslyn et al. (1974) and used in a later replication (Newcombe & Liben, 1982) averages the number of intervening items named between critical pairs of objects in the space. While this measure can reveal persistent overestimates or underestimates, it can obscure large and meaningful differences among target positions and across subjects. That there are indeed such differences becomes readily apparent when correlational analyses are substituted (see Liben & Newcombe, in preparation).

In short, the tasks, the measures used to evaluate performance on those tasks, and the techniques used to analyze the resulting data must be chosen with caution, and with close attention to the kinds of inferences one may justifiably draw.

DEVELOPMENTAL CONTRIBUTIONS

The definitional and methodological issues discussed above are relevant for both developmental and nondevelopmental approaches to spatial cognition. They take on particular importance in developmental work, however, because confused definitions or inappropriate methodologies may grossly distort the conclusions one draws about what children of different ages can accomplish. Thus, careful attention to these issues is critical if one is attempting to describe age-linked accomplishments on the basis of empirical data.

The contribution of a developmental approach to the study of spatial cognition, however, extends beyond its role in highlighting definitional and methodological troublespots in empirical work. First, at the descriptive level, a developmental approach necessarily involves a progressive ordering of accomplishments in a particular domain since there is a presumption that the child comes to acquire the adult skill level only gradually. By examining the child en route to adult mastery, it should be possible to learn something about the foundations upon which mature skills are built.

Importantly, the identification of prerequisite and component skills that is inherent in a developmental approach proves useful not only for understanding gradual mastery, but also for exploring individual differences among mature individuals. As a result, it may be possible to go beyond simply labeling adults as having good or poor spatial abilities by exploring their mastery of basic spatial concepts identified in developmental research. Research of this kind has, in fact, revealed large variability among adults. For example, many adults have been found to have difficulty on the shadow projection and water-level and plumb-line tasks designed by Piaget and Inhelder (1956) to test children's projective and Euclidean concepts (e.g., Barsky & Lachman, 1986; Liben, 1978b; Liben & Golbeck, 1980, 1984; Meehan & Overton, in press; Merriwether & Liben, 1985; Thomas, Jamison, & Hummel, 1973).

From a practical viewpoint, the identification of weaknesses in component concepts may be useful for designing educational interventions to overcome these deficits. More generally, these findings emphatically point to the need to study, rather than to hide, individual differences in performance. In the barrier studies discussed earlier, for example, only *some* adults showed strikingly lower accuracy in their judged rank order than in their map-derived rank orders (Liben & Newcombe, in preparation). Apparently, individual subjects are differentially able to deal with the processing demands of the ranking task, and/or use qualitatively different strategies to do so. The need to study individual differences in spatial processes has been argued before (e.g., see Downs, 1981; Underwood, 1975), and has been the focus of some empirical work (e.g., Pellegrino & Goldman, 1983). But predominately, differences among subjects continue to be treated as noise in the data and hidden in aggregate analyses. Perhaps the recognition that some adults have serious difficulty on tasks designed for young children will help to change that tradition.

Second, at the explanatory level, developmental psychologists are interested in identifying the causal agents of change. Because many of the probable agents change naturally over the course of ontogeny, developmental investigations provide opportunities for testing the role of these hypothesized agents. For example, one mechanism often thought to play a critical role in the acquisition of various spatial functions is self-induced locomotion. Comparisons of spatial skills in children who can versus cannot locomote independently through the environment (e.g., same-aged toddlers who do versus do not walk, see Acredolo, Adams, & Goodwyn, 1984; Acredolo, this volume) may shed light on the role of self-directed movement in spatial cognition. It must, of course, be acknowledged that there may be some unknown differences between children of the same age who have mastered self-locomotion versus those who have not. It is even possible that more advanced spatial skills encourage greater locomotion. Nevertheless, the contrast is at least as defensible as manipulation of active versus passive movement through space used in traditional experimental paradigms.

Finally, at the theoretical level, developmental psychology is also useful since, unlike theories devised to model highly limited domains (such as subjects' performance on mental rotation tasks), the theories formulated in developmental psychology attempt to integrate an extremely wide range of phenomena. As such, the theoretical formulations have the potential for making predictions about new phenomena, and for explaining phenomena from diverse domains. One such comprehensive developmental theory is that formulated by Piaget and Inhelder (1956). They proposed that children first master topological concepts (spatial relationships such as order, proximity, enclosure), followed by mastery of projective relationships (the understanding of the relativity of spatial viewpoints) and Euclidean relationships (encompassing notions of parallelity, metric distance, etc.). More recently, Olson and Bialystok (1983) have formulated a highly integrative developmental theory of spatial cognition focused on structural descriptions of representation. Both of these systems have been applied to an incredibly broad range of tasks and phenomena, including cross-modal recognition of objects; comprehension of spatial language; perspective-taking; use of coordinate axes; mental rotation; and understanding of congruent forms. They could similarly be used to organize an even wider range of spatial phenomena such as those discussed elsewhere in this volume. The point here is neither to attempt to provide an overview of these theoretical systems, nor to endorse one or another of them. Instead it is to suggest that an integrative framework of this kind—like attention to the definitional issues raised earlier—would be valuable in providing greater coherence to an otherwise fragmented area of inquiry.

General theories of cognitive development have, in addition, another important function: they provide a context in which individual empirical findings may be monitored. For example, the conclusion reached by Blaut and Stea (1971) that even preschoolers can understand aerial photographs does not mesh well with the more general picture of preschoolers' cognitive skills found in Piagetian theory. Recent work formulated in response to this discrepancy (Downs & Liben, in press) has, in fact, shown that preschoolers' understanding of aerial photographs is limited in ways that are compatible with Piagetian theory. A three-year old girl, for example, having correctly identified a road on an aerial photo, next identified an area immediately next to the road as "cheese." While adults find the identification of many details in an aerial photograph difficult, they do not make errors of this kind which suggest a failure to appreciate the scale and representational relationships between the two-dimensional representation and the actual space.

In summary, a developmental approach to the study of spatial cognition is valuable not only because it catalogues age-linked changes in spatial functioning, but also because it provides useful ways of identifying prerequisite and component skills for advanced levels of spatial functioning; suggests areas in which to examine individual differences in adult functioning; allows for the evaluation of selected causal mechanisms that are hypothesized to be important in the mastery of spatial skills; and finally, provides theoretical systems that are useful for generating predictions about spatial phenomena, integrating behaviors across a wide range of phenomena, and monitoring conclusions from individual empirical studies.

CONCLUSIONS

Viewed in one light, the thrust of this chapter may be interpreted as pessimistic. There is an implied accusation that we have been too ready to accept any conclusions offered. In the first section of the chapter, it was argued that we need to re-examine some of the implicit and explicit definitions underlying work on the development of spatial cognition. A failure to recognize some distinctions—such as between abstract space and particular place—may have led to the inappropriate use of data from one realm to draw conclusions about another. At the same time, classic distinctions—such as that routinely drawn between large-scale and small-scale space—may have led us to ignore potentially relevant generalizations across research traditions.

In the second section of the chapter, several reasons to question conclusions drawn by particular investigators were discussed. Conclusions may be questioned because the tasks given to subjects are inappropriate for the concept of interest; because the dependent measures used to assess subjects' performance on the selected task are inappropriate; because the statistical treatment of the data obtained from these dependent measures obscures rather than illuminates findings; and/or because baseline or component skills are neither recognized nor systematically measured. What is especially disturbing about these criticisms is that they have been illustrated by reference to studies that are undoubtedly considered to be among the classics in the literature on the development of spatial cognition. Not only do these studies serve as cornerstones within developmental work, they are cited extensively by those working on adult cognition as if these were the "facts" of developmental psychology.

While it may be necessary to reject some of our existing conclusions, it is not necessary to begin our empirical work *de novo*. It is in this light that the present chapter may be viewed as forward-looking and optimistic. That is, the criticisms of various empirical studies do not undermine the scientific value of the data. Rather, they question the interpretation of those data. By more careful attention to definitions of underlying constructs and how they may be measured, the extensive data base that already exists may be salvaged.

Many of the problems discussed in this chapter arise from the shotgun nature of much of the empirical work in spatial cognition. It is difficult to identify meaningful questions and appropriate methodologies without theoretical direction. Correlatively, it is difficult to recognize the potential flaws in conclusions about isolated phenomena. When evaluated from the context of a broad theoretical framework, however, anomalies may become readily apparent. Fortunately, the field of cognitive development already offers a number of integrative theories for this purpose, and thus as with empirical data, is also unnecessary to start *de novo* in the generation of useful theory. In short, by directing attention to definitional and methodological issues, approached within the context of integrative developmental theories, we should be in a position not only to reinterpret existing data, but also to inform the collection and interpretation of additional data in future work.

These points may be reiterated by returning to our metaphorical elephant. Investigators studying the development of spatial cognition—like the blind men approaching the elephant—are all groping at isolated parts. If one blind man describes the tail under the misapprehension that he is observing the leg, the theory of locomotion that he generates will be grossly inadequate. Only if we can correct our interpretation of which pieces we are observing, and organize those pieces into a coherent whole, will we advance our understanding of the conceptual beast. In summary, while it has been argued that many of the conclusions in the literature are misleading, the data base itself and the theoretical traditions that are already in place provide viable mechanisms to reinterpret past work and to direct our future research efforts productively.

ACKNOWLEDGMENTS

This material is based, in part, upon work supported by the National Institute of Education under Grant Number NIE-G-83-0025. Any opinions, findings, and conclusions expressed in this publication are those of the author and do not necessarily reflect the views of the Institute or the Department of Education.

I would like to express my deep appreciation to Roger Downs and Nora Newcombe for their helpful comments on earlier drafts of this chapter.

REFERENCES

Acredolo, L. P. 1979. Laboratory versus home: The effect of environment on the 9-month-old infant's choice of spatial reference system. *Developmental Psychology.* 15:666-667.

Acredolo, L. P. 1981. Small- and large-scale spatial concepts in infancy and childhood. In L. S. Liben, A. H. Patterson, & N. Newcombe (Eds.), *Spatial representation and behavior across the life span: Theory and application.* 63-81. New York: Academic Press.

Acredolo, L. P., Adams, A., & Goodwyn, S. W. 1984. The role of self-produced movement and visual tracking in infant spatial orientation. *Journal of Experimental Child Psychology.* 38:312-327.

Appleyard, D. A. 1976. *Planning a pluralistic city.* Cambridge, MA: MIT Press.

Barsky, R. S., & Lachman, M. E. 1986. Understanding of horizontality in college women: Effects of two training procedures. *International Journal of Behavioral Development.* 9:31-43.

Blaut, J. M., & Stea, D. 1971. Studies of geographic learning. *Annals of the Association of American Geographers.* 61:387-393.

Cassirer, E. 1944. *An essay on man.* New Haven: Yale University Press.

Downs, R. M. 1981. Maps and mappings as metaphors for spatial representation. In L. S. Liben, A. H. Patterson, & N. Newcombe (Eds.), *Spatial representation and behavior across the life span: Theory and application.* 143-166. New York: Academic Press.

Downs, R. M., & Liben, L. S. (in press). Children's understanding of maps. In P. Ellen, & C. Thinus-Blanc (Eds.), *Cognitive processes and spatial orientation in animal and man.* Dordrecht, Holland: Martinus Nijhoff.

Downs, R. M. & Stea, D. 1977. *Maps in minds.* New York: Harper & Row.

Gardner, H. 1978. Commentary on animal awareness papers. *Behavioral and Brain Sciences.* 4:572.

Gibson, E. J., & Spelke, E. S. 1983. The development of perception. In J. H. Flavell & E. M. Markman (Eds.), *Cognitive development* (Vol. III) of P. H. Mussen (Ed.), *Handbook of child psychology.* 1-76. New York: Wiley.

Girgus, J. S. 1973. A developmental approach to the study of shape processing. *Journal of Experimental Child Psychology.* 16:363-374.

Girgus, J. S., & Hochberg, J. E. 1970. Age differences in sequential form recognition. *Psychonomic Science.* 21:211-212.

Golbeck, S. L. 1983. Reconstructing a large-scale spatial arrangement: Effects of environmental organization and operativity. *Developmental Psychology.* 19:644-653.

Hart, R. A. 1981. Children's spatial representation of the landscape: Lessons and questions from a field study. In L. S. Liben, A. H. Patterson, & N. Newcombe (Eds.), *Spatial representation and behavior across the life span: Theory and application.* 195-233. New York: Academic Press.

Herman, J. F., & Siegel, A. W. 1978. The development of cognitive mapping of the large-scale environment. *Journal of Experimental Child Psychology.* 26:389-406.

Huttenlocher, J. A., & Newcombe, N. 1984. The child's representation of information about location. In C. Sophian (Ed.), *The origins of cognitive skills.* Hillsdale, NJ: Lawrence Erlbaum Associates.

Huttenlocher, J. A., & Presson, C. 1979. The coding and transformation of spatial information. *Cognitive Psychology.* 11:375-394.

Ittelson, W. H. 1973. Environment perception and contemporary perceptual theory. In W. H. Ittelson (Ed.), *Environment and cognition.* New York: Seminar Press.

Jammer, M. 1954. *Concepts of space.* Cambridge, MA: Harvard University Press.

Kosslyn, S. M., Pick, H. L., & Fariello, G. R. 1974. Cognitive maps in children and men. *Child Development.* 45:707-716.

Landau, B., Gleitman, H., & Spelke, E. 1981. Spatial knowledge and geometric representation in a child blind from birth. *Science.* 213:1275-1278.

Landau, B., Spelke, E., & Gleitman, L. 1984. Spatial knowledge in a young blind child. *Cognition.* 16:225-260.

Liben, L. S. 1978a. Perspective-taking skills in young children: Seeing the world through rose-colored glasses. *Developmental Psychology.* 14:87-92.

Liben, L. S. 1978b. Performance on Piagetian spatial tasks as a function of sex, field dependence, and training. *Merrill-Palmer Quarterly.* 24:97-110.

Liben, L. S. 1981. Spatial representation and behavior: Multiple perspectives. In L. S. Liben, A. H. Patterson, & N. Newcombe (Eds.), *Spatial representation and behavior across the life span: Theory and application.* 3-36. New York: Academic Press.

Liben, L. S. In preparation. The blind inference of spatial knowledge.

Liben, L. S., & Belknap, B. 1981. Intellectual realism: Implications for investigations of perspective-taking in young children. *Child Development.* 52:921-924.

Liben, L. S., & Golbeck, S. L. 1980. Sex differences in performance on Piagetian spatial tasks: Difference in competence or performance? *Child Development.* 51:594-597.

Liben, L. S., & Golbeck, S. L. 1984. Performance on Piagetian horizontality and verticality tasks: Sex-related differences in knowledge of relevant physical phenomena. *Developmental Psychology.* 20:595-606.

Liben, L. S., Moore, M. L., & Golbeck, S. L. 1982. Preschoolers' knowledge of their classroom environments: Evidence from small-scale and life-size spatial tasks. *Child Development.* 53:1275-1284.

Liben, L. S., & Newcombe, N. 1981. Inferring Euclidean spatial knowledge in a young blind child. Unpublished manuscript. University of Pittsburgh.

Liben, L. S., & Newcombe, N. (In preparation). Barrier effects in children and adults.

Light, P., & Nix, C. 1983. "Own view" versus "good view" in a perspective-taking task. *Child Development.* 54:480-483.

Mandler, J. M. 1983. Representation. In J. H. Flavell & E. M. Markman (Eds.), *Cognitive development.* (Vol III) of P. H. Mussen (Ed.), *Handbook of child psychology.* 420-494. New York: Wiley.

Meehan, A. M., & Overton, W. F. (in press). Gender differences in expectancies for success on Piagetian spatial tasks. *Merrill-Palmer Quarterly.*

Merriwether, A. M., & Liben, L. S. 1985. Adult performance on projective and Euclidean tasks: Inaccuracies and interrelationships. Paper presented at the 15th Annual Symposium of the Jean Piaget Society, Philadelphia.

Newcombe, N. 1985. Methods for the study of spatial cognition. In R. Cohen (Ed.), *The development of spatial cognition.* 277-300. Hillsdale, NJ: Lawrence Erlbaum Associates.

Newcombe, N., & Liben, L. S. 1982. Barrier effects in the cognitive maps of children and adults. *Journal of Experimental Child Psychology.* 34:46-58.

O'Keefe, J., & Nadel, L. 1978. *The hippocampus as cognitive map.* Oxford: Oxford University Press (Clarendon).

Olson, D. R., & Bialystok, E. 1983. *Spatial cognition.* Hillsdale, NJ: Lawrence Erlbaum Associates.

Pellegrino, J. W., & Goldman, S. R. 1983. Developmental and individual differences in verbal and spatial reasoning. In R. F. Dillon & R. R. Schmeck (Eds.), *Individual differences in cognition.* 1:137-180. New York: Academic Press.

Piaget, J. 1954. *The construction of reality in the child.* New York: Basic Books.

Piaget, J., & Inhelder, B. 1956. *The child's conception of space.* New York: Norton.

Piaget, J., Inhelder, B., & Szeminska, A. 1960. *The child's conception of geometry.* New York: Basic Books.

Pylyshyn, Z. W. 1978. When is an attribution of beliefs justified? *Brain and Behavioral Sciences.* 1:592-593.

Rozin, P. 1976. The evolution of intelligence and access to the cognitive unconscious. In J. M. Sprague & A. A. Epstein (Eds.), *Progress in psychobiology and physiological psychology.* Vol. 6. New York: Academic Press.

Siegel, A. W. 1981. The externalization of cognitive maps by children and adults: In search of ways to ask better questions. In L. S. Liben, A. H. Patterson, & N. Newcombe (Eds.), *Spatial representation and behavior across the life span: Theory and application.* 167-194. New York: Academic Press.

Siegel, A. W., & Schadler, M. 1977. Young children's cognitive maps of their classroom. *Child Development.* 48:388-394.

Thomas, H., Jamison, W., & Hummel, D. 1973. Observation is insufficient for discovering that the surface of still water is invariantly horizontal. *Science.* 181:173-174.

Underwood, B. J. 1975. Individual differences as a crucible in theory construction. *American Psychologist.* 30:128-134.

CHILDREN'S VERBAL REPRESENTATION OF SPATIAL LOCATION

9

JUDITH R. JOHNSTON
University of Indiana

INTRODUCTION

Language studies of spatial representation in children have focused on predicates which specify the location of objects. In English these predicates are prepositions such as *in* or *behind*, but across languages locative expressions vary in grammatical form. A number of investigators have reported on children's use of stative locatives in comprehension and production tasks. Despite differences in observational contexts and acquisition criteria, these reports present a remarkably consistent developmental picture. Table 9.1 summarizes data from nineteen studies for a representative group of locatives. The locatives are listed there by lexical families. *In, on,* etc., designate any one of the surface forms which express these spatial relationships. IN BACK OF and IN FRONT OF are listed twice since research has suggested that children first use these locatives with reference objects which have back and front features (F), and only later use them in their deictic sense. There is obvious strong agreement among these studies as to the age at which specific locatives are typically acquired. Where wide age ranges do occur, they seem to reflect differences among languages in characteristics of the loca-

Table 9.1.
Age range within which various locatives are acquired in English, German, Hebrew,
Italian, Japanese, Portuguese, Russian, Serbo-Croatian, and Turkish.

Location	Age of Comprehension	Age of Elicitation	Investigators*	Language
IN	under 2;0	2;0-2;4	2,3,5,9,10,13,15	E,H,I,P,S,T
ON	2;0-2;3	1;9-2;4	2,3,5,9,10,13,15	E,H,I,P,S,T
UNDER	2;0-2;9	2;0-2;8	2,3,5,9,10,13,16	E,H,I,P,R,S,T
NEXT-TO	2;0-3;0	2;4-3;6	5,7,9,10,13,14,18	E,G,I,P,S,T
BETWEEN	3;0-3;8	3;4-4;0	2,6,10,18	E,I,S,T
BACK (F) FRONT (F)	2;0-3;6	4;0-4;6	1,7,9,10,11,12,13,15,18	E,G,I,P,S,J
BACK FRONT	3;0-4;8	after 4;8	4,8,9,10,12,13,17	E,I,S,T

* Reference key follows:
1. Akiyama, 1976
2. Ames and Learnerd, 1948
3. Clark, E., 1972
4. Cox, 1978
5. Dromi, 1979
6. Durkin, 1981
7. Grimm, 1973
8. Holmes, 1932
9. Johnston, 1984

10. Johnston and Slobin, 1979
11. Kubena, 1975
12. Kuczaj and Maratsos, 1975
13. Pinto, 1982
14. Prather, 1975
15. Sinha and Walkerdine, 1975
16. Sokhin, 1966
17. Tanz, 1976
18. Washington and Naremore, 1978

tive system such as lexical diversity, synonymity, homonymity, and etomological transparency (Johnston & Slobin, 1979).[1]

In addition to the results cited in Table 9.1, several studies have tested children of a restricted age range on locatives purportedly acquired by younger children. These data too are largely consistent with Table 9.1 (Washington & Naremore, 1978; Holzman, 1981; Durkin, 1980; Akiyama, 1976; Stern & Stern, 1928; Walkerdine & Sinha, 1974; Harris & Strommen, 1972; Harris, 1972). Studies

---

[1] Durkin (1981) notes dramatic differences in children's responses to various BETWEEN arrays. Similar differences were observed, though not reported, in our cross-linguistic study (Johnston & Slobin, 1979). Factors such as the proximity and similarity of the reference objects seem to affect the likelihood that a child will interpret arrays as instances of BETWEEN. This suggests some pattern of meaning development which needs further study. The ages listed in Table 9.1 reflect performance in the "easier" contexts. Pinto (1982) used only one elicitation array, similar to our more difficult array, and reports a somewhat later acquisition point.

which report order of acquisition without mentioning ages add further confirmation (Hess & Cook, 1975; Conner & Chapman, 1985; Windmiller, 1973; Museyibova, 1961; Silliman & Bohne, 1978).

The strongest tests of ordered acquisition are found in the Johnston and Slobin (1979) and Johnston (1984) analyses. In the first study, English speaking children from 2 years to 4 years 8 months (2;0 to 4;8) were tested in comprehension and elicitation tasks for each of the locatives in Table 9.1. Gutman scale analyses of the resulting data yielded reproducibility indices of .88 and .93, respectively, supporting the hypothesis that these locatives are acquired in the order in which they are listed in Table 9.1. Scale analyses of independent elicitation data in the Johnston (1984) study virtually replicate these findings. Equally interesting, Johnston and Slobin's data from Turkish, Italian and Serbo-Croatian speaking children performing comparable locative tasks also scaled. Moreover, elicitation scales for the four languages resembled each other: *In, on, under* and *next to* consistently preceded *between* and *in back of/in front of* for featured reference objects; these in turn consistently preceded *in back of* and *in front of* for non-featured reference objects.

COGNITIVE PREREQUISITES

These facts about early verbal representations of location are both curious and compelling. Locative terms are apparently learned at predictable ages, in a predictable order, across a span of years. This systematicity extends to changes in the meanings of surface lexemes as well as to their initial acquisition (Conner & Chapman, 1985; Halpern, Corrigan, & Aviezer, 1981; Johnston, 1984). While linguistic and experiential factors undoubtedly influence locative acquisition patterns, these data are most valuable for what they reveal about the relationships between verbal and nonverbal spatial cognition. The "universality" and protracted nature of locative learning suggest that nonverbal conceptual development plays a major determining role (Johnston, 1985).

Direct empirical tests have thus far confirmed this hypothesis. At least three studies have compared children's performance on related nonverbal and verbal tasks and have found that success on the nonverbal problem preceded verbal proficiency. Halpern et al. (1981) scaled performance on nonverbal and verbal tasks which demanded knowledge of UNDER relations. Problems involving nonverbal block manipulations were reliably solved prior to problems requiring linguistic comprehension or expression. Levine and Carey (1982) looked at children's understanding of *back* and *front* as it related to knowledge of object features. In the nonverbal tasks two- and three-year-olds were asked to place objects with inherent fronts and backs in a parade line, and also to place these objects so that they could talk to a doll. Virtually all of the children oriented the objects appropriately in the nonverbal tasks though many of the children subsequently failed to point to the fronts or backs of these same objects on command. Johnston (1979) investigated children's use of the lexical families *in front of* and *in back of* as a function of their understanding of various spatial notions hypothesized to comprise the meanings of these terms. Early "featured" uses of these prepositions seem to express meanings like NEXT-TO-THE-FRONT/BACK-OF while later, deictic, uses seem to express meanings like FIRST/ SECOND-IN-THE-LINE-OF-SIGHT. This being so, it was hypothesized that the younger children should control notions of PROXIMITY and OBJECT-FEATURE, while the older children should additionally understand ORDER and PROJECTIVE relations. Thirty-three children ages 31 to 54 months performed in a variety of tasks designed to test this hypothesis. Subsequent scale analyses indicated that spatial concepts and linguistic proficiencies emerged in the predicted parallel orders: PROXIMITY, OBJECT-FEATURE < ORDER, PROJECTIVE RELATIONS, and *in front/back of* in featured contexts < *in front/back of* in nonfeatured contexts. Moreover, children who used these spatial terms in one or the other senses could indeed solve the nonverbal problems requiring application of the pertinent spatial concepts. Not all children who succeeded in the nonverbal tasks, however, demonstrated the correlate linguistic knowledge. (See Table 9.2.) This study is particularly useful because it demonstrates that the ontogenetic precedence of nonverbal knowledge obtains systematically, across a conceptual field, at different developmental points.

Table 9.2
Percentage of children failing either a given locative task or its related nonverbal task (but not both) who showed the pass-nonverbal, fail-verbal pattern.

Tasks	Fail Verbal/Fail either
Proximity & Object Feature/BACK (f)	95%
Proximity & Object Feature/FRONT (f)	96%
Order/BACK	86%
Order/FRONT	100%
Projective Relations/BACK	89%
Projective Relations/FRONT	100%

EARLY DEVELOPMENT OF SPATIAL CONCEPTS

It seems, then, that the facts of locative acquisition point to a developing nonverbal spatial cognition. Children learn new words and new usages as their repertoire of spatial concepts expands. How shall we characterize the course of this underlying development? Psycholinguists have appealed to either physical laws or to geometries in building their models of meaning. Halpern et al. (1981, following H. Clark, 1973), for example, distinguish between concepts of UNDER according to their compliance with gravity and object shape. Other researchers (e.g., Parisi & Antinucci, 1970; Windmiller, 1973) have borrowed the Piagetian metaphor (Piaget & Inhelder, 1967; Laurendeau & Pinard, 1970) and distinguished among topological, projective and Euclidean concepts. Whichever set one chooses, physical or geometric, descriptive categories are merely the starting point of a developmental model. Verbal and nonverbal data point to locational concepts which emerge in a reliable order (Johnston, 1981); our models must explain this order. Why are spatial concepts of one sort constructed before those of another sort? Why should gravity compliance or rubber sheets serve as launch sites for spatial cognition?

Consider the NEXT TO < IN BACK OF developmental sequence as an illustrative case. Children reliably produce "next to," "by" or "beside" before they use "in back of" or "behind" in their deictic senses. Likewise, in my own studies of nonverbal cognition (Johnston, 1979), children who inferred that a hidden object was proximal to a landmark frequently failed to realize that objects placed along the projective axis were invisible to a blocked viewer. Piagetians might see this as a clear instance of the priority of topological concepts. But is there some reason why topological relations should emerge prior to projective relations? An analysis of the NEXT TO and IN BACK OF relations suggests an answer. NEXT TO judgments require single decisions about the proximity of two points (objects, etc.); IN BACK OF judgments require this same decision about proximity, coordinated with the imposition of an imaginary axis, the designation of a point of origin on that axis, and an order judgment vis a vis the three point series. Thus decomposed, the IN BACK OF judgment proves two ways complex: it involves multiple elements in its calculation and it entails other, more primitive, spatial relations. This seems to be the sort of argument implicit in Inhelder's explanation that certain topological relations are later "integrated into more specific operations and notions of both Euclidean and projective geometry" (1969, p. 35).

Such an explanatory model would account for the locative development facts while still accommodating recent evidence that some aspects of the supposedly later projective and Euclidean systems (Piaget & Inhelder, 1967) are constructed early. Developmental predictions within this model are based on the number of reasoning steps or the availability of specific relational notions, not on any general system property such as projectivity. The basic elements of all three conceptual geometries may well emerge simultaneously. Flavell's work (Lempers, Flavell & Flavell, 1977; Flavell, Shipstead & Croft, 1978) points to the two-year-old's knowledge of lines-of-sight (projective system), and Gelman's work, among others (Gelman & Gallistel, 1978; Wagner & Walters, 1982) establishes relative magnitude judgments (Euclidean system) within this same period—one which haptic perception tasks (Laurendeau & Pinard, 1970) would identify as merely "topological." There are, on the other hand, certain topological relations such as ORDER which are themselves clearly derivative and emerge later, during the fourth year (Johnston, 1979). It is only when we ask about the child's ability to represent locations that the priority of topological notions emerges. This is true, not because the topological *system* is developmentally prior, but because the locational notion of PROXIMITY within this system is both primitive and uncoordinated.

This account of the NEXT TO < IN-BACK-OF sequence may well be wrong. I offer it not so much to assert its validity as to illustrate the sort of explanatory reasoning that our growing descriptive literature now demands. Even if this account were valid, it would leave two important questions unanswered. First, the picture I have sketched focuses on integrative aspects of development; conceptual primitives of all sorts are coordinated into increasingly complex calculations. What of the character and origins of the primitives themselves?

Piaget and Inhelder claim that "thought has the task of reproducing at its own level (of representation as distinct from direct perception) everything that perception has so far achieved within the limited field of direct contact with the object" (1967, p.13). Here as elsewhere in the Piagetian literature we find a clear line being drawn between the mental schemata of infancy and the subsequent "notions" of representational thought. Sensorimotor thought is viewed as presentational, successive, and non-reflective; the infant reacts to objects-of-the-moment without anticipation or contemplation. Representational thought, on the other hand, is free of space and time, reasons and reflects on imaginary states, and operates in a world of abstracted relations quite apart from their embodiment in any particular object or event.

The Piagetian literature is notably murky in its discussion of the conceptual reconstitution of sensorimotor schemes. It is clear, however, in its assertion that this distinction must be preserved if we wish to understand mental development. The locative data cited earlier support this view. They speak to major changes in spatial cognition which occur during the preschool years. Claims "that the child knows all about space before he begins to learn about language" (H. Clark, 1973, p.61) may thus be misleading insofar as they ignore the unique status of conceptual, as opposed to sensorimotor, spatial representation. Until the space of movement and perception has become the object of reflection, the child seems unable to discover the meaning of those linguistic symbols which signify spatial relations.

We have as yet few accounts of this transformation in spatial thought. Foreman's study of early block play suggests a "gradual atemporalization of successive states" and a "disassociation of the logical from the contingent" (1982, p. 133). Movements such as banging a block on the table are "frozen" when one block is released on top of another. Similarly, when inductive rules for centering stacked blocks are applied in contexts where no mishap is likely (e.g., small blocks on large ones), order becomes distinguishable from consequence. In both cases the child's actions lead to products which can be studied as instantiated relations and ultimately compared.

Such reflective comparison seems critical to the emergence of higher level thought. Sugarman (1983) argues from her data on children's class groupings that representational thought develops from judgments to coordinated judgments about judgments. She focuses especially on the mental coordination implicit in her 2 1/2 year olds' simultaneous construction of two arrays having different bases of similarity, e.g. red vs. blue. Some higher level equivalence judgment seems to facilitate the child's easy movement from one sort of comparative judgment (i.e. same in redness) to another (i.e. same in blueness) and back. Analogous arguments could be made at an earlier phase characterized by successive iteration. Sugarman's two-year olds tended to group all objects that were similar in a given attribute (e.g. red) before moving to group by a second scheme (e.g. blue). Even in this simpler classificatory behavior, we can see the child expressing an equivalence judgment (i.e. same in redness) about prior attributions (i.e. X is red). Such internal organization and reflection seems central to conceptual thought.

The micro-histories of Foreman and Sugarman clarify the evolution of spatial thought by pointing to the probable origin and structure of conceptual representation, i.e. action products and judgments on judgments. The spatial primitives which support early locative learning, e.g. IN, ON, NEXT TO, are certainly discoverable in the static products of object manipulation. Likewise, comparisons across object arrays can invite equivalence judgments (e.g. same in on-ness) about prior relational judgments (e.g. X is on Y). The forces promoting such reflection remain, as always, mysterious.

To raise my second question, let me note that this chapter purports to be a discussion of verbal representation, and indeed began with data on locative acquisition. The child language facts led me quickly, however, to a consideration of early nonverbal spatial concepts. This does not seem to be a case where the study of linguistic "spatial products" involves an "unabashed concern with the representational medium itself" (Liben, 1981, p.12). Why not? Does the developmental significance of spatial language reduce to that of underlying nonverbal thought? Claims that linguistic schemes are one of the two basic sorts of mental representation would suggest otherwise (Olson, 1975). As Kosslyn (1980) notes, however, many features of "verbal" thought are due to its propositional rather than its linguistic character. So viewed, language again loses its special place. Or does it? Even if we assume that spatial concepts are constructed prior to their linguistic mapping and thus are essentially nonverbal, words, once available, may constitute convenient interpretive programs that streamline real time processing. Given the constraints of a limited capacity system, verbal thought may achieve what propositional thought cannot. I know of no developmental research which addresses this point, but the importance of verbal representations of space may be far greater than patterns of locative acquisition would imply.

ACKNOWLEDGMENT

My thanks to Robin Chapman for her encouragement and assistance in this project.

REFERENCES

Akiyama, M. 1976. Personal correspondence.
Ames, L. B., & Learnerd, J. 1948. The development of verbalized space in the young child. *Journal of Genetic Psychology*. 72:63-84.
Clark, E. 1972. Some perceptual factors in the acquisition of locative terms by young children. *Proceedings of the Chicago Linguistic Society*. 8:431-439.

Clark, H. 1973. Space, time, semantics and the child. In T. Moore (Ed.), *Cognitive development and the acquisition of language.* New York: Academic Press, 27-63.

Conner, P., & Chapman, R. 1985. The development of locative comprehension in Spanish: Harder when locatives lack object part labels? *Journal of Child Language.* 12:109-123.

Cox, M. 1978. *Young children's understanding of 'in front of' and 'behind' in the placement of objects.* Unpublished paper, University of York.

Dromi, E. 1979. More on the acquisition of locative prepositions: analysis of Hebrew data. *Journal of Child Language.* 6:547-562.

Durkin, K. 1981. Aspects of late language acquisition: School children's use and comprehension of prepositions. *First Language.* 2:47-59.

Durkin, K. 1980. The production of locative propositions by young school children. *Educational Studies.* 6:9-30.

Forman, G. 1982. A search for the origins of equivalence concepts through a microanalysis of block play. In G. Forman (Ed.), *Action and thought: From sensorimotor schemes to symbolic operations.* New York: Academic Press. 97-136.

Flavell, J., Shipstead, S., & Croft, K. 1978. Young children's knowledge about visual perception: Hiding objects from others. *Child Development.* 49:1208-1211.

Gelman, R., & Gallistel, C. 1978. *The child's understanding of number.* Cambridge, Mass: Harvard University Press.

Grimm, H. 1973. *On the child's acquisition of semantic structure underlying the wordfield of prepositions.* Unpublished paper, University of Heidelberg.

Halpern, E., Corrigan, R., & Aviezer, O. 1981. Two types of "under"? Implications for the relationship between cognition and language. *International Journal of Psycholinguistics.* 8:37-56.

Harris, L. 1972. Discrimination of left and right and development of logic of relationships. *Merrill-Palmer Quarterly.* 18:307-320.

Harris, L., & Strommen, E. 1972. The role of front-back features in children's "front", "back", and "beside" placements of objects. *Merrill-Palmer Quarterly.* 18:259-271.

Hess, C., & Cook, D. 1975. *An investigation of the acquisition of ten prepositions denoting spatial relationships.* Paper presented at the American Speech and Hearing Association convention.

Holmes, T. C. 1932. Comprehension of some sizes, shapes, and positions by young children. *Child Development.* 3:269-273.

Holzman, M. 1981. Where is under: From memories of instances to abstract featural concepts. *Journal of Psycholinguistic Research.* 10:421-439.

Inhelder, B. 1969. Some aspects of Piaget's genetic approach to cognition. In H. Furth (Ed.), *Piaget and knowledge.* Englewood Cliffs, NJ: Prentice-Hall, Inc. 22-40.

Johnston, J. 1984. Acquisition of locative meanings: Behind and In front of. *Journal of Child Language.* 11:407-422.

Johnston, J. 1985. Cognitive prerequisites: The evidence from children learning English. In D. Slobin (Ed.), *The cross linguistic study of language acquisition*: Vol. 2. *Theoretical issues*. Hillsdale, NJ: Lawrence Erlbaum Associates. 961-1004.

Johnston, J. 1981. On location: Thinking and talking about space. *Topics in Language Disorders*. 2:17-32.

Johnston, J. 1979. *A study of spatial thought and expression: In back and in front*. Ph.D. dissertation, University of California, Berkeley.

Johnston, J., & Slobin, D. 1979. The development of locative expressions in English, Italian, Serbo-Croatian, and Turkish. *Journal of Child Language*. 6:529-545.

Kosslyn, S. 1980. *Image and mind.*. Cambridge, Mass.: Harvard University Press.

Kubena, M. 1975. *An experimental study of the comprehension and expression of prepositions of location and direction of movement in the speech of children*. Paper presented at the American Speech and Hearing Association convention.

Kuczaj, S., & Maratsos, M. 1975. On the acquisition of front, back and side. *Child Development* 46:202-210.

Laurendeau, M., & Pinard, A. 1970. *The development of the concept of space in the child*. New York: International Universities Press.

Lempers, J., Flavell, E., & Flavell, J. 1977. The development in very young children of tacit knowledge concerning visual perception. *Genetic Psychology Monographs*. 95:3-53.

Levine, S., & Carey, S. 1982. Up front; the acquisition of a concept and a word. *Journal of Child Language*. 9:645-658.

Liben, L. 1981. Spatial representation and behavior: Multiple perspectives. In L. Liben, A. Patterson, & N. Newcombe (Eds.), *Spatial representation and behavior across the life span*. New York: Academic Press. 3-38.

Museyibova, T. 1961. The development of an understanding of spatial relations and their reflection in the language of children of preschool age. In Anan'yev, B. and Lomov, B. (Eds.), *Problems of spatial perception and spatial concepts*. Moscow: Izdatel'stvo Akademii Pedagogicheskikh Nauk RSFSR. (NASA Technical Translation F-164, 1964, 121-129.)

Olson, D. 1975. On the relations between spatial and linguistic processes. In J. Eliot & N. Salkind (Eds.), *Children's spatial development*. Springfield: Charles C. Thomas. 67-110.

Parisi, D., & Antinucci, F. 1970. Lexical competence. In G. Flores d'Arcais, & W.V.U. Levelt (Eds.), *Advances in psycholinguistics*. Amsterdam: North-Holland Publishing Co. 197-210.

Piaget, J., & Inhelder, B. 1967. *The child's conception of space*. New York: W. W. Norton and Co., Inc.

Pinto, M. da Graca. 1982. *A study on locative expressions in Portuguese*. Paper presented to the Linguistic Society of America, College Park.

Prather, E. 1975. *Structured test elicitation vs. spontaneous occurrence of plurals, prepositions and conjunctions*. Paper presented at the American Speech and Hearing Association convention.

Silliman, E., & Bohne, S. 1978. *The effect of objects and pictures as variables on comprehension and production of spatial terms.* Unpublished paper, Hunter College, NY.

Sinha, C., & Walkderdine, V. 1975. *Functional and perceptual aspects of the acquisition of spatial relational terms.* Unpublished paper, University of Bristol.

Stern, C., & Stern, W. 1907. *Die Kindersprache: Eine psychologische und sprachtheoretische Untersuchung.* Darmstadt: Wissenschaftliche Buchgesellschaft, Leipzig: Barth (4th rev. ed., 1928).

Sugarman, S. 1983. *Children's early thought: Developments in classification.* Cambridge: Cambridge University Press.

Tanz, C. 1976. *Studies in the acquisition of deictic terms.* Unpublished Ph.D. dissertation, University of Chicago.

Wagner, S., & Walters, J. 1982. A longitudinal analysis of early number concepts: From numbers to number. In G. Forman (Ed.), *Action and thought: From sensorimotor schemes to symbolic operations.* New York: Academic Press. 137-164.

Walkerdine, V., & Sinha, C. 1979. *Spatial and temporal relations in the linguistic and cognitive development of young children.* Manuscript, University of Bristol.

Washington, D., & Naremore, R. 1978. Children's use of spatial prepositions in two and three dimensional tasks. *Journal of Speech and Hearing Research.* 21:151-165.

Windmiller, M. 1973. *The relationship between a child's conception of space and his comprehension and production of spatial locatives.* Ph.D. dissertation, University of California at Berkeley.

INTERRELATION OF LOGICAL AND SPATIAL KNOWLEDGE IN PRESCHOOLERS

10

AGELIKI NICOLOPOULOU
University of California, San Diego

Research in developmental psychology has focused mainly on the development of cognitive abilities within a specific domain of knowledge (e.g., either of number, space, or causality). However, theoretical formulations of development which emphasize the self-constructive and self-organizing process of knowledge acquisition through the individual's actions are concerned with a systemic whole as their unit of analysis of the mind (see Glick, 1983; Langer, 1969, 1980; Werner, 1926/1948). Research that attempts to capture a whole at any stage of development must include interfunctional relationships of domains of knowledge rather than simply concentrate on development within a single domain of knowledge (see also Turiel, 1983; Turiel & Davidson, 1985). The inclusion of more than one domain provides the conditions for observing the nature of their initial interrelations and thus for identifying initial phases of a cognitive equilibrated system. In contrast, when development is traced within a single domain, one can identify only the disequilibrating factors that guide development; that is, we only observe the lack of interrelation at the initial stages, without identifying also its stable equilibrated points.

The present chapter reviews research motivated from a systemic and interactionist framework that emphasizes the self-constructive and self-organizing aspect of children's actions in their development of cognition.[1] Preschoolers' use of spatial relations (contact and separation) to express logical relations (similarity and difference) was investigated in an open-ended, quasi-naturalistic play setting with semi-structured materials. The research addresses two issues that will be discussed in some detail here. First, the methodology that the research adopts allows for inferences about children's knowledge to be drawn based on their actions. This methodology speaks to the concern of some investigators in spatial cognition to find an experimental task that best taps children's spatial representation. Second, the research seeks to determine the form of the interrelation between logical and spatial domains of knowledge, if present, and to trace its development. For instance, at the initial stages, the interrelation between the domains of knowledge either could be undifferentiated and uncoordinated or some initial forms of differentiation and coordination could be present.

SPATIAL REPRESENTATION VERSUS SPATIAL KNOWLEDGE

Some investigators of spatial cognition have been concerned with developing experimental tasks that will best capture children's spatial knowledge, and especially, their ability for spatial representation (e.g., Downs, 1981; Downs & Siegel, 1981; Siegel, 1981). The concern centers around the fact that findings derived from many of the traditional spatial tasks (e.g., paper-and-pencil drawings, small- or large-scale reproductions of either a spatial area like a hometown, the layout of a model village, city, or of certain spatial relations among a limited number of objects) are replete with inaccuracies due to "performance" factors that prevent tapping and accessing the "true" spatial representation or cognitive map of children. One approach to the continuously elusive discrepancy between competence and performance has been to simplify the task demands and present children with tasks that they can perform readily. However, the cognitive demands of simpler tasks differ from those of more complex tasks and thus may not tap the same cognitive functions.

In attempting to provide as complete a description of children's spatial knowledge as possible, one should not attempt simply to find easier tasks, for this amounts only to "discovering" that children

---

[1] The framework presented in this chapter is similar in character with the organismic-developmental approach of Werner's theory. Instead of merely calling this approach "organismic", different terms were sought that would highlight the key assumptions that the approach makes.

have more advanced spatial knowledge than previously acknowledged. An alternative approach is to provide children with
numerous tasks that vary in difficulty such that this variation
assesses spatial knowledge in diverse situations. Ultimately this
will enable us to explain the conditions or dimensions that determine a task's ease or difficulty by mapping out precisely how
children's behavior differs under differing task conditions and dimensions. In turn, these conditions or dimensions need to be incorporated in our models of children's developing spatial knowledge to
see if they capture the general dimensions by which spatial
knowledge develops (see Newcombe, 1981, for a similar argument).

The approach adopted in the present research project was that of
taking the structural properties articulated in children's spatial constructions as an expression of their cognitive abilities. (For a similar
approach see Langer, 1980, 1986; Sugarman, 1982, 1983). Children's
spatial knowledge was inferred from the way they incorporate the
structural properties present in the materials given to them in their
spatial constructions. The materials consisted of both same and
different objects which could be placed either in contact or separation. The research addressed the question how children of various
ages express such relations (same/different, contact/separation) in
their constructions. The objective of this approach is to capture spatial knowledge in its *use*; it is not intended to tap some preformed
representation in the head of subjects. (For a similar perspective on
spatial knowledge see Cassirer, 1957; Wapner, Kaplan, & Ciottone,
1981; Werner, 1926/1948). Optimally, the study of children's uses of
space must involve many spatial behaviors, including but not limited to reproduction through various symbolic means (drawings,
small- or large-scale reproductions, etc.). Furthermore, it must
involve the way space (i.e., geometrical spatial relations) is used in
expresssing other domains of knowledge such as logic, causality, etc.
The interactions of spatial and non-spatial uses of space have rarely
been investigated.

Within this framework, one way to account for the difficulties that
young children have with certain spatial tasks has been advanced by
Piaget and Inhelder (Inhelder & Piaget, 1959/1969; Piaget &
Inhelder, 1948/1967). They claim that young children around 3 to 5
years of age do not differentiate between spatial and logical operations. This hypothesis, in turn, can explain some of the "performance" difficulties seen by some investigators. One investigator
(Siegel, 1973), for instance, claimed that scoring children's small-
scale reproduction of their classroom cannot accurately capture the
preschoolers' spatial knowledge of their classroom. He argued that

their reproductions, which often consisted of placing all of the objects together in a spatial aggregate, did not capture their "true" knowledge about space in that the children were fully capable of walking through space without bumping into the various objects.

From the perspective of *uses* of space, these two behaviors (i.e., walking and reproduction) express different types of knowledge about space. Some investigators see these as manifestations of the same underlying competence, and go so far as to say that one of them (walking) comes closer than the other to tapping the competence of the child. However, the activity of successful walking around space does not necessitate invoking a conceptual and flexible representation of spatial relations among objects and the self, but only a unidirectional relation between an object and the self. Furthermore, this unidirectional relation need not be conceptual in the strict sense of the term as it is occurring always in the presence of objects. Moreover, the observations on spatial abilities based on young children's reproductions can best be explained by the hypothesis advanced by Piaget and Inhelder: the difficulties and "errors" in reproductions of space can be seen as an expression of children's confusion between spatial and logical analyses with the task at hand. Before closely examining this hypothesis, it is necessary to define logical and spatial operations.

LOGICAL AND SPATIAL OPERATIONS

Knowledge of objects, or more generally knowledge of the world, always involves two elements: the element of the sensual given and ineffable presentation, and the element of conceptual interpretation which represents the mind's response (Lewis, 1929). A study of mental operations focuses on the conceptual interpretation of the mind. More specifically, "operations" are mental cognitive acts that create conceptual relations among the sensual given and also combine to establish a strongly structured whole. In other words, these cognitive acts derive their meaning only in relation to a virtual set of all the other cognitive acts that constitute and complete the structure. In psychological terms, an operation can be analyzed into two distinct but closely related processes: analysis (i.e., cognize parts from the whole) and synthesis (i.e., cognize the whole from the parts). In a systemic framework, a mental operation always involves both of these complementary processes, but for brevity's sake we will concentrate on analysis rather than both.

A logical operation is used to conceptually relate objects with one another according to either their similarities (which form the basis of classes or symmetrical relations) or their differences (which form the basis of series or asymmetrical relations). In other words, logical operations are expressed when children deal with discrete objects, by gathering them into classes, relating differences between them, adding or subtracting them, etc. Specifically, children carry out logical acts as a function of abstracting out certain perceptual qualities that objects possess (e.g., red beads vs. blue beads; or red beads vs. wooden beads). It is a function of these unique qualities that objects are united by classes, that classes are nested, and that, afterwards, they are added or subtracted. Furthermore, the objects are cognized as discrete such that they form discontinuous elements. This also means that a class is cognized if subjects can separate the arbitrary subclasses (i.e., red vs. blue) irrespective of the spatial arrangement in which the elements are formed. In other words, the spatiotemporal organization of the elements within a class is irrelevant. The logical relations between objects in a class are maintained regardless of their particular spatiotemporal organization. A logical operation then "deals with individual objects considered as invariant and is concerned with linking them together or interrelating them irrespective of their spatiotemporal location" (Piaget & Inhelder, 1948/1967, p. 458; see also Grize, 1964).

In contrast to logical operations, spatial operations conceptually relate objects in terms of contact (or very close proximity) and segregate them in terms of separation (distance). Spatial operations are expressed when children deal with continuous objects that they partition and then reconstruct through the use of spatial coordinates. Here, objects are either spatial figures or the empty space that the figures occupy. These spatial objects are formed by an assembly or a division of individual elements, which themselves were the "objects" of the logical operations. The point is that each analysis defines its own "object" of inquiry. Continuous spatial objects are formed either by fusing the parts of an object into a single whole or by arranging them in a specific spatial order. Thus, continuous objects are formed not as a function of certain spatial qualities that they satisfy (i.e., by uniting points, lines, planes, or other geometrical objects), but because the elements of continuous objects are contacting and coexistent (cofigural). A figure can, nevertheless, possess certain spatial abstractions (point, line, etc.) as internal properties. But the fundamental aspect of spatial analysis is the establishment of spatiotemporal continuity among the elements of this analysis, and not the abstraction of spatial properties. It is this activity that bears on the figures per se that Grize (1964) calls "intrafigural." An intrafigural analysis compares the elements of a single figure without any external spatial reference. On the other hand, interfigural analysis results in the construction of spatial coordinates. This enables the subject to partition and separate these continuous objects and also to reconstruct them. The coordination of intrafigural and interfigural analyses implies that spatial objects have certain positional relations within them, while they can also be partitioned and related within a general frame of reference which reestablishes a single spatial object at a different level of abstraction (Grize, 1964; Montangero, 1976; Piaget & Inhelder, 1948/1967).

From one perspective, expressed by Piaget and Inhelder (1948/1967, pp. 457-460) logical and spatial operations are not comparable. They hold that linking objects together to form either objects or classes of objects according to either contact or similarity entails a fundamental contradiction regarding their mode of conjunction. Linking objects together on the basis of contact results in unitary wholes whose ultimate outcome is continuity. But bringing items together on the basis of similarity results in discontinuous systems. For this reason, they hold that spatial operations are not equivalent to logical operations. This perspective, however, is based on a partial consideration of the content of each analysis in that it considers only similarity for logical operations and only contact for spatial operations and ignores their complementary constructions of difference and separation, respectively.

From another perspective logical and spatial operations are comparable if we recognize that spatial analysis deals with geometrical propositions and not with observations concerning objects in space. As Cassirer (1950) points out, not every observation of a spatial object, and not every proof bearing upon it, has the characteristics of a geometrical proposition. Nongeometrical proofs can, for example, relate to the position of an object in space or to some particular shape such as a triangle with sides of specified length. These propositions belong to a science (like topography or geography) which individualizes each point and conceives the entities of importance to this science as separate, and thus, not concerned with creating spatial relations that can encompass an increasingly number of objects and that can be ultimately extended to a general space. Only properties that are characterized by an invariance with respect to certain transformations can be called geometrical. Thus, "[geometry] is an inquiry into all those properties of a spatial figure that remain invariant throughout all the motions of space [e.g., slide, rotation, flip] and its similarity transformations [e.g., affine, projective] and through the process of reflection as well as throughout all transformations compounded of these" (Cassirer, 1950, p.31). Such invariances are independent of the position that the figure under investigation occupies in space as well as its absolute size or the specific order in which its parts are arranged. Geometries and, in our case the stages characterizing the development of spatial cognition, differ only with respect to the system of transformations upon which they are based and upon which they establish the totality of their invariant properties (Beilin, 1984; Laurendeau & Pinard, 1970; Piaget & Inhelder, 1948/1967; Weinzweig, 1978).

In essence, research on the development of spatial knowledge maps the gradual development of what is regarded by children as the "same" and "not the same" under spatial transformations. For instance, tasks that require children to produce a spatial map of their hometown (e.g., Hart, 1981; Piaget, Inhelder, & Szeminska, 1948/1960) or to judge if a spatial relation between the child and an object has been rotated or altered (e.g., Acredolo, 1976, 1977, 1978; Acredolo & Evans, 1980; Piaget & Inhelder, 1948/1967; Pick & Lockman, 1981; Pick & Rieser, 1982) assess conceptions of "same" or "different." Conversely, the present research's inquiry into logical knowledge informs an understanding of spatial cognition in that children's conceptions of "same" and "different" are studied under the transformations of contact and separation. It is important to reemphasize that in the view expounded here, spatial and logical operations differ in terms of the system of transformations by which invariances are established. More specifically, logical transformations entail perceptual dimensions, while spatial transformations entail our motions in space.

LACK OF DIFFERENTIATION
BETWEEN SPATIAL AND LOGICAL OPERATIONS

Piagetian theory has provided developmental psychology with the theoretical framework which establishes that invariances, whether logical, physical, spatial, etc., are necessary for the development of knowledge (e.g., Piaget, 1972; Piaget, 1975/1977). Equally, Piagetian theory and research has aptly and repeatedly demonstrated that the establishment of any concept or relation requires the coordination of its dichotomous components (e.g., similarity and difference if logical, or contact and separation if spatial). The theory holds, however, that the establishment of this coordination (which insures conceptual invariance) occurs only around 7 to 8 years of age (end of concrete operations) (e.g., Inhelder & Piaget, 1959/1969; Piaget, 1941/1965; Piaget, 1975/1977; Piaget & Inhelder, 1948/1967). Since each individual concept is not fully formed until this age, Piaget and

Inhelder hold that logical and spatial operations are also not independent of one another—especially between 3 and 5 years of age (preoperational period) (Inhelder & Piaget, 1959/1969; Piaget & Inhelder, 1948/1967).

Specifically, Piaget and Inhelder (1948/1967) report that when young children are asked to reproduce the diagrammatic layout of a model village, a few of the youngest ones (3 to 4 years) placed identical objects together in close proximity even though they were far apart in the model. Because these children did not reproduce the spatial separation of identical objects but instead made a logical class marked by proximity, they claim that a lack of differentiation exists between the logical operation that relates objects on the basis of similarity and the spatial operation that connects objects on the basis of proximity. However, only a few young children were tested and responses were not analyzed systematically.

Inhelder & Piaget (1959/1969) postulated a similar lack of differentiation between logical and spatial operations when explaining the character of the graphic collections stage of classificatory development. Specifically, they claimed that young children are guided by what they perceive and, thus, instead of sorting objects solely on the basis of similarity, children abandon one-dimensional linear arrangement of "same" objects in favor of placing the given objects (same and different) in two dimensions. These dimensions are graphic rather than logical. By strengthening the inclusion and making as many elements as possible belong simultaneously to an immediate whole, children tend to forget about the similarities between the elements. In contrast, when children pay attention to similarities, they tend to forget the graphic properties of the whole.

It is possible, however, that young children prior to the operational coordination of similarity and difference relations or metric contact and separation (7 or 8 years) have achieved other interrelations of the components of each of these relations. Such interrelations, however, are necessarily at a different level of abstraction. Equally children might have achieved some initial coordination of the spatial and logical domains given that children have forms of knowledge which, from a theoretical standpoint, require these interrelations. These, if found, can only be precursory to the later forms of coordination.

The research presented here reassesses the hypothesis that preschool aged children lack differentiation between logical and spatial relations (Inhelder & Piaget, 1959/1969; Piaget & Inhelder, 1948/1967). This investigation is important for two reasons. First, previously used methods have relied on verbal reports with young children who may not have been able to adequately express themselves through language. To remedy this difficulty, the present study relied on young children's actions to infer their cognitions, as they made and remade spatial constructions with particular objects that embodied a clear logical class structure. Therefore, children's conceptions of the logical relations of similarity and difference were expressed through their spatial constructions rather than what they said about "same" and "different." Second, previous investigations have emphasized only one of the components of logical (i.e., similarity) and spatial (i.e., contact/proximity) operations. At best, they have only speculated about difference and separation. In contrast, the present study focuses on both relations necessary for the development of spatial cognition (i.e., contact/proximity and separation) as well as on both of those necessary for the development of logical cognition (i.e., similarity and difference). Therefore, this fourfold analysis provides a complete and general characterization of logical and spatial cognition at 3 to 5 years of age, in addition to tracing changes in that characterization across development.

The investigation consisted of analyzing the spontaneous spatial constructions of eight children at each of three age levels (3, 4, and 5 years) playing with a set of geometrically shaped objects made out of colored cardboard. The set of materials contained four classes with four identical objects in each class. Each of the four shapes that formed the classes differed from the others in color as well, but objects of the same shape were also of the same color. This set of materials allowed constructions that consisted of either identical objects or different objects. The number of classes and objects per class were selected such that it gave children enough objects to play with and also provided equal opportunities for placing identical objects or different objects together. The children were presented with a random array of 16 objects and were asked to "make something" with them, rather than to either classify or seriate them. The number of constructions expected was not specified. The entire session was videotaped.

The systematization of children's behavior, as they engaged in making spontaneous constructions, constitutes the major phase of this research. Previous research on classification (Denney, 1972a, 1972b; Fisher & Roberts, 1980; Inhelder & Piaget, 1959/1969; Kofsky, 1966; Langford & Berrie, 1974; Pieraut-Le Bonniec, 1972) analyzed children's final products; that is, the final set of constructions that children made was examined without taking into account previous constructions that were destroyed or altered in the course of construction. Because the question posed by these investigators was whether children could classify or not, they specified which behaviors indexed successful classification using a priori criteria. Some even went as far as categorizing children's behavior into "pass" or "fail" (e.g., Fisher & Roberts, 1980; Kofsky, 1966), while others were more sensitive to children's own capabilities and indicated degrees by which children's constructions differed from "desired" final criteria (e.g., Denney, 1972a, 1972b; Inhelder & Piaget, 1959/1969). The main objective of the present study was to let children's spontaneous actions express their cognitive organizational abilities. Thus, children were allowed to behave freely in a semi-naturalistic situation. As previously noted, a fundamental assumption of this research is that children's constructions are taken to be an expression of their cognitive abilities in the same way that language itself is, *inter alia*, such an expression. Thus, this measure is independent of language at an age when children are limited in their ability to express themselves linguistically. In addition, the actions chosen for observation are typical of children's everyday repertoire, at least in Western cultures, since they often engage in making constructions with various materials during play. For these reasons, every attempt a child made, whether successful or not (from the child's point of view), was as informative as the rest. The focus then was on the ways children go about expressing logical relations through action, rather than language, as manifested in the constructions they make, the changes or corrections they make, as well as the final products of their organizational efforts.

After detailed transcripts of the videotapes were complete, spontaneous behavior was segmented into individual constructions. Both the transcription and segmentation of behavior into individual constructions were mainly based on a system developed by Langer (1980; 1986) and associates (e.g., Jacobsen, 1984; Slotnick, 1984; Sugarman, 1983). The minimal requirements for a construction were that at least two objects are brought together into contact and that the exact same spatial relation among contacting objects (e.g., next to, in, on) is maintained if the child adds more objects to the construction. Many children did not just make a single construction at one time, but they sometimes left intact an already made construction and went on to make other constructions.

Children's spontaneous spatial constructions were analyzed in two major ways. One analysis scored individual constructions defined solely by contact relation. The second analysis scored multiple, spatiotemporally coexistent constructions defined by contact within the objects of individual constructions and separation between constructions. A summary of the coding scheme follows, but for further details see Nicolopoulou (1984).

I. Contact relations. Contact relations define a construction by requiring that a series of objects be spatially arranged so that there is a path that passes from any object to any other object of the construction by traversing only contacting objects and not empty space. In this analysis, all spatial constructions that each child made were scored irrespective of what finally happened with each specific construction. For example, some constructions were destroyed after they were made; others were remade using the same objects; and others were left intact while children went on to make more constructions with other objects. Constructions defined through a contact relation could have different logical properties: they could be by similarities, differences, or no logical pattern.

(a) Similarity. A construction was by similarity when all its contacting points among objects were by similarities. In other words, children used a single logical criterion when making these constructions. For this reason, they were called *uniformity* constructions to emphasize the uniform logical criterion among the objects in a single construction. It should also be noted that similarity in this task entailed identical objects (Figure 10.1).

(b) Difference. A construction was by differences when children alternated logical criteria in making the construction as long as the alternation was arranged such that the objects showed some spatial regularity. For this reason, constructions by differences were called constructions by *alternations*. In fact, we accepted any construction conforming to the above criterion, whether the classes involved in the alternation were presented by an equal (complete alternation; see Figure 10.2) or by an unequal number of objects (Incomplete alternation; see Figure 10.3).

(c) No pattern. There was no apparent logical pattern observed in these constructions (Figure 10.4).

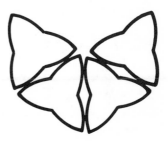

Figure 10.1. Similarity (uniformity).

   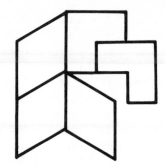

Figure 10.2. Difference (complete alternation).   **Figure 10.3.** Difference (incomplete alternation).

The criteria for similarity and difference relations were defined such that they took account of all possible differences in the strategies available to the child in generating the two types of relations. Specifically, while we adopted the strict criterion of similarity—all same contacting objects—we did not adopt the strict criterion of difference—all different contacting objects—because the kinds of strategies the child must employ to reach each of these criteria are not equivalent. Children can successfully generate constructions by similarity that exhaust all objects by relying on a simple matching strategy that relates an object to its next one and thus simply reflects local pairwise criteria. That is, children generate similarity relations by matching a red square to another red square, etc., without having the concept of either "red" color as it contrasts with

Figure 10.4. No pattern.

other colors, or the concept "shape" as it contrasts with other shapes (see Brown & Bellugi, 1964, for a similar argument). In contrast, a similar local matching strategy (e.g., pairs of different objects) would not ensure constructions by differences (defined by the strict criterion) that can exhaust all given objects. Because more than two classes were present in the array and each class was represented by several objects, children must adopt a rather sophisticated strategy that not only relates an object to its next one (local level) but also classes of objects (global level). For instance, children can include only one object from each class and cannot return to that class until all other classes are equally represented in the construction. Or they restrict themselves in including the same two classes, at first, and only later include the two other classes. Although this strategy might appear to be pairwise, it also reflects that the children are consistent in excluding the same two classes. That is, to avoid making mistakes, they cannot randomly start shifting between any two classes without taking into account how many classes and how many objects have not yet been included. These requirements demonstrate that the strict criterion for difference constructions does not simply reflect local but also global criteria. For this reason, this criterion was relaxed so that it could be equivalent to the simple pairwise strategy used for constructions by similarity.

II. Contact and Separation. These spatial relations define multiple spatiotemporally coexisting constructions as follows: (a) there is contact of the objects within a construction, and (b) there is separation (spatial distance) between constructions. This analysis includes all the constructions that children made while they went on to make new constructions and left others intact on the table. These two spatial relations might appear to not be independent of one another in that a construction that was scored as an individual construction can also be scored in multiple constructions if it meets the requisite criterion. However, the emphasis of each analysis is at different levels: individual constructions are analyzed at a local level, while multiple constructions are analyzed at a global level. This difference is also reflected in the shift of terminology from similarity/difference to equivalence/nonequivalence.

Constructions defined spatially through contact and separation could have different logical properties; they could be by equivalences, or nonequivalences.

(a) Equivalences. A set of constructions were by equivalences when two criteria were met: First, there is consistency in their logical cri-

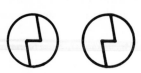

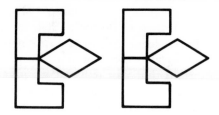

Figure 10.5. Equivalence by similarities (exact replication of uniform construction).

Figure 10.6. Equivalence by differences (exact replication of alternation).

terion across constructions; that is, children repeat the same logical criterion of either uniformity or alternation. And, second, the children also replicate the exact spatial arrangement within objects. Thus, equivalence can be achieved by (i) the exact replication of uniform constructions (Figure 10.5), and (ii) the exact replication of alternation constructions (Figure 10.6).

(b) Nonequivalences—All. A set of constructions were by nonequivalences when one or both of the above criteria were not met across *all* constructions, thus resulting in degrees of nonequivalence. **(b1) Weak criterion**: Children repeat only the same logical criterion but not the exact spatial arrangement of objects across constructions. For example, constructions were all-by-uniformity (Figure 10.7), or they were all-by-alternation (Figure 10.8). **(b2) Strong criterion**: There is even lack of repetition of the same logical relation across constructions. For example, a set of constructions were by uniformity + alternation, when about half of the constructions were by uniformities and the rest by alternations (Figure 10.9); or some were by uniformities and the rest by no-patterns.

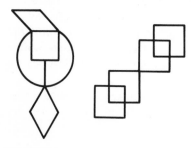

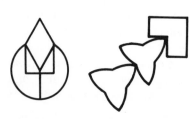

Figure 10.7. Nonequivalence by similarities (all-by-uniformity).

Figure 10.8. Nonequivalence by differences (all-by-alternation).

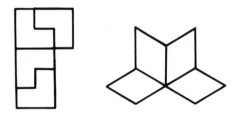

Figure 10.9. Nonequivalence by differences (uniformity-and-alternation).

(c) Nonequivalences—Some. For this set of constructions the above logical and spatial criteria were met among *some* of the constructions, but not among all of them. For example, the repetition of the same logical criterion and the exact same spatial arrangement of objects within constructions were observed between two of the constructions but not among all of them. Depending upon the logical relation holding between the replica constructions and the rest, these multiple constructions were also generated by either weak or stong criteria. **(c1) Weak criterion**: the same logical criterion was repeated between replicas and the rest (e.g., replicas and the rest were by similarity). **(c2) Strong criterion**: there was a shifting of the logical criterion between replicas and the rest (e.g., replicas were by alternation and the rest of constructions by uniformity).

THE INTERRELATION OF SPATIAL AND LOGICAL OPERATIONS

Comparing the results of the two analyses (a) individual constructions and (b) multiple, coexistent constructions, it was found that when we focus on the contact relation between objects that form individual constructions, three-year-olds made most of these constructions by uniformities (70%) (see Table 10.1). Thus, contact relation at this age group marks similarity (i.e, similarity from all points of view in this task). On the other hand, when we also consider spatial separation as manifested in coexistent constructions, most of these

Table 10.1
Mean Percentages of Logical Categories in Single Constructions

		Logical Categories		
Age	Uniformity	Complete Alternation	Incomplete Alternation	No Pattern
3	69.50	15.38	8.75	6.50
n = 8	(140)*	(25)	(11)	(17)
4	45.88	8.63	25.50	20.13
n = 8	(108)	(21)	(84)	(9)
5	49.75	12.25	38.25	—
n = 8	(153)	(24)	(91)	

* Numbers in parentheses indicate the number of constructions.

constructions were by a relation of nonequivalence (see Table 10.2).[2] Nonequivalence, however, was expressed mainly by weak criteria of all-nonequivalence constructions (49%), and all of these constructions were all-by-uniformity. Thus, at age three, while contact marks similarity, separation marks nonequivalence.

At age four, individual constructions were about equally likely to be by uniformity (46%) and by alternation (34%). Thus, a contact relation comes to mark both similarity and difference relations.

Table 10.2
Mean Percentages of Logical Categories in Multiple Constructions

Age (years)	Equivalences All	Nonequivalences			
		Some		All	
		Weak	Strong	Weak	Strong
3	9	12	6	49	24
n = 6	(13)*	(23)	(8)	(39)	(38)
4	10	23	—	34	33
n = 5	(15)	(26)		(48)	(42)
5	3		4	25	69
n = 7	(5)		(13)	(54)	(82)

* Numbers in parentheses indicate the number of constructions.

---

[2] This shift in terminology from similarity or difference relations to equivalence or nonequivalence indicates that the criteria are second order. The question is whether a specific relation (similarity or difference) is consistent or not over time and space.

Most multiple coexistent constructions continue to express none-quivalence. This nonequivalence is expressed equally by weak and strong criteria for nonequivalences—all (34% and 33%, respectively) as well as by weak criteria for nonequivalences—some constructions.

At age five, individual constructions continue to be equally marked by uniformity (50%) and by alternation (50%). Thus, a contact relation continues to mark both similarity and difference relations. Coexistent constructions still marked nonequivalence and this relation was basically expressed through constructions that half were by uniformity and the rest by alternation. Thus, separation still marks nonequivalence but five-year-olds come to express this relation basically through a strong form that marks both spatial and logical differences.

In sum, logical similarity and difference relations and spatial contact/proximity and separation relations interact and inform one another (see Langer, 1985, and Piaget, 1971/1974 for similar developmental models applied to different domains). At three years of age, spatial and logical operations are detached from each other in that similarity is uniquely marked by contact and difference (here nonequivalence) by separation. This detachment, however, is still only minimal because neither is similarity differentiated from contact nor nonequivalence from separation. The developmental progression observed is for the contact relation to become detached from its singular logical expression and, thus, to begin to mark both similarity and difference relations. On the other hand, there seems to be no developmental progression with the spatial relation of separation because it mainly expresses nonequivalence. There is, however, an internal shift from generating nonequivalences by weak criteria at 3 years to generating them by strong criteria at 5 years. Thus, 5-year-olds mainly generate coexistent constructions that besides being unrelated in spatial terms, they are also unrelated in logical terms; that is, some constructions are by uniformity and some by alternation. Children, then, shift logical criteria of similarity and difference in making such coexistent constructions. It is these constructions with their internal contradiction (i.e., relating them spatially by leaving them unrelated logically) that we hypothesize will be the impetus for the next developmental progression. Specifically, the developmental change will be that separation comes to mark a relation of equivalence. Only then can we say that logical and spatial operations are totally differentiated and coordinated with one another.

In conclusion, these results do not support a strong version of the lack of differentiation hypothesis between logical and spatial operations around 3 to 5 years of age. The strong interpretation of this hypothesis as expressed by Piaget and Inhelder (Inhelder & Piaget, 1959/1969; Piaget & Inhelder, 1948/1967) implies that children, during a task or activity, shift sometimes to a logical analysis (i.e., similarities and differences) and at others to a spatial analysis (i.e., contact and separation). In contrast, the present results demonstrate that preschoolers' logical relations are tied to specific spatial expressions as early as three years. By this young age, a structural restriction is evident in children's cognitive system; namely, at first, similarity is expressed by contact and difference by separation (see Nicolopoulou, 1984, for further support of this claim). Therefore, an initial coordination is apparent between logical and spatial operations. However, this coordination between domains is only minimal and there is still some lack of differentiation within logical relations and within spatial relations. This is evident from the fact that the spatial relation of contact expresses only similarity and not the difference relation; equally, the logical relation of difference is only expressed by separation and not additionally by contact. The developmental progression is characterized by a gradual shift toward freeing logic from its one-way spatial expression; that is, to a further differentiation and coordination of the operations of the domains of knowledge under consideration.

The initial coordination between logical and spatial domains became apparent when we allowed children's organizational abilities to structure the open-ended task at hand. Observing children's constructions, it became evident that we could not capture the richness of their behavior unless we included both a spatial and logical analysis. For each of the analyses, we included each of its logically inversely related component (i.e., similarity and difference as well as contact and separation). These concerns were motivated by a theoretical framework whereby development must be described as a multistructured and recursive model rather than a linear model (see Langer, 1986, in press, for further discussions of this distinction). A linear model of development does not emphasize a system from the beginning but assumes that one of the logically inversely related components leads in development and the other follows until both become reciprocally or inversely related (i.e., coordinated) at the next level of development. Similarly, when dealing between domains of knowledge, the linear model assumes that they are undifferentiated and uncoordinated. In contrast, a multistructured and recursive model emphasizes a systemic whole as its unit of analysis and accepts that linear sequences might be limited to development within specific domains. Further, if we look at a larger cross section of children's cognition that allows for possible interrelations between domains, we can see expressions of both of the logically inversely related components.

It is apparent, then, that the evidence we have provided must be incorporated into our understanding of children's development of both spatial and logical cognition. On the one hand, the interpretation offered above serves as a parsimonious alternative explanation of the dualistic conceptual organization of "collections" and taxonomies offered by Carbonnel (1978) and by Markman and associates (e.g., Markman, 1981, 1983; Markman, Horton, & McLanahan, 1980; Markman & Seibert, 1976). For Carbonnel, collections emphasize mainly a spatial component. For Markman, they are part-whole relations and include a spatial component plus some other characteristics that result in providing collections with greater psychological cohesion than classes. Both investigators found that young children's logical inferences were enhanced when the problems in question were presented to them in terms of collections rather than classes. Based on this evidence, they hypothesized two principles of conceptual organization: one informed by taxonomic relations (logic) and the other by collections (some linear relational organization reflected in spatial relations). The results presented here offer evidence against the hypothesis that these two principles of conceptual organization are distinct at the origins since neither one is independent of the other during the period under consideration. In fact, logical relations are tied to specific spatial relations and development entails a gradual detachment of the logical relations from their specific spatial expressions. It should be noted, however, that these results should not be interpreted to mean that spatial relations are the only expressions that logical relations can take at the ages studied. Rather, the point is that logical relations are tied to specific relations of some expressive medium (here space) and only gradually detach themselves from it and become flexible. (See Stiles-Davis, this volume, for how children express similarity relations when spatial relations are hindered.)

On the other hand, the perspective adopted in the present research can generate useful hypotheses when we analyze children's spatial reproductions. For instance, they allow us to score not only "accuracy" when children reproduce a spatial relation or a set of them, but provide us with useful insights to explain children's "erroneous" behavior. More importantly, the results generated from this type of research can provide a rich background against which we can interpret the findings of restricted experimental situations where most ecological constraints have been removed. The guiding principle of the approach outlined here is to let practical spatio-temporal action of *situated subjects* guide our investigation. The inferences we can draw from these activities are directed to the description of children's knowledge manifested in interactions with the world around them. There is no denial of internalization of thought (see Furth, 1969; Wertsch & Stone, 1985) or of the ability to represent space in thinking, or, even, the possible usefulness of mechanistic metaphors like information-processing models that attempt to be precise and explicit about the various components or features necessary for the specification of the character of mental representations. One objection, however, is that these mechanistic models emphasize and are precise about a static and rigidified moment of the interaction of subjects with the world and, thus, cannot generate the relevant dynamical relational concepts that equally encompass both poles of the interaction, a concern fundamental to a developmental perspective. In contrast, the systemic and interactionist approach advocated here encompasses both aspects of the interaction, inferring knowledge from the practical actions of situated subjects.

ACKNOWLEDGMENTS

Preparation of this chapter was supported in part by a National Research Service Award from NICHD postdoctoral fellowship (5T32HD07196) to the author at the Graduate Center of the City University of New York. I would like to thank Joe Becker, Richard Beckwith, Harry Beilin, Julie Gee, Virginia Marchman, Sylvia Scribner, Joan Stiles-Davis, Susan Sugarman, and especially Jonas Langer for helpful comments on earlier versions of this chapter.

REFERENCES

Acredolo, L. P. 1976. Frames of reference used by children for orientation in unfamiliar spaces. In G. Moore & R. Golledge (Eds.). *Environmental knowing*. Stroudsburg, Pennsylvania: Dowden, Hutchinson, & Ross.

Acredolo, L. P. 1977. Developmental changes in the ability to coordinate perspectives of a large-scale space. *Developmental Psychology*. 13:1-8.

Acredolo, L. P. 1978. Development of spatial orientation in infancy. *Developmental Psychology*. 14:224-234.

Acredolo, L. P. & Evans, D. 1980. Developmental changes in the effects of landmarks on infant spatial behavior. *Developmental Psychology*. 16:312-318.

Beilin, H. 1984. Cognitive theory and mathematical cognition: Geometry and space. In B. Gholson & T. Rosenthal (Eds.), *Applications of cognitive-developmental theory.* (pp.49-93). New York: Academic Press.

Brown, R. W., & Bellugi, U. 1964. Three processes in the child's acquisition of syntax. *Harvard Educational Review.* 34:133-151.

Carbonnel, S. 1978. Classes collective et classes logiques dans la pensee naturelle. *Archives de Psychologie, XXVI,* 177:1-19.

Cassirer, E. 1950. *The problem of knowledge: philosophy, science, and history since Hegel.* New Haven: Yale University Press.

Cassirer, E. 1957. *The philosophy of symbolic forms. Volume 3: The phenomenology of knowledge.* New Haven: Yale University Press.

Denney, N. W. 1972a. A developmental study of free classification in children. *Child Development.* 43:221-232.

Denney, N. W. 1972b. Free classification in preschool children. *Child Development.* 43:1161-1170.

Downs, R. M. 1981. Maps and mappings as metaphors for spatial representation. In L. S. Liben, A. H. Patterson, & N. Newcombe (Eds.), *Spatial representation and behavior across the life span: Theory and application.* 143-166. New York: Academic Press.

Downs, R. M. & Siegel, A. W. 1981. On mapping researchers mapping children mapping space. In L. S. Liben, A. H. Patterson, & N. Newcombe (Eds.), *Spatial representation and behavior across the life span: Theory and Application.* 237-248. New York: Academic Press.

Fisher, K. W. & Roberts, R. J. 1980. A developmental sequence of classification skills in preschool children. Manuscript submitted for publication.

Furth, H. G. 1969. *Piaget and knowledge: Theoretical foundations.* New Jersey: Prentice Hall.

Glick, J. A. 1983. Piaget, Vygotsky, and Werner. In S. Wapner and B. Kaplan (Eds.), *Toward a holistic developmental psychology.* 35-52. New Jersey: Lawrence Erlbaum Associates.

Grize, J. B. 1964. Remarques sur la structure de la geometrie elementaire. In V. Bang, P. Greco, J. B. Grize, V. Hatwell, J. Piaget, G. N. Seagrim et E. Vurpillot (Eds.), *Etudes d'epistemologie genetique: XVIII L'epistemologie de l'espace.* 41-92. Paris: Presses Universitaires de France.

Hart, R. A. 1981. Children's spatial representation of the landscape: Lessons and questions from a field study in L. S. Liben, A. H. Patterson, & N. Newcombe (Eds.), *Spatial representation and behavior across the life span: Theory and application.* 195-233. New York: Academic Press.

Inhelder, B. & Piaget, J. 1969. *The growth of logic in the child.* New York: The Norton Library (Original French edition published in 1959).

Kofsky, E. 1966. A scalogram study of classificatory development. *Child Development.* 37:191-204.

Jacobsen, T. A. 1984. The construction and regulation of early structures of logic: A cross-cultural study of infant cognitive development in rural Peru. Unpublished dissertation, University of California, Berkeley.

Langer, J. In press. A note on the comparative psychology of mental development. In S. Straus (Ed.) *Ontogeny and history.* Norwood, N.J.: Ablex Press.

Langer, J. 1986. *The origins of logic: One to two years.* New York: Academic Press.

Langer, J. 1985. Necessity and possibility during infancy. *Archives de Psychologie, 53,* 61-75.

Langer, J. 1980. *The origins of logic: six to twelve months.* New York: Academic Press.

Langer, J. 1969. *Theories of development.* New York: Holt, Rinehart & Winston.

Langford, P. E. & Berrie, N. 1974. Stage in the development of classification concepts. *Archives de Psychologie.* 42:459-472.

Laurendeau, M. & Pinard, A. 1970. *The development of the concept of space in the child.* New York: International Universities Press.

Lewis, C. I. 1929. *Mind and the world order: Outline of a theory of knowledge.* New York: Dover Publications.

Markman, E. 1983. Two difference kinds of hierarchical organization. In E. K. Scholnick (Ed.), *New trends in conceptual representation: Challenges to Piaget's theory?* 165-184. Hillsdale, New Jersey: Lawrence Erlbaum Associates.

Markman, E. 1981. Two principles of conceptual organization. In M. E. Lamb & A. L. Brown (Eds.), *Advances in developmental psychology.* Hillsdale, New Jersey: Lawrence Erlbaum Associates.

Markman, E. M., Horton, M. S., & McLanahan, A. G. 1980. Classes and collections: Principles of organization in the learning of hierarchical relations. *Cognition.* 8:227-241.

Markman, E. M. & Seibert, J. 1976. Classes and collections: Internal organization and resulting holistic properties. *Cognitive Psychology.* 8:561-577.

Montangero, J. 1976. Recent research on the child's conception of space and geometry in Geneva: Research work on spatial concepts of the International Center for Genetic Epistemology. *Space and geometry.* 99-128. Columbus, Ohio: ERIC Center for Science, Mathematics & Environmental Education.

Newcombe, N. 1981. Spatial representation and behavior: Retrospect and Prospect. In L. S. Liben, A. H. Patterson, & N. Newcombe (eds.), *Spatial representation and behavior across the life span: Theory and application.* 373-388. New York: Academic Press.

Nicolopoulou, A. 1984. Young children's development of similarity and difference relations and their implications for the origins of negation. Ph.D. dissertation. University of California, Berkeley.

Piaget, J. 1980. *Etudes d'epistemologie genetique: Vol 37. Recherches sur les correspondances.* Paris: Presses Universitaires de France.

Piaget, J. 1977. *The development of thought: Equilibration of cognitive structures.* New York: Viking Penguin Inc. (Original French edition published in 1975).

Piaget, J. 1974. *Understanding causality.* New York: The Norton Library. (Original French edition published in 1971).

Piaget, J. 1972. *Essai de logique operatoire* 2eme edition du *Traite de logique, essai de logistique operatoire.* Etablie par J. B. Grize, Paris: Dunod (coll. "Sciences du Comportement").

Piaget, J. 1965. *The child's conception of number.* New York: The Norton Library. (Original French edition published in 1941).

Piaget, J. Inhelder, B. 1967. *The child's conception of space.* New York: The Norton Library. (Original French edition published in 1948).

Piaget, J. Inhelder, B., & Szeminska, A. 1960. *The child's conception of geometry.* New York: Harper & Row Publishers, Inc. (Original French edition published in 1948).

Pick, H. L., Jr. & Lockman, J. J. 1981. From frames of references to spatial representations. In L. S. Liben, A. H. Patterson, & N. Newcombe (Eds.), *Spatial representation and behavior across the life span: Theory and application.* 237-248. New York: Academic Press.

Pick, H. L., Jr. & Rieser, J. J. 1982. Children's cognitive mapping. In M. Potegal (ed.). *Spatial abilities: Development and physiological foundations.* 107-128. New York: Academic Press.

Pieraut-Le Bonniec, G. 1972. Recherche sur l'evolution genetique des operations de classification. *Archives de Psychologie.* 41:89-117.

Siegel, A. W. 1981. The externalization of cognitive maps by children and adults: In search of ways to ask better questions. In L. S. Liben, A. H. Paterson, & N. Newcombe (Eds.), *Spatial representation and behavior across the life span: Theory and application.* 167-194. New York: Academic Press.

Slotnick, C. F. 1984. The organization and regulation of block constructions: A comparison of autistic and normal children's cognitive development. Unpublished dissertation, University of California, Berkeley.

Sugarman, S. 1983. *Children's early thought. Developments in classification.* Cambridge: Cambridge University Press.

Sugarman, S. 1982. Developmental change in early representational intelligence: Evidence from spatial classification strategies and related verbal expression. *Cognitive Psychology.* 14:410-449.

Turiel, E. 1983. *The development of social knowledge: Morality and convention.* Cambridge: Cambridge University Press.

Turiel, E. & Davidson, P. 1985. Heterogeneity, inconsistency, and asynchrony in the development of cognitive structures. In A. Levine (Ed.) *Stages and structure.* Norwood, N.J.: Ablex Press.

Wapner, S., Kaplan, B., & Ciottone, R. 1981. Self-world relationships in critical environmental transitions: Childhood and beyond. In L. S. Liben, A. H. Patterson, & N. Newcombe (Eds.), *Spatial representation and behavior across the life span: Theory and application.* 251-282. New York. Academic Press.

Weinzweig, A. I. 1978. Mathematical foundations for the development of spatial concepts for children. *Recent research concerning the development of spatial and geometric concepts.* 105-176. Columbus, Ohio: ERIC Center for Science, Mathematics & Environmental Education.

Werner, H. 1948. *Comparative psychology of mental development.* New York: International University Press, Inc. (Original German edition published in 1926).

Wertsch, J. V. & Stone, C. A. 1985. The concept of internalization in Vygotsky's account of the genesis of higher mental functions. In J. V. Wertsch (Ed.) *Culture, communication, and cognition: Vygotskian perspectives.* 162-179. Cambridge: Cambridge University Press.

DRAWING THE BOUNDARY: THE DEVELOPMENT OF DISTINCT SYSTEMS FOR SPATIAL REPRESENTATION IN YOUNG CHILDREN

11

DENNIS WOLF
Harvard University

INTRODUCTION: KINDS OF SPATIAL REPRESENTATION

In her book about a severely autistic child, Nadia, Lorna Selfe includes two facts that should startle anyone interested in questions of spatial representation: At five, Nadia drew like a gifted young adult, turning out complex scenes of galloping horsemen—however, she could not perform simple sorting tasks in which she had to place similar items in the same location (Selfe, 1977). This pair of facts highlights how many different, and potentially independent, aspects there are to human spatial cognition: motoric plans and performances (such as knowing how to grasp the pencil and move it along the paper surface); conscious operations (like sorting), and knowledge of conventional symbol systems skills like drawing (Liben, 1981).

Since Thurstone's (1938) pioneering efforts to isolate different spatial abilities, psychologists have been trying to analyze the broad notion of spatial cognition into its component parts. Through careful task design and testing, a number of investigators have come to the conclusion that humans possess at least several independent types of spatial representational skills such as: (1) the ability to visualize spatial transformations (e.g., inversions, rotations, etc.) and (2) the ability to understand relative orientations among parts or landmarks (Fleishman & Dusek, 1971; McGee, 1979).

But the area in which the analysis of spatial skills has progressed most rapidly is probably that of neuropsychology. Based on work with both normal and special populations, researchers have developed an increasingly fine picture of the independent elements or strands within spatial representation. For example, work with brain-damaged patients suggests that we may have separate spatial abilities to deal with overall forms and details. Patients suffering insult to the right hemisphere have difficulty drawing the overall gestalt of a three-dimensional model, while they can often reproduce the separate details or features that characterize an object or scene. By comparison, left hemisphere patients may reproduce the overall form, yet struggle and fail to capture the details of a model (Gardner, 1983). Research on children who are acquiring American Sign Language (ASL) indicates that distinct types of spatial representation may support referential abilities in different modalities. While these children show no impairment in their ability to navigate large spaces or produce drawings, they do not learn how to use selected aspects of the spatialized reference system of ASL easily (Loew, 1984).

Findings such as these leave little doubt about the differentiated way in which spatial information is stored and processed (Kritchevsky, this volume; Neville, this volume). But neuroanatomy describes only one kind of patterning of spatial abilities. Atop our biologically given variety of spatial skills we impose what might be called a *semiotic* variety. Following a trip through a neighborhood, we can create a landscape drawing, a scale model, an aerial map, a route map or a diagram of crowded and deserted areas. In other words, as human beings, we have the option of encoding our experience in any one of a number of different symbol systems. In contrast to the brain-based differentiation of spatial abilities, this semiotic variety of spatial skills is a by-product of considerable social and cultural learning.

Figure 11.1A and 11.1B illustrate how, as late as their third year, children use similar, rather than differentiated systems for depicting the features and locations of parts within a larger whole, independent of whether they are given markers and paper or building blocks. In both her block model and her drawing of a house, this child simply accords a block or a mark for each item she wishes to represent in a way that records rough location and number but nothing about external contour or volume. In other words, her drawing lacks the distinctive two-dimensional, or graphic, strategies for representing a volume with space around it. At the same time, her block construction is only uni-dimensional (a pile of items) rather than a fully three-dimensional construction.

However, by the age of 5, children learn to distinguish between the two systems of spatial representation. In Figure 11.2A, a 5-

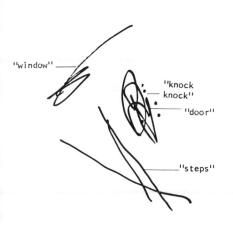

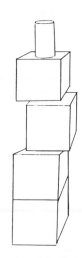

Figure 11.1A.   A drawing without distinctive
two-dimensional characteristics.

Figure 11.1B.   A model without distinctive
three-dimensional characteristics.

year-old selectively uses two-dimensional or pictorial strategies to
depict the volume of a house. She uses a contour line to distinguish
the "figure" of the house from the surrounding "ground" of the
paper and depicts the several facets of volume in left-to-right
arrangement on the page. In Figure 11.2B, another 5 year-old constructs the volume of a house: making use of a central cavity and

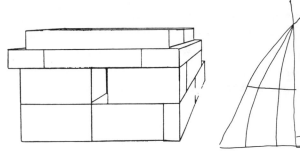

Figure 11.2A.   A drawing with two-dimensional
characteristics.

Figure 11.2B.   A model with three-dimensional
characteristics.

construction along three axes to portray the shape of the form in space. It is this development of a responsiveness to the demands of different systems of spatial representation, such as drawing and construction, that is the focus of this chapter.

The chapter is based on observations of spontaneous building and drawing in children between the ages of 1 and 5. Using these observations, I will first describe the development of a constructional, or three-dimensional system for representing information about volumes in space. Second, I will summarize major points in the evolution of a graphic, or two-dimensional system for representing volumes. By comparing the major steps in the representation of dimensionality within these two systems, I will argue that between the ages of one and five years children gradually construct the distinctive rules of at least these two systems of spatial representation.

The data reviewed in this paper come from a longitudinal study of 9 middle-class children (3 M, 6 F) who were the subjects in an intensive study of early symbolic development. Between the ages of 1 and 3 the children were visited weekly in their homes; between the ages of 3 and 7, they were seen twice a month. During these visits observers watched as children engaged in free play, elicited their responses to open-ended tasks ("Draw a house." "Build a house.") and asked them to participate in more structured tasks (e.g., copying models, completing figures, etc.) (Shotwell, Wolf & Gardner, 1980).

THE EVOLUTION OF THREE-DIMENSIONAL SYMBOLIZATION

Based on our observations, it appears that the process of translating blocks from a physical material into a symbolic medium carrying particular rules may take place in several phases: the making of small-scale models, uni-dimensional, planar, and volumetric representations. (Except where noted, this sequence of acquisitions was observed in all nine longitudinal subjects. The mean age at which each strategy appeared is indicated in parentheses.)

Small-scale Models: (Mean Age of Acquisition: 1;5 years)

Within the compass of the first year, children begin to give significance to particular positions and places. For example, in order to start a clapping game, a child may pull his mother's hands into what he knows is the starting position for that game. Children can search for objects in their customary places: pointing to the refrigerator where milk may be stored or straining toward a bureau top where a favorite blanket is usually kept. In fact, the meanings associated with particular locations may be so well learned as to become an obstacle. At least one interpretation of the infant's perseveration in searching for an object at its original hiding place, even when it has been visibly displaced, is that the original site comes to have the "meaning" of the place where things are found (Freeman, 1980).

Space becomes a modality for encoding still more explicit and complex forms of knowledge during the second year. For instance, Riccuiti (1965), Sugarman (1983), and Stiles-Davis (this volume) have demonstrated the manner in which young children's serial touching and spatial groupings of objects reflect early forms of categorical knowledge. Perhaps more germane to our concerns with spatially rendered representation of *spatial* knowledge is the fact that during the second year, children begin to act on and combine objects in both large- and small-scale re-duplications of actual spatial relationships (Jackowitz & Watson, 1980; Winner, 1979). Thus, a child may turn a stool into an oven, treating the top surface as if it had burners and using the open space between the legs like an oven. On a smaller scale, a shell on top of another object can be a cat on top of a wall or an upright puzzle piece pushed across the surface of the table can be labeled: "boat."

This kind of object-based metaphor-making transfers easily to the palpable world of blocks: a long flat block is a "road," the same rectangle held upright can be a "house." But the fact that each and every block already has height, width, and depth gives the child a too-convenient way of representing volumes in space. Whereas the challenge of drawing is to use the two-dimensional paper plane to represent the depth and volumes of the spatial world, the challenge in blocks is to stop using just the volume of individual blocks in favor of learning to construct larger volumes from many blocks.

Uni-dimensional Representations of Three-dimensional Information: (Mean Age of Acquisition: 2;0 years)

At the outset of their third year, children begin to combine several blocks into stable structures. The forms that occur are, at most, linear. Typically, in linear forms, only two facets of a block are matched and the remaining surfaces figure directly in the shape and outline of the structure. Thus, even in linear structures, individual elements are prominent in the profile of the final structure. The child achieves a sense of volume or mass only accidentally — because the blocks themselves happen to have bulk. If asked to build a house at this time, a child is likely to produce a stack in which each additional block stands for a single feature ("door," "kitchen," "my room," etc.).

Two-dimensional Representations of Three-dimensional Information: (Mean Age of Acquisition: 3;4 years)

In the course of building different types of towers and lines, children eventually discover the possibility of creating an overall shape from block elements. For example, in building a tower an unevenly placed or smaller topmost block can be read as "roof" or "chimney." Thus, children begin to "overlook" the boundaries between individual blocks, building extended horizontal lay-outs or vertical facades in which individual blocks contribute to the overall shape without contributing to the outline of the structure. Thus, they begin to depict the surface or the extent of forms. Asked to build a house, one child, aged 2;6 produced the planar layout of his "room" shown in Figure 11.3. As detailed as the construction is, child does not place blocks in such a way that more than four of the six available facets are joined. The result is still, therefore, fundamentally a two-dimensional representation of what is, in fact, a three-dimensional form.

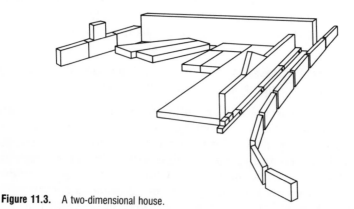

Figure 11.3. A two-dimensional house.

Three-dimensional Representation:
(Mean Age of Acquisition: 4;0 years)

About the age of 4 years, children pass three milestones in being able to construct fully three-dimensional representations of forms. First, children build along all three possible axes. Second, in order to build in three-dimensions, children position at least some individual blocks so that many, and occasionally all, of their facets are joined to other blocks. In this way, children can build the interior bulk of a form, not just its outside surfaces. Finally, children begin to construct enclosed vacant spaces. Such interior spaces are analogous to the interior blocks in volumetric building: they contribute to the form of the whole without figuring in the external surface of the structure. A house built by a child with these skills begins to approximate what we think of as a genuinely three-dimensional model of a volume in space.

Thus, between one and four, children gradually develop at least an implicit set of rules for what is involved in making a three-dimensional model of a form in space. While the longitudinal data presented here reflect only the development of nine subjects, quite similar sequences of constructional development have been observed in much larger and more diverse populations (Gesell, 1925; Guanella, 1934; Reifel, 1984).

THE DEVELOPMENT OF TWO-DIMENSIONAL REPRESENTATIONS OF SPACE

Across any number of years and theories, it has been assumed that graphic representation occurs in children's drawings with the onset

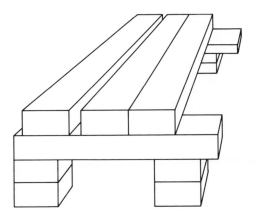

Figure 11.4. A volumetric house.

of their ability to produce simple look-alike forms or what might be called "pictures": a rough circle enclosing a few dots can stand for a face; an oblong atop two small circles can be used to represent a car or truck. In other words, we do not usually accord representational status to children's marks until they produce forms that encode the relative sizes, spatial locations, and shapes of objects in ways that echo the conventions of Western pictorial drawing. Given the amount of eye-hand coordination and planning required for even simple look-alike drawings of this kind, it has long been observed that children under the age of three make only what Burt called "purposeless pencillings" and what others have labeled "scribbles" or "sensory-motor explorations."

This description of early drawing is suspect on a number of grounds:

1. Between the ages of one and three years, children exhibit a "rampant" exploration of symbolization. During these two years normal children construct not only the basic rules for both linguistic and symbolic play forms of reference, they develop both gestural and constructional representations (such as the early block structures just described).

2. There is strong evidence that children between one and three "read" graphic representations with a fair degree of sophistication. While they may not be able to interpret information about perspective and diminishing size, young children are able to make sense of highly stylized line drawings of the kind that they might produce themselves (Wolf & Gardner, 1980).

3. Moreover, as mentioned earlier, data on early metaphor and symbolic play suggest that children can "discover" meaning in quite a wide range of visual patterns which were in no way specifically tailored to picture information. Thus a two-year old can bite into a cookie, produce a crescent, hold it up and call it "moon" (Jackowitz & Watson 1980; Winner, 1979). It requires a highly specific and focused concept of symbolization to imagine that children exhibiting this range of representational productions and perceptions treat their own marks only as scratches, traces, or scribbles.

Consequently, in analyzing the drawings of the children we followed, we looked for evidence of *any* kind of representational behaviors associated with the drawing process. Thus, beyond watching for the usual look-alike forms, we indexed the use of drawing tools or gestures in symbolic play; verbal labeling of the tools, paper, or marks; any systematic way of encoding visual-spatial information into spatial or graphic patterns.

Representations Based on Position or Motion: (Mean Age of Acquisition: 1;8 years)

As a result of broadening the definition of early graphic representation, we observed a number of types of pre-picturing strategies for encoding visual-spatial information. In the middle of the second year, roughly co-temporous with the onset of simple language and symbolic play abilities, children begin to handle the marker and paper precisely as they handle other objects in the course of short episodes of symbolic play. Thus, while the child uses the tool and marking surface to represent some other referent, there is nothing especially *graphic* about this type of spatial representation. For example, a child may make a mark, scrub over it with additional marks and comment, "All gone" or "Bye bye." The notion of the mark disappearing or being hidden has a great deal in common with the events and spatial relations which occur when a child drops a blanket down over a doll or a scarf over her father's face in a game of peek-a-boo. In an allied type of pre-picturing representation, it is the *process* of making lines and shapes that carries meaning. For example, one child used the marker as if it stood for a rabbit hopping. As she moved the marker, it created traces or "footprints" of hopping or driving which led away from a point of origin. While this gestural strategy occurred in only four of our subjects, it is important to point out that it has been observed by other investigators who have watched very early drawing development even more intensively than we did (Athey, 1980; Matthews, 1983).

While these strategies hardly yield conventional drawings, the products do have several novel qualities, when compared to purely object-based representations: Meaning has been transferred to marks. Those marks occur on the horizontal plane of a marking surface. Some primitive spatial relations such as "next to," "past," or "connected to," are being represented. Obviously, there are limits on these traces as effective or conventional graphic symbols: Children are encoding position and/or motion, not the static visual aspects of objects such as size, shape, color, or volume. Consequently, positional characteristics and gestural properties such as speed, emphasis, and pause are the vehicles for meaning. Although these properties carry meaning for the maker, they may be invisible to other perceivers who see only the finished product.

Point-plot Representations: (Mean Age of Acquisition: 2;7 years)

During the third year, an additional, and more nearly conventional, strategy for the graphic representation of spatial information arises. If children are provided with (or can generate) a list of relevant features for an object, they can turn out a spatially systematic plotting of these features using the drawing surface as a background. Frequently, children plot single points for features like tummy, head, or face, while they plot two points for eyes and feet, and multiple marks for hair. For example, in Figure 11.1a, there is primitive attempt at this by a child aged 2;6. Since not all of the nine children in our study spontaneously exhibited this strategy, it is important to indicate the robustness of the phenomenon. A recent experimental study by Fucigna (1985) confirms the existence of such strategies in a much larger population of two and three year-olds. Additionally, studies of older blind children and adults making raised-line drawings for the first time indicate that similar point-plot systems of representation emerge in these individuals prior to anything resembling the kinds of connected contour drawings we typically think of as "drawings" (Kennedy, 1983; Millar, 1975).

Again, there are marked limits to this form of graphic representation: There is no vocabulary of differentiated forms and each feature is rendered only as a point on a surface. Further, there is no concept of a line to mark the outside edge of an object; consequently the paper is treated as a surface on which to locate features rather that a pictorial space in which to portray the volumes or three-dimensional relations among objects.

The Emergence of Figure-Ground Relations:
(Mean Age of Acquisition: 3;0 years)

Children's understanding of an explicitly graphic system for representing spatial information becomes sharply articulated between the ages of 3;0 and 5;0. During these years, children develop both the notion of depicting figures in a pictorial space and the rudiments of a system for condensing the volumes and in-depth relations between objects into the two dimensions of the conventional drawing surface.

The first step in the development of a pictorial space occurs as the earlier point-plot system gives way to an incipient system for the representation of surface inherent in the contrasting use of points and patches as shown in Figure 11.5. Between 3;0 and 3;6, children apply their picture-reading skills to their own drawings with increasing frequency and aptness. Once they perceive a partial, accidental

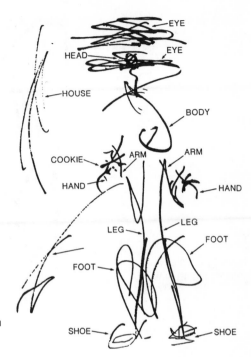

Figure 11.5. A drawing using a system of patches and points.

visual-spatial "likeness" in a drawing, they often pursue it. Thus one child happens to create a legible outline, which he labels a "pelican kissing a seal." He pursues what he has read into the visual pattern, making an even more readable, if simple, picture from it by adding eyes and freckles as shown in Figure 11.6.

The discovery of the contour line to describe the boundary of a surface marks a major turning point in drawing development (Arnheim, 1974; Freeman, 1980; Golomb, 1974). In a sense, the child ceases to treat the physical surface of the paper as an underlying object *on* which to locate features. Instead she treats the paper as a pictorial space *in* which to locate objects. Not surprisingly, this opens the way to complex problems in two dimensional representations of spatial information, notably the problems of depicting the third dimension.

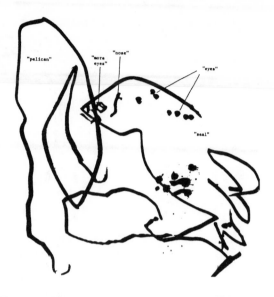

Figure 11.6. A drawing with a discovered contour line.

Rudimentary Systems for Rendering Scenes and Three-dimensional Information: (Mean age of acquisition for scenic drawings: 4;0 years; for scenic drawings with rudimentary depth: 5;2 years)

Once children have created pictorial spaces, they begin to draw partial scenes that occur in their experience such as "me and my sister" where two figures are portrayed side by side. At the outset, it is not uncommon for the child to include several such scenes within the same drawing surface. It is not really until their fifth year that children begin to use the areas between figures to represent different locations within a continuous space. Once this concept of the drawing surface as "a window on a world" emerges, children can portray genuine scenes in which transitive spatial relations apply both left-to-right and top-to-bottom directions. However, even in the most complex scenic drawing, a child can (and often does) avoid depicting such difficult three-dimensional relations as "in front of" or "behind."

It is not until almost a year later that most children spontaneously work out even a partial system for portraying aspects of the third dimension. Their initial attempts to capture depth relations take the form of what has been called "tipping the picture plane." The backpack on a hiker is not portrayed jutting out a little above the figure's shoulders, instead, it is drawn just above the figure. Children devise still other ways to portray the volume of individual objects, such as coloring them in or enlarging their outside contours. Viewed from an adult perspective, these are primitive strategies. Nevertheless, they are significant because they signal the child's awareness that when drawing, she must find two-dimensional means to represent even the three-dimensional aspects of her spatial experience.

THE DIFFERENTIATIONS OF DRAWING AND CONSTRUCTION AS SYSTEMS FOR REPRESENTING SPATIAL KNOWLEDGE

Between one and three, children have little sense of the distinctions or *boundaries* which their particular culture draws between various formats or systems for representing spatial information. In these years, drawing is neither a profoundly two-dimensional system nor is block-building a fully three-dimensional system for representing spatial information. Only between the ages of three and five do children make a fundamental differentiation between the rules for representing all three dimensions of spatial experience in drawing and block-building. This occurs only as children develop the notions of (1) a pictorial space and (2) the rudimentary rules for condensing volume and depth into two dimensions in their drawings and (3) the means to represent the volume of a referent in their block constructions.

The effort to refine the boundaries between two- and three-dimensional continues for a number of years. As they continue drawing, children eventually turn in older "burying" or "hiding" strategies for occlusion as a means to portray how one object obscures another. Similarly, they continue to work out devices to portray the solid volumes of objects. At six, one of the children we observed was struggling to depict the difference between a red disk and a red sphere. She added a layer of red, then orange, then red, claiming that the three layers of color made that particular drawing "fat," and thus, a good representation of the volume of the sphere. She had yet to discover the devices of shading, elliptical lines, or cast shadows that can act, in more conventional drawing systems, as indicators of volume.

In closing, it is important to point out that what young children work out with respect to the different rule system for drawing and block-building is not unique. Throughout the life-span, individuals acquire new forms for representing their spatial experience. In middle childhood, children work out the boundaries between drawings and maps. Still later, as adults, we grapple with the fact that engineers' and artists' drawings may abide by different rules and that chemists and architects use three-dimensional models in varying ways.

REFERENCES

Arnheim, R. 1974. *Art and visual perception: A psychology of the creative eye.* Berkeley: University of California Press.

Athey, C. 1980. *From marks to meaning: The language of lines.* Roehampton, U.K.: Froebel Institute.

Fleishman, J. & Dusek, R. 1971. Reliability and learning factors associated with cognitive tests. *Psychological Reports.* 29:523-530.

Freeman, N. 1980. *Strategies of representation in young children.* New York: Academic Press.

Fucigna, C. 1985. Children's earliest representational strategies in drawing. Unpublished Masters thesis. Tufts University, Medford, MA.

Jackowitz, E. & Watson, M. 1980. Development of object transformations in early pretend play. *Developmental Psychology.* 16:543-549.

Gardner, H. 1983. *Frames of mind: The theory of multiple intelligences.* New York: Basic Books.

Gesell, A. 1925. *The mental growth of the preschool child: A psychological outline of normal development from birth to the sixth year.* New York: Macmillan.

Guanella, F. 1934. Block building activities of young children. *Archives of Psychology.* 174:1-92.

Golomb, C. 1974. *Young children's sculpture and drawing.* Cambridge, MA: Harvard University Press.

Kennedy, J. M. 1983. What can we learn about pictures from the blind? *American Scientist.* 71:19-26.

Liben, L. S. 1981. Spatial representation and behavior: Multiple perspectives. In L. S. Liben, A. H. Patterson & N. Newcombe (Eds.), *Spatial representation and behavior across the life span.* New York: Academic Press.

Loew, R. 1984. Roles and reference in American Sign Language: A developmental perspective. Ph.D. dissertation, University of Minnesota.

Matthews, J. 1983. Children drawing: Are young children really scribbling? Paper presented at the British Psychological Society International Conference on Psychology and the Arts, Cardiff, Wales.

McGee, M. 1979. *Human spatial abilities: Sources for sex differences.* New York: Praeger Press.

Millar, S. 1975. Visual experience or translation rules? Drawing the human figure by blind and sighted children. *Perception.* 4:363-371.

Reifel, S. 1984. Block construction: Children's developmental landmarks in representation of space. *Young Children.* 61-67.

Riccuiti, H. 1965. Object grouping and selective ordering behavior in infants 12 to 24 months old. *Merril-Palmer Quarterly of Behavioral Development.* 11:129-148.

Selfe, L. 1977. *Nadia: A case of extraordinary drawing ability in an autistic child.* London and New York: Academic Press.

Shotwell, J., Wolf, D. & Gardner, H. 1980. Styles of achievement in early symbolization. In M. Foster & S. Brandes (Eds.), *Universals and constraints in symbol use.* New York: Academic Press.

Sugarman, S. 1983. *Children's early thought: The development of classification.* New York: Cambridge University Press.

Thurstone, L. L. 1938. *Multiple factor analysis: A development and expansion of "The vectors of the mind".* Chicago: University of Chicago Press.

Winner, E. 1979. New names for old things: The emergence of metaphoric language. *Journal of Child Language.* 6(3):469-491.

Wolf, D. & Gardner, H. 1980. On the structure of early symbolization. In R. Schieffelbusch & D. Bricker (Eds.), *Early language intervention.* University Park, MD.: University Park Press.

PART III

EFFECTS OF DIFFERENT EARLY EXPERIENCES

INTRODUCTION

The first section presented recent advances in neurobiology and neuropsychology which lead to a deeper understanding of the brain bases of spatial cognition in adults. The second section reviewed studies of the development of spatial cognition in normal children. This section of the book is concerned with how spatial cognition in children is affected by different early experiences such as right hemisphere brain damage, Williams Syndrome, and the absence from birth of auditory or visual inputs.

In the first chapter, Stiles-Davis discusses the development of spatial cognition in young children with focal brain lesions. She reports evidence of spatial cognitive deficits in children with injury to the right, but not the left, hemisphere. The implications of these findings for the normal development of spatial cognition, and for theories of early brain plasticity are discussed.

In the next chapter, Bellugi, Sabo and Vaid examine the effects of Williams Syndrome, a rare metabolic disorder, on the development of spatial cognition. This little known disorder has onset in infancy and leads to severe cognitive deficits yet remarkable sparing of expressive language. The children with Williams Syndrome described in the chapter show severe spatial cognitive deficits but unimpaired visuoperceptive abilities, underscoring the separability of these two domains in development.

In the following chapter, Petitto and Bellugi describe aspects of languages that have developed in the spatial domain: the sign languages of deaf people. American Sign Language is a primary linguistic system that has evolved independently of spoken languages. They find that sign language is acquired by young deaf children of deaf parents at the same rate and with the same milestones as are the spoken languages of the world. The relation between sign language and its spatial cognitive substrate is discussed.

Neville, in the following chapter, focuses on cerebral organization for spatial cognition, separating out the effects of early auditory deprivation and the acquisition of a visual language on the specialization of cortical areas important for spatial cognition. Her experiments suggest that different sensory and language experiences have specific effects on the development of the neural systems that mediate aspects of spatial cognition. For example, she finds that attention to peripheral visual space is superior in deaf subjects and is mediated by different neural systems than in hearing subjects. She also finds principled differences between deaf and hearing signers even when both groups learned sign language as a native language from their parents.

In her chapter, Landau examines the construction of spatial knowledge in children with a different sensory deprivation, the absence of vision. She finds that blind children develop the ability to solve some spatial problems at ages compatible with that of sighted children. Based on her evidence, she argues that some basic principles of children's developing knowledge systems arise independently of the nature or degree of particular experiences with the physical world. Both blind and sighted children alike use these principles to construct a spatial world.

In the final chapter, Witelson and Swallow focus on neuropsychological aspects of spatial cognitive development. They consider possible definitions of spatial cognition, and then review the neuropsychological literature from both normal and brain-damaged populations on the early development of spatial understanding. Finally, they consider patterns of variation in spatial ability that exist within the normal population, focusing on sex differences.

The chapters in this section discuss the effects of dramatically different early experiences on the development of spatial cognition. Taken together, the data suggest that the brain damage associated with right hemisphere lesions or with the metabolic disorder of Williams Syndrome can produce well-defined deficits of spatial cognition, though these are somewhat different from those seen in brain damaged adults. In contrast, children with specific sensory deprivation, such as deafness or blindness, in the presence of normal cerebral functioning, are shown to have essential preservation of spatial cognitive abilities.

SPATIAL DYSFUNCTIONS IN YOUNG CHILDREN WITH RIGHT CEREBRAL HEMISPHERE INJURY

12

JOAN STILES-DAVIS
University of California, San Diego

Until recently, it had been unclear whether it is possible to document, in the first few years of life, specific cognitive disorders associated with focal brain lesions. Most of the available data indicated that the consequences of early localized brain injury are minimal, at least over the long run. Children appear to be quite resilient, compared to adults, in that they recover, or more precisely acquire, cognitive functioning following injury to the brain that would leave adults permanently impaired (Alajouanine & Lhermitte, 1965; Brown & Jaffe, 1975; Carlson, Netley, Hendrick, & Pritchard, 1968; Gott, 1973; Hammill & Irwin, 1966; Krashen, 1973; Lenneberg, 1967; McFie, 1961; Reed & Reitan, 1971).

However, in the past few years, detailed retrospective studies of adults and older children whose injuries occurred early in life have provided evidence of subtle persistent cognitive deficits within the general pattern of recovery (Day & Ulatowska, 1979; Dennis, 1980; Dennis & Kohn, 1975; Dennis & Whitaker, 1976; Kohn, 1980; Kohn & Dennis, 1974; Rudel & Teuber, 1971; Rudel, Teuber, & Twitchell, 1974; Vargha-Khadem, O'Gorman, & Watters, 1983, 1985; Woods, 1980; Woods, & Carey, 1979). These data suggested that it might be possible to identify cognitive deficit in young children with focal brain injury. Recent prospective studies of young children with congenital or early acquired focal brain lesions support this view.

Aram and her colleagues (Aram, Ekelman, Rose, & Whitaker, 1985; Aram, Ekelman, & Whitaker, 1986; Aram, Rose, Rekate, & Whitaker, 1983; Rankin, Aram, & Horwitz, 1981) have reported data from cross-sectional studies of children under five years of age which demonstrate linguistic and cognitive deficits in children with early acquired focal brain injury. Recent longitudinal data from our laboratory (Stiles-Davis, 1983; Stiles-Davis, Sugarman, & Nass, 1985) have identified spatial-constructive deficits associated with right hemisphere injury in children as young as 2 to 3 years of age. Together, these studies support the view that it is possible to identify specific cognitive deficits in young children with localized brain injury, and that the deficits can be associated with side of injury.

The documentation of specific deficits associated with early localized brain injury has important implications for our understanding of both early cognitive functioning and brain plasticity. In the course of normal development, many aspects of cognitive functioning develop simultaneously, and it is difficult to determine how or if the development of one function interacts with the development of another. In observing the concurrent development of cognitive functions in normal children, the question remains as to whether individual developments are independent parallel events, or obligatorily linked and interdependent events. One potentially useful source of data relating to this question comes from children with specific deficits of cognitive functioning. These children represent a kind of "natural experiment" for observing the dissociation of cognitive functions during development.

The identification of specific cognitive deficits in very young children with localized brain injury has important implications for a second issue, that of early functional plasticity in the developing brain. Data identifying specific cognitive deficits in young children suggest that even very early in life the developing brain is not equipotential for all functions, and they argue against the strong form of the early brain plasticity hypothesis. The development of cognitive functioning is affected adversely by early injury. However, data on the development of cognitive functioning in these children are limited, and we do not know yet how their development will proceed. We do not know whether the impairment thus far documented represents developmental delay or deficit, or even whether the delay/deficit dichotomy represents an appropriate approach for describing impairment in this population. A range of outcomes is possible. These children could simply overcome the early form of deficit showing a delayed, but normal sequence of development, or their deficit could take a different form later in development (Goldman-Rakic, Isseroff, Schwartz, & Bugbee, 1983). Retrospective analyses that look only at the outcome of development can tell us *if* functioning is impaired, but not how the particular form of impairment arose. A more complete description of what constitutes impairment in these children requires a prospective investigation of cognitive functioning, one in which testing is initiated early in life and continues at regular intervals across the target developmental period.

The remainder of this chapter will review the data from our laboratory on spatial deficits in young children with localized right cerebral hemisphere lesions, and then consider the implications of these findings for our understanding of normal development and early brain plasticity. The data review will focus on a brief presentation of our original work (Stiles-Davis, 1983; Stiles-Davis et al., 1985) in which a general form of spatial-constructive deficit was identified. Some preliminary results from an extended longitudinal data pool will also be considered. The data from our original work identifying a spatial constructive deficit bear directly on both the issue of dissociating cognitive function in development, and that of early brain plasticity. The preliminary data from subsequent longitudinal studies provide suggestive evidence on the long-term course of functional recovery in brain damaged children and raise questions concerned with the issue of cognitive deficit versus developmental delay.

IDENTIFICATION OF A SPATIAL-CONSTRUCTIVE DEFICIT

The focus of our original study in children with localized brain lesions was on the development of classification skills within a spatial domain. A series of manipulative classification tasks was used to test young children's ability to organize small sets of toys into class consistent spatial groupings. The children were presented with toy sets containing from two to five classes of identical objects (e.g. four blue blocks and four orange plates), and their play activities were videotaped. The tasks were based on procedures used by Sugarman (1982, 1983a, b) in her study of the development of classification in normal children. Sugarman's work demonstrated a marked developmental trend for spatial grouping activities, one that differentiated the 1 to 4 year age span that we were interested in studying (Riccuiti, 1965; Sugarman, 1983a, b). The developmental trend Sugarman found is characterized by systematic, age-related

change in the ways in which children generate more and more complicated procedures for constructing class consistent spatial groupings. To review her findings briefly, children of 18 months group
only one kind of object. For example, given a set of toys containing
four blue blocks and four orange plates they might group all the
blocks and simply ignore the plates. By 24 months children group
more than one class of objects, but do so sequentially, for example,
clustering all the blocks and then all the plates. By about 30
months the children shift back and forth between classes in the process of constructing separate spatial groupings. For example, they
might stack two blocks, then two plates, then put another block on
the block stack, a plate on the plate stack, and so on until all the
objects are arranged in class consistent spatial groups. Thus, change
in the child's conceptualization of class relations is evidenced as systematic changes in spatial grouping activities.

Eight children with unilateral brain lesions were tested in our
study: four had right cerebral hemisphere injury, and four had
lesions in the left side of the brain. The results of standardized
behavioral and neurological examinations for each subject are indicated in Table 12.1. Data from the brain damaged children were
compared with previous results from normal children between 18
and 42 months (Sugarman, 1983a, b). The brain damaged children
were between two and three years of age when first tested; they were
tested at six month intervals.

Our preliminary analysis indicated that performance of the right
hemisphere damaged children on manipulative classification tasks
was impaired relative to that of same age normal children. When
presented with toy sets, the right hemisphere damaged children
spontaneously ordered the objects, but they were limited in the ways
in which they did it. For example, in contrast to normal children,
the right hemisphere damaged children rarely grouped similar
objects together in clusters. Children with left hemisphere injury
did not show a comparable pattern of impairment. We did not know
whether the restricted range of observed behaviors for children with
right hemisphere injury indicated a general impairment of their
ability to mentally construct class relations, or whether we were seeing selective impairment of some ways in which children express
class relations.

A principal way children express class relations in manipulative
classification tasks is by organizing objects into class consistent
groupings in space. Spatial deficits, and in particular spatial-
constructive deficits, have been associated with right hemisphere
injury in adults (e.g. Arrigoni & De Renzi, 1964; Belleza, Rappaport,

Table 12.1

Neurological and Behavoral Examinations for the Brain-Damaged Children

Subject	Age at lesion	CAT scan	Seizures	EEG	Age at first testing	Intelligence test scores
	Right-hemisphere damage					
C	3 Months, hemophiliac-spontaneous hemorrhage	Right frontal porencephaly	Yes	Right spike focus	29 Months	Stanford-Binet = 80 Wechsler (WPPSI) FIQ = 73, VIQ = 69, PIQ = 82
K	Prenatal, normal birth history	Right parietal temporal infarction	Yes	Right slowing and spikes	27 Months	Stanford-Binet = 127 Wechsler (WPPSI) FIQ = 98, VIQ = 100, PIQ = 96
M	Prenatal, normal birth history	Right lateral ventricular enlargement	No	Mild generalized slowing	29 Months	Stanford-Binet—not available Wechsler—not available Denver Developmental = mild delay 29 months
A	Perinatal, premature	Normal	Yes	Right spike focus	30 Months	Stanford-Binet—not available Wechsler (WPPSI) FIQ = 87, VIQ = 101, PIQ = 74
	Left-hemisphere damage					
B	Perinatal, premature	Normal	No	Normal	28 Months	Stanford-Binet = 113 Wechsler (WPPSI) FIQ = 110, VIQ = 115 PIQ = 104
L	1 Year: Right focal status, but already left-handed	Normal	Yes	Left focal abnormalities	27 Months	Stanford-Binet = 61 Wechsler (WPPSI) FIQ = 59, VIQ = 52, PIQ = 61
Q	Perinatal meconium	Left parietal temporal occipital infarction	Yes	Mild generalized slowing	27 Months	Stanford-Binet = 135 Wechsler (WPPSI) FIQ = 118, VIQ = 130 PIQ = 101
V	Prenatal, normal birth history	Left-hemisphere porencephaly	Yes	Left focal abnormalities	30 Months	Stanford-Binet = 124 Wechsler (WPPSI) FIQ = 111, VIQ = 120 PIQ = 100

Kenneth, & Hall, 1979; Benton, 1979; De Renzi, 1982; Kritchevsky, this volume; Ratcliff, 1982). We hypothesized that the impairment we observed in the way right hemisphere damaged children grouped objects might relate to problems they have with the construction of spatial, rather than class, relations.

To tease apart the possible sources of difficulty encountered in the spatial grouping tasks, two different types of classification measures were incorporated into the testing procedure. One set of tasks involved the organization of objects into class consistent spatial groupings; the other assessed the order in which children selected objects belonging to different classes from the collection of objects presented. Sugarman (1983a, b) had shown that for normal children both kinds of tasks tap comparable levels of developmental change in the child's understanding of class relations during the 1 to 4 year age range. The children in our study were tested on a total of seven manipulative classification tasks. Tasks 1-5 involved grouping objects in space. Tasks 6 and 7 involved sequential selection of objects. For Tasks 1-5 the children were presented with toy sets containing from 2 to 5 classes of identical objects. They were encouraged to play, and their spontaneous spatial grouping activities were videotaped. For Tasks 6 and 7, children were presented with toy sets containing either 4 or 5 classes of objects. Brightly colored stickers were affixed to the bottom of objects from two classes of objects within each set. The children were shown the stickers on the bottom of one exemplar from each tagged class, and were then encouraged to search for more stickers. The order in which the children selected objects from the stimulus array was videotaped.

Transcripts of videotapes were analyzed for the kinds of class and spatial relations the children constructed. We had two principal measures of classification: The first was a measure of *spatial* classification; how did the children organize objects by class into spatial groupings in Tasks 1-5? The second measure of classification was a temporal selection measure; in what order did the children select objects from the stimulus array for Tasks 6 and 7? We also analyzed the kinds of *spatial* relations the children constructed when grouping objects. That is, for Tasks 1-5, we observed whether the children placed objects in, on, or next to other objects.

Our results indicated that on temporal measures of classification the right hemisphere damaged children appear to be developing normally in their understanding of class relations. But, on measures that require them to form class consistent spatial groupings, they appear to be impaired. Furthermore, these children produce a more restricted range of spatial relations than do normal or left hemisphere damaged children.

On the classification tasks, impairment was evident in the failure of the right hemisphere damaged children to arrange objects in class consistent spatial groupings at levels comparable to same age normal children (See Table 12.2). The most advanced spatial grouping procedure produced by the children at age 33 to 36 months was that of normal 24 month old children. These children were restricted also in the range of *spatial* relations they constructed (See Table 12.3). As late as 30-36 months they almost always grouped objects by placing them in or on other objects, they rarely placed objects next to each other. As young as 18-24 months, both normal and left hemisphere damaged children regularly placed objects next to other objects in their constructions.

Furthermore, the failure of the right hemisphere damaged children to construct next to relations could account for limitations we had observed earlier in their class grouping activities. The more advanced class grouping procedures require children either to shift between classes when forming class groupings, or to integrate objects into larger spatial patterns. Both of these procedures require the child to place objects next to other objects, which the right hemisphere damaged children almost never do.

Table 12.2
Spontaneous Classification Tasks-Summary

Normal children	Brain-damaged children*
18 Months: One relation at a time	
Correspondence grouping: construct object pairs	C at 29 months
	K at 27 and 33 months
	M at 29 and 35 months
	A at 30 and 36 months
Identity grouping: cluster dolls, ignore rings	M at 29 and 35 months
24 Months: Multiple relations, in sequence	
Correspondence grouping: construct object pairs, then integrate them into a larger spatial pattern	C at 36 months
Identity grouping: cluster dolls, then cluster rings	C at 29 and 36 months
	K at 27 and 33 months
	A at 30 and 36 months
30 Months: Multiple relations shifting between relations	
Correspondence grouping: shift between construction of object pairs and integration of pairs into larger spatial patterns	
Identity grouping: construct two class groupings by shifting between classes	

* Developmental level achieved by ages specified.

Table 12.3
Proportions of Constructions Containing Each Type of Spatial Relation

	Mean across sessions for each child with right-hemisphere damage				Mean across children
	C	K	M	A	
In	.41	.37	.30	.28	.34
On	.39	.37	.39	.49	.41
Next to	.04 ⎫ .12	.05 ⎫ .05	.02 ⎫ .02	.04 ⎫ .09	.04 ⎫ .07
Mixed-next to	.08 ⎭	0.0 ⎭	0.0 ⎭	.05 ⎭	.02 ⎭
Mixed	.08	.22	.30	.13	.18

	Mean across sessions for each child with left-hemisphere damage				Mean across children
	B	L	Q	V	
In	.20	.40	.18	.41	.30
On	.37	.32	.36	.32	.33
Next to	0.0 ⎫ .27	.13 ⎫ .25	.21 ⎫ .39	.12 ⎫ .28	.12 ⎫ .30
Mixed-next to	.27 ⎭	.12 ⎭	.18 ⎭	.16 ⎭	.18 ⎭
Mixed	.17	.03	.08	0.0	.07

	Mean proportions for normal children in each age group				Mean across ages
Age (months)	18	24	30	36	
In	.33	.32	.37	.35	.34
On	.35	.30	.19	.17	.25
Next to	.33	.38	.44	.48	.41

Finally, the right hemisphere damaged children showed evidence of normal development in their understanding of class relations on the *temporal* selection measures. At ages comparable to their normal peers they selected from more than one class, and they shifted among classes in doing so. Together these results suggest that the limitations we observe in the right hemisphere damaged children's class grouping activities are a function of limitations in their understanding of spatial rather than class relations.

In summary, within the context of the classification tasks, we found evidence for a specific cognitive deficit in 2 to 3 year old children with localized brain injury. The deficit is specific in two ways: first, it affects children with right, but not left, cerebral hemisphere injury; and second, it selectively affects their ability to construct spatial relations, but not logical relations in the classification tasks. The children do not appear to be impaired generally in their ability to conceptualize relations between objects; rather the deficit appears specifically to involve spatial relations. On classification tasks that do not require the spatial organization of objects the children perform at age appropriate levels.

In addition, the children are not globally impaired in their ability to generate spatial relations. Their deficit involves limitations on the range of spatial relations generated in the block arrangement tasks. Unlike normal children or children with left hemisphere injury, the children with right hemisphere injury place objects in and on other objects, but they rarely place objects next to one another. The findings of our study point to limitations in the spatial cognitive domain, but those limitations are not global. We are left with the question of why the children have difficulty constructing next to relations but not stacking or containment relations.

It is unlikely that the spatial constructive deficit we have observed in the children with right hemisphere injury lies in the construction of next to relations, per se. Rather, within the context of the spatial construction task, the next to relation presents a more difficult or complex problem for the child, one that requires more analysis of the spatial array than does the construction of stacking or containment relation. On this point, it should be noted that, like brain damaged children, normal children begin to produce next to relations later than they produce stacking or containment relations. They stack and contain by 12 months, but do not begin to generate next to relations until about 18 months. It may be that whatever factors make the next to relation difficult for normal children, pose more extreme problems for the right hemisphere damaged children who rarely generate next to relations even at 36 to 42 months.

In what ways do stacking and containment relations differ from the next to relation? Both stacking and containment relations are well defined. That is there is only one way to stack or contain objects, and the construction process centers around a single spatial locus. Furthermore, the act of construction provides functional feedback for construction: In stacking, the elements in the construction provide support for new items; in containment, the container item can serve as a guide for placement of new items (Johnston, 1981; Sugarman, 1983a, b). Next to relations are not defined in any of these ways: New items may be placed in any position around other items; a next to relation may include multiple spatial loci; and the placement of a new object need not involve a functional relation between objects, the items can simply be juxtaposed. In short, there are many more factors to be considered in producing a next to relation than there are in the production of a stacking or containment relation, and it may be this greater complexity that accounts for the later acquisition in normal children, and poses more extreme problems for the children with right, but not left, hemisphere injury.

If this hypothesis is correct, the spatial deficit children with right hemisphere injury should not be restricted to the construction of next to relations. The children should show impairment on any measure of spatial cognition that requires them to analyze a complex spatial array. One way to assess a child's analysis of the spatial array is to adopt a microanalytic approach employing multiple, detailed and possibly converging indices of spatial understanding and development. A comparison at such a detailed level of analysis of the ways in which normal and brain damaged children go about organizing objects in a space may provide a more complete definition of the impairment observed in the right hemisphere damaged children.

We have begun to use such a microanalytic approach to examine the components of the spatial construction process, assessing both the kinds of spatial groupings children produce and the procedures used to generate them. Our preliminary data provide suggestive evidence of the dimensions along which spatial construction ability differs in the right hemisphere damaged children, and tentatively provide converging evidence of spatial deficit.

Because the available data on the construction of spatial groupings among young normal children are very limited, we began our assessment of spatial construction abilities with a set of studies testing normal children. A series of studies were devised aimed at analyzing in detail the early development of spatial cognition that incorporated multiple indices of spatial construction behavior. These indices were intended to assess normal developmental change in the 1 to 4 year age range. Very briefly, we have found evidence for developmental change in: (1) the kinds of relations children generate among individual elements in the array, for example whether objects are placed in, on, or next to other kinds of objects; (2) in the number of different kinds of relations children combine in a single construction, for example, do they stack all objects, or do they stack some items and place others next to one another; (3) the number of spatial loci incorporated into a single grouping, for example whether the grouping is built around a single point in space, or several; (4) the number of directions elements extend from a spatial locus, for example does the child build in one direction or more; (5) the kind of end-product groupings the children produce, for example, whether lines, stacks, or arches are produced. For all these measures, we find with increasing age, greater diversity and flexibility in the number and kind of spatial relations generated. These trends reflect developmental change in the ways in which children analyze and conceptually define a spatial array.

Preliminary data from three children with right hemisphere injury suggest that all these measures of spatial development can serve as indices of spatial impairment, and possibly also of recovery. Only one right hemisphere damaged child under age 42 months has been tested in this new series of studies. On all measures the child, at age 36 months, performed at the level of a normal eighteen month old. That is, he constructed in and on, but rarely next to relations; he usually included only one kind of relation in his groupings; the groupings were centered around a single spatial locus; they extended out in single direction in space; and the final products tended to be stacks, rather than more complex constructions. Two other children were 52 and 56 months when tested on the new series of tasks. These two were somewhat more advanced than the 36 month old for all the spatial construction measures; however they had not reached the 42 month level of performance for any of the measures.

As observed in our original study, spatial deficits for all three children were evident in the restricted range of spatial relations generated. Within the context of the new tasks, the restricted range of behaviors was evident across the range of behavioral indices. In addition, data from the older children point, at least tentatively, to developmental change in the form of the deficit. Both children were performing well above the 18 month level on all measures of spatial construction ability, including construction of next to relations. In our original study neither of these children, as late as age 36 months, spontaneously generated next to relations. The new data on these children are preliminary, but they point to the possibility that the children are developing, in that they appear to be mastering tasks that previously served as indices of their impairment. Detailed analysis of data from a larger sample of children, spanning the 1 to 5 year age range, may provide clues as to what aspects of spatial understanding are changing and when. By comparing closely the patterns of development for normal children with brain damaged children we should be able to determine whether the patterns are similar but offset in time, or whether the patterns of development for the two groups are in fact different.

One final recent set of data on early spatial deficit in young children with right hemisphere injury comes from a case study report of the ability to draw in a five year old child with right hemisphere injury. Drawings were solicited from two children, both with localized brain injury. Both are drawings of a house (Figure 12.1). The

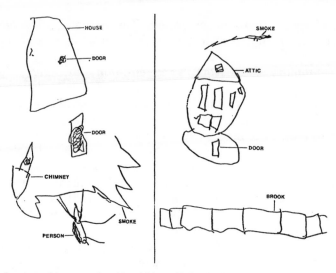

Figure 12.1. Drawings of house produced by children with localized brain injury. The drawing on the left was done by a child with right hemisphere injury; the drawing on the right was done by a child with left hemisphere injury.

drawing on the left was done by a child with right hemisphere injury, the one on the right by a child with left hemisphere injury. The labels identify parts of the house as indicated by the children. The right hemisphere damaged child was 62 months when this drawing was made, he has an IQ of 101 as measured by the Stanford-Binet, and comes from a middle SES home. The child with left hemisphere injury was 55 months when this drawing was made, she has an IQ of 110, and also comes from a middle SES home. The contrast between the drawings is marked. Most notably the drawing of the child with right hemisphere injury lacks cohesion, the parts of the house are scattered around the page. They are not configured into a coherent whole. Such configurational anomalies are reminiscent of those found in the drawings of adult patients with right parietal injury (Ratcliff, 1982). The drawing data provide additional, convergent evidence of spatial impairment for the right hemisphere damaged child.

Together, the data presented in this section suggest that specific deficits of spatial cognition can be identified in young children with right cerebral hemisphere injury. A specific form of spatial deficit was identified in our original study. Preliminary data from our recent studies indicate that it may be possible to provide convergent data, based on multiple indices of development, that will define more completely the parameters of spatial impairment. By following the children longitudinally we have at least suggestive evidence that the particular form of deficit identified early in development may change with age. By 4.5 to 5 years of age two children with right hemisphere injury had begun to generate some, but not all, of the spatial forms that emerge in normal development by age three. These findings have implications for both the study of normal cognitive development, and for questions related to early brain plasticity.

SPECIFIC COGNITIVE DEFICITS AND THE DISSOCIATION OF COGNITIVE FUNCTIONS IN DEVELOPMENT

The children with specific cognitive deficits associated with localized brain injury represent a potentially important population for testing the dissociation of cognitive functions during development. The study of adults with brain lesions for assessing localization of function has a long history. The logic of such experiments is that if the mediation of a particular cognitive function is associated with a specific brain area, then injury to that area should result in impairment or loss of the associated cognitive function.

The logic underlying the study of children with specific deficits has a similar, if not somewhat more complex, basis. The complexity of the logic arises from the fact that the questions we are asking involve not simply dissociation of functions, but dissociation of functions within the context of development, that is, within the context of a continuously changing individual. It is possible that the association of functions in the developing child is very different from what it is in adults. The young child may rely on information from one cognitive domain to achieve early developmental milestones within another domain, or development in two or more domains may be linked to a common third source (Bates, Benigni, Bretherton, Camaioni, & Volterra, 1977). Development may entail a kind of obligatory bootstrapping that may or may not be required in adulthood. Patterns of interaction and interdependencies of cognitive functioning that might be evident early in development need not extend to the adult state. Indeed, dissociations evident in the final state may not capture, or adequately represent, the developmental process.

The identification of specific deficits in the young child provides an arena for testing the necessary interaction of cognitive functions in development. The dissociation of functions in early development would be evident in data verifying normal patterns of development for one cognitive function, function A, and impaired development for another function, function B. The dissociation of functions in this way would demonstrate that the normal development of function A does not depend on function B.

Our original study illustrated the dissociation of logical and spatial functions in young children with localized brain injury. Children with right hemisphere injury were selectively impaired in their ability to construct some kinds of spatial relations, but they were developing normally in their ability to form class relations when the expression of class relations did not require spatial grouping. These results help to clarify some disparate findings in the literature on the development of logical and spatial relations in normal children.

For example, some studies of normal children suggest that the development of children's early understanding of logical relations depends upon their ability to conceptualize those relations spatially (Hughes, 1980; Inhelder & Piaget, 1964; Riley & Trabasso, 1974; Trabasso, 1975, 1977; Trabasso, Riley, & Wilson, 1975), while other work with normal children suggests that these two aspects of cognition develop independently (Markman, Cox, & Machida, 1981). Our findings support the later view. The dissociation of developmental patterns for spatial and class relations among the right hemisphere damaged children (Stiles-Davis, 1983; Stiles-Davis et. al., 1985) indicates that the development of these two functions is not necessarily related. Children can develop normally in their understanding of class relations without necessarily expressing those relations spatially.

It should be noted that the above dissociation excludes only the condition of necessary association between functions. It does not preclude the possibility that the functions may interact in a noncontingent way during the course of normal development. The findings of our study should not be interpreted as meaning that the two functions cannot, or do not, interact during normal development. Class relations can be expressed by grouping objects into spatial clusters. Nicolopoulou (See chapter this volume) has demonstrated the possible relation between the development of class and spatial relations early in life. The point here is that while development of the two functions may sometimes, even frequently, be related, that relation is not necessary for the development of classification. A more extensive examination of how development proceeds in children with specific cognitive deficits could provide insight into the interactions of cognitive functions during development.

EARLY FUNCTIONAL PLASTICITY OF THE DEVELOPING BRAIN

The identification of a specific deficit of spatial cognition in right hemisphere damaged children under 3 years of age constrains possible theories of early functional plasticity in the developing brain. If the brain were equipotential for cognitive functions, specific deficits should not be detectable early in life. An intact and unallocated brain region would presumably assume the mediation of function normally carried out by the injured brain area and sparing of function should be seen. The strong form of the equipotentiality hypothesis cannot account for the present data identifying specific deficits of spatial cognition in children under three years of age. However, the data above cannot be taken as support for a strong early localization of function position. The deficits we have identified are subtle compared to adults with comparable injury, and they appear to be changing with the development of the child. Some form of recovery, or rather development, does appear to be taking place. We do not yet know what the nature or extent of that development will be within this population of children. But, at least thus far, we have not seen a stable level of impairment emerging. The observed patterns of developmental change indicate that some form of recovery or redirection of functions is taking place and, as such, we cannot rule out the possibility that some form of neural reorganization is mediating the continuous change.

A variety of mechanisms for recovery of function following early injury have been proposed including, substitution, hierarchical representation, diaschisis, and retraining (e.g., Hecaen & Albert, 1978; Stein, Rosen & Butters, 1974). Behavioral studies alone cannot distinguish between the various neural mechanisms of recovery. However, they can provide insight into subtle performance differences that may serve as markers of variation in either level of cognitive functioning, or in strategies for carrying out a particular cognitive task. For young children a crucial aspect of their behavioral data base is the assessment of behavioral change over time.

In the young child deviation from normal developmental patterns is an important measure of behavioral variation. Measurement at a single point in time can serve as an index, a means of detecting, abnormal cognitive functioning. However, longitudinal examination involving periodic assessment of the child's behavior has the potential for providing a much more detailed profile of what constitutes deviant cognitive functioning, and also recovery of function in the child. Where we find evidence of both impairment and developmental change in cognitive functioning, detailed longitudinal assessment allows us to ask whether development follows the same sequence as that of normal children but at slower pace, or whether the developmental pattern deviates from the norm.

Such assessment goes beyond the global distinction often drawn between developmental deficit and delay. The pattern of development involving a delayed and abnormal developmental sequence is frequently labeled deficit, and a normally sequenced but slower paced pattern is labeled delay. While the terms deficit and delay may in a broad sense capture some aspects of the difference between the two developmental patterns, they may also obscure important issues in the assessment of early cognitive impairment in neurologically damaged populations. First, both patterns represent deficit in the development of cognitive functioning at some level. Delayed acquisition is often a marker for impaired development. Second, achievement of developmental milestones within the context of either a delayed or deviant developmental sequence may or may not reflect the same underlying cognitive functioning found in unimpaired populations. The brain damaged children may be adopting alternative cognitive strategies for solving problems that pose difficulties. More precise definition of impaired development is needed, one that incorporates multiple measures of cognitive functioning administered repeatedly over a time span of years.

Our original study of spatial understanding in young children with focal brain lesions employed a longitudinal design. The children were tested on the same measures at six month intervals. However, we incorporated only a single measure of spatial construction ability. On the basis of that single measure, we knew that the children produced a restricted range of spatial relations, but we could not tell what that limited behavior reflected about their ability to analyze the spatial array. From the measures employed, we could not address the question of why the children did not generate "next to" relations.

In our new study we have attempted to remedy this assessment problem by incorporating into our analysis multiple measures of spatial construction ability. The preliminary data suggest this more detailed, multi-measure approach may provide a more precise picture of development in the children with right hemisphere injury. Analyses of the measures taken individually yield common developmental patterns across measures. Specifically, the pattern for each measure indicates a normal sequence of development, but with delayed acquisition. However, comparing across measures the developmental profile for the group of children with right hemisphere injury differs from that of normal children. In particular, the relative timing for acquisition of developmental milestones across measures differs from normal patterns. For example, we compared the performance of the two children in our preliminary study with normal children on the "directions in space" and the "spatial loci" measures. The directions in space measure assessed the number of directions in space blocks extended from one or more spatial loci. For example, a line could be constructed by building in either one or two directions depending on whether the child placed each new block to the right of the original block, or whether some blocks were added to the right of the first block and others to the left. The spatial loci measure assessed the number of loci incorporated into a construction. For example, a construction containing a single stack was scored as having a single spatial locus, the bottom block, while a construction containing two stacks would contain two loci. Both children in our original study were more advanced on the "directions in space" measure than on the "spatial loci" measure. By 52 and 56 months they had begun to build in more than one direction from a single spatial locus, but they only occasionally built from more than one locus in space. Such a pattern was not typical of normal children who either achieve both milestones simultaneously or begin incorporating multiple spatial loci in their constructions slightly ahead of building in more than one direction in space. Anomalous sequences of development on the spatial construction tasks are thus evident in the comparison across measures, rather than in the independent assessment of individual measures where only developmental delay is apparent.

The data suggesting an anomalous pattern of development are preliminary, and at this point difficult to interpret. Furthermore, the differences are subtle and evident only by comparing the relative timing of developmental milestones across different measures of spatial constructive activity. Within this context, the issue of what constitutes developmental deficit versus developmental delay is ambiguous. The data suggest that the deficit/delay dichotomy may not be the best approach to describe impairment of development in the population of children with specific cognitive impairment associated with localized brain injury. What is needed is a much more detailed analysis of cognitive development in this population to be able to define more precisely what factors contribute to the differences observed in developmental patterns. The data suggest the possibility that development may be proceeding along a divergent course. Such deviant patterns in turn suggest that, although children with specific impairment of spatial cognition appear to be developing, part of that development may entail devising new strategies for solving problems that pose difficulty.

SUMMARY

The group of children with specific spatial constructive deficits related to localized right cerebral hemisphere injury present an interesting and unique perspective on the issue of the early development of spatial cognition. The patterns of impairment and development evidenced in this population have implications for several different issues in the areas of human neuropsychology and cognitive developmental psychology.

I have suggested that experimental observation of children with specific spatial constructive deficits represents a potential opportunity for a kind of natural experiment in the area of early cognitive development. The approach of observing development in children with specific cognitive disorders to understand more about normal development is analogous to studying adult patients with specific cognitive deficits associated with localized lesions in the hope of understanding the neural substrates of cognitive function in the terminably differentiated state. The dissociation of cognitive functions in development, within the context of specific early occurring deficits of cognitive functioning, provides the opportunity for identifying necessary dependencies and interaction between cognitive functions in development. When a child manifests normal development for one cognitive function and specific deficit for another cognitive function, it can be inferred the development of the normal function does not depend upon the other function. The dissociation of classification and spatial construction was demonstrated within the population of children with right hemisphere lesions. The study of children with focal brain lesions offers a unique means of addressing questions about the development (and possibly the re-direction of development) of cognition that is precluded in the study of normal populations.

The data on spatial constructive deficits in brain damaged children also have implications for questions relating to early brain plasticity in the developing brain. Our original study (Stiles-Davis et al., 1985), which examined the effects of early localized brain injury on cognitive functioning, represents the first experimental documentation of a specific deficit of spatial cognition associated with lesions of the right hemisphere in children under three years of age. The data are consistent with retrospective studies of the effects of early brain injury on cognitive functioning, but place the origins of identifiable deficit early in the developmental period. The data constrain theorizing about the extent of early brain plasticity. The developing brain is clearly not equipotential for all functions. However, the extent of cognitive dysfunction in young children with localized injury is less extreme than it is for adults with comparable injury. The deficits identified are subtle, and appear to change with development. Some form of "recovery," or more appropriately cognitive development (or redirection of development), appears to occur. The data collected thus far, which are behavioral data, cannot alone specify the neural bases for this development, but they do have the potential for offering a detailed description of the behavioral components of cognitive functioning in this population of children. Such detailed descriptions of what constitutes cognitive impairment in neurologically disordered children are an essential part of our understanding of the recovery process. Before we can make the associations between the development of cognitive functioning and the change in neural substrate, we must first know more at the level of cognitive functioning about exactly what is developing, and how that development is proceeding.

ACKNOWLEDGMENTS

This work was supported by a grant from the John D. and Catherine T. MacArthur Foundation Network on the Transition from Infancy to Early Childhood.

REFERENCES

Alajouanine, T. & Lhermitte, F. 1965. Acquired aphasia in children. *Brain*, 88:553-562.

Aram, D.M., Ekelman, B.L., Rose, D.F., & Whitaker, H.A. 1985. Verbal and cognitive sequelae following unilateral lesions acquired in early childhood. *Journal of Clinical and Experimental Neuropsychology*, 7:55-78.

Aram, D.M., Ekelman, B.L. & Whitaker, H.A. 1986. Spoken syntax in children with acquired unilateral hemisphere lesions. *Brain and Language*, 27:75-100.

Aram, D.M., Rose, D.F., Rekate, H.L., & Whitaker, H.A. 1983. Acquired capsular/striatal aphasia in childhood. *Archives of Neurology*, 40:614-617.

Arrigoni, G., & De Renzi, E. 1964. Constructional apraxia and hemispheric locus of lesion. *Cortex*, 1:170-197.

Bates, E., Benigni, L., Bretherton, I., Camaioni, L. & Volterra, V. 1977. From gesture to first word: On cognitive and social prerequisites. In M. Lewis and L Rosenblum (Eds.), *Interaction, Conversation, and the Development of Language*, New York: Wiley, 247-307.

Belleza, T., Rappaport, M., Kenneth, H. & Hall, K. 1979. Visual scanning and matching dysfunction in brain-damaged patients with drawing impairment. *Cortex, 15*, 19-36.

Benton, A.L. 1979. Visuoperceptual, visuospatial, and visuoconstructive disorders. In K.M. Heilman & E. Valenstein (Eds.), *Clinical Neuropsychology*. New York: Oxford University Press.

Brown, J. & Jaffe, T. 1975. Hypothesis on cerebral dominance. *Neuropsychologia*, 13:107-110.

Carlson, J., Netley, C., Hendrick, E., & Pritchard, J. 1968. A reexamination of intellectual abilities in hemidecorticated patients. *Transactions of the American Neurological Association*, 93:198-201.

Day, P.S. & Ulatowska, H.K. 1979. Perceptual, cognitive, and linguistic development after early hemispherectomy: Two case studies. *Brain and Language*, 7:17-33.

Dennis, M. 1980. Capacity and strategy for syntactic comprehension after left or right hemidecortication. *Brain and Language*, 10:287-317.

Dennis, M. & Kohn, B. 1975. Comprehension of syntax in infantile hemiplegics after cerebral hemidecortication: Left hemisphere superiority. *Brain and Language*, 2:472-482.

Dennis, M. & Whitaker, H.A. 1976. Language acquisition following hemidecortication: Linguistic superiority of the left over the right hemisphere. *Brain and Language*, 3:404-433.

De Renzi, E. 1982. *Disorders of Space Exploration and Cognition*. New York: Wiley.

Goldman-Rakic, P.S., Isseroff, A., Schwartz, M.L., & Bugbee, N.M. 1983. The neurobiology of cognitive development. In M.M. Haith & J.J. Campos (Eds.), *Handbook of Child Psychology: Infancy and Developmental Psychobiology*, Vol. II, New York: Wiley, 281-344.

Gott, P.S. 1973. Cognitive abilities following right and left hemispherectomy. *Cortex*, 9:266-274.

Hammill, D. & Irwin, O.C. 1966. I.Q. differences of right and left spastic hemiplegic children. *Perceptual and Motor Skills*, 22:193-194.

Hecaen, H. & Albert, M. 1978. *Human Neuropsychology*, New York: Wiley.

Hughes, F.P. 1980. The relationship between spatial and logical functioning in the child. *Journal of Genetic Psychology*. 137:63-77.

Inhelder, B. & Piaget, J. 1964. *The Early Growth of Logic in the Child*, New York: Norton.

Johnston, J. 1981. On location: Thinking and talking about space. *Topics in Language Disorders*, 2:17-32.

Kohn, B. 1980. Right hemisphere speech representation and comprehension of syntax after left cerebral injury. *Brain and Language*, 9:350-361.

Kohn, B. & Dennis, M. 1974. Selective impairments of visuospatial abilities in infantile hemiplegics after right cerebral hemidecortication. *Neuropsychologia*, 12:505-512.

Krashen, S. 1973. Lateralization, language learning, and the critical period: Some new evidence. *Language Learning,*. 23(1):63-74.

Lenneberg, E. 1967. *The Biological Foundations of Language.* New York: Wiley.

Markman, E., Cox, B., & Machida, S. 1981. The standard object sorting task as a measure of conceptual organization. *Developmental Psychology*, 17:115-117.

McFie, J. 1961. Effects of hemispherectomy on intellectual function. *Journal of Neurology, Neurosurgery, and Psychiatry*, 24:240-249.

Rankin, J.M., Aram, D.M., & Horwitz, S.J. 1981. Language ability in right and left hemiplegic children. *Brain and Language.* 14:292-306.

Ratcliff, G. 1982. Disturbances of spatial orientation associated with cerebral lesions. In M. Potegal (Ed.), *Spatial Abilities: Development and Physiological Foundations*, New York: Academic, 301-331.

Reed, J.C. & Reitan, R.M. 1971. Verbal and performance differences among brain-injured children with lateralized motor deficits. *Neuropsychologia*, 9:401-407.

Riccuiti, H. 1965. Object grouping and selective ordering behavior in infants 12 to 24 months old. *Merrill-Palmer Quarterly.* 11:129-148.

Riley, C.A. & Trabasso, T. 1974. Comparatives, logical structures, and encoding in a transitive inference task. *Journal of Experimental Child Psychology.* 17:187-203.

Rudel, R.G. & Teuber, H.L. 1971. Spatial orientation in normal children and in children with early brain damage. *Neuropsychologia.* 9:401-407.

Rudel, R.G., Teuber, H.L., & Twitchell, T. 1974. Levels of impairment of sensorimotor function in children with early brain damage. *Neuropsychologia.* 12:95-108.

Stein, D.G., Rosen, J.J., & Butters, N. 1974. *Plasticity and Recovery of Function in the Central Nervous System*, New York: Academic.

Stiles-Davis, J. 1983. Construction of spatial and class relations in four children with right cerebral hemisphere damage. Ph.D. dissertation, Princeton University.

Stiles-Davis, J., Sugarman, S., & Nass, R. 1985. The development of spatial and class relations in four young children with right cerebral hemisphere damage: Evidence for an early spatial-constructive deficit. *Brain and Cognition*, 4:388-412.

Sugarman, S. 1982. Developmental changes in early representational intelligence: Evidence from spatial classification and related verbal expressions. *Cognitive Psychology.* 14:410-449.

Sugarman, S. 1983a. *Children's Early Thought: The Development of Classification*, NY: Cambridge.

Sugarman, S. 1983b. The development of inductive strategy in children's early thought and language. *The Quarterly Newsletter of the Laboratory of Comparative Human Cognition*, UCSD, San Diego, Ca.

Trabasso, T. 1975. Representation, memory and reasoning: How do we make transitive inferences? In A.D. Pick (Ed.), *Minnesota Symposia on Child Psychology*. 9. Minneapolis: University of Minnesota Press.

Trabasso, T. 1977. The role of memory as a system in making transitive inferences. In R.V. Kail & J.W. Hagen (Eds.), *Perspectives on the Development of Memory and Cognition*, Hillsdale, N.J.: Lawrence Erlbaum Associates.

Trabasso, T, Riley, C., & Wilson, E. 1975. The representation of linear and spatial strategies in reasoning: A developmental study. In R.J. Falmagne (Ed.), *Reasoning, Representation and Process in Children and Adults*, Hillsdale, N.J.: Lawrence Erlbaum Associates.

Vargha-Khadem, F., O'Gorman, A. & Watters, G. 1983. Aphasia in children with "prenatal" versus postnatal left hemisphere lesions: A clinical and CT scan study. Paper presented at the 11th meeting of the International Neuropsychological Society, Mexico City.

Vargha-Khadem, F., O'Gorman, A. & Watters, G. 1985. Aphasia and handedness in relation to hemispheric sides, age at injury and severity of cerebral lesion during childhood. *Brain*. 108:667-696.

Woods, B. T. 1980. The restricted effects of right-hemisphere lesions after age one: Wechsler test data. *Neuropsychologia*. 18:65-70.

Woods, B. & Carey, S. 1979. Language deficits after apparent clinical recovery from childhood aphasia. *Annals of Neurology*. 6:405-409.

SPATIAL DEFICITS IN CHILDREN WITH WILLIAMS SYNDROME

13

URSULA BELLUGI
Salk Institute for Biological Studies

HELENE SABO
Cornell Medical Center

JYOTSNA VAID
Texas A&M University

INTRODUCTION

Clearcut cases of selective impairment in cognitive development are relatively rare, since mental retardation frequently results in cognitive functions being similarly depressed in all domains. We have recently been presented with an intriguing new population with a metabolic disorder which appears to result in just such an uneven profile of cognitive abilities; language functions appear to be relatively intact while spatial cognitive functions are profoundly impaired.

Much of our knowledge of spatial cognition comes from studying the spatial abilities of normal adults and the patterns of disabilities of adults with brain-damage. The study of brain-damaged individuals offers a particularly revealing vantage point for understanding the organization of language and nonlanguage functions. In related research from our laboratory, we have been examining dissociations between language and spatial cognition from the special perspective of deaf signers with unilateral left or right cerebral lesions (Poizner, Klima & Bellugi, in press). We find that right cerebral lesions in deaf signers lead to deficits in spatial cognitive functions, although spatial language remains intact. Conversely, left cerebral lesions in deaf signers lead to sign language aphasias, but leave spatial cognitive functions largely spared. In hearing patients also, some spatial cognitive functions are disrupted with right hemisphere damage, as some of the chapters in the first section of this book describe.

In some new studies, we are engaged in a line of investigation which links a specific neuropsychological profile with a specific metabolic disorder. The population that we are studying has Williams Syndrome (otherwise known as Infantile Hypercalcemia). Williams Syndrome is a rare clinical disorder of hitherto unknown etiology which appears to affect language and spatial cognition in highly specific ways. Of great interest to us is the apparent dissociation between language and cognitive functions, and it is this unusual separation that first captured our attention. In this chapter, we describe the severe spatial cognitive deficit exhibited by these children, and some aspects of the uneven neuropsychological profile which they exhibit. The particular pattern of spatial cognitive abilities, but spared linguistic functions exhibited by these children will be examined. We are currently examining the brain basis of this unusual behavioral profile through studies of brain function and structure. These studies should illuminate brain organization for language and spatial cognitive functions using evidence from a rare metabolic disorder as a model.

Williams Syndrome was first identified and so named after a clinical study by Williams, Barrett-Boyes and Lowe (1961), who described four patients with supravalvular aortic stenosis in association with mental retardation and a peculiar facial appearance. Black and Bonham-Carter (1963) associated the characteristic facial appearance of these children with that found in Infantile Hypercalcemia, as the syndrome is known in Great Britain. The syndrome first came to public attention in the early 1950's in Great Britain, when cases of unexplained infantile hypercalcemia began to appear. These cases were first thought to be correlated with the excessive fortification of dried milk and other foods with Vitamin D. It was suggested that maternal or fetal hypersensitivity to increased Vitamin D intake might be an etiologic factor. More recent studies implicate abnormal production of the hormone, calcitonin, as a marker (Culler, Jones & Deftos, 1985). What was noticed early on was that the children shared physical and medical characteristics including cardiac defects (heart murmur, intracardiac defects, supravalvular aortic stenosis), mental retardation, and alterations of facial features. The physical characteristics have been documented across a group of Williams Syndrome children in a paper by Jones and Smith (1975). According to their report, the unusual facial characteristics of the children are the most consistent feature in the recognition of this sporadically occurring disorder, consisting of a stellate pattern in the iris, medial eyebrow flare, depressed nasal bridge, and thick lips with an open mouth posture. Furthermore, the children tend to have pre- and post-natal growth deficiency, mild microcephaly, and a hoarse voice.

Figure 13.1 shows photographs of Williams Syndrome children, courtesy of the Williams Syndrome Association, which we have made into a collage. Note the striking similarity of facial features across the children.

The medical/clinical symptoms of this disorder have been well described and documented. However, to date there have been very few studies of the neuropsychological characteristics in this special population, and those few that appear have presented some contradictory results (Arnold & Yule, 1985; Bennett, LaVeck, & Sells, 1978; Frank, 1983; Neale, 1980). Our studies across a range of Williams Syndrome children suggest a characteristic neuropsychological profile which is discontinuous from normal. There appears to be a marked discontinuity between linguistic functions and other cognitive functions—a marked sparing of grammatical capacities in the face of general mental deficiency. Furthermore, our studies suggest that Williams Syndrome children show an unusual sensitivity to classes of sounds, and may evidence abnormal brain organization. We are currently embarked on a program of studies that includes neuropsychological, electrophysiological, brain imaging, and neurobiological studies (Bellugi, Sabo, Neville & Culler, 1985).

We are now embarked on a major program of studies with Williams Syndrome children. This report is based on findings from the first three children that we studied. Since this was a new area of interest to us, we began with an in-depth case study of one child (age 15 at the time) with this disorder. Her mother brought the child to our laboratory every week for almost a year, for two-hour sessions; we used a battery of tasks as well as experimental probes in a variety of domains (linguistic functioning, cognitive functioning, visuospatial functioning, and motor and sensory functioning, among others). We found that although Crystal's score on a standardized IQ test was low (IQ 49), her performance across domains was not uniform; in fact it was dramatically uneven, with surprisingly preserved abilities in some areas and gross deficits in others. One domain in which we found a specific deficit was in spatial cognitive tasks, although language functions were much higher than one would expect from her other aspects of mental deficiency. This led us to examine two other Williams Syndrome children across a selected range of tasks involving language and visuospatial abilities. We present here a first report on studies across three children with Williams Syndrome ranging in age from 11 to 16. We focus on the

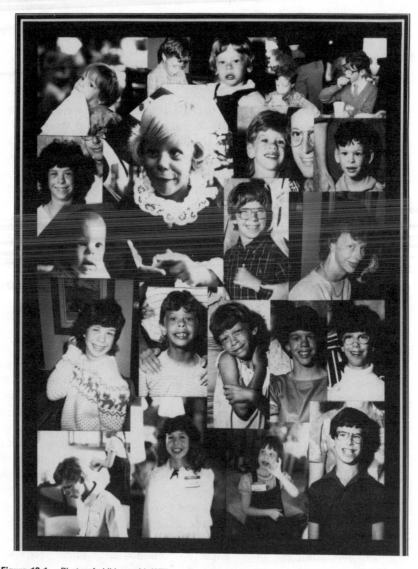

Figure 13.1. Photo of children with Williams Syndrome.

spatial deficits exhibited by this group of children, and the uneven pattern of abilities even within this domain.

We chose older children for our first study because we wanted to examine the children first in the "steady state" of development, after milestones of motor, language, cognitive, and sensory development had been achieved. We have extensive data on their language and visuospatial functioning as well as on a range of neuropsychological tests, in addition to medical and educational background information and parental reports on their development. In the course of a widespread evaluation of one child, 15 at the time of testing, certain dissociations of functions were evident and characterized her profile as unique. We selected the most revealing probes and developed a test battery which we have now used with other Williams Syndrome children of comparable ages. Crystal was diagnosed as having Williams Syndrome at the age of 5 months, and has been enrolled in classrooms for the trainable mentally retarded throughout her school years. Ben, at 16 years of age, is the oldest of our three subjects. In addition to exhibiting the characteristic symptomatology of Williams Syndrome, Ben was diagnosed as hyperactive. He too has been placed in classrooms for the trainable mentally retarded throughout his schooling. The third subject, Van, is 11 years old. Parental reports suggest a similar developmental history and shared behavioral characteristics with our other subjects. Van has been attending special schools for the retarded since the age of 10 months and is currently enrolled in a learning handicapped classroom.

We present our findings of striking behavioral similarities across the children, focusing on their visuospatial functions which stand in sharp contrast to their spared language functions.

Developmental Milestones. From medical and parental reports we noted that the children were severely delayed in both language and motor milestones. During the first year, all the children suffered from colic, severe constipation and recurrent vomiting, often resulting in a failure to thrive in infancy. Parental reports suggest that all the children were delayed in learning to walk, ranging from 2 to 3-1/2 years. Parental reports also suggested that none of the children began using single words before the age of 2, that none began using phrases until 4, and that the transition to complete sentences developed slowly, requiring 3 years or more. Furthermore, our own studies of the emergence of language in a young Williams Syndrome child show an even more delayed onset. By the age of 3:2, the child entered therapy because she had not yet started to develop language.

By the age of 5:5 she has only begun to put two words together in simple phrases. What is remarkable, as we will indicate, is the language used by the older children we studied, after such initial delays in milestones of language development.

Handedness. The parents of all three Williams Syndrome children reported that the children were slow to develop hand preferences; Crystal was reported to develop a hand preference only around 8 to 10 years of age, and Van not until 5 years of age. Handedness in our sample of children was assessed empirically with reference to four measures: the Edinburgh Hand Preference Inventory (Oldfield, 1971), the Grooved Pegboard Test (Lewis & Kupke, 1977), and two subtests of the Harris Tests of Lateral Dominance (Harris, 1974)— the Dot Tapping Test and Simultaneous Writing Test. The measures all show a lack of strong right handedness, and a tendency toward mixed results (right hand better in one task, left hand in another) in measures of hand performance and preference.

COGNITIVE FUNCTIONING IN WILLIAMS SYNDROME CHILDREN

Intelligence Quotients. On traditional intelligence tests, such as the Wechsler Intelligence Scale for Children (Revised, 1974), the children perform at low levels: ranging from 43 to 66, corresponding to mild to moderate levels of mental retardation. These findings are in accord with those reported by Jones and Smith with Williams Syndrome children (IQ scores ranging from 41 to 80). The children's chronological ages were 11, 15, and 16 at the time of testing; however, their mental ages were all below 7 years, according to the IQ test results. These depressed IQs are also consonant with the children's educational placement; none of the children attend normal classes, and all three are instead in special classes for the educable or trainable mentally retarded child.

We observed an interesting pattern when we examined mental age scores derived from IQ scores made at different points in time across the three Williams Syndrome children; we found that over a relatively long period of time, the children's mental ages showed very little change; thus the degree of delay increased (see Figure 13.2). Although the chronological ages of our subjects range from 11 to 16, their mental ages appear to be fairly uniform, and furthermore, stabilized across time.

Other aspects of cognitive functioning in Williams Syndrome children have not been examined before, to our knowledge. We admin-

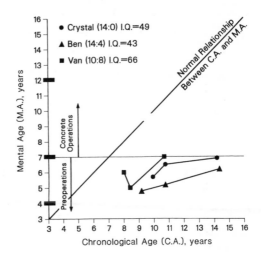

Figure 13.2. Mental age score graph in children with Williams Syndrome.

istered several cognitive tasks, within a Piagetian framework, several of which have been purported to be linked to language development. The children who are now in their second decade are still functioning within the pre-operational stage of cognitive development, normally acquired between the ages of 18 months and 6 years. On a range of tasks, the children performed very poorly. They were unable to perform tasks reflecting knowledge of conservation, seriation, and multiple classification, skills which are attained by normal children far younger in age. The Williams Syndrome subjects failed across the board on the conservation tasks we administered; only in the case of number conservation did two of the children indicate that two rows of objects were the same although they were in different arrays, and this the children accomplished not by reasoning, but by counting the objects in the arrays (see Figure 13.3). Thus it seems that the Williams Syndrome children attend to the irrelevant perceptual features of the task such as height, width, size, and shape, and not to the relevant dimension of actual amounts. Although there are occasional correct answers, none of the children were able to say why they chose a particular response.

It has been suggested that certain cognitive concepts are prerequisite to the attainment of certain linguistic structures (Ingram, 1975; Sinclair, 1975). In particular, the attainment of concrete operational thinking has been considered necessary for the acquisition of many complex linguistic structures. Based on the results of

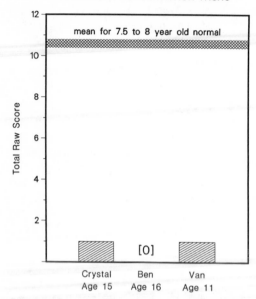

Figure 13.3. Failure of conservation in children with Williams Syndrome.

the cognitive tasks given, it appears that these older Williams Syndrome children do not yet demonstrate evidence of concrete operational behavior, normally acquired by the age of 7. In fact, their level of performance in these nonlanguage cognitive areas suggests that they are demonstrating a preoperational level of behavior. Clearly, the Williams Syndrome children exhibit major deficits in cognitive functioning. We now turn to examining the children's surprising linguistic facility.

LANGUAGE: AN ISLAND OF SPARING

On Crystal's first visit, the first time we met a Williams Syndrome child, we had prepared a list of questions to elicit spontaneous language, together with a battery of formal and informal tests. During the two-hour session, we never had to resort to the list of questions—language flowed freely and spontaneously, and Crystal kept up her end of the conversation without any prompting whatsoever. An anecdote may give a sense of the odd juxtaposition of mental deficiency and language ability. Crystal is unable to read; at the age of 15 she reads less than twenty words. She is at the level of a much younger child in many of the cognitive tasks that we gave her. One day she talked to us about her "aims in life," in these words:

"You are looking at a professional bookwriter.
I am going to write books, page after page, stack after stack.
I'm going to start on Monday."

Clearly this is unusual language for a mentally retarded child. While not noted for its plausibility, this incident exemplifies one aspect of the children's apparent dissociations. Their language only occasionally shows such confabulation; in contrast, it *characteristically* shows grammatical well-formedness, even when there is grammatical complexity.

There have been some recent linguistically informed studies of language development in a group of children who are mentally retarded, namely children with Downs Syndrome (Fowler, 1981). According to Gleitman (1983), three adolescent children with Downs Syndrome were studied in detail. They were selected because they had presumably reached some steady, final state of language development. These children had mental functions at about the level of six-year-old children, and language functions (assessed by a variety of standard psycholinguistic instruments) about like those of 2-1/2-year-old normal controls. Their mean length of utterance was between 3.0 and 3.5, usually achieved by normal children between the ages of 2 and 3. Gleitman describes a case history of one individual with Downs Syndrome, called "Jenny," whose language learning has been studied for about three years. She began to speak very late, at about 5 years of age. When the child reached a mean length of utterance of about 3.5 (and had traversed the stages of language development outlined in Brown, 1973), her learning came to a halt and no further progress was seen. Gleitman suggests that these individuals may exhibit a case of diminished endowment; and that the progress of these children, constrained as it is, suggests a very low level automatic process at work to determine what she calls the "rock bottom" aspects of linguistic functioning.

Despite the delay in the onset of language development, the level of linguistic functioning exhibited by the older Williams Syndrome children far outstrips what we might expect based on their cognitive abilities. Their sentences are long, complex, usually grammatically well-formed, and show a great range of grammatical structures with complex embeddings, as well as unusual vocabulary. In fact the level of sophistication of linguistic structure is surprising in the face of the mental deficits. As one index of language output, the average sentence length in morphemes ranged from a low of 8.6 to 13.5, showing a striking contrast with the Downs Syndrome children reported by Gleitman (1983). The children with Williams Syndrome, like the Downs Syndrome subjects in Gleitman's study, were mildly to moderately mentally retarded. However, the language functioning of the two groups appears to be extremely dissimilar. While the language of the Downs Syndrome children appeared to plateau at a very early stage of development, the language of our adolescent Williams Syndrome subjects becomes highly developed, and after the initial delay in fact, becomes the children's dominant mode of functioning. We are currently engaged in contrasting Williams and Downs Syndrome children, matched in chronological and mental ages, across our range of tasks, thus documenting the profound difference between the two groups in linguistic functioning.

With the three Williams Syndrome subjects described here, we have used a battery of tests of language processing and production at each of the major linguistic levels (phonology, morphology, syntax, semantics, and pragmatics) to address issues involving Williams Syndrome children's mastery of language functions as well as their appreciation of and ability to reflect on these forms. We report on these studies separately, focusing on the sparing of language abilities in Williams Syndrome in the face of general cognitive impairment. Here we present only an instance of that dissociation.

The difference between the children's performance in the cognitive and linguistic domains is shown dramatically by contrasting the results of two different probes. The three Williams Syndrome children were completely unable to perform relatively simple cognitive tasks, as was mentioned above, such as conservation (refer to Figure 13.3). All three children failed on this task, as they failed almost across the board on the conceptual tasks. In great contrast, consider their responses on a complex linguistic item, shown in Figure 13.4. The children are presented with four pictures, three depicting a horse and a man and one depicting a horse and a dog. They are asked to point to the picture in which, "the horse is chased by the man." This is a nontrivial task, and normal adults may hesitate and search the array of pictures before replying. Yet all three children answered correctly on this item and on a variety of other items that involved such complex syntactic information. It is this remarkably preserved ability, not just to produce complex sentences freely and creatively but also to process them correctly, entirely on the basis of their syntactic form, that is striking. In general, on tests of their ability to process complex morphological and syntactic structures, the children performed quite well. As Figure 13.4 shows, the

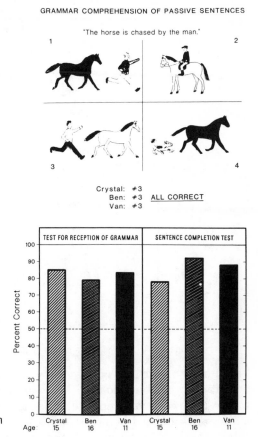

Figure 13.4. Linguistic ability in children with Williams Syndrome.

children showed a relatively high level of performance on the Test for Reception of Grammar (Bishop, 1983) and on a test of sentence completion which we devised. Furthermore, they performed well across a range of probes for components of language structure and showed some preserved metalinguistic abilities as well. Their striking language abilities in the face of general cognitive deficits are one facet of a highly uneven profile, suggesting an autonomy of systems, a dissociation between language and other cognitive functions.

THE AUTONOMY OF LANGUAGE

A striking dissociation between language and visuospatial functions is shown in Figure 13.5. We asked each child to draw a bicycle free-

A) FREEHAND DRAWINGS
OF A BICYCLE

B) DRAWINGS WITH CHILDREN'S
VERBAL LABELS ATTACHED

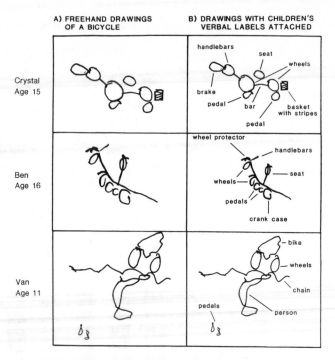

Crystal
Age 15

Ben
Age 16

Van
Age 11

Figure 13.5. Drawings of a bicycle by three Williams Syndrome children.

hand, after ascertaining that they all had bicycles in their homes
and knew what one looked like. The labels were added by the examiner from the children's remarks as they drew. Each one of the
children verbalized before and while drawing, as if "talking themselves through the drawing," the examiner noted. In the drawings,
parts of a bicycle are represented and labeled (wheels, handlebars,
pedals, seat, basket, wheel protectors, crankcase, chain) and the children could explain the parts as well as label them ("It has wheel protectors like this and that; the wheel protectors are against dirt and
rust."). Note again the lack of integration of parts; for example, the
chain stretched out below the wheels in Van's drawing, and the
pedals floating below the "person."

In addition, note the children's use of language to verbally "cue"
themselves through the spatial task of drawing. When asked to
draw a flower, Crystal took the pencil and began to draw, slowly and
laboriously, all the while talking to herself. "It's a line, and a circle.
It's a circle, a line," she said. Then we asked her to copy a drawing
of a flower from a model. She looked carefully and long at the
model, began to speak again, and then to draw: "Hmmm... circle,
and these. Those are two leaves, right? The line goes all the way

up." (And then she drew the stalk of the flower.) "Then the circle," drawing the "face" of the flower. We had the impression that she considered the task one of copying lines and circles, rather than making a graphic representation of a flower.

The examples of the children talking while drawing again demonstrate the dissociation between language and visuospatial skills. The children would often name the various parts of the model, and draw them as they named them, one next to the other. The drawings consist of separate parts that show no integration into functional objects. It is interesting to note how they use their relative strengths in language to mediate in this visuospatial task on which they perform so poorly.

SPATIAL COGNITIVE DEFICITS IN WILLIAMS SYNDROME

While damage to either hemisphere can produce spatial impairments, one can select tests which maximally discriminate performance of patients with right as opposed to left brain-damage. We have shown that deaf signers with right brain lesions, in contrast to those with left brain lesions, indeed show characteristic impairment in specific spatial cognitive tasks such as drawing with or without a model, block design, facial recognition, and line orientation (Poizner, Klima & Bellugi, in press). What often differentiates the performance of right and left lesioned patients is not the degree of absolute impairment that they show, but rather the different types of errors that they make and the different strategies they use in performing the tasks.

To date, there is no evidence of gross structural damage to either the right or the left hemisphere from the available neurological data of children with Williams Syndrome. However, despite the lack of evidence for gross structural damage, our first investigation of Williams Syndrome children suggests a striking difference between their expressive language and their abilities in certain spatial cognitive functions. The first task we gave them, that of drawing a bicycle, gave startlingly uniform results and led to the administration of a wide variety of spatial cognitive tasks. Even within these tasks we found some interesting and tantalizing dissociations, suggesting a domain-specific spatial deficit, which we expand on below.

Drawing. To investigate the children's performance on a well known test of drawing ability as well as their ability to depict visuospatial organization, we selected a subtest of the Boston Diagnostic Aphasia Examination (Goodglass & Kaplan, 1972). The children were first asked to draw some common objects (a cross, a cube, a flower, a house, and an elephant) without a model and then to draw the same objects again with a model. Patients with left hemisphere lesions characteristically draw a general contour or configuration, but leave out internal details and features. Their drawings generally display correct spatial relationships but appear simplified. By contrast, the drawings of patients with damage to the right hemisphere are replete with details but lacking in overall spatial organization. This test thus can be a sensitive indicator of intact or impaired hemispheric functioning.

The drawings by Williams Syndrome children often showed the parts of the object scattered on the page with no integration into functional objects. However, neither medical history nor recent brain images show evidence of gross structural damage. To draw a house, Ben made two lines for the house, a square beside it for the door, and then a series of separate squares to the left for the "windows," all unattached to the house. In addition to the lack of integration, the drawings made by all the children are simple, have altered orientations, and lack any attempts at representation of depth, resulting in the various dimensions all being represented next to each other, completely lacking in perspective (see Figure 13.6). In fact the drawings by Ben and Van would be almost completely unrecognizable as efforts to copy the figures above. Van has the highest IQ score of the three children and yet his drawings are in many ways the poorest, indicating that the drawing deficits seen in this population do not seem to be a function of IQ.

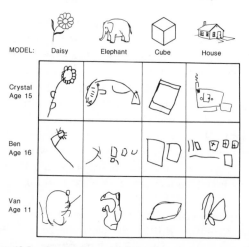

Figure 13.6.   Drawing from a model by Williams Syndrome children.

Spatial Attention. Because of the children's drawing impairment, we administered a test which taps aspects of the attentional capacities of the two hemispheres: a test of unilateral visual neglect (see Albert, 1973). This test examines spatial attention and its distribution across the environment, and whether or not it is asymmetrical. The test is frequently used with brain-damaged individuals to assess the presence or absence of visual neglect in one half of the visual field. Subjects are required to cross out 40 lines that are arranged pseudorandomly on a page. Albert reports that nonbrain-damaged controls cross out every line while patients with neglect cross out fewer lines in the neglected half of the page than in the other, and in fact, we found that some deaf signers with right hemisphere damage showed left neglect. None of the Williams Syndrome children showed any evidence of visual neglect. They crossed out every line on the page appropriately.

Copying Geometric Shapes. The drawing test from the Boston Diagnostic Aphasia Examination involves drawings of complex objects (an elephant, a house) requiring representations of depth and perspective, which none of the children could begin to approach. We thus turned to a drawing task which has been normed on much younger children, the Developmental Test of Visual-Motor Integration (Beery & Buktenica, 1967). On this test, subjects are required to copy a set of figures from a model. The items range from straight lines and triangles, to cubes and more complex three-dimensional figures.

The children were able to draw straight lines and circles, but none of them could copy a triangle, and they failed completely on representing any of the more complex shapes. The children only successfully completed the first eight of the 24 items which are sequenced in order of difficulty. From the simple representation of a triangle onward to the drawings of intersecting lines, a circle of dots, a cube, etc., the children failed completely. The children's scores were all the same, despite their advanced ages (11 to 16), and comparable only to the level of a normal child of age 4:11, thus showing uniformly severe spatial deficits in this simplified drawing task (see Figure 13.7). Note that the children are quite unable to keep the overall configurations of the drawings they are copying, failing to organize the drawings so that the parts are in contact. In drawings that are hierarchically organized (a triangle made out of circles, as shown in the figure), the children represent only the local internal details, without organizing them into the appropriate global whole.

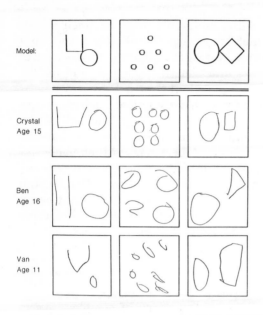

Figure 13.7. Selected Visual-Motor Integration Test items.

In another attempt to understand the children's difficulty with copying simple shapes, we asked them to simply *trace* the figures on this test at a later date, rather than copy them. Crystal's traced versus copied drawings are represented in Figure 13.8 and are typical of the differences between the traced and copied drawings of the children. Crystal was able to trace all the figures (including the three-dimensional items) quite well, despite her inability to copy them. This would suggest that the Williams Syndrome children's extreme difficulties in drawing—whether from a model or without one—are not simply due to motor difficulties.

The fact that the children can all write their names and write words apparently without difficulty, as well as trace drawings that they are otherwise unable to represent, again supports the idea that the deficits are not just motor in nature, but rather appear to derive specifically from a visuospatial deficit.

Spatial Construction. To investigate whether the children are able to copy visuospatial patterns without requiring them to draw, we turned to a different task. We asked them to copy a visuospatial array—block designs—when given the blocks to assemble. A subtest of the Wechsler Intelligence Test for Children-Revised was used (WISC-R; Wechsler, 1974). In the Block Design Test, the subject is required to reproduce patterns of three-dimensional blocks whose surfaces are colored red, white, or half-red, half-white, to match a

Figure 13.8. Impairment of visuospatial (not visuomotor) abilities in a child with Williams Syndrome (Crystal, Age 15).

two-dimensional model of the top surface. The adult version of this test (Block Design subtest of the WAIS-R) has proved a sensitive distinguisher of left from right brain-damage. Typically, right hemisphere damage impairs the maintenance of the overall configuration and increases the likelihood of a piecemeal approach to the problem. Adequate performance on the block design task requires the integrity of both cerebral hemispheres, and a lesion to either one produces a distinctive performance that reflects the contribution of the nondamaged hemisphere. Our results with right and left lesioned deaf signers brought out this difference dramatically (Poizner, Kaplan, Bellugi & Padden, 1984).

Figure 13.9 shows the performance of the three children with Williams Syndrome on a sample item, one of the earliest and simplest (item #2). The test is designed to commence with administration of item #3 for normal children between the ages of 8 and 16 and therefore, it is expected that by age 8, children should be able to reproduce design #2 correctly. The children uniformly failed to show an

BLOCK DESIGN TEST

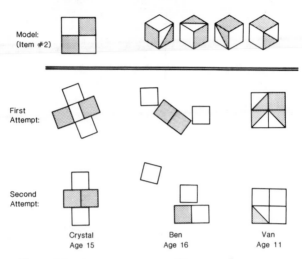

Figure 13.9. Spatial disability in children with Williams Syndrome.

integrated performance. Across the board, their attempts at assembling the blocks to reproduce a design failed from the very earliest stages. In this visuospatial task, even at a very simple level, the children's performances showed distinct and profound impairment. Thus the task shows their inability to copy visuospatial patterns without a drawing component, and points to a specific kind of impairment in the Williams Syndrome children.

Line Orientation. In order to examine the children's apparent visuospatial deficit in the absence of a motor component, even one as simple as arranging blocks in a design, we turn to a spatial cognitive task which has no constructional element. The Benton Line Orientation test, developed by Benton, Varney, and Hamsher (1978), requires the subject to match the angular orientations of two simultaneously presented lines to a choice display consisting of 11 lines oriented 18 degrees apart. Five practice items consist of a pair of lines that are shown in full length. The 30 test items consist of a pair of lines of partial length, representing either the upper, middle, or lower segments of the response-choice lines. Subjects are asked to match the spatial orientation of lines to those presented in an array. The task involves a component which is purely orientational along with a component that involves extrapolation of the oriented lines.

On this test, the three children with Williams Syndrome were again markedly and dramatically impaired. Their scores are severely defective (Crystal completed only 37% of the items correctly; Ben scored even lower, with only 20%). In fact one child, Van, was not able to perform correctly even on the practice items and thus the test was discontinued (see Figure 13.11 below). This test shows again a profound visuospatial impairment in children with Williams Syndrome.

Spatial Transformations. We administered a spatial task that involves different orientations of forms and requires the subject to perform mental spatial transformations. The Ayres Space Visualization Test involves perception of stimuli composed largely of spatial elements, including the mental manipulation of space or space visualization (Ayres, 1980). The subject is asked to determine which of two plastic blocks will fit into either an egg-shaped or diamond-shaped formboard with pegs inserted in four possible positions. The first four items of the test involved only form-perception, that is, distinguishing an oval shape from a diamond shape, and the children had no difficulty with this simple form perception task. The other items involve discriminating between similar shapes with different peg locations and/or altered orientations, thereby requiring visuospatial transformations. The responses are scored for accuracy, and only the subject's first choice is accepted. The children performed very poorly on those items requiring purely spatial rotation and space visualization, with their performance approaching the level of chance.

SELECTIVE PRESERVATION OF FORM AND FACE PERCEPTION

Thus it appears that the children with Williams Syndrome have a spatial cognitive deficit involving a range of dysfunctions, including deficits in drawing, block design, line orientation, spatial transformations, and spatial memory. Some of the tasks involved a constructional component while others did not; the result was the same—striking evidence of impairment in this battery of spatial cognitive tasks. However, there was a hint in our data that the children were not impaired across all tasks that are relevant to right hemisphere functioning in brain-damaged adults. Where the tasks involved aspects of object recognition or form perception (such as the items in the Ayres test), the children appeared to perform well. As a first approximation, we thus hypothesize that there may be in children with Williams Syndrome a distinction between those spatial cognitive functions described above and cognitive functions involving perception of faces, which we explore in two tasks: one a task of visual closure, and the other a complex task of facial recognition.

Visual Closure. In a test of perceptual closure, the Mooney Faces Test, subjects must discriminate photographs of human faces from nonfaces, where the photographs have highly exaggerated shadows and highlights. For photographs identified as faces, subjects are to specify identity in categories: boy, girl; man, woman; old man, old woman. In order to identify the photographs accurately, the subject must achieve a configurational percept from fragmentary information, an ability that has been associated with intact right hemisphere functioning (Newcombe & Russell, 1969). The test has been normed on different populations, including children and brain damaged as well as normal subjects (Lansdell, 1968, 1970; Mooney, 1957; Newcombe, 1969).

Figure 13.10 shows examples of three of the faces which all of the children identified correctly. The three children with Williams Syndrome all performed within the normal range on this test, and in fact performed better than average for normal subjects, showing

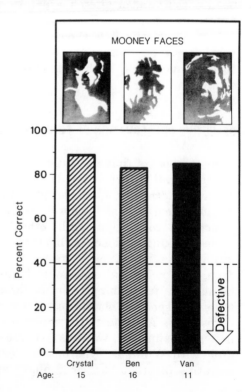

Figure 13.10. Performance of Williams Syndrome children on a visual closure task.

preserved abilities to perceive and differentiate shape and form. Defective performance on this task is below 39% correct. Crystal identified 89% of the faces correctly; Ben, 83%; and Van attained 85% correct. Thus the children are within the normal range for neurologically normal adults. They show intact abilities to perceive and differentiate shape and form in this complex task.

Facial Recognition. To assess the children's discrimination of unfamiliar faces, a standardized test of face recognition was used (Benton, Van Allen, Hamsher & Levin, 1978). The Benton Test of Facial Recognition has been standardized on a large number of left and right lesioned patients and controls; patients with right hemisphere damage show substantially more defective performance than patients with left hemisphere damage. The test consists of three parts. In the first part, the subject is shown a single front-view photograph of a face and asked to identify it in a display of six photographs appearing below the target face. In the second part, the target face appears three times in a display of six photographs of three-quarter-view faces. In the third part, a single photograph must be identified from an array of faces photographed under different lighting conditions.

The three children with Williams Syndrome all performed well within the normal range on this difficult test of facial recognition, showing no impairment whatsoever in the ability to recognize and discriminate unfamiliar faces (Crystal had 74% correct; Ben, 87% correct; and Van, 80% correct). The children responded quickly and with ease, and performed well on this complex task, as well as on the task of closure above. Thus it appears that there is no impairment of object recognition even under conditions of deformation (closure tasks, recognition of faces with different lighting and orientation conditions).

A dramatic contrast between two tasks, neither of which involve any constructional component, is seen in comparing the children's scores on the Benton Line Orientation (described above) and Benton Facial Recognition tests, shown in Figure 13.11. We see that the children show gross deficiencies in determining the spatial orientation of lines, but show no impairment in the complex task assessing the ability to recognize and discriminate unfamiliar faces under different conditions of lighting and orientation.

In great contrast to their performance on the nonlanguage spatial tasks where they are severely impaired, they show remarkably spared abilities in tasks involving perception of form, and to recognize faces even under conditions of different spatial orientation and

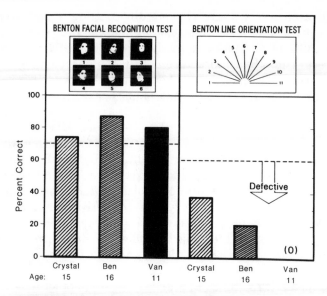

Figure 13.11. The contrast between facial recognition and spatial perception in children with Williams Syndrome.

lighting. On the other hand, the children are strikingly impaired on many visuospatial and visuoconstructive functions, beyond what might be predicted from their general cognitive limitations, implicating a *specific spatial cognitive deficit*.

CONCLUSIONS

Williams Syndrome is a diffuse metabolic disorder that has hitherto been little explored. We have developed a broad program of studies to investigate the neuropsychological profile exhibited by children with this disorder. We are finding marked patterns of dissociations; so far the most striking of which is the dissociation between generally impaired cognitive abilities and remarkably spared expressive linguistic abilities. It is well known from lesion data that language can be selectively destroyed. Here we investigate a metabolic disorder in which there appears to be a marked discontinuity between linguistic and other cognitive functions—a marked sparing of language capacities in the face of general mental deficiencies. This pattern is currently being examined in a series of studies.

In this chapter we have confronted another interesting dissociation in the neuropsychological profile of Williams Syndrome children. The children appear to show a marked and specific spatial cognitive deficit, not accounted for by their general retardation in other cognitive domains. Their performance on drawing tasks, judgment of line orientation, spatial construction, and spatial transformations is dramatically impaired, not unlike the performance of patients with right hemisphere lesions. However, there is no indication that Williams Syndrome is associated with gross structural damage to either of the hemispheres; nor is there any indication of deficits in spatial attention, or any other signs associated with right hemisphere lesions. This unusual pattern of dysfunction appears not to be the effect of gross cortical lesions, but is a developmental deficit. Despite their severe spatial cognitive deficits, the Williams Syndrome children exhibit unimpaired performance on certain visual tasks such as recognition of unfamiliar faces under different conditions of lighting and orientation. This report presents the beginning investigation of these issues, using largely standardized tests. We are currently exploring the nature and level of the uneven neuropsychological profile of these children, working with larger groups of Williams Syndrome children, and contrasting Williams and Downs Syndrome children, matched in mental and chronological age.

The unusual pattern of deficits seen in this population allows for the specification of the various subcomponents of spatial cognition and their interrelationships in development. The apparent separation between certain visuoperceptive functions which are relatively spared, and other visuospatial functions which are profoundly impaired may turn out to be characteristic of this special population of children, but the basis for the distinction is not yet understood. Despite their impaired abilities on certain tasks, the children are able to perform other visual tasks, including those that involve perception of form, recognition of unfamiliar faces, and closure. In marked contrast, they are unable to perform across the board on tasks involving visuospatial cognitive functions, whether these have a motoric aspect (such as drawing or block design) or simply involve responses such as pointing (judgment of line orientation). These findings are consonant with a distinction that has been made recently in terms of the nonlanguage visuospatial domain. One basis for the cleavage in performance would implicate what have been called the "two visual systems," described in Morrow and Ratcliff and in Neville (this volume), as well as in Newcombe (1985). This is one possible basis for the interesting dissociation presented here. Another intriguing facet of the Williams Syndrome children's performance is the apparent inability to maintain two hierarchically organized levels in their drawings, as suggested by the results of the

Visual-Motor Integration Test. The children appear to handle the internal details but not the overall configuration. Delis, Robertson, and Efron (in press) have recently shown that right hemisphere damaged patients are impaired on tasks involving such hierarchically organized stimuli. We are currently pursuing directions which should pinpoint the nature and level of the deficits shown by these children.

We are examining a range of other specific behaviors in Williams Syndrome children, including language functioning, motor functioning, memory, and attention. Our studies so far suggest that the acquisition of both language and hand preference is delayed in Williams Syndrome children. Together with Helen Neville, we have been engaged in electrophysiological studies of brain activity with language and nonlanguage processing, and preliminary results suggest that there may be an abnormal pattern of cortical functioning in children with Williams Syndrome (Bellugi, Sabo, Neville & Culler, 1985). These studies will be combined with thorough investigations of the underlying basis for the disorder, including metabolic, neurological, and electrophysiological studies and neuroimaging techniques (CT scans and magnetic resonance imaging). In addition, in a separate series of studies together with Floyd Culler, we are investigating a possible genetic basis for the disorder.

Thus Williams Syndrome appears to affect behavior, language, and learning in highly specific ways. We report here one facet of a multidisciplinary study which should, in the long run, provide some clues to the neurological basis of the disorder. We have focused on the children's spatial cognitive deficits and the apparent dissociations between some visuospatial and visuoperceptual functioning. Such studies of specific dissociations in development among special populations may make a contribution toward understanding the components of spatial cognition and their underlying brain basis.

ACKNOWLEDGMENTS

This work was supported in part by National Institutes of Health Grants #NS15175, #NS19096, and #HD13249, the John D. and Catherine T. MacArthur Foundation Network on the Transition from Infancy to Early Childhood, and National Institutes of Health Grant #P 50 NS22343 as Project 4 of the Center for the Study of the Neurological Basis of Language, Behavior and Learning.

The photographs of Williams Syndrome children are provided courtesy of the Parents Group of the Williams Syndrome Association. We are very grateful to the children and parents who have taken part in our studies. In particular, we thank the children (pseudonyms Crystal, Ben, and Van) and their parents for their participation in our studies.

REFERENCES

Albert, M.L. 1973. A simple test of visual neglect. *Neurology*, 23:658-664.

Arnold, R., & Yule, W. 1985. The psychological characteristics of Infantile Hypercalcemia: A preliminary investigation. *Developmental Medicine and Child Neurology*, 27:49-59.

Ayres, A.J. 1980. *Southern California sensory integration tests.* Los Angeles: Western Psychological Services.

Beery, K.E., & Buktenica, N.A. 1967. *Developmental test of visual-motor integration.* Modern Curriculum Press: Cleveland, Ohio.

Bellugi, U., Sabo, H., Neville, H., & Culler, F.L. 1985. Language and visuospatial functions in children with Williams Syndrome. American Speech-Language-Hearing Association, Washington, D.C.

Bennett, F.C., LaVeck, B., & Sells, C.J. 1978. The Williams Elfin Facies Syndrome: The psychological profile as an aid in syndrome identification. *Pediatrics*, 61:303.

Benton, A.L., Van Allen, M.W., Hamsher, K. deS, & Levin, H.S. 1978. *Test of facial recognition, Form SL.* Iowa City, Iowa: Benton Laboratory of Neuropsychology, University of Iowa.

Benton, A.L., Varney, N.R., & Hamsher, K. deS. 1978. Visuospatial judgement: A clinical test. *Archives of Neurology*, 35:364-367.

Bishop, D.V.M. 1983. *Test for reception of grammar.* University of Newcastle upon Tyne.

Black, J.A., & Bonham-Carter, R.E. 1963. Association between aortic stenosis and facies in severe Infantile Hypercalcemia. *Lancet*, 2:745-749.

Brown, R. 1973. *A first language.* Cambridge, Mass.: Harvard University Press.

Culler, F.L., Jones, K.L., & Deftos, L.J. 1985. Impaired calcitonin secretion in patients with Williams Syndrome. *The Journal of Pediatrics*, 107(5):720-723.

Delis, D.C., Robertson, L.C., & Efron, R. In press. Hemispheric specialization of memory for visual hierarchical stimuli. *Journal of Clinical and Experimental Neuropsychology*.

Fowler, A.E. 1981. Language learning in Downs Syndrome children. University of Pennsylvania, Ms.

Frank, R. 1983. Speech language characteristics of Williams Syndrome: Cocktail party speech revisited. Paper presented at American Speech-Language-Hearing Association.

Gleitman, L.R. 1983. Biological dispositions to learn language. In W. Demopoulos and A. Marras (Eds.), *Language learning and concept acquisition.* Norwood, NJ: Ablex Publishing Corp.

Goodglass, H., & Kaplan, E. 1972. *Assessment of aphasia and related disorders.* Philadelphia: Lea and Febiger.

Harris, A.J. 1974. *Harris tests of lateral dominance* (3rd ed.) New York: The Psychological Corporation.

Ingram, D. 1975. If and when transformations are acquired by children. In D.P. Data (Ed.), *Developmental psycholinguistics: Theory and applications.* Washington, DC: Georgetown University Press.

Jones, K.L., & Smith, D.W. 1975. The Williams Elfin Facies Syndrome: A new perspective. *Journal of Pediatrics,* 86:718-723.

Lansdell, H. 1968. Effect of extent of temporal lobe ablations on two lateralized deficits. *Physiology and Behavior,* 3:271-273.

Lansdell, H. 1970. Relation of extent of temporal removals to closure and visuomotor factors. *Perceptual and Motor Skills,* 31:491-498.

Lewis, R., & Kupke, T. 1977. *The grooved pegboard.* Lafayette, IN: Lafayette Instrument Co.

Mooney, C.M. 1957. Age in the development of closure ability in children. *Canadian Journal of Psychology,* 11(4):219-310.

Neale, M.M. 1980. A description of the psycholinguistic abilities of a Williams Syndrome population. Ph.D. dissertation, The American University.

Newcombe, F. 1985. Neuropsychology qua interface. Presidential address to International Neuropsychology Society. *Journal of Clinical and Experimental Neuropsychology,* 7:663-681.

Newcombe, F. 1969. *Missile wounds of the brain.* London: Oxford University Press.

Newcombe, F., & Russell, W.R. 1969. Dissociated visual perceptual and spatial deficits in focal lesions of the right hemisphere. *Journal of Neurology, Neurosurgery, and Psychiatry,* 32:73-81.

Oldfield, R. 1971. The assessment and analysis of handedness. The Edinburgh inventory. *Neuropsychologia,* 9:97-113.

Poizner, H., Kaplan, E., Bellugi, U., & Padden, C. 1984. Visuospatial processing in deaf brain-damaged signers. *Brain and Cognition,* 3:281-306.

Poizner, H., Klima, E.S., & Bellugi, U. In press. *What the hands reveal about the brain.* Cambridge, MA: MIT Press/Bradford Books.

Sinclair, H. 1975. The role of cognitive structures in language acquisition. In E.H. Lenneberg and E. Lenneberg (Eds.), *Foundations of language development,* Vol. 1. New York: Academic Press.

Wechsler, D. 1974. *Wechsler intelligence scale for children—revised.* New York: The Psychological Corporation.

Williams, J.C.P., Barrett-Boyes, B.G., & Lowe, J.B. 1961. Supravalvular aortic stenosis. *Circulation,* 24:1311-1318.

SPATIAL COGNITION AND BRAIN ORGANIZATION: CLUES FROM THE ACQUISITION OF A LANGUAGE IN SPACE

14

LAURA A. PETITTO
McGill University

URSULA BELLUGI
Salk Institute

Intensive research over the past two decades has been directed at determining whether natural language is specific to the spoken modality. This research has uncovered the existence of natural languages residing entirely outside of the realm of sound, sign languages that are instead expressed and perceived in the visual-spatial modality. American Sign Language (ASL), a naturally evolved language that is used by most North American deaf persons, is the most closely understood of these visual-spatial languages. As a result of studies by Stokoe (1960), Klima and Bellugi (1979) and others, the basic organizational structure and grammatical components of ASL have been identified. Analyses of ASL have revealed that it exhibits formal organization at the same two levels found in spoken languages, including a sublexical level of structuring internal to the sign (analogous to the phonemic level; Battison, 1978; Bellugi, 1980; Stokoe, 1960), and a level that specifies the precise ways that meaningful units are bound together to form complex signs and signs to form sentences (analogous to the morphological and syntactic levels; Klima & Bellugi, 1979; Bellugi, 1980; Padden, 1981, 1982, 1983; Supalla, 1982; Wilbur, 1979; Wilbur & Petitto, 1981, 1983). ASL also shares important underlying principles of organization with spoken languages (e.g., constrained systems of features, rules based on underlying forms, recursive grammatical processes). Thus, research on ASL yields the surprising conclusion that human languages are not restricted to the speech channel.

The existence of signed languages presents a natural experiment providing data relevant to several essential problems in the study of human cognition, the fundamental one being how modality influences the knowledge and use of language. Until recently, the human linguistic capacity was studied exclusively with respect to spoken languages. Some researchers have argued that the structural properties of spoken languages reflect constraints imposed by the perceptual, cognitive and motoric capacities that subserve speech and hearing (e.g., Bellugi & Studdert-Kennedy, 1980). For example, the linear, sequential ordering of phonemes universally observed in spoken languages may be a consequence of biological constraints on the production of sound. However, a different set of constraints might be relevant to languages in the visual-gestural modality. On the one hand, it would seem that signed and spoken languages should differ in fundamental ways; they involve different types of signals (visual-gestural vs. auditory), they are differentially adapted to conveying various kinds of information (e.g., imagistic, analogic), perceived through different sensory systems, remembered using different memory structures, and may be subserved by different neural structures. On the other hand, both spoken and signed languages convey identical kinds of linguistic information and are used to perform the same communicative function. Because of the linguistic status of signed languages, several fundamental questions can be addressed, including how modality influences the structure of language, and how differences in the way information is represented in the two modalities affect the acquisition, processing, and neural representation of language. In particular:

- Are the properties of the Universal Grammar hypothesized by Chomsky (1965, 1975) "modality-independent?" Specifically, do these properties require an aural-oral basis, or can they be expressed in gesture and space?

- Which properties of languages are incidental consequences of the modality of transmission, and which are essential and modality-free?

- Do the differences in how information is represented in the two modalities affect how the languages are structured and processed? The visual-gestural channel affords greater potential for the perception and production of simultaneous sources of information; perception and production in the speech channel may make greater use of linear and temporal contrasts between discrete sources of information.

- Is the course of the acquisition process similar for languages in the two modalities or does acquisition differ because of modality-specific properties (e.g., the potential for iconic or indexical structures in a signed language)?
- Does the pattern of cerebral specialization for language differ depending on modality? Is the pattern of cerebral specialization for language speech-dependent, or is it neurologically modifiable depending on the mode of language transmission?

Moreover, signed languages make it possible to investigate the human capacity to process visual-spatial information from a wholly different vantage point, because they use space in an extraordinary way, incorporating it into the language in a conventional manner. The unique role of space in signed languages is perhaps their most significant distinguishing aspect, and one that is crucial for understanding spatial cognition. In ASL, for example, the space in front of the signer's body functions as a central component of the grammar of the language. Specifically, ASL makes *linguistic* use of visual-spatial information that is otherwise used only for *non-linguistic* functions in hearing (speaking) persons (such as negotiating within a three-dimensional world, etc). Interestingly, unlike spoken languages, ASL displays a marked preference for layered (as opposed to linear) organization of linguistic information in space, a situation that no doubt arises out of the very different possibilities of the visual-gestural mode (Bellugi & Studdert-Kennedy, 1980). The elements that distinguish signs (handshapes, movements, places of articulation) occur in contrasting spatial arrangements; grammatical mechanisms exploit the possibility of simultaneous and multidimensional articulation in the signing space. In the lexical items, the morphological processes, the syntax and discourse structure of ASL, such multi-layering of linguistic elements in space is a pervasive characteristic (Bellugi, 1980; Poizner, Klima, Bellugi & Livingston, 1983).

Because space is used linguistically, we can determine which aspects of the human capacity to process this information are due to the *form* of the information, and which are due to the *functions* it subserves. If it is the form of the information that matters, we should expect to see commonalities between both the linguistic and non-linguistic uses of space. These might be realized as commonalities in perception, learning, or memory that reflect a common neurological substrate. If it is the functions that are crucial, there may be differences in the representation of linguistic and non-linguistic uses of space, despite the fact that the nature of the information that informs these functions shares a common sense modality (i.e., visual-spatial).

LINGUISTIC USE OF SPACE IN ASL

Knowledge of the several important ways in which ASL uses space is critical to an understanding of this language and to the issues discussed above. The linguistic distinctions that are marked by spatial devices in ASL occur at all levels of language structure. Some ways that space functions linguistically in ASL are represented in Figure 14.1, and discussed below.

Lexical Use of Space. ASL uses space to differentiate between formationally identical signs. Signs in ASL are structurally differentiated by specifying the values of a closed set of three formational elements (or parameters), analogous in function to the phonemic inventory of a spoken language: hand configuration, movement of the hand(s), and spatial location of the hand(s) in front of the signer's body. Thus, signs that are formationally the same on other parameters, but differ only in terms of spatial location, are minimally differentiated by this spatial feature. For example, spatial locus minimally differentiates the lexical signs SUMMER, UGLY, DRY made with the same handshape and movement at the forehead, nose and chin (shown in Figure 14.1a. See Appendix for notation conventions).

Morphological Use of Space. Aspects of the space in front of the signer's body actually serve as morphological units in the language, conveying such grammatical information as person, number, and temporal aspect (specific information about the nature of the passage of time). For example, to indicate the grammatical subject and object in the phrase "I give to you," the ASL sign GIVE is positioned first at the space in front of the signer's body that indicates first person or subject (the signer's body), and then moves to the space denoting second person or object (a point that is directly in front of the signer). These spatial and movement changes on the root form of signs are obligatory components of ASL's structure, similar in function to grammatical inflections in spoken language (see Klima & Bellugi, 1979). They co-occur with the sign stem, using dimensions unique to a visual-spatial language. Some sample inflections on the single sign GIVE are shown in Figure 14.1b, including inflections for person, number, distributional aspect, temporal aspect, e.g., convey-

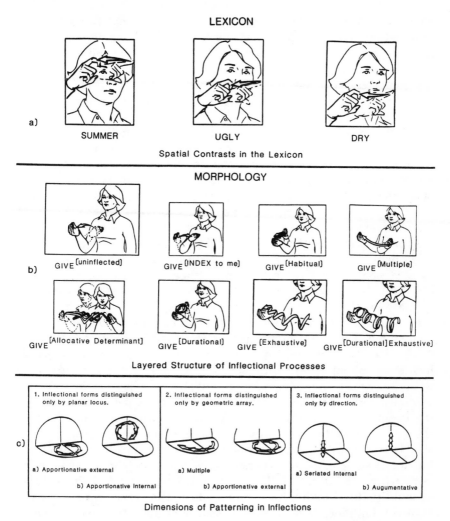

Figure 14.1. Lexical and morphological spatial contrast in ASL. (a) Spatial contrast in the lexicon; (b) Layered structure of inflectional processes; (c) Dimensions of patterning in inflections.

ing the meanings "give to me," "give regularly," "give to them," "give to certain ones at different times," "give over time," "give to each," "give over time to each in turn."

Dimensions of Patterning. In the kinds of distinctions that are morphologically marked, ASL is like many spoken languages; in the degree to which morphological marking is a favored form of patterning in the language, ASL is again similar to some spoken languages, but unlike English. In the *form* by which its lexical items are systematically modified in the sentences of the language, ASL has aspects that are unique. Figure 14.1c shows some of the dimensions of patterning, specific to a visual spatial language, used to build up morphological contrasts in ASL; planes in signing space; different geometric contours (lines, arcs, circles); directions of movement.

Syntactic Use of Space. A most striking and distinctive use of space in ASL is its role in syntax and discourse, especially in pronominal reference, verb agreement, and the anaphoric referencing systems. In this language, person indexing and re-indexing is accomplished primarily by manipulating the space in front of the signer's body. To refer to referents that are physically present in the discourse environment a signer may point directly to self, when indicating first person, and directly to others, when referencing either second or third person. However, an abstract use of space occurs when reference is made to referents that are either physically or temporally distant. Here, nominal referents are established at arbitrary and spatially distinct loci along an imaginary horizontal plane in front of the signer's body. Subsequent pronominal referencing is accomplished by pointing (gazing or shifting the body) to the previously established spatial locus. Further, the establishment of spatial loci is an obligatory syntactic device that interacts in complex ways with the verb agreement and anaphoric referencing systems, whereby verb signs move between established spatial loci in specifying grammatical relations such as subject of the verb and object of the verb. Thus, the linguistic manipulation of the space in front of the signer's body is used to denote central and universal features of human language: person, person roles, and anaphoric referencing (e.g., Klima & Bellugi, 1979; Padden, 1983; Bahan & Petitto, 1980; Wilbur, 1979). Finally, the language has other grammatical devices such as classifiers, size-and-shape specifiers and other means which are also used for representing *literal* (topographic) spatial relations (e.g., description of the layout of one's room, description of the size and shape of objects as in Supalla, 1982).

In sum, ASL is unique in its use of space at all levels of linguistic organization: lexical, morphological, syntactic, and discourse. While ASL is the most thoroughly analyzed of the signed languages of the world to date, other signed languages examined (e.g., Lange des Signes Quebecoise, the language used by most French Canadian deaf persons; Petitto, 1985) suggest that these characteristics may turn out to be universal characteristics of signed languages.

In addition to their use of space, signed languages are unique in the extent and degree of "motivatedness" between meaning and form. Characteristically, ASL lexical items themselves are often globally iconic, their form resembling some aspect of what they denote. At the morphological and syntactic levels also, there is often some congruence (motivatedness) between form and meaning. Spoken languages are not without direct clues to meaning (reduplication processes and ideophones provide direct methods of reflecting meaning through form, for example). But in sign language such transparency is pervasive. ASL thus bears striking traces of its representational origins, but at the same time it is fully grammaticized.

In this chapter we will focus on how the spatial properties of ASL influence its acquisition in deaf children of deaf parents who are learning sign language as a native language. By examining the acquisition of specifically linguistic space in ASL (as opposed to other types of more general spatial cognitive knowledge), important information about both the representation and the organization of space in development may be uncovered.

THE ACQUISITION OF LINGUISTIC SPATIAL DEVICES IN ASL

Like hearing children, deaf children must be able to negotiate within the spatial environment of a three-dimensional world; that is, they possess a comparable (if not identical) spatial representational system as that found in hearing people, one that is rich enough to support the full range of general, cognitive (and actual) manipulations of visual-spatial information (e.g., knowledge of routes, landmarks, and relations among objects, ability to shift perspective, ability to view and manipulate mental images, etc.). However, it is the specific, linguistic use of space where the most dramatic differences between signed and spoken languages are found. Here, the space in front of the child's body must be carved out and used in the service of the language. How the deaf child comes to acquire a linguistic as well as a general cognitive representation of space is one of the most elusive, yet important questions in the study of sign acquisition today.

One might have every reason to believe that such surface differences between signed and spoken language will influence the course of language acquisition. Given the surface differences between signed languages and spoken languages, the task that the deaf child faces in learning sign language may be radically different from that faced by the hearing child. If, for instance, the mapping between meaning and form is more direct than in spoken language, then this might allow the child a more direct route into the language at all levels. Not only are there differences in the surface structure of the languages, but also differences in the channels used for production and perception. Would these spatial, iconic aspects of ASL influence the course of acquisition?

Over the course of a decade, we have studied the acquisition of sign language by deaf children of deaf parents by obtaining monthly videotapes of mother-child interaction in the home, augmented by experimental interventions. Longitudinal studies of ten children between the ages of one year and eight years have been undertaken and the course of acquisition of different grammatical domains (e.g., pronominal reference, verb agreement, inflectional processes, derivational processes) across the same children has been charted. There are cross sectional studies with deaf children of deaf parents between the ages of two and ten years old, as well as formal tests for each of the grammatical processes found in ASL (for phonological, lexical, inflectional, derivational, and compounding processes as well as syntax (Lillo-Martin, Bellugi & Poizner, 1985). These tests have been normed with young deaf adults and are being used with deaf brain damaged signers in studies of the effects of left and right hemisphere lesions on a visual spatial language (Poizner, Klima & Bellugi, in press). Further, acquisition studies have led to the investigation of the interplay and separation between the acquisition of a spatial language and its spatial cognitive underpinnings.

As a result of these studies, the basic course of language acquisition in signing deaf children of deaf parents is now fairly well understood. There are detailed accounts of the child's acquisition of "phonology," the stages of manual articulation (Boyes-Braem, 1973, 1981; McIntire, 1977; Petitto, 1980); acquisition of complex verb morphology (Bellugi & Klima, 1982; Lillo-Martin, 1984 and in press; Meier, 1982; Newport & Supalla, 1980; Supalla, 1982); development of grammatical and semantic categories (Launer, 1982; Newport & Ashbrook, 1977); and studies of the acquisition of pronominal and anaphoric referencing (Bellugi, in press; Bellugi & Klima, 1980; Hoffmeister, 1978; Lillo-Martin, Bellugi, Struxness & O'Grady, 1985; Loew, 1982, 1983; Petitto, 1977, 1980, 1983a & b, and in press). These studies have established that despite the differences in modality, deaf children acquire ASL as a first language in ways that are remarkably similar to those of hearing children acquiring spoken language. For an excellent overview, see Newport and Meier (1986).

Several studies, however, are especially revealing with regard to the acquisition of spatial and iconic properties of sign language. These studies will be summarized below.

The Transition from Gesture to Symbol

A study of the acquisition of personal pronouns in deaf children (Petitto, 1983 a & b, and in press) provides a striking demonstration of unexpected similarities between deaf and hearing children's acquisition of language. Three noteworthy features characterize hearing children's acquisition of pronouns. First, they are acquired in a particular order. Beginning around 16-20 months children begin producing the pronoun *me*, followed by *you* around 22 months, and then third person pronouns (e.g., Charney, 1978; MacNamara, 1982). Second, prior to the acquisition of these forms children and their mothers use proper nouns (e.g., "Jane do something" instead of "I do something"), rather than use the pronoun *I* or *me*. Third, around the time when *you* enters the child's lexicon some children— although not all—engage in systematic pronoun reversal errors. For example, mother might say to the child "Do *you* want to go to the store?" and the child would reply "Yes, *you* want to go store." Similarly, the child may understand and produce *me* to refer to the adult rather than to herself; although it is uncommon for symmetrical *you-me* error pairs to co-occur. Some researchers have proposed that these children initially regard pronouns as having fixed or stable referents like names (i.e., *you* is equivalent to child, or *me* is equivalent to addressee) rather than having changing or "unstable" referents that depend upon the speaker role (Charney, 1978; Chiat, 1981, 1982; Clark, 1978).

Although the use of personal pronouns in ASL is constrained by the grammar of the language, they are not formed by arbitrary symbols. Rather, they are represented by pointing directly to the addressee (e.g., YOU), or self (e.g., ME). Thus, the formational aspects of the functional equivalent of personal pronouns in ASL resemble extra-linguistic pointing gestures which commonly accompany speech and are used pre-linguistically by hearing and deaf children. This provides a means for investigating the deaf child's transition from pre-linguistic gestural communication to linguistic-symbolic communication because gesture and symbol are virtually identical in form.

Petitto (1983, a & b) investigated deaf children's acquisition of personal pronouns both experimentally and in spontaneous mother-child interactions. She found that despite the transparency of the pointing gesture deaf children acquire knowledge of personal pronouns over a period of time, displaying errors similar to those of hearing children. Although deaf children begin pointing at around 9 months, they do not use the pointing form to indicate "you" and "me" until around 17-20 months, the precise range that hearing children first begin to use verbal pronouns systematically. Soon after the sign ME has been established, deaf children gain productive control over the YOU pronoun (around 22-23 months), followed by third person pronouns. Like hearing children, they also use full proper nouns prior to the productive use of pronouns despite the fact that they use the pointing form in a rich, varied and communicative fashion. Surprisingly, the children used the pointing form to refer to aspects of their caretaker's body but seemed to avoid the use of the pointing form to indicate the adult. For example, one child (age 1:11) used the pointing form to refer to a spot on her mother's bathing suit but did not use it to refer to her mother as "you," not even in an experimental task specifically designed to elicit this and other pronouns. Although the phenomenon of "avoidance" has been noted previously in child language literature (e.g., Ferguson & Farwell, 1975), this case is especially intriguing because the children avoided a particular *function* of a form rather than the *form* itself. Further, like hearing children, the deaf children initially exhibited confusion over which pronouns were appropriate given a particular linguistic context, and they produced pronoun reversal errors as well. See Figure 14.2a for illustrations of some pronoun reversal errors.

Petitto's results provide dramatic evidence of the transition from gesture to linguistic symbol in a signed language. The child shifts from conceptualizing person pointing as part of the class of deictic gestures to viewing them as elements within the linguistic, grammatical system of ASL; this constitutes one form of evidence that the transition from gesture to sign requires a reorganization of the child's knowledge. Despite differences between the modalities that might be relevant to acquisition, both deaf and hearing children showed very similar performance in acquiring personal pronouns. The study provides evidence for a *discontinuity* in the child's transition from pre-linguistic gesture to linguistic communication system, even when they share a single channel of expression and the forms are wholly transparent. It appears to make little difference whether pronominal terms are symbolized by arbitrary streams of sound segments as in spoken language or by pointing signs which are indistinguishable in form from pointing gestures. Indeed, this study provides strong evidence that the structure of a gesture as a linguistic unit, rather than the iconicity of its form, determines the course of acquisition.

Acquisition of Verb Agreement for Present Referents

When expressing relations among present referents, a specific class of ASL verbs must "agree" with their noun arguments. Specifically,

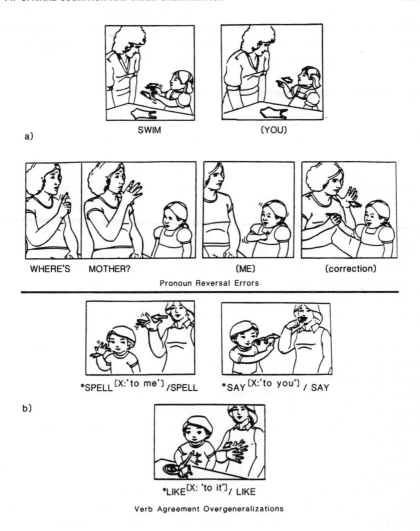

Figure 14.2. Young deaf children's acquisition of ASL. (a) Pronoun reversal errors; (b) Verb agreement overgeneralizations.

verb agreement in ASL is accomplished by moving an indexible verb from the spatial locus established for the subject to the spatial locus of the object (Padden, 1983). Some indexible verbs have obligatory double-argument agreement (i.e., the verb must inflect for both subject and object), some verbs can agree only with a single argument, and some undergo optional agreement. In all cases, however, the general mechanism for verb agreement is the same: the path movement of the verb "incorporates" the spatial loci that is associated with noun arguments, be they present in the signing environment or abstract spatial loci (Klima & Bellugi, 1979; Padden, 1983). Recall the example of the verb GIVE cited earlier. To express the meaning "I give to you," the verb is moved from a locus in a horizontal plane of space near the signer to a locus in that plane on the direction of the addressee. Similarly, to express "You give to me," the verb moves from the addressee to the signer.

Although the structural regularity in the ASL verb agreement system has led to its analysis as a morphological component of the language, aspects of the system nonetheless have an iconic basis. In particular, sentences using verb agreement with a verb such as GIVE could be said to resemble the iconic mime and action of giving and receiving. How do children acquire a morphological system which is grammaticized but which nevertheless displays a large amount of iconicity? A priori, one might expect the morphological variants of forms such as GIVE would be acquired relatively early; that the transparency in the forms of the sign would facilitate their acquisition, regardless of the fact that these are analyzed as morphologically inflected forms.

Meier (1981, 1982) analyzed the acquisition of the verb agreement system both longitudinally and experimentally, uncovering several stages. First, Meier noted that deaf children using two to three signs (around age two) do not make use of the inflectional apparatus of ASL. Instead, they use the *uninflected* (or citation) form of the verb. Interestingly, inflections are omitted even from the child's imitations of parental utterances. Additionally, Newport and Ashbrook (1977) show that young deaf children initially favor the use of sequential ordering of signs rather than spatial organization to mark grammatical relations in their signing.

Second, deaf children between the ages of two and three begin to produce inflected forms of verbs. However, children make revealing errors during this time. Although information about subject and object (i.e., the grammatical arguments of the verb) is reflected in verb's *path movement*, deaf children have been observed to include personal pronouns in their sentences involving such verbs nonetheless (Petitto, 1977, 1980, 1983a; Meier, 1981, 1982). For example, one girl (age 2:3) studied by Petitto (1983a) attempted to convey to her mother that grandmother gave her (the child) a book by signing the following: *GRANDMA GIVE [X: "to you"] ME. Despite the potentially mimetic and transparent quality of the sign sentence "give to me," the deaf child appears neither to perceive nor to exploit this iconicity, signing "give to you" instead. Rather, the child appears to analyze segments of her language morpheme-by-morpheme, and to integrate such segments into her linguistic system over time. (In this case, it appears that the child has realized that a verb's path movement is linguistically relevant, but she appears not to know that *direction* in addition to *path movement* is critical to mastering the verb agreement system.)

By age three to three and a half, deaf children master and consistently use the verb agreement system with present referents in required contexts (Meier, 1982). However, they inflect some verbs for subject and object which do not accept such inflections in the adult language. By inflecting non-indexible verbs, deaf children are exhibiting the same type of morphological overgeneralizations that are typically observed in hearing children with comparable linguistic competence (see Figure 14.2b for overgeneralizations of verb agreement in ASL).

Thus, we have seen that deaf children's mastery of the verb agreement system in ASL occurs at the same age as mastery of comparable linguistic processes in hearing children, despite the seemingly mimetic nature of the forms presented to them.

The Integration of the Lexical and Morphological Systems: Spatially Organized Syntax and Discourse

Evidence suggests that despite obvious differences in surface structure and modality, the time course of the acquisition of ASL is remarkably similar to that for spoken languages (Bellugi & Klima, 1982; Newport & Meier, 1986). We now turn to the acquisition of a domain in which the nature of the apparatus used in ASL may have its most striking effect: the means by which relations among signs are stipulated in sentences and in discourse. Languages have different ways of marking grammatical relations between their lexical items. In English, it is primarily the order of the lexical items that marks the basic grammatical relations; in other languages, it is the morphology of case marking or verb agreement that signals these relations. ASL, by contrast, specifies relations among signs primarily through the manipulation of sign forms in space. In sign language, space itself carries linguistic meaning. The most striking and distinctive use of space in ASL is in its role in syntax and discourse, especially in nominal assignment, pronominal reference, verb agreement, anaphoric reference and the referential spatial framework for discourse. In this section, we turn to some of the spatial cognitive, memorial, and linguistic requirements involved in a language whose syntax is essentially spatial, and then consider the consequences of these requirements for acquisition of such a language.

Consider a review of the use of spatial loci for referential indexing, coreference, verb agreement, and the fixed and shifting spatial
framework underlying sentences and discourse. Nominals introduced into ASL discourse may be assigned to arbitrary reference
points in a horizontal plane of signing space. In signed discourse,
pointing again to a specific locus clearly "refers back" to a previously established nominal, even with many other signs intervening.
This spatial indexing allows explicit coreference and may reduce
ambiguity: In ASL, coreferential nominals must be indexed to the
same locus point, both within and across sentences. Verb signs
move between such points in specifying grammatical relations, thus
the ASL systems of verb agreement is also essentially spatialized.
Classes of verbs bear obligatory markers for person (and number) via
spatial indices (see Figure 14.3 for an example sentence requiring
spatial agreement).

The same signs in the same order, but with a reversal in direction
of spatial endpoints of the verb, would indicate different grammatical relations. Because verb agreement may be given spatially, sentences whose signs are made in different temporal orders can still
have the same meaning. The verb agreement system in ASL can be
extended to complex embeddings as diagrammed in Figure 14.3b, an
illustration of the spatial arrangement of an ASL sentence meaning
"John encouraged him to urge her to permit each of them to take up
the class." In function, this system is like grammatical devices in
spoken languages. However, in its form—marking connections
between spatial points—spatially organized syntax in ASL bears the
imprint of the mode in which the language evolved (Padden, 1983;
Bellugi & Klima, 1982; Lillo-Martin, 1985).

The horizontal plane in front of the signer's torso is the locus for
indices of definite reference (that is, if the speaker has already introduced a referent into the discourse). Different spaces may be used to
contrast events, to indicate reference to time preceding the utterance, to express hypotheticals and counterfactuals. It is also possible
to embed a subspace within another subspace, as in embedding past-
time context within conditional subspace, illustrated in Figure 14.3c.

Creating a spatial referential framework for syntax and discourse
is complicated by some interacting mechanisms. Whereas the
referential system described above is a fixed system in which nominals remain associated with specific points in space until "erased,"
the spatial referential framework sometimes shifts; third person
referents may be assigned to the locus in front of the signer's torso
which otherwise denotes self reference. When this shift occurs, the
whole spatial plane rotates, and previously established nominals are

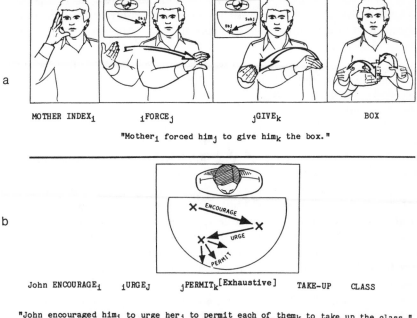

MOTHER INDEX$_i$ $_i$FORCE$_j$ $_j$GIVE$_k$ BOX

"Mother$_i$ forced him$_j$ to give him$_k$ the box."

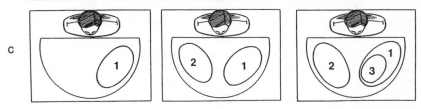

John ENCOURAGE$_i$ $_i$URGE$_j$ $_j$PERMIT$_k$[Exhaustive]   TAKE-UP   CLASS

"John encouraged him$_i$ to urge her$_j$ to permit each of them$_k$ to take up the class."

Spatial reference can be embeded, one subspace in another.

Figure 14.3. Spatially organized syntax in ASL. (a) ASL sentence requiring spatial agreement; (b) Complex embedding and spatial indices; (c) Spaces embedded in spaces in ASL discourse.

now associated with new points. In this system a fixed referential framework may be implied for the addressee, but it is not spatially fixed, thus adding complexity to the spatial cognitive requirements of the language (Bahan & Petitto, 1980; Padden, 1982, 1983, in press).

A Deaf Child's Storytelling. Petitto (1977, 1980) and Loew (1982, 1983) have completed studies of deaf children's spontaneous narratives, examining in particular the acquisition of the systems underlying anaphoric reference. For example, Petitto finds the following stages in the acquisition of storytelling in one signing child:

—At 3:0 Jason freely and happily told stories about non-present referents despite the fact that they were extremely difficult to understand, due to ambiguous spatial referencing. Although he was fully capable of indexing verbs to present referents at this time (i.e., verb agreement), he was not able to do so grammatically when it required that he first establish a nominal in space for non-present referents. Instead, Jason signed all story characters at a single, center space, using *uninflected* verbs to denote relations among characters, all signed in a list-like fashion. Unfortunately, the participants in conversation with Jason were left in a quandary as to who did what to whom, because none of the obligatory establishment and co-referencing procedures had been observed.

—At 3:9, Jason's first use of a grammatical spatial device in his referencing on non-present story characters was observed. For the first time, the child used double argument *inflected* verbs in reference to non-present characters, but did not first establish the identity of the nominals that he was expressing verbal relations about. Nor did he use space differentially, as he still favored the use of center space.

—At 4:3 a unique phenomenon occurred. Jason began to (1) explicitly establish referents in the signing space, (2) differentiate the signing space by using gross spatial distinctions (i.e., *left, center*, and *right* spatial regions in front of his body), and (3) use inflected verbs in storytelling, but did so in a most unusual way. Instead of establishing story characters at discrete spatial indices in front of his body, Jason recounted the "Wizard of Oz" story by establishing all 11 of his characters at a signed, undifferentiated *right* space, reserving the *left* space as the point of introduction of some characters; for example, he had the "Wicked Witch of the West" enter from a high left space and "land" and remain at the space to his right. Further, all of his indexible verbs were inflected with an onset point in right space and an endpoint in center space. Jason also used center space for the ongoing description of the story's plot. Thus, what has come to be known as the "stacking phenomenon" (Petitto, 1977, 1980) occurred, whereby the child stacks referents up at a *single* location, thus still leaving reference unclear and ambiguous. Loew (1983) describes another child's first use of abstract spatial loci, in which the course of acquisition is nearly identical to Jason's. Finally, it is intriguing to note that Jason did not yet explicitly establish his characters by using the indexical point, one linguistic means for pronominal reference in ASL. Instead, all characters were established either non-manually with explicit eye-gaze shifts to the right space (i.e., using the "pronominal sight-line"), or by inflecting verbs from right space. It was not until later that Jason was first observed using the pointing form to establish non-present referents in the signing space.

The importance of such findings is the following. At a time when the child appears to possess (a) the individual spatial components necessary to construct grammatically correct anaphoric referencing in storytelling, and (b) the ability to cognitively comprehend and convey events about non-present referents (albeit in ungrammatical ways), he does not seem able to *integrate* these devices into a rule-governed linguistic system at the discourse level. Indeed, at age five, Jason begins to establish referents at distinct points along the horizontal arc in front of his body—using sight-line and verb agreement—thereby establishing referents and differentiating space at the sentence-level, but fails to consistently maintain the identity of the previously established spatial loci.

In summary, the deaf child's knowledge of the linguistic use of space in ASL necessarily has to include information on the (a) general differentiation of the signing space, (b) explicit establishment of nominals at discrete spatial loci, (c) consistent spatial identity of loci, and (d) contrastive use of established loci in sentences and in discourse. Children appear to acquire this knowledge over time and it appears not to be until around ages 7-10 that the fully mature anaphoric referencing system is mastered in syntax and discourse.

These findings raise several important questions which are being addressed in a separate series of studies (Bellugi, in press). Central to these issues is the relationship between cognition and language. In a spatially organized language, the relationship between acquisition in such an alternative medium and the development of its non-linguistic spatial cognitive substrate is crucial. As Newport and Meier put it in their excellent review article, "it has sometimes been suggested that spatial representation is conceptually difficult for the child, and therefore is a cognitively complex medium in which to signal linguistic functions. On this view, the acquisition of morphological devices in ASL should occur somewhat later than the acquisition of formally similar devices in spoken languages, where spatial representation is not involved" (Newport & Meier, 1986). In fact, the available evidence suggests that spatial representation itself does not constrain the acquisition process—the acquisition of morphological devices in ASL occurs on a strikingly similar time table to the acquisition of spoken language devices that are formally similar in complexity. We are now comparing the acquisition of discourse functions (anaphoric reference and discourse organization) across hearing and deaf children in the same sets of tasks as part of our ongoing research (Lillo-Martin, Bellugi, Struxness & O'Grady, 1985; Bellugi, in press).

The Comprehension of Spatially Organized Syntax

In a series of studies, the spatially organized syntax has been broken down into component parts, to investigate the young child's processing and comprehension of separate aspects of linguistic structure (Lillo-Martin, Bellugi & Poizner, 1985). The first findings are reported here asking whether the young signing child can understand that nominals may be abstractly associated with arbitrary points in space, even when he is not producing such spatial mechanisms regularly in his ongoing signing. This question was examined with sixty-eight deaf children of deaf parents between the ages of one and ten, using a formal language test devised to examine in particular the association of nominals with spatial loci (Bellugi, in press). The Nominal Establishment Test examines perception, comprehension, and memory for spatial loci associated with specific nominals. In the test, nominals are assigned to arbitrary loci in the horizontal plane of signing space that serves for definite reference. Two kinds of questions are asked: (a) where a certain nominal has been established (to which the child answers by pointing to a specific locus); and (b) what nominal has been established at a certain locus (to which the child answers by signing the nominal). Two and three nominals are used in different parts of the test. In associating loci with their nominal referents, this test assesses a key aspect of coreference structure in ASL syntax and discourse, and has been used with deaf children, with deaf adults of different language background, and with left and right brain-lesioned deaf signers (Poizner, Klima & Bellugi, in press. Figure 14.4 presents sample test items and results with sixty-eight deaf children of deaf parents.

When we attempted to test one and two-year-old deaf children, they were quite unable to deal with the test. When the deaf experimenter signed "Where's the doll?" (after previously associating an arbitrary locus with the sign DOLL), these young children looked around the room as if looking for an actual doll; one ran to her bedroom to take one out. When asked "What is at point X?" (an arbitrary point in space previously associated with the sign BOY), the children seem nonplussed. Thus one-year-olds and most two-year-olds fail the test; but importantly, already by the age of three, deaf children perform well on the task, even with two and three nominal

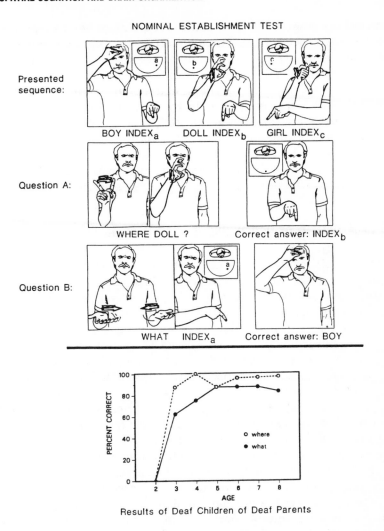

Figure 14.4. Results of the nominal establishment comprehension test. (a) Sample test items on nominal establishment comprehension test; (b) Results of test with deaf signing children between two and ten.

assignments to abstract points in a plane of signing space (Lillo-Martin, Bellugi, Struxness & O'Grady, 1985). This is despite the fact that such nominal establishment to spatial loci is not reported in deaf children's signing before the age of four and a half (e.g., Loew, 1983).

Such results suggest that the deaf child by the age of three does understand that in this language a nominal can be associated with

an arbitrary point in abstract space; furthermore he is adept at processing this aspect of the language structure, and can handle two
and three nominals at a time at different spatial loci with ease and
facility. We have since found that young deaf children can also process the spatial syntax of the language in sentences involving
minimal pairs, distinguished only by different spatial endpoints of
the verb for subject and object marking (Bellugi, in press). To identify the source of the difficulty in deaf children's discourse structures
we shall have to look further, and thus are investigating the
comprehension of co-reference and shifting spatial frameworks as
well as contrasting hearing and deaf children's narratives.

THE DEVELOPMENT OF NONLINGUISTIC SPATIAL COGNITIVE ABILITIES

At the same time, we are tracking the developmental course for the
acquisition of the spatial cognitive underpinnings which may form
the prerequisites for the mastery of linguistic system. In this manner
we will investigate whether the acquisition of spatially organized
syntax is yoked in particular ways to the development of its nonlanguage substrate; that is, to aspects of spatial cognition. So far
our early studies suggest that deaf children who have early exposure
to processing spatial relationships in a linguistic system perform at
the same level (and in some cases even show early enhancement)
compared to norms for hearing children (Bellugi, O'Grady, Lillo-
Martin, O'Grady, van Hoek & Corina, in press). The studies suggest that deprivation of auditory experience from birth and exposure
to a spatially organized linguistic system in no way impedes development of spatial cognition. In fact, the studies so far suggest that
there may even be some *enhancement* of certain spatial cognitive
abilities. These results are consistent with the studies by Neville of
deaf and hearing adults showing that in a spatial attention task,
deaf subjects are superior to hearing subjects (Neville, this volume).

THE BREAKDOWN OF SYNTAX AND SPATIAL COGNITION WITH BRAIN LESIONS

We find that despite the surface differences between signed and spoken languages, the acquisition process in deaf children is remarkably like that of the acquisition of spoken languages. Yet spoken
and signed languages are very different in surface organization.
One difference that we have highlighted is that processing linguistic
structure in ASL implies processing complex spatial cognitive under-

pinnings as well, aspects that would be irrelevant to processing linguistic structure in spoken languages. We are currently studying the interplay between spatial syntax and spatial cognition from the special perspective of the intertwining of the two in a visual spatial language.

In a separate series of studies, the effects of unilateral lesions in deaf signers are being investigated (Poizner, Klima & Bellugi, in press; Bellugi, Poizner & Klima, 1983; Poizner, Kaplan, Bellugi & Padden, 1984). Since ASL displays the complex linguistic structure found in spoken languages, but conveys much of its structure by manipulating spatial relations, it exhibits properties for which each of the hemispheres of hearing people shows a different predominant functioning. The study of brain damaged deaf signers offers a particularly revealing vantage point for understanding the organization of the brain for language and spatial cognitive functions and addressing the central issue of whether they can be dissociated in deaf signers.

Subjects for these studies carried out at the Salk Institute are right handed prelingually deaf signers who have had either right or left hemisphere lesions and matched controls. Subjects are administered a battery of tests specially designed to assess their capacities with respect to each of the levels of ASL linguistic structure, as well as a version of a standardized aphasia battery adapted for ASL (the Boston Diagnostic Aphasia Battery). In addition, tasks which are sensitive distinguishers of visuospatial performance in right hemisphere damaged hearing patients are administered.

On spatial cognitive tasks, there were clear cut differences in performance between left hemisphere damaged signers and right hemisphere damaged signers across a range of tasks. In nonlanguage spatial tasks, the right hemisphere damaged signers were severely impaired; they tended to show severe spatial disorganization, were unable to indicate perspective, neglected the left side of space, reflecting the classic visuospatial impairments seen in hearing patients with right hemisphere damage. These nonlanguage data suggest that the right hemisphere in deaf signers develops cerebral specialization for nonlanguage visuospatial functions (Poizner, Kaplan, Bellugi & Padden, 1984).

On linguistic tasks and in analyses of ongoing signing, the two groups of patients were also markedly different. The signers with right hemisphere damage were not aphasic. They exhibited fluent, grammatical virtually error-free signing, with good range of grammatical forms, no agrammatism, and no signing deficits. This preserved signing ability existed in the face of marked deficits in their processing of nonlanguage spatial relations. The signers with left hemisphere damage, in great contrast, were not impaired in non-language visuospatial tasks. The signers with left hemisphere strokes were, however, impaired in language functions—they showed frank sign language aphasias, including impairment of spatially organized syntax. Thus language functions in deaf signing adults are lateralized to the left hemisphere, even though ASL's linguistic units are visuospatial in nature (a function typically associated with the right hemisphere). Other important findings include the observation that the left hemisphere damaged signers exhibit selective loss of linguistic function, e.g., impairment in lexicon or in grammar (Bellugi, Poizner & Klima, 1983; and Poizner, Klima & Bellugi, in press).

These studies of brain damaged deaf signers suggest that hearing and speech are not necessary for the development of hemispheric specialization; furthermore, the data show that in these deaf signers it is the left hemisphere that is dominant for sign language. In addition, there is a complementary right hemisphere specialization for visuospatial nonlanguage functioning. This principled separation between brain organization for nonlanguage functioning and for language functioning—even in this unusual instance in which both involve visuospatial processing—is important, and supports from a new perspective the studies of impairment in spatial cognitive functions in the normal adult brain (Morrow & Ratcliff, this volume).

SUMMARY OF THE ACQUISITION OF SPATIAL SYNTAX AND SPATIAL COGNITION

In general, despite radical differences in language modality, deaf and hearing children show a dramatically similar course of development. The deaf child, as does his hearing counterpart, analyzes out discrete components of the language presented to him. Even when the modality and the language offer possibilities that seem intuitively obvious (for example, pointing for deictic pronominal reference), the deaf child appears to ignore their directness.

The study of the acquisition of American Sign Language in deaf children brings into focus some fundamental questions about the representation of language and the representation of space. Are these distinct forms of knowledge, or are these the manifestations of a general cognitive capacity that subserves both of them (i.e., language and space)? On the latter view, one's ability to use language or perceive spatial relationships may be governed by general cognitive processes (e.g., memory, learning) implicated in all types of knowledge, rather than domain-specific types of knowledge. Signed languages provide a way to address this issue because linguistic and non-linguistic information are in the same visual-spatial mode. Comparative studies of the structure and processing of signed languages provide important information about the biologically governed, modality-free versus channel-specific constraints on the human language faculty. Further, differentiation between linguistic and non-linguistic use of visual-spatial information in language acquisition as well as language breakdown provides important behavioral evidence for the existence of domain-specific types of knowledge including distinct language faculty that exists irrespective of the mode of language transmission.

Sign languages offer a powerful way to explore the links between language and visual-spatial knowledge, and their organization in the brain. Comparative study of aphasias among signing and speaking persons provides a way to determine whether it is the *type* of information which is relevant to cerebral organization (e.g., language versus non-language), or the *modality* in which it is produced and perceived (visual-spatial versus oral-aural). Further, comparative studies of how children acquire (or "build up") a representation of their language and how this knowledge breaks down in brain-injured deaf adults are especially revealing.

The data from studies of brain damaged deaf persons show that hearing and speech are not necessary for the development of hemispheric specialization: sound is *not* crucial. Further, the data show that in these deaf signers, it is the left hemisphere that is dominant for sign language. In addition, there is a complementary right hemisphere specialization for visuospatial functioning. The fact that much of the grammatical information is conveyed via spatial manipulation appears not to alter this complementary specialization.

Aspects of the data from acquisition studies show very similar patterns of dissociations between linguistic and non-linguistic forms of knowledge. For example, we observed that deaf children did not acquire pronouns earlier than hearing children, even though the linguistic means for expressing this information is of the same form as children's non-linguistic pointing gestures (Petitto, 1983a). The child's linguistic knowledge (concerning, for example, the relationship between form and meaning) is not merely constructed out of the non-linguistic materials at hand. In this sense, the language acquisition process in signing children is strikingly discontinuous with other forms of knowledge, and, thus, can also be viewed as being modular.

Taken together, these data suggest that in deaf children who are deprived of auditory experience but exposed to a natural visuospatial language by deaf parents from birth, language and spatial cognitive functions unfold normally and without deficit. These findings are in sharp contrast with studies across a different group of children with a specific metabolic disorder that results in a fractionation of language and spatial cognitive functioning (Bellugi, Sabo & Vaid, this volume). Moreover, the data presented both from the acquisition and breakdown of spatial language and spatial cognition suggest that biological foundations underlying language rest not on the form of the signal but rather in the linguistic function it subserves.

ACKNOWLEDGMENTS

This research was supported in part by National Institutes of Health grants #NS15174, #NS19096, #HD13249, National Science Foundation Grant #BNS 8309860 to Ursula Bellugi at the Salk Institute for Biological Studies; by a University Research Fellowship from Natural Science and Engineering Research Council and a grant from the Quebec Ministry of Education to Laura Petitto at McGill University; and by MacArthur Foundation Research Network on the Transition from Infancy to early Childhood to Elizabeth Bates at U.C.S.D. Laura Petitto was a Post Doctoral Fellow at Salk Institute under the MacArthur Network, and has currently established an independent laboratory at McGill University. The two authors have an indebtedness to Prof. Roger Brown of Harvard University as a common mentor (separated by a generation or two). Research presented in this paper draws on several sources including Bellugi, in press; Petitto, in press; and Bellugi, Poizner and Klima: Annual Report from the Salk Institute, 1985. Illustrations were drawn by Frank A. Paul, copyright Ursula Bellugi. We are grateful to Mark Seidenberg, Diane Lillo-Martin, Edward S. Klima, and Howard Poizner for their helpful comments on this chapter and the research on which it is based; and to Lucinda O'Grady, Maureen O'Grady, and Dennis Schemenauer for their aid in some of the experimental studies and analyses. We are also grateful to the deaf parents and children in our studies, as well as the staff of the California School for the Deaf in Fremont, California, for their spirited participation in several of the studies presented here.

REFERENCES

Bahan, B., & Petitto, L. A. 1980. Aspects of rules for character establishment and reference in American Sign Language storytelling. Ms., The Salk Institute for Biological Studies.

Battison, R. 1978. *Lexical borrowing in American Sign Language.* Silver Spring, Md.: Linstok Press.

Bellugi, U. In press. The acquisition of a spatial language. In F. Kessel (Ed.), *The development of language and language researchers.* Hillsdale, NJ: Lawrence Erlbaum Associates.

Bellugi, U. 1980. The structuring of language: Clues from the similarities between signed and spoken language. In U. Bellugi and M. Studdert-Kennedy (Eds.), *Signed and spoken language: Biological constraints on linguistic form.* Dahlem Konferenzen. Weinheim/Deerfield Beach, Fla.: Verlag Chemie, 115-140.

Bellugi, U., & Klima, E. S. 1982. The acquisition of three morphological systems in American Sign Language. *Papers and Reports on Child Language Development.* Stanford, California: Stanford University, 21:1-33.

Bellugi, U. & Klima, E. S. 1980. Morphological processes in a language in a different mode. In W. F. Hands, C. Hofbauer, and P. R. Clyne (Eds.), *The elements: Linguistic units and levels.* Chicago, Ill.: Chicago Linguistic Society, 21-42.

Bellugi, U. & Studdert-Kennedy, M. (Eds.). 1980. *Signed and spoken language: Biological constraints on linguistic form.* Dahlem Konferenzen. Weinheim/Deerfield Beach, Fla.: Verlag Chemie.

Bellugi, U., O'Grady, L., Lillo-Martin, D., O'Grady, M., van Hoek, K. & Corina, D. In press. Enhancement of spatial cognition in deaf children. In V. Volterra & C. Erting (Eds.), *From gesture to language.* Berlin: Springer-Verlag.

Bellugi, U., Poizner, H., & Klima, E. S. 1983. Brain organization for language: Clues from sign aphasia. *Human Neurobiology, 2:155-170.*

Boyes-Braem, P. 1981. Features of handshape in American Sign Language. Ph.D. dissertation, University of California, Berkeley.

Boyes-Braem, P. 1973. The acquisition of handshape in American Sign Language. Ms., The Salk Institute for Biological Studies.

Charney, R. 1978. The development of personal pronouns. Ph.D. dissertation, University of Chicago.

Chiat, S. 1981. Context-specificity and generalization in the acquisition of pronominal distinctions. *Journal of Child Language*, 8:75-91.

Chiat, S. 1982. If I were you and you were me: The analysis of pronouns in a pronoun-reversing child. *Journal of Child Language*, 9:359-397.

Chomsky, N. 1965. *Aspects of the theory of syntax.* Cambridge, Mass.: M.I.T. Press.

Chomsky, N. 1975. *The logical structure of linguistic theory.* New York: Plenum Press.

Clark, E. V. 1978. From gesture to word: On the natural history of deixis in language acquisition. In J. S. Bruner and A. Garson (Eds.), *Human growth and development*. Oxford: Clarendon Press.

Ferguson, C. & Farwell, C. 1975. Words and sounds in early language acquisition. *Language*, 51:419-39.

Hoffmeister, R. J. 1978. The acquisition of American Sign Language by deaf children of deaf parents: The development of demonstrative pronouns, locatives, and personal pronouns. Ph.D. dissertation, University of Minnesota.

Klima, E. S. & Bellugi, U. 1979. *The signs of language*. Cambridge, Mass.: Harvard University Press.

Launer, P. 1982. Acquiring the distinction between related nouns and verbs in American Sign Language. Ph.D. dissertation, City University of New York.

Lillo-Martin, D. In press. Effects of the acquisition of morphology on syntactic parameter setting. In *Proceedings of North Eastern Linguistic Society*, Montreal.

Lillo-Martin, D. 1985. Null pronouns and verb agreement in American Sign Language. In S. Berman, J. Cohe and J. McDonough (Eds.), *Proceedings of the North Eastern Linguistic Society*, 15:302-318.

Lillo-Martin, D. 1984. The acquisition of task-specific word formation devices in American Sign Language. *Papers and Reports on Child Language Development*, Stanford University Press. 23:74-81,

Lillo-Martin, D., Bellugi, U. & Poizner, H. 1985. Tests for American Sign Language. Ms., The Salk Institute for Biological Studies.

Lillo-Martin, D., Bellugi, U., Struxness, L., and O'Grady, M. 1985. The acquisition of spatially organized syntax. *Papers and Reports on Child Language Development*, Stanford University Press. 24:70-78.

Loew, R. 1983. Roles and reference in American Sign Language: A developmental perspective. Ph.D dissertation, University of Minnesota.

Loew, R. 1982. Roles and reference. In F. Caccamise, M. Garretson, and U. Bellugi (Eds.), *Proceedings of the Third National Symposium on Sign Language Research and Teaching*, 40-58.

McIntire, M. 1977. The acquisition of American Sign Language hand configurations. *Sign Language Studies*, 16.

MacNamara, J. 1982. *Names for things*. Cambridge, Mass.: Bradford Books/M.I.T. Press.

Meier, R. 1982. Icons, analogues, and morphemes: The acquisition of verb agreement in American Sign Language. Ph.D. dissertation, University of California, San Diego.

Meier, R. 1981. Icons and morphemes: Models of the acquisition of verb agreement in American Sign Language. *Papers and Reports on Child Language Development*, 20:92-99.

Newport, E.L. & Ashbrook, E. 1977. The emergence of semantic relations in American Sign Language. *Papers and Reports on Child Language Development*, 13:16-21.

Newport, E. and Meier, R. 1986. Acquisition of American Sign Language. In D.I. Slobin (Ed.), *The crosslinguistic study of language acquisition.* Hillsdale, NJ: Lawrence Erlbaum Associates, Vol. I, pt. 2.

Newport, E., & Supalla, T. 1980. The structuring of language: Clues from the acquisition of signed and spoken language. In U. Bellugi and M. Studdert-Kennedy (Eds.), *Signed and spoken language: Biological constraints on linguistic form.* Dahlem Konferenzen. Weinheim/Deerfield Beach, Fla.: Verlag Chemie, 187-212.

Padden, C. In press. Grammatical theory and signed languages. *Linguistics: The Cambridge study.* Cambridge, England: Cambridge Univ. Press.

Padden, C. 1983. Interaction of morphology and syntax in American Sign Language. Ph.D. dissertation, University of California, San Diego.

Padden, C. 1982. Syntactic spatial mechanisms. Ms., The Salk Institute for Biological Studies.

Padden, C. 1981. Some arguments for syntactic patterning in American Sign Language. *Sign Language Studies.* 32:239-259.

Petitto, L. A. In press. Language in the pre-linguistic child. In F. Kessel (Ed.), *The development of language and language researchers.* Hillsdale, NJ: Lawrence Erlbaum Associates.

Petitto, L. A. 1985. Deaf people in Canada: A look at their sign language and culture. In Parker (Ed.), *Encyclopedia of deaf people and deafness.* NY: McGraw-Hill.

Petitto, L. A. 1983a. From gesture to symbol: The relationship between form and meaning in the acquisition of personal pronouns in American Sign Language. Ph.D. dissertation, Harvard University.

Petitto, L. A. 1983b. From gesture to symbol: The relationship between form and meaning in the acquisition of American Sign Language. *Papers and Reports on Child Language Development,* 22:100-107.

Petitto, L. A. 1980. On the acquisition of anaphoric reference in ASL: Report on research in progress. Ms. The Salk Institute for Biological Studies.

Petitto, L. A. 1977. The acquisition of pronominal reference in American Sign Language. Ms. The Salk Institute for Biological Studies.

Poizner, H., Kaplan, E., Bellugi, U. & Padden, C. 1984. Visual-spatial processing in deaf brain-damaged signers. *Brain and Cognition,* 3:281-306.

Poizner, H., Klima, E. S., & Bellugi, U. In press. *What the hands reveal about the brain.* Cambridge, Mass.: Bradford Books/MIT Press.

Poizner, H., Klima, E. S., Bellugi, U. & Livingston, R. 1983. Motion analysis of grammatical processes in a visual-gestural language. In *Motion: Representation and Perception,* New York: The Association for Computing Machinery, 148-171.

Stokoe, W. 1960. Sign language structure: An outline of the visual communication systems of the American deaf. *Studies in Linguistics, Occasional Papers 8,* University of Buffalo.

Supalla, T. 1982. Structure and acquisition of verbs of motion and location in American Sign Language. Ph.D. dissertation, University of California, San Diego.

Wilbur, R. 1979. *American Sign Language and sign language system: Research and applications.* Baltimore: University Park Press.

Wilbur, R. & Petitto, L. 1981. Discourse structure of American Sign Language conversations. *Discourse Processes,* 6(3):225-241.

Wilbur, R. & Petitto, L. 1983. How to know a conversation when you see one: Discourse structure in American Sign Language conversations. *Journal of the National Student Speech Language Hearing Association,* 91:66-81.

APPENDIX

We use the following notation in this chapter:

SIGN = Words in capital letters represent English labels (glosses) for ASL signs. The gloss represents the meaning of the unmarked, unmodulated, basic forms of a sign out of context).

SIGN[X:] = A form that has undergone indexical change. The form or meaning may be specified, as in INFORM[X:1 to 2] or INFORM[X:I to you].

SIGN[N;M] = A form that has undergone inflection for number and distributional aspect or for temporal aspect, focus or degree.

SIGN[D:] = A form that has undergone derivational process.

*SIGN = An asterisk preceding a sign form indicates that it is ungrammatical within adult ASL.

CEREBRAL ORGANIZATION FOR SPATIAL ATTENTION

15

HELEN J. NEVILLE
Salk Institute for Biological Studies

Anatomical, physiological and behavioral research on non-human animals has documented an important role for early sensory experience in the functional development and organization of neurosensory systems. Similarly, in humans, several lines of evidence suggest that the nature and timing of early language experience impacts the organization of language relevant brain systems. However, very little evidence exists on the effects of early experience on the development of the cerebral systems that mediate different aspects of spatial cognition. In this chapter I will discuss evidence which suggests that both early sensory experience (auditory deprivation since birth) and early language experience (acquisition of a visual, sign language) have different and specific effects on the specializations of cortical areas important for visual spatial attention. Two large sets of literature provide background information relevant to this issue.

The first includes behavioral studies of humans conducted over the last century that have attempted to verify experimentally the idea that early unimodal deprivation may lead to compensatory enhancement of abilities in remaining modalities. Many such studies have employed tests which measure rather elementary sensory functions such as thresholds and acuity. Taken as a whole these results do not provide clear evidence for compensatory enhancement following early auditory or visual deprivation (reviewed by Burnstine,

Greenough & Tees, 1984). However, more recently a few studies have focused on the possibility that the effects of altered early sensory experience may be primarily upon higher order perceptual and attentional processes. Thus, there are reports that attention to and localization of auditory, cutaneous and kinesthetic information are superior in blind as compared to sighted individuals, while more elementary sensory functions may not be (Niemeyer & Starlinger, 1981; Starlinger & Niemeyer, 1981; Bagdonas, Kochyunas & Linyauskaite, 1980). These results suggest Diderot (1749) may have been very prescient when he attributed the greater sensitivity to sounds demonstrated by the blind to superior *attentional* capabilities. However, very little evidence is available concerning the possible neural mechanisms that might mediate such behavioral changes.

On the other hand, the second large literature relevant here is the studies of experimental animals describing neuroanatomical and neurophysiological changes following altered early sensory experience. These results suggest several possible neural mechanisms whereby compensatory behavioral changes might occur. For example, there are reports of enhanced neural activity and increases in several neuronal structures in cortical areas associated with remaining modalities ("compensatory hypertrophy"). Additionally, there is evidence suggesting that cortical areas that would normally subserve functions that are lost may process information from remaining modalities ("functional reallocation") (Burnstine, Greenough & Tees, 1984). In theory either or both of these types of changes might underlie compensatory changes in behavior. Typically in this literature the observed neural changes have not been related to performance measures. However two lines of evidence suggest that structures and functions of the "primary" visual system (the geniculo-striate pathway hypothesized to mediate the discrimination of structural features of objects), the "focal" system (Trevarthen, 1968) or the "what" system (Schneider, 1969) may be less affected by altered early visual experience than is the "secondary" visual system (the retino-collicular pathway which includes projections to parietal cortex; the "ambient" or "where" system). According to Hyvarinen (1982), dark-rearing in monkeys has only minimal effects on neurons in striate cortex but leads to very pronounced changes in the functional properties of neurons in parietal cortex (area 7). Moreover, Hyvarinen (1982), Regal, Boothe, Teller and Sackett (1976) and Riesen (1958) report that the behavioral effects of dark-rearing are less evident on measures of visual acuity and discrimination than they are on visual orientation and attention. Additionally, it is of interest to note that the Y cells of the retina, which are more prominent in the retinal periphery and whose projections include the superior colliculus and parietal cortex, are more susceptible to the effects of early visual deprivation than are the X cells (which are most prevalent in area centralis and project to the lateral geniculate and striate cortex) (Sherman, Hoffmann & Stone, 1972). These results might be seen as consistent with the studies of humans mentioned above that report more pronounced effects of early experience on functions such as spatial localization, attention and orientation than on tasks requiring discrimination and identification.

Also in agreement with the animal studies are results of a recent study of ours (Neville, Schmidt & Kutas, 1983) comparing visual evoked potentials from congenitally deaf and hearing adults. Whereas in normal hearing subjects visual evoked potentials were small and refractory over temporal brain regions, deaf subjects' visual evoked potentials were large and displayed faster recovery cycles. Significantly, these group differences were only observed in visual evoked potentials to *peripheral* visual stimuli. In order to further explore the possibility that early auditory deprivation might significantly affect the activity of functions hypothesized to be subserved by the second visual system we assessed behavioral and electrophysiological indices of focused attention to central and peripheral regions of visual space. We compared event-related brain potentials (ERPs) to attended and unattended stimuli in a paradigm similar to that used in past research in which ERPs have proven to be a sensitive index of the timing and nature of selective attention (Hillyard, Munte, & Neville, 1985; Hillyard, Simpson, Woods, Van Voorhis & Munte, 1984; Hillyard & Munte, 1984). In order to try and bring into play the functions of the secondary visual system subjects were required to detect the direction of motion of stimuli at specific attended locations. We first compared attention to different regions of visual space in normal hearing adults to test the hypothesis, raised by several different lines of evidence, that central visual information is attended to and processed in a fundamentally different fashion than are peripheral inputs. These data were compared with results from a group of profoundly and congenitally deaf adults who had acquired American Sign Language (ASL) as a first language, from their deaf parents. In order to separately assess the roles of auditory deprivation and acquisition of a visual language in producing differences between deaf and hearing individuals, we studied a group of normally hearing individuals who also had acquired ASL as a first language, from their deaf parents (termed "hearing of deaf"). The results from these experiments are fully reported in Neville and Lawson, in press, a, b and c.

METHODS

Subjects

Twelve normal hearing adults, 12 congenitally deaf adults and 12 hearing of deaf subjects, all between the ages of 17-26, were paid to participate in the experiment. All had normal or corrected vision and all but one were right handed. In each group half were female. All subjects were of normal neurological status, except for the hearing loss in the deaf subjects. Since each of the deaf subjects had deaf parents the etiology of the deafness was most likely hereditary, in which case the CNS was probably not directly affected by the disease.

STIMULI, PROCEDURES, AND DATA ANALYSIS

The stimuli were white squares (0.6 degree) presented with an ISI of 200-400 msec, 18 degrees to the left (lvf) and right (rvf) of a central fixation point (peripheral stimuli) and just above the fixation point (central stimuli). Eighty percent of the stimuli were single presentations of the squares for 33 msec ("standards"). Twenty percent of the stimuli consisted of one 33 msec presentation of a square in the same position as the standards, followed immediately by the illumination of one of eight adjacent squares for 33 msec. The appearance of the second square produced a clear illusory movement in the direction of the second square (i.e., along the vertical, horizontal or diagonal axes).

During each of six blocks of trials subjects foveated the fixation point and focused their attention on the stimuli in only one of three locations, in order to detect the direction of motion of the targets in that location. Subjects kept their finger on the center button of a 3 × 3 array and pressed one of eight surrounding buttons to indicate the direction of motion of targets that occurred at the attended location. Half of subjects pressed with the left and half with the right hand. Hearing subjects received spoken instructions. Deaf and hearing of deaf subjects received instructions in ASL. Scalp electrical activity was recorded from homologous points over left and right occipital, parietal, temporal, anterior temporal and frontal regions. Recordings from these electrodes and the vertical EOG recorded from the left inferior orbital ridge were referred to the linked mastoids, and were amplified with a band pass of 0.01-100 Hz (time constant 8 seconds). The horizontal EOG was recorded between electrodes placed on the left and right external canthi, and was amplified with a D.C. amplifier and high frequency half-amplitude cut-off of 60 Hz.

The EEG and EOG were digitized for 100 msec prior to and 924 msec following each stimulus presentation at a rate of 1 point/4 msec. Trials in which excessive eye movement or muscle artifact occurred were excluded (approximately 10% of all trials, range 0-15%). Event-related brain potentials were averaged separately for standards and targets at each location (3), attention condition (3), hemisphere (2) and electrode site (5). ERP "difference" waves were formed by subtracting, point by point, ERPs recorded during different attention conditions.

Event-related brain potential component amplitudes were quantified by computer as either peak or area amplitudes within a specified latency range. Event-related brain potentials from each group of subjects were analyzed with a five-way analysis of variance with repeated measures on the factors of location, attention, hemisphere and electrode. Comparisons of hearing, deaf and hearing of deaf subjects added group as a factor.

Behavioral measures of percent correct reaction time and d′ and B were also scored by computer.

RESULTS

Hearing Subjects

All stimuli elicited ERPs that displayed a prominent negative component around 150 msec (N1) followed by broad shifts in amplitude whose polarity depended on direction of attention. Attention to both peripheral and central stimuli significantly enhanced the amplitude of N1, i.e., compared to the amplitude of the response to the same stimuli when attention was directed away from them. However this effect of attention occurred over different brain areas with attention to central and peripheral space. As seen in Figure 15.1a attention to the lvf was associated with enhanced N1 amplitudes over parietal and temporal regions of the contralateral, right hemisphere. This increase was not observed over the occipital regions, or over the ipsilateral, left hemisphere. Attention to the rvf was associated with a mirror-image pattern of results. By contrast attention to the central stimuli produced increased N1 amplitudes over the occipital regions of both hemispheres. The different distributions of the N1 attention effect for central and peripheral attention are shown in Figure 15.2.

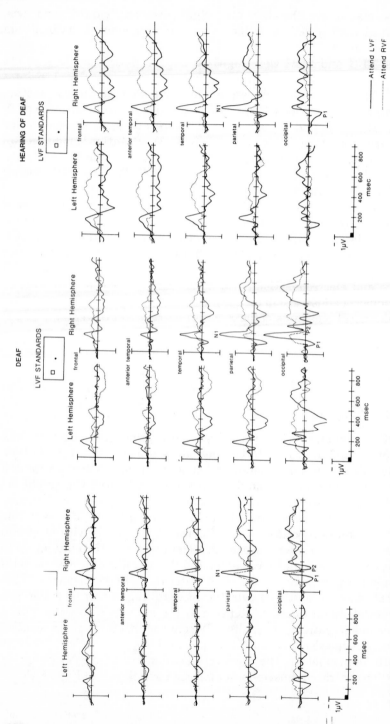

Figure 15.1. Event-related potentials averaged across 12 hearing subjects (left panel), 12 deaf subjects (center panel) and 12 hearing of deaf subjects (right panel) to standard stimuli presented to the left visual field (lvf) when attended (attend lvf) and when inattended (attend rvf). Recordings from left and right frontal, anterior temporal, temporal, parietal and occipital cortex.

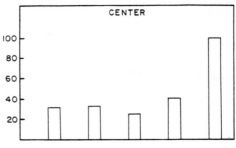

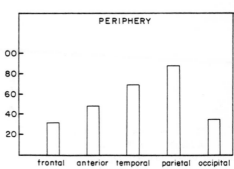

Figure 15.2. Percent increase in N1 Amplitude with Attention (Standards). Percent by which N1 amplitude was increased from inattend to attend conditions. *Top:* Center standards, mean of left and right frontal, anterior temporal, temporal, parietal and occipital sites. (reprinted from Neville and Lawson, in press a) *Bottom:* Peripheral standards, mean of contralateral frontal, anterior-temporal, temporal, parietal and occipital sites. (reprinted from Neville and Lawson, in press a)

Further differences in the ERPs to peripheral and central stimuli occurred in their lateral asymmetries. Whereas for central stimuli N1 amplitude and its increment with attention were symmetrical from over the two hemispheres, for both peripheral stimuli N1 amplitude and the effect of attention on N1 were larger from over temporo-parietal regions of the right hemisphere (see Figure 15.3). Additionally, attention-related changes in the subsequent slow waves were also larger from over the right hemisphere, and the detection of direction of motion was more accurate after lvf than rvf presentation.

These data suggest that in hearing subjects attention to peripheral and central visual space may be mediated by different neural systems that include a greater role for parietal cortex in attending the visual periphery, and a greater role for bilateral occipital areas for central attention. They also suggest that the special role of the right hemisphere in visual attention may be reserved for peripheral stimuli.

Deaf Subjects

The morphology of the ERPs to these stimuli was similar in deaf and hearing subjects. Moreover with attention to the central stimuli, the

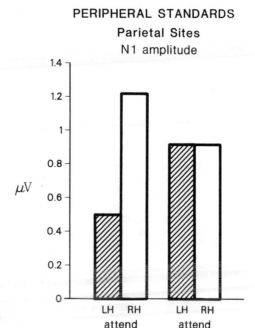

PERIPHERAL STANDARDS
Parietal Sites
N1 amplitude

Figure 15.3. Peripheral standards. Mean amplitude in uV of N1 across lvf and rvf stimuli from left (LH) and right (RH) parietal sites under attend lvf and attend rvf conditions.

increase in N1 amplitude was similar in the two groups. However, attention to both peripheral stimuli produced attention effects that were several times larger in deaf than in hearing subjects. Additionally, there were highly specific group differences in the distribution of the peripheral attention effects, and these occurred independently of which periphery was attended. As seen in Figure 15.2 (compare a and b) over the right temporal and parietal regions the attention-related changes were similar in the two groups. However, in contrast to the hearing subjects, the deaf subjects displayed large attention effects over the occipital regions of both hemispheres. The deaf subjects also displayed considerably larger effects over the left temporal and parietal regions than did the hearing subjects. Further group differences occurred in asymmetries of the ERPs and in behavior. Whereas in hearing subjects N1 amplitude and the increase in N1 with attention were larger from over the right than the left hemisphere, the deaf subjects displayed larger amplitudes over the left hemisphere (see Figure 15.4). Consistent with these results, detection of direction of motion was superior following lvf presentations in hearing subjects, but was better following rvf presentations in deaf subjects. Deaf subjects also responded more quickly (70 msec) than hearing subjects.

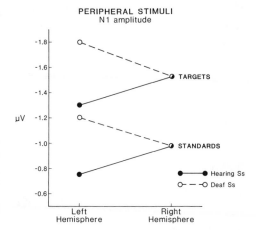

Figure 15.4. Peripheral Stimuli. Amplitude of N1 from the left and right hemispheres for hearing and deaf subjects. Mean amplitude across all conditions, for standards and targets separately. (reprinted from Neville and Lawson, in press b)

These data suggest that attention to central space is similar in deaf and hearing subjects, but that attention to peripheral visual space is superior and is mediated by different neural systems in deaf subjects. The specific changes with peripheral attention include (1) increased activity of the occipital regions of both hemispheres, and (2) a greater role for the left temporo-parietal regions in deaf than in hearing subjects.

In order to assess the possibly separate roles of early auditory deprivation and acquisition of a visual language in producing these group differences we tested the hearing of deaf subjects in the same paradigm.

Hearing of Deaf

ERPs from the hearing of deaf subjects displayed a similar morphology to those of the hearing subjects and deaf subjects. Attention to the center was associated with a similar pattern of changes as seen in the other two groups. As seen in Figure 15.1, with attention to the peripheral stimuli all three groups displayed similar ERPs over the right temporal and parietal regions. However, over the occipital regions the hearing of deaf subjects, like the hearing subjects and in contrast to the deaf subjects, displayed very small attention effects. These results suggest the bilateral increase in occipital activity with peripheral attention in the deaf subjects was not a consequence of acquiring ASL, but occurred secondary to auditory deprivation.

On the other hand, over the left temporal and parietal regions the hearing of deaf subjects displayed results similar to those of the deaf subjects—i.e., attention effects much larger than those observed in the normal controls. The behavioral data were also consistent with a greater role for the left hemisphere in peripheral attention in the hearing of deaf and deaf subjects. As seen in Figure 15.5, whereas hearing subjects displayed a lvf advantage in detecting the direction of motion, both hearing of deaf and deaf subjects displayed a rvf advantage. These results imply that the early acquisition of ASL was an important factor in the increased role of the left hemisphere in peripheral attention in the deaf subjects.

DISCUSSION

These results suggest that the cerebral systems that mediate attention to and detection of motion in peripheral visual space are modified both by auditory deprivation and by the acquisition of ASL. Since the deaf subjects displayed attention-related activity over the left and right occipital regions that was several times larger than that observed in both the hearing and the hearing of deaf subjects, this effect is not attributable to the acquisition of ASL but may be a consequence of auditory deprivation. We have observed other bilaterally symmetric differences in the distribution of ERPs to peripheral visual stimuli between deaf and hearing subjects, and these were also attributed to compensatory increases in the activity of the visual system following auditory deprivation (Neville et al., 1983, Neville and Lawson, in press c). Studies of experimental animals suggest several possible mechanisms that may underlie this type of

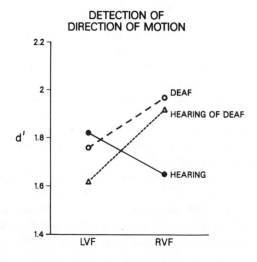

Figure 15.5. Detection of Direction of Motion. Detection (d′) of motion of targets in the left and right visual fields (lvf and rvf) for hearing, deaf, and hearing of deaf subjects. (reprinted from Neville and Lawson, in press c)

change. For example, there are reports of increased growth and activity of cortical areas associated with remaining sensory modalities following early blindness and deafness (Ryugo, Ryugo, Globus and Killackey, 1975; Gyllensten, Malmfors and Norrlin, 1965; Postnikova, 1978). A related possibility is that cells responsive to auditory input, which have been observed in posterior visual areas (Morrell, 1972; Spinelli, Starr and Barrett, 1968; Fishman and Michael, 1973), are taken over by visual afferents when auditory input is absent.

On the other hand, the similar pattern of lateral asymmetries displayed by the deaf and hearing of deaf subjects suggests that the acquisition of ASL may have been the factor that contributed to the departure from the pattern observed in the hearing subjects. While there is evidence that hemispheric specialization for language depends in part on specific parameters of early language experience (for example, individuals who acquire an ideographic script may rely more on structures of the right hemisphere during reading than do those who have acquired phonetic scripts) (Hatta, 1978, 1981; Endo, Shimizu and Hori, 1978), bilinguals may display less asymmetrical cerebral organization than monolinguals (Vaid, 1983, 1984; Albanese, 1985) and individuals who acquire language later than normal may display abnormal patterns of asymmetries between the hemispheres (Curtiss, 1977; Neville, 1977; Neville, 1985a) little is known about the role that early language experience might play in the development of cerebral specializations related to non-language cognitive processing. However, in hearing individuals the left hemisphere plays a greater role in the perception of temporal order of non-language auditory information, a result that may be attributed to the fact that the perception of fine differences in temporal order is critical for the perception and production of speech (Albert, 1972; Swisher and Hirsh, 1972; Lackner and Teuber, 1973; Efron, 1963a; Carmon and Nachshon, 1971). Additionally, some evidence suggests that certain cognitive skills which depend more on the right hemisphere in hearing subjects who speak English are mediated by the left hemisphere in individuals who have acquired a language whose lexicon or grammar makes use of those skills. For example, whereas English speakers display either right hemisphere or bilateral involvement in pitch discrimination, speakers of Thai, Chinese, and Vietnamese, languages in which differences in pitch are linguistically significant, display a greater role for the left hemisphere on such tasks (VanLancker and Fromkin, 1973, 1978; Naeser & Chan, 1980; Hecaen, Mazaro, Rannier, Goldblum & Merienne, 1971). Similarly, deaf subjects who have acquired ASL, a language in which hand location and facial expression provide grammatical and lexical information, display evidence for left hemisphere specialization for picture identification, dot localization and the recognition of faces, tasks on which hearing subjects without knowledge of ASL show right hemisphere predominance (Neville, 1977; Neville & Bellugi, 1978; Corina, 1985). The results from the studies described here, showing left hemisphere specialization for the perception of peripheral motion in both deaf and hearing individuals who have acquired ASL, a language in which motion is significant, are compatible with these studies. These results, in conjunction with the data that suggest the left hemisphere is specialized for the processing of both spoken and signed languages (Neville & Bellugi, 1971978; Virostek & Cutting, 1979; Bellugi, Poizner & Klima, 1983; Neville, 1985b), suggest that the left hemisphere is innately predisposed to serve as the substrate for the acquisition of language, but that critical parameters of the language play a role in specifying other functions that the left hemisphere will mediate, and those which the right hemisphere subserve. Thus these data are similar to many other results in neurobiology and suggest that certain features of the final pattern of cortical specializations important for spatial cognition are influenced by aspects of both early sensory and early language experience.

REFERENCES

Albanese, J-F. 1985. Language lateralization in English-French bilinguals. *Brain and Language,* 24:284-296.

Albert, M.L. 1972. Auditory sequencing and left cerebral dominance for language. *Neuropsychologia,* 10:245-248.

Bagdonas, A.P., Kochyunas, R.B., & Linyauskaite, A.I. 1980. Psychoacoustic functions in visually normal and impaired and blind subjects. *Human Physiology,* 6:108-113.

Bellugi, U., Poizner, H., & Klima, E.S. 1983. Brain organization for language: Clues from sign aphasia. *Human Neurobiology,* 2:155-170.

Burnstine, T.H., Greenough, W.T., & Tees, R.C. 1984. Intermodal compensation following damage or deprivation: A review of behavioral and neural evidence. In C. R. Almli and S. Finger (Eds.), *Early brain damage, Vol. 1, Research orientation and clinical observations.* New York: Academic Press, pp. 3-34.

Carmon, A., & Nachshon, I. 1971. Effect of unilateral brain damage on perception of temporal order. *Cortex,* 7:410-418.

Corina, D.P. 1985. Hemispheric specialization for affective and linguistic facial expression in deaf signers. Presented at *Annual Conference on Research in the Neuropsychology of Language.* Ontario, Canada.

Curtiss, S. 1977. *Genie: A psycholinguistic study of a modern day "wild child."* New York: Academic Press.

Diderot, D. 1916. Letter on the blind for the use of those who see, 1749. In: M. Jourdain (Ed. and Transl.) *Diderot's early philosophical works.* New York: Burt Franklin, pp. 68-141.

Efron, E. 1963a. Temporal perception, aphasia, and deja vu. *Brain,* 86:339-342.

Endo, M., Shimizu, A., & Hori, T. 1978. Functional asymmetry of visual fields for Japanese words in kana (syllable-based) writing and Japanese shape-recognition in Japanese subjects. *Neuropsychologia,* 16:291-297.

Fishman, M.C., & Michael, C.R. 1973. Integration of auditory information in the cat's visual cortex. *Vision Research,* 13:1415-1419.

Gyllensten, L., Malmfors, T., & Norrlin, M.L. 1965. Growth alteration in the auditory cortex of visually deprived mice. *Journal of Comparative Neurology,* 126:463-470.

Hatta, T. 1978. Recognition of Japanese kanji and hirakana in the left and right visual field. *Japanese Psychological Research,* 20:51-59.

Hatta, T. 1981. Differential processing of kanji and kana stimuli in Japanese people: Some implications from Stroop test results. *Neuropsychologia,* 19:87-93.

Hecaen, H., Mazaro, G., Rannier, A., Goldblum, M., & Merienne, L. 1971. Aphasie croisee chez un sujet droitier bilingue. *Revue Neurologique,* 124:319-323.

Hillyard, S.A., and Munte, T.F. 1984. Selective attention to color and locational cues: An analysis with event-related brain potentials. *Perception and Psychophysics,* 36:185-198.

Hillyard, S.A., Munte, T.F., & Neville, H.J. 1985. Visual-spatial attention, orienting and brain physiology. In M. I. Posner & O. S. Marin (Eds.) *Mechanisms of attention: Attention and performance XI.* Hillsdale, NJ: Lawrence Erlbaum Associates, pp. 63-84.

Hillyard, S.A., Simpson, G.V., Woods, D.L., Van Voorhis, S., & Munte, T. 1984. Event-related brain potentials and selective attention to different modalities. In F. Reinoso-Suarez & C. Ajmone-Marsan (Eds.) *Cortical Integration.* New York: Raven Press, pp. 395-414.

Hyvarinen, J. 1982. *The parietal cortex of monkey and man.* New York: Springer-Verlag.

Lackner, J.R., & Teuber, H.L. 1973. Alterations in auditory fusion thresholds after cerebral injury in man. *Neuropsychologia,* 11:403-412.

Morrell, F. 1972. Visual system's view of acoustic space. *Nature,* 238:44-46.

Naeser, M., & Chan, S.W-C. 1980. Case study of a Chinese aphasic with the Boston Diagnostic Aphasia Exam. *Neuropsychologia,* 18:389-410.

Neville, H.J. 1977. Electroencephalographic testing of cerebral specialization in normal and congenitally deaf children: A preliminary report. In S. Segalowitz & F. Gruber (Eds.) *Language development and neurological theory.* New York: Academic Press, pp. 121-131.

Neville, H.J. 1985a. Effects of early sensory and language experience on the development of the human brain. In J. Mehler & R. Fox (Eds.)

Neonate cognition: Beyond the blooming buzzing confusion. London: Lawrence Erlbaum Associates, pp. 349-363.

Neville, H.J. 1985b. Biological constraints on semantic processing: A comparison of spoken and signed languages. *Psychophysiology. Volume 22,* p. 576.

Neville, H.J., & Bellugi, U. 1978. Patterns of cerebral specialization in congenitally deaf adults: A preliminary report. In P. Siple (Ed.) *Understanding language through sign language research.* New York: Academic Press, pp. 230-257.

Neville, H.J., & Lawson, D. Attention to central and peripheral visual space in a movement detection task: An event-related potential and behavioral study. I. Normal hearing adults. *Brain Research,* in press a.

Neville, H.J., & Lawson, D. Attention to central and peripheral visual space in a movement detection task: An event-related potential and behavioral study. II. Congenitally deaf adults. *Brain Research,* in press b.

Neville, H.J., & Lawson, D. Attention to central and peripheral visual space in a movement detection task. III. Separate effects of auditory deprivation and acquisition of a visual language. *Brain Research,* in press c.

Neville, H.J., Schmidt, A., & Kutas, M. 1983. Altered visual-evoked potentials in congenitally deaf adults. *Brain Research,* 266:127-132.

Niemeyer, W., & Starlinger, I. 1981. Do the blind hear better? Investigation on auditory processing in congenital or early acquired blindness. *Audiology,* 20:510-515.

Postnikova, N.N. 1978. The formation of a defensive conditioned reflex to acoustic stimuli in rabbits after early visual deprivation. *Zhurnal Vysshei Nervnoi Deyatel'nosti Imeni I. P. Pokavlova,* 28:293-297.

Regal, D.M., Boothe, R., Teller, D.Y., & Sackett, G.P. 1976. Visual acuity and visual responsiveness in dark-reared monkeys (Macaca nemestrina). *Vision Research,* 16:523-530.

Riesen, A.H. 1958. Plasticity of behavior: Psychological aspects. In H. Harlow & C. N. Woolsey (Eds.) *Biological and Biochemical Bases of Behavior.* Madison, Wisconsin: University of Wisconsin Press, pp. 425-450.

Ryugo, D.K., Ryugo, R., Globus, A., & Killackey, H.P. 1975. Increased spine density in auditory cortex following visual or somatic deafferentation. *Brain Research,* 90:143-146.

Schneider, G.E. 1969. Two visual systems. *Science,* 163:895-902.

Sherman, S.M., Hoffmann, K.P., & Stone, J. 1972. Loss of a specific cell type from dorsal lateral geniculate nucleus in visually deprived cats. *Journal of Neurophysiology,* 35:532-541.

Spinelli, D.N., Starr, A., & Barrett, T.W. 1968. Auditory specificity in unit recordings from cat's visual cortex. *Experimental Neurology,* 22:75-84.

Starlinger, I., & Niemeyer, W. 1981. Do the blind hear better? Investigations on auditory processing in congenital or early acquired blindness. *Audiology,* 20:503-509.

Swisher, L., & Hirsh, I.J. 1972. Brain damage and the ordering of two temporally successive stimuli. *Neuropsychologia,* 10:137-152.

Trevarthen, C.B. 1968. Two mechanisms of vision in primates. *Psychol. Forsch.*, 31:299-337.

Vaid, J. 1983. Bilinguals and brain lateralization. In S. Segalowitz (Ed.) *Language functions and brain organization.* New York: Academic Press, pp. 315-339.

Vaid, J. 1984. Visual, phonetic, and semantic processing in early and late bilinguals. In M. Paradis & Y. Lebrun (Eds.) *Early bilingualism and child development.* Amsterdam: Lisse, Swets & Zeitlinger, 174-191.

VanLancker, D. & Fromkin, V. 1973. Hemispheric specialization for pitch and "tone": Evidence from Thai. *Journal of Phonetics*, 1:101-109.

VanLancker, D. & Fromkin, V. 1978. Cerebral dominance for pitch contrasts in tone language speakers and in musically untrained and trained English speakers. *Journal of Phonetics,* 6:19-23.

Virostek, S., & Cutting, J.E. 1979. Asymmetries for Ameslan handshapes and other forms in signers and non-signers. *Perception and Psychophysics,* 26:505-508.

THE CONSTRUCTION AND USE OF SPATIAL KNOWLEDGE IN BLIND AND SIGHTED CHILDREN

16

BARBARA LANDAU
Columbia University

It is hard to imagine how we could exist without the ability to extract and use spatial information about objects and their layouts in the physical world. Perhaps it is partly this fact, and the intuition that vision is a rich source of spatial information, that has led psychologists to ask whether the blind could ever come to have the same understanding of space as do the sighted. Certainly, this question has practical significance, for it is obvious that the blind require special aids to perform many spatially controlled activities that are simple for the sighted) e.g. reading text or negotiating public transportation). No one would disagree with the notion that on a practical level, the spatial worlds of the blind and sighted differ.

But the issue of space in the blind has historically served another significant agenda: it has provided a testing ground for two radically different theories of the development of human knowledge. Rationalists long have argued that the nature and form of knowledge are relatively independent of the particular avenue of experience through which one gains information about the world. In contrast, empiricists have argued that all knowledge originates with sensory experience. Hence, they argue, the form and nature of that knowledge must be affected by the particular sensory access. Proponents of each view suggested examples concerning the blind. Descartes (1637) offered the example of a blind man exploring objects with a stick, who must construct their spatial configurations and relationships by referring sequential tactual impressions to a unitary spatial framework structured by the principles of Euclidean geometry. Descartes argued that the task of any perceiver was identical to that of the blind man: constructing a spatial world from the partial and fragmentary information gained through experience. He reasoned from the degraded and variable nature of experience and the ultimate similarity in knowledge between blind and sighted that the principles underlying spatial knowledge must be innate and accessible to any sensory mode.

The empiricists' counter-claim proposed enormous differences between spatial ideas born of sight and those born of touch. Bishop Berkeley (1709) held that the ideas of touch and of sight must be "wholly distinct" as their sensory source differs. Similarly, Locke (1690) replied to Molyneux's question by stating that a person born blind whose sight had been restored would be unable to identify by sight an object which he had hitherto experienced by touch alone. Locke further proposed that the blind could never truly come to know about things visual—such as color—for visual experience was both a necessary and sufficient condition for the development of those ideas.

These two positions have shaped our thinking about the nature of spatial ideas and their development. The blind remain an important test case as they differ so obviously from the sighted in the sensory means by which they confront the world. Do these obvious differences mean that the ideas of the blind must inevitably differ from those of the sighted?

In this chapter, I will argue that the blind and sighted share the same spatial ideas, that these ideas are produced by a rich and articulated system of *spatial knowledge*, and that this knowledge system arises early in life under informal, naturally occurring conditions of learning. Further, I will provide evidence that the proper analysis of spatial knowledge and its development leads to the conclusion that both blind and sighted children face identical problems in coming to understand space. Accordingly, we find that blind children can develop impressive competence and close comparability to the sighted, despite differences in their sensory accesses to the world. And we find that sighted children do not always have an advantage when visual information is present, for by itself such information is not sufficient to guide spatial thinking. Spatial knowledge is dependent on an underlying structure which serves to organize information obtained through any modality; but spatial knowledge does not itself depend on information obtained through any particular modality.

Before proceeding, I would like to stress what this view does and does not entail. It does entail rejection of some extremely strong extensions of the empiricist view, notably those that propose that the blind have no sense of space whatsoever. This view was first put forth by Senden (1932), based on his observations of congenitally blind individuals who had had their vision restored as adults. He argued that the blind live in a world determined by time rather than space. He concluded that "by tactual perception alone the patient is unable to acquire an awareness of space, that this is solely dependent on visual perception" (p.309). More recent proponents of such a view suggest that blind children are particularly unable to construct a spatial world. In Fraiberg's (1977) landmark study of ten congenitally blind infants, she argued that the lack of vision causes widespread and severe deficits in the development of various spatial concepts such as object permanence, and various linguistic concepts served by space, such as appropriate pronoun use. Similarly, in a recent book on infant development, Bower (1977) states "The congenitally blind child apparently never acquires a spatial framework for judgements about the relative position of objects. The spontaneous framework he uses instead is a temporal one" (p.160). As the remainder of this chapter will show, these extreme views must be rejected, for they do not accord with the facts.

In contrast, the view taken in this chapter does not entail complete identity between the blind and sighted in *all* aspects of spatial functioning. For example, some questions have arisen about the extraction and retention of spatial information by the haptic and visual systems. Perhaps these systems "specialize" in the kinds of information they can best extract; or perhaps their memory stores have different retention characteristics (Millar, 1974; Gilson & Baddeley, 1969; Sullivan & Turvey, 1972). As another example, perhaps the blind differ from the sighted in the kinds of information they select to guide their actions in space. Blind adults are known to use echolocation in determining the size, distance, and material of objects (Kellogg, 1962), yet the sighted typically do not. Since the blind seem to have less information about the positions of objects at a distance, they may tend to use body-based reference systems, rather than external (object-based) reference systems—especially where using such egocentric reference systems typically has been successful in past similar tasks (Landau & Spelke, 1985; see also Rieser, Lockman, & Pick, 1980; and Strelow, 1985, for a recent review).

Such differences between the blind and sighted are plausible. But the issue addressed in this chapter concerns the spatial knowledge system that one can develop in the absence of vision. Here we find that certain principles of spatial knowledge arise independently of the particular avenue of experience. That is, the blind and sighted develop identical principles rather early in life, despite their very different encounters with the world.

WHAT IS SPATIAL KNOWLEDGE?

For our purposes, spatial knowledge is a system of rules and representations that allows the perceiver to plot spatially their sequential experiences (haptic or visual) relative to a unitary framework, and then to perform inferences on that description, predicting properties of the spatial layout that have not been directly experienced (Landau, Spelke, & H. Gleitman, 1984). Two examples may clarify this notion. First, consider the following navigation problem (and see Section 3 for evidence with the blind child). A traveller starts at point A, and proceeds to walk straight ahead to some point B, which is not visible from A. He then makes a 90 degree right-hand turn, and walks straight ahead to some point C, not visible from B. Now he is asked to return to A, which is not visible from C. In order to accomplish this, he must record the angle and distance relationships between points A and B, and B and C, and must be able to infer the angle and distance relationships between C and A. In other words, from the experience of travelling along two paths in a triangular array, he must be able to deduce the third path. The geometric elements forming the premises (A-B, B-C), and the inference rules producing the conclusion (A-C) are what is meant here by a system of spatial knowledge.

A second example will show that the need for such a knowledge system is not restricted to problems of navigating through large arrays. It must also be invoked in cases where the perception of a form requires integration over successive glances. Consider for example, the sequential presentation of visual information using a successive aperture-viewing technique (Hochberg, 1968). In one such case, the experimenter moves a cross-shaped figure behind an aperture, so that the subject receives successive views of parts of the figure. If the figure is moved at the proper pace, subjects immediately perceive the views as parts of a whole—specifically, a whole cross moving behind an aperture. In fact, the perception is so compelling, that if the experimenter takes a "short-cut" across one of the arms of the cross, the subject has no difficulty perceiving it as just that. Apparently, the subject has been able to construe the sequence as a spatially coherent whole; and he can use that representation to make predictions about parts of the configuration that will appear upon taking a novel turn through the figure. Much of our visual perception of shapes (as well as larger layouts) seems to require mental organization, or putting together of the piece-meal view we receive of the world (Hochberg, 1978). Such assembly seems to require a spatial knowledge system.

Spatial knowledge, then, must be invoked in describing the solutions to various spatial problems, including perceiving objects whose configurations must be explored over multiple glances or grasps, and navigating by short-cuts and detours through larger arrays. Moreover, it seems to be implicated in the support of other symbolic functions and systems, such as the understanding and use of physical representations of space (drawings and maps), and the development and use of the language of space (see also O'Keefe & Nadel, 1978; Jackendoff, 1983; Talmy, 1983). The following sections describe some recent findings on blind and sighted children's development and use of the spatial knowledge system, as evidenced in these four domains.

EXPLORING AND RECOGNIZING OBJECTS THROUGH TOUCH

Students of touch long have noted that much information about objects is available through active exploration as we move through space (Katz, 1925/ in Krueger, 1970; Gibson, 1962). We can discover the shapes, textures, temperatures, and substances of objects by hand. But such discoveries seem highly dependent on haptic activity (Gibson, 1962). If the hand remains passive as an object is pressed into it, recognition is much poorer than if the subject is permitted to explore freely. In a way, this seems puzzling, for as the hand moves, different parts of the object stimulate the same parts of the hand, and the same parts of the object stimulate different parts of the hand. Of course, the same problem exists for visual exploration of an array, for the eyes and head move as we visually explore an object. This problem makes clear that, in recognizing an object by haptic (or visual) exploration, the perceiver must be plotting the sequentially exposed parts of the object in a common framework that will yield a single shape (c.f. Jeannerod, 1983).

Are infants and young children capable of the active haptic exploration that would yield such information about objects? From work on the sighted, we know that even infants can extract information about shape and substance by manual or oral touch, and that this information is accessible to cross-modal transfer (Gibson &

Walker, 1984; Rose, Gottfried, & Bridger, 1981). But reports on young blind children have suggested serious deficiencies in this area.

Fraiberg's (1977) description of congenitally blind children was particularly bleak. Her earliest case studies focused on the extreme passivity of the blind, especially in haptic exploration. She described children whose hands remained shoulder height in a stereotyped fashion. The hands could serve to feed, but were unable to engage in directed exploration of the world. It was these observations that led Fraiberg to suggest that the ordinary route of development only enables active haptic exploration and perception as it serves and is guided by vision. She argued that without specific intervention, the blind infant's development would be permanently derailed, resulting in wideranging cognitive deficiencies.

Clearly, if vision were necessary for adequate development of the haptic system, blind children would be seriously limited in their ability to extract spatial information about objects and their layouts. But we now know that Fraiberg's view was overly pessimistic. First, some new evidence suggests that blind toddlers engage in systematic and efficient haptic exploration that could allow them to extract important object properties early in life. Second, it seems likely that both the texture and shape of objects can be detected by the blind rather early in development, although the likelihood of detecting one rather than the other seems to depend on the exploratory activities performed by the child.

The Nature of Early Haptic Exploration

It has been claimed that the haptic system lags behind vision in development (Piaget & Inhelder, 1948/1967; Zaporozhets, 1965; see Gibson & Spelke, 1983; and Warren, 1982 for reviews). Sighted infants can visually explore and perceive three-dimensional forms (Gibson & Spelke, 1983). Yet as Piaget, as well as other investigators (Zaporozhets, 1965; Abravanel, 1968) have noted, sighted toddlers who are required to explore objects by hand alone tend not to systematically scan the objects with the fingertips as they attempt to understand its shape. Rather, they tend to grasp and palpate the object, as one would in using a tool. Some investigators have concluded from this that systematic haptic exploration awaits later development. For Piaget, the child would not be able to construct shapes haptically until mental operations came to guide his exploration.

Such conclusions about early haptic exploration are problematic. First, one cannot reason from the supposed inadequacy of such exploration in the sighted to the inadequacy of haptic exploration in general. One can only draw conclusions about how the haptic system functions in the absence of usual visual guidance. Any conclusions about nature and effectiveness of non-visually guided haptic exploration early in development must come in part from blind subjects, for whom it has adaptive significance. Second, the children's haptic activities—grasping, palpating—are often assumed to be deficient (relative to scanning with the fingertips). But such activities are phenomenally described as most important in detecting object shapes (Gibson, 1962). Some evidence from blind adults suggests that these activities also give rise to better recognition of objects.

In particular, Davidson (1972) studied blind and sighted but blindfolded adults, who explored a series of curved rods, each cemented to a heavy base that could not be lifted. Blind subjects showed better accuracy at detecting the curvatures than the sighted subjects. More importantly, they also showed quite different patterns of exploration from the sighted subjects, especially more gripping of the rod with several fingers at a time. Sighted subjects tended more to scan the length of the rod with a single fingertip, or to "pinch" the top with thumb and two fingers. When the sighted subjects were trained to use the same strategies as the blind, their detection of curvature significantly improved.

Now, the key issue is whether haptic exploration by blind toddlers and infants is like that of these blind adults. In our own lab, we are beginning to study this question. We are videotaping blind toddlers and sighted controls between 18 and 36 months, as they explore familiar and unfamiliar objects. These videotapes are then analyzed for quantity and quality of exploration. So far, the results are quite striking. They suggest that by 18 months, the haptic system is well adapted to extracting important object properties. The blind toddler evolves an impressive repertoire of exploratory activities, which he uses with relish as he encounters both familiar and novel objects. In terms of sheer amount of time spent in exploration, we find that the blind toddlers explore even familiar objects more thoroughly than do the sighted. As an example, the blind 18-month-old is handed a bottle (plastic, with nipple) which he then proceeds to rotate, mouth, and squeeze for more than 60 seconds. In contrast, the 18-month-old sighted child takes the same bottle, looks at it for 15 seconds, and rejects it. One interpretation is that the blind child does not recognize the bottle, while the sighted child does. But this will not do; for the blind toddler sucks on the bottle nipple within the first 5 seconds. Clearly, he recognizes it as a bottle; but still wishes to explore it.

Does this lengthy exploration seem systematic, and designed to extract important object information? Yes indeed. We have developed coding categories based on second-by-second analysis of the videotapes. These categories cohere as manipulations that can extract information about overall configuration (rotate, grasp, palm, transfer), surface properties (scratch, finger, rub, handle), and material or substance (press, squeeze, clap, bend). While the kind of exploration must depend in part on the particular object, so far it seems that the blind child most frequently performs activities to extract overall configuration, with material second, and surface last. Most fascinating, despite the differences between the blind and sighted toddlers in sheer amount of time spent in exploration, they show great similarities in the nature of their exploration—even though the sighted subjects are tested with full vision. For example, both blind and sighted toddlers explore a heavy rope ring by compressing and expanding its sides (presumably exploring the flexibility of the material); they explore a flat metal ring with holes in the surface by inserting the fingers into the holes repeatedly (presumably to explore the shape).

While we must be tentative, then, it seems that blind toddlers are well equipped to extract information about objects through haptic exploration. From the similarity of the exploratory activities of blind and sighted, it seems likely that they both may be detecting similar properties. Information on slightly older children suggests that two such properties—shape and texture—are indeed extractable by both blind and sighted.

Extracting Texture and Shape Information

Touch is particularly well suited to detecting texture (Lederman, 1978), so it would not be surprising if blind children were able to extract this property from spatial arrays. Indeed, some have suggested that the blind extract textural information at the expense of shape information (Millar, 1978). But the facts show that the nature of the extracted property depends on the exploratory strategy the subject can use.

In several experiments, Susanna Millar (1978) presented Braille letters and other small dot-type arrays to blind and sighted children, and then tested them in a recognition task. She found more confusions based on density than on shape, suggesting that the children were coding the letters more by something akin to texture than by shape. This might suggest a generalized preference for texture coding, but if so, then it would indeed be true that the blind would experience the world differently from the sighted. For the sighted, object kinds are primarily differentiated by their shape, not texture.

However, Millar's findings do not suggest a generalized preference for texture coding, for the arrays she used were more or less two-dimensional (Braille dot patterns), requiring exploration with the fingertip. Recent evidence suggests that spatial integration does not occur during fingertip exploration of such arrays as it does when the hand freely explores three-dimensional objects (Bliss, 1978). The question then becomes whether children are more likely to extract shape than texture when they are permitted to freely explore three-dimensional objects with their hands.

An experiment conducted by Abravanel (1970) with sighted children suggests an affirmative answer to this question. Abravanel set out to discover whether previous findings of sighted children's preference for texture over shape might not be due to the characteristics of the stimulus items. Previous experimenters had used two-dimensional stimuli, and had found texture preference in matching and discrimination tasks (Gliner, Pick, Pick, & Hales, 1969). Abravanel argued that using three-dimensional objects might yield shape preferences. He presented preschoolers with three-dimensional objects, permitting the children to pick up and explore the objects freely. A subsequent matching task showed that the children had coded these objects on the basis of shape, not texture. Like Davidson, Abravanel suggested that the nature of the exploration (partly determined by the stimulus) was a crucial determinant of the properties one could extract—here, with shape extractable by palpating the object, but not by scanning the outline shape with the fingertip (see also, Abravanel, 1968).

Can blind toddlers extract shape information, if allowed to use appropriate exploratory activities? The standard form recognition experiments have simply not been done here, with this population. Evidence from older blind subjects is conflicted, apparently due to the wide variety of tasks and stimuli that have been used (see Warren, 1982, for review). However, there is compelling evidence available from the language learning literature, suggesting that blind toddlers can indeed extract the shapes of objects through naturally developing haptic exploration. Blind toddlers develop a vocabulary completely comparable to the sighted, at roughly the same age unless additional complicating factors (such as prematurity) are involved (Landau & Gleitman, 1985; see Mulford, 1985, for a review of such evidence on more than a dozen congenitally blind toddlers; also, see below). These words are primarily object labels, words for people, animals, toys, food, and clothes (the same vocabulary one finds universally in young sighted children, see Gentner, 1982). One could hypothesize that the blind child does not identify instances of these items on the basis of shape; but this seems to be false. For, as Andersen, Dunlea & Kekelis (1984) have shown, where there are overgeneralizations in the vocabulary of blind children, they are based on much the same properties as those of the sighted—shape and texture. By 18 months, the blind child has extracted important information about objects, and can use that information in language learning.

LARGER SPATIAL LAYOUTS

It seems intuitively obvious that the blind must construct a representation of any large spatial array sequentially. The hands move as they sequentially explore any shape larger than the fist, and the body moves as it sequentially explores arrays that surround us. Whereas such sequentially gained information is primary and predominant for the blind, the sighted also may be able to gain simultaneous visual-spatial information. This difference has suggested to some that the spatial representations of the blind must be different from those of the sighted. For example, some have claimed that the blind must rely on sequential coding of the layout—derived, supposedly, from the sequential kinesthetic experience they have as they move through space (Millar, 1975); or that the blind have less access to a spontaneous reference system, in the way that the sighted do (Warren, Anooshian & Bollinger, 1973). Such differences might then give rise to more sequential, or more fragmentary spatial representations.

Yet, as I have emphasized, the same problem exists in principle for the sighted. The eyes move in the head, the head moves on the body, and the body moves through space. This means that we must piece together information about spatial arrays in much the same way the blind man must, as he moves through space. This analysis suggests that the blind should be no less able than the sighted to construct spatially unified layouts over distances. A line of research conducted in our own laboratory addresses this issue.

Spatial Inferences in the Blind Child

Landau, Spelke and H. Gleitman (1984) studied a 2-year-old congenitally blind child's ability to navigate independently through space. They asked whether she could assemble such successive walks along parts of a triangular layout into a unified spatial whole. The child was tested on a variety of spatial inference tasks requiring locomotion through triangular layouts in an 8' × 10' room (see Figure 16.1). In a first experiment, the child was led from a starting point (M) along three separate paths linking the starting point with three other objects. She was led along M-P, then M-T, then M-B and back again. When she returned to M, she was taken to T and tested on her ability to travel along paths connecting P, T, and B on her own. Over all paths, she performed significantly better than chance, suggesting that she had indeed used the experience travelling along the three paths to assemble one unified layout, which could then be used as the basis for generating new routes through the layout. Various alternative explanations were ruled out in subsequent experiments (echolocation, subtle room cues, experimenter bias). Sighted but blindfolded children performed at approximately the same level as the blind child. These results suggest that the blind child (as well as the sighted child) could indeed construct a unified spatial layout from sequential travel through some of its parts, and that she could use that construction to determine properties of the layout she had not directly experienced.

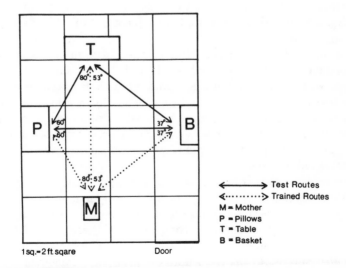

Figure 16.1. Layout for spatial inference task. (Reprinted from Landau, Spelke, & H. Gleitman, 1984, by permission of the publisher.)

Spatial Inferences in the Sighted Child

Those who maintain that there are significant differences between visually and haptic-kinesthetically gained information about a layout might still argue that the task is very different when performed with vision — that is, that when one visually explores an array, the information is somehow more directly or simultaneously given, and the need for mental assembly disappears or is weakened. But if the problems are truly different with and without vision, we should see superior inference performance after visual exploration of layout, relative to performance after haptic-kinesthetic exploration of that layout. An investigation of sighted children either visually or haptic-kinesthetically exploring an array, and then performing spatial inferences suggests that this is not the case.

Knapp, Gleitman and Landau (1984) tested sighted 4-year-olds' ability to make spatial inferences under several different conditions. All children were tested on their ability to navigate among three objects in a $6' \times 6' \times 8'$ triangular array, ABC. In the Visual (V) condition, children were brought into the testing room with their eyes open, were seated at A, and were shown the parts of the array from their seated position. The experimenter pointed to B, commenting "There's the telephone," and pointed to C, commenting "There are the coins for the telephone." In the Kinesthetic (K) condition, children were brought into the room blindfolded, were seated at A, and were shown the parts of the array by walking them to point B and back again, then to point C and back again. All children were then tested blindfolded.

Testing took two forms. Half of the children in each condition were asked to walk along paths AB and AC (which they had either seen or walked during training), and were then asked to find BC on their own (which they had neither seen nor walked before). The other half of the children in each condition were led to point B and asked to find path BC only. Directional accuracy was assessed for each subject and path, using measures similar to those described by Landau et al. (1984).

Results showed that 11 of 12 children tested on previously travelled paths AB and AC were successful in moving towards the goal (i.e. in a directionally appropriate manner): 6 in Visual condition, and 5 in the Kinesthetic condition. Of these same 12 children, only 3 in the Visual condition and 2 in the Kinesthetic condition were also successful on the inference path BC. However, of the 16 children tested on path BC only, 11 were successful: 5 in the Visual condition, and 6 in the Kinesthetic condition. This suggests that children in both conditions (V, K) could equally well reconstruct the experienced path and the inference path. The relatively poor performance of the children who were tested on all three paths was probably due to forgetting, since they were always tested on the experienced path before the novel path.

This somewhat surprising set of results suggests that, whether children obtain information by vision alone or by kinesthesis alone, they are equally capable of integrating the successive "glances" into a whole. Despite our intuitions about the supremacy of vision for rapidly gaining information over large spatial arrays, the problem of mentally assembling the parts into a whole exists equally for one who explores by vision alone and one who explores by kinesthesis alone.

Summary

These experiments provide definitive evidence for the existence of a spatial knowledge system by the age of about 2 years. That is, given sequential haptic-kinesthetic or visual information about a set of routes connecting objects in space, the child tends naturally to assemble this information in accordance with a geometric mental map that indicates the spatial relationships among objects in a layout. This map is apparently the product of an abstract, amodal spatial knowledge system that incorporates geometric properties such as angle and distance, and inference rules corresponding to straightforward geometric computations (see Landau et al., 1984, for further discussion). This spatial knowledge system can guide navigation through the world early in development. Moreover, it seems to be implicated in the support of apparently more abstract functions such as the use and understanding of physical representations of space, and learning the language of space. We now turn to evidence that both blind and sighted toddlers are also capable of using spatial knowledge in the service of these functions.

UNDERSTANDING PHYSICAL REPRESENTATIONS OF SPACE

Understanding physical representations of space such as pictures and maps seems to require several elements. First, one must be able to form two unified spatial ideas, one of the representational object (the picture or map), and one of the represented object (the object or object layout). As has been argued in previous sections, this ability is dependent on a spatial knowledge system which is no less accessible to the blind or sighted, as each sequentially explores the world. Second, one must be able to put into correspondence these two products of spatial knowledge. Third, one must be able to recognize a "stand for" relationship between the elements used in the representational object, and those they correspond to in the represented object.

In the sighted child, the development of these elements does not seem to depend on extensive specific experience using particular representational materials. The ability to understand line drawings seems to be immediately accessible by 2 years of age. Hochberg and Brooks (1962) studied a young child who had had extremely restricted experience viewing either pictures or line drawings of objects, and had never heard such drawings labelled. At 19 months, the child was shown a set of line drawings of familiar objects, and was asked to label them—a task which he accomplished with no difficulty. This suggests that the mapping between the two mental objects (the representation of the object, and of the drawing) arose as a natural and straightforward function of the child's spatial knowledge system.

If the blind also develop a spatial knowledge system early in life, then what might we predict about their ability to achieve this correspondence between two products of the spatial knowledge system? In principle, there seems to be no reason to predict a difference, for both the blind and sighted face precisely the same task: inferring a relationship between two mental entities. In fact, it is well known that blind adults can use three-dimensional maps to guide locomotion. Leonard and Newman (1957) showed that blind adolescents could use three-dimensional maps to follow previously travelled routes, as well as to construct new routes between known landmarks. Current investigations of map use in blind adults assume some such basic competence, and therefore revolve around the question of what physical elements can best convey information to the blind—not whether they can use maps at all (Berla, 1982).

Yet, one might wonder whether the early development of this knowledge in the blind is as spontaneous and immediate as it apparently is in the sighted. Perhaps the blind require years of formal training or considerably more metacognitive ability than is available to toddlers. Indeed, some investigators have argued that blind *children* have difficulty achieving various presumptive symbolic functions. For example, Fraiberg (1977) suggested that blind children were particularly delayed in their achievement of such milestones as Piagetian object permanence, representational play, and use of personal pronouns (see also Bower, 1977). Based on such observations, one might expect delays or difficulties in the blind child's use and understanding of physical representations of space. And, while blind adults might eventually come to understand some basic map concept, one might still suspect (along with Locke) that they would never come to understand the physical representation of those spatial properties that are embodied only in the visual system (e.g. the two-dimensional representation of visual occlusion). However, current evidence suggests that the blind child can rapidly and easily understand physical representations of space; that blind adults can rapidly understand even representations of visual-spatial properties; and that these accomplishments are not dependent on lengthy practice or formal training. Rather, much like Hochberg and Brooks' subject, the blind can come to interpret and use simple three-dimensional maps and raised line drawings without any previous experience in doing so.

Early Map Use in the Blind Child

Evidence on the blind child comes from Landau (1986), who extended the observations on spatial knowledge in the blind child to include a map task (see also, Landau et al., 1984). The child had shown that she could make spatial inferences in navigation tasks (see above), so clearly had a system of spatial knowledge. However, she had had no experience with maps of any kind. Moreover, as is reportedly common for blind children, she was clearly delayed in other so-called representational activities, such as playing with standard symbolic objects (see Landau & L.R. Gleitman, 1985, for a non-deviant interpretation of this delay). Could she interpret and use a simple three-dimensional map to guide her locomotion? If so, how much training would she require?

The child (who was now 4 years old) was brought into a room, where a target object was placed approximately three to four feet from a small chair. She was seated in the chair, and shown a simple two-object map: one wooden block represented her own position in the chair, and a second wooden block represented the target object, positioned to represent its location relative to the chair. The child was told that the map would "show you where things are in the room," and she was allowed to explore it. She was then asked to use the map to locate the target in the room. Over twelve trials, she performed significantly better than chance, navigating in the proper direction. In subsequent experiments, she was shown the same map, but under various transformation conditions: horizontal translation (e.g. the map—hence both wooden blocks—to her left, but the target to her right in space), front-behind translation (i.e., the map held in front of her, but the target behind her), and vertical rotation (the map held upright, as in reading a book). In each condition she succeeded in locating the target on a significant proportion of trials. Her accuracy could have been based only on her use of the map, since no other useful cues were available in the testing room. In sum, the blind child required no formal training or extended experience with maps or like objects in order to interpret and use a simple map. At an early age, the blind child can use physical representations of space—as well as mental representations of space—to guide her locomotion.

Appreciation of Line Drawings in the Blind Adult

Evidence from blind adults comes from work by John Kennedy (1978; 1982), who has shown that congenitally blind adults are able to understand raised line drawings on their first encounters with such materials. These adults had no experience interpreting or producing such drawings before they were tested, and apparently, many were quite sure that they would be unable to perform such tasks. However, they were successful. Many of them could identify the line drawings of familiar objects, and many could produce line drawings that were reasonable approximations to target objects. These adults, therefore, could understand the means by which one conveys three-dimensional spatial relationships in two dimensions. Moreover, they were not confined to expressing or understanding only those spatial relationships that can be experienced non-visually. For example, some of the subjects understood that a two-dimensional representation should include only what is "visible" from the front (e.g. the front face of a cube should be represented by four straight lines arranged as a square). And they understood that if the object was rounded, then the occluding bound should be represented by a curved line. As Kennedy (1978) has pointed out, haptic exploration might give rise to detection of the linear edges on the front face of a sharply bounded object (such as a cube), but no such clear boundaries are detected when one haptically explores a sphere. The sharp boundaries in a two-dimensional representation of a sphere exemplify spatial properties afforded only by vision; yet without formal training, the blind seem capable of inferring that they exist, and seem to understand how to convey them in a separate physical representation of space.

Summary

The blind child and adult seem quite capable of understanding and using physical representations of space. No formal training or extensive specific experience with particular materials seems necessary to effect the crucial translations between two products of spatial knowledge. Kennedy's demonstrations suggest that, by adulthood, the blind can even appreciate spatial properties they have never experienced first-hand (i.e. those given through vision). As the next section will show, this appreciation develops quite early in life, and may depend in part on the intimate relationship between spatial knowledge and language.

SPATIAL KNOWLEDGE AND LANGUAGE LEARNING

For the sighted child, it seems obvious that first language learning depends in part on adequate construal of the spatial world—understanding of objects and object layouts, and the spatial relationships embodied in events. This is usually referred to as the "context" for language learning, but also can be considered explicitly in spatial terms (see also, Talmy, 1983; Jackendoff, 1983; Landau & L.R. Gleitman, 1985). For example, in order to understand the sentence "John gave the book to Mary," the child must be able to understand the spatial relationships among the three objects/arguments, John, Mary, and the book; and the spatial transformation that occurs as the book moves from one party (source) to the other (goal). Such understanding seems necessary (though by no means sufficient) for learning the mapping between forms and meanings. Many investigators of first language learning have argued that some such semantic bootstrap is necessary for the child to begin the task of language learning (Braine & Hardy, 1982; Maratsos, 1983; Gleitman & Wanner, 1982; Pinker, 1984). While the semantic categories usually invoked are, e.g., agents, actions, and objects, the spatial description seems like a necessary first step in constructing these higher level categories (and may turn out to be quite directly mappable onto them, see Landau & Gleitman, 1985).

Given the importance of spatial context, some have suggested that blind children will inevitably be deficient in their language learning, as they are supposed to lack normal contextual support (Bloom, 1983; Werth, 1983; Andersen et al., 1984). However, this argument is faulty on two grounds. First, it assumes that the blind must have difficulty in constructing a spatial world populated by objects and the spatial relationships inherent in actions and events. Evidence that this is not true has been adduced in previous sections. Second, the argument assumes that context somehow is sufficient for language learning. But of course it is not. For, as many have pointed out, any given context (or scene) can be described linguistically by a large number of sentences; and any given sentence can describe a great many different scenes. Therefore, knowledge about context cannot be equivalent to knowledge about language. The puzzle is just how the child manages to discover the intricate correlations that exist between the forms of language and the meanings. If context is important, then *how* is it important? What is its role in helping the child to crack the linguistic code?

Landau and Gleitman (1985) attempted to gain some insight into these problems by studying language learning in blind children. To us, as to all, it seemed obvious that the context for language learning by blind children somehow differs from the normal case. For example, the blind child will often be unable to understand what is going on around him, simply because there is less information about scenes occurring at a distance. More importantly, for certain terms and structures—visual words—the blind child will apparently lack important contextual support because he has no first-hand visual experience. Therefore, we were particularly interested in discovering how the blind child would come to learn such visual terms as *look* and *see*, as well as other visual verbs and adjectives (color terms). In a set of investigations, we were able to show that blind children develop normally the gross milestones of language, including early vocabulary, thematic relations, and syntax. Moreover, we found that the blind child comes to have rich and articulated representations for the spatial properties of visual verbs. This latter development—as well as the acquisition of other spatial verbs— appears to be highly dependent on the joint use of spatial and linguistic knowledge. The next sections briefly describe the findings that led to this conclusion (see Landau & Gleitman, 1985, for details of rationale and findings).

Knowledge of Spatial Properties of Visual Verbs

A single congenitally blind child, Kelli, served as subject in the study of visual verbs. At around age 2, she began using visual terminology spontaneously (this accords with sighted norms for use of perception verbs, see Bloom, Lightbown, & Hood, 1975). In particular, the word *see* was used extensively in contexts that suggested the child wanted to come in contact with an object. For example, she said "see camera" when the video camera was being assembled, and was content after being allowed to touch it. Similarly, Kelli's mother often said the word *look* to her, usually in settings where she was about to show Kelli some object (a fact to which I return below). Kelli typically responded to this word by reaching out in space, as if searching for the object of attention. These two observations provided the setting within which we began to ask what the words *see* and *look* meant to Kelli.

In a series of experiments beginning when Kelli was three years old, we were able to show that she developed two different meanings for these visual verbs: one meaning as used of herself, and one as used of sighted others. First, we found that Kelli used *look* of herself to mean roughly, "explore with the hands in a spatially appropriate manner." In a first experiment, we gave her spatially modified commands to *look*, and she responded in spatially appropriate ways. For example when we gave her the command "look up," she raised her hands straight up in the air, without moving her head; when we gave her the command "look in front of you," she moved her hands about in the space in front of her (see Figure 16.2). When sighted but blindfolded controls were given the same commands, they moved their heads (and unseeing eyes) in spatially appropriate ways (e.g. tilting their heads upward to "look up") (see Figure 16.3). This already suggests that, by age three, the blind and the sighted child have appropriately mapped spatial prepositions onto spatial directions, and that they seem to construe the verb *look* as spatial and

Figure 16.2. Kelli's response to "look up." (Reprinted from Landau & L. R. Gleitman, 1985, by permission of the publisher.)

Figure 16.3. A blindfolded sighted child's response to "look up." (Reprinted from Landau & L. R. Gleitman, 1985, by permission of the publisher.)

tied to a specific modality (haptic for the blind; visual for the sighted).

In another experiment, we modified *look* and *touch* commands, to determine whether the two had the same meaning for Kelli. These modifications yielded clear results: *look* commands yielded spatial exploration while *touch* yielded mere contact. For example, when we told Kelli to "look behind you" she explored the space behind her; but when told to "touch behind you," she tapped her back. When we told her to "look real hard," she explored the target object all over; but when we said "touch real hard," she hit the object with her hand, just once. Sighted blindfolded controls responded to *touch* commands by contacting the target with their hands; but to *look* commands by performing visual-type responses (e.g., orienting the eyes and head though blindfolded). Along with several controls that support this interpretation, these experiments confirmed that Kelli's meaning for *look* as applied to herself concerned spatial exploration with the organ most likely to extract object information—the hands. The sighted children apparently meant much the same thing—except that for them, the most important exploratory organ is the eye.

A second set of experiments showed that by age three, Kelli had also differentiated the sighted meanings of visual verbs. Manipulating the spatial configurations of various target object layouts, we were able to show that Kelli appreciated three spatial properties of vision, specifically, the distance, orientation, and barrier structures that would lead to seeing with the eyes. For example, when asked to "let Mommy see the doll," Kelli held up the doll for the mother's inspection, even though the mother was stationed at quite a distance from her. When asked to "let Mommy see the front of your pants" or "let Mommy see the back of your pants," Kelli always moved so as to position the object of viewing in her mother's line of sight (see Figure 16.4). For example, if she started out facing the mother, she remained in that position to let her mother see the front of her pants, but turned around 180 degrees to let her mother see the back of her pants. Finally, she knew how to prevent her mother from seeing some object (by concealing it), as opposed to preventing her from hearing some object (by silencing it). In addition to these spatial properties, Kelli also recognized the difference between the active verbs *look/listen* and the stative verbs *see/hear*, as evidenced by her judgments that her mother might have looked, but not seen some object; or listened, but not heard some sound.

Kelli's spontaneous use of the visual verbs also showed that she had mastered the syntax of *look* and *see* as well as that of the other verbs she commonly used. In most cases, she used *look* and *see* in simple sentences with noun phrase objects, for example "Let me look at the doll" or "Let Mommy see the horse." In all such cases, Kelli properly included the preposition for *look (at),* and properly omitted any such preposition for *see.* Furthermore, she obeyed the syntactic restrictions for interjectives using active *look* and stative *see,* saying "Look!" and "See?" but never "Look?" or "See!" Kelli's spontaneous use of these verbs was always appropriate in context, so far as could be determined.

Figure 16.4. Kelli's response to "Let me see the back of your pants." (a) The command here is given while the child is facing the experimenter; (b) Her response is to turn around and pluck at her pants, saying, "This is the back of my pants." (Reprinted from Landau & L. R. Gleitman, 1985, by permission of the publisher.)

These findings as a whole motivated us to search for the possible bases of Kelli's learning. We assumed that she had extracted the appropriate form-meaning relationships from the ambiant linguistic and non-linguistic environment provided by the mother, who used these terms freely. Since Kelli had obeyed spatial as well as syntactic restrictions on the use of *look* and *see*, we considered both the spatial and linguistic contexts of the mother's uses as possible information sources. The corpus used for analysis consisted of all the mother's use of visual verbs as well as other verbs commonly used by the mother, from the earliest language samples up until the time experimentation began on Kelli's knowledge of *look* and *see*. This corpus contained over 1500 of the mother's utterances.

The Spatial Analysis

We first considered a purely spatial analysis of the situations accompanying the mother's use of *look* and see, as well as other verbs she commonly used. We assumed that Kelli might be able to extract important spatial properties of looking and seeing by analyzing the spatial contexts that accompanied sentences containing *look* and *see*. For example, if Kelli heard *look* and *see* (but no other verbs) in contexts where she was holding an object, or where the mother was offering her an object, she might come to understand that those verbs meant something having to do with exploring an object. (This leaves aside the question of how she constructed the *visual* spatial properties as well; but seems a first clear step in ascertaining how she could have constructed *any* meaning for *look*.) We therefore analyzed the situations accompanying the mother's use of all common verbs (including *look* and *see*) in terms of where the target object was when *look* or *see* was uttered. Three coding categories were used: target object near Kelli, far from Kelli, or no target object at all (e.g. "You look funny").

Ten verbs were analyzed: *look, see, come, get, give, go, have, hold, play*, and *put* (chosen because each occurred with a frequency greater than 10 in the mother's corpus). The spatial analysis revealed that *look* occurred 73% of the time when an object was near Kelli, 9% of the time when an object was far from her, and 18% of the time when no target object was present. This suggested that Kelli's mother did indeed use *look* in conditions where "haptically explore" might have been a reasonable construal. But the results for the rest of the verbs made it impossible to argue that Kelli was using this one spatial source of information to completely ascertain the meanings of *look* and *see* as verbs of perception, in contrast to various other verbs.

First, the results for *give, hold, play,* and *put* showed that these verbs occurred either as often or more often than *look* in near-object contexts. For example, *hold* occurred 100% of the time when an object was near (being held, or about to be held). Second, *see*, which should have patterned spatially like *look* (in order to provide useful information about the similar meanings of the two verbs) did not. It occurred in the near-object context 39% of the time. Thus, these results suggest that the spatial analysis of the situation could provide only rough indications of the verb meanings (e.g. that *look* had something to do with exploring nearby objects). It could not in principle have provided Kelli with *sufficient* information for grouping the verbs together on the basis of their meanings. This finding motivated a search for a spatial analysis amplified by syntactic information contained in the mother's sentences, that could have further aided Kelli in determining the meanings of these verbs.

Syntactic Analysis

Our general question here was whether any stable information about the meanings of the verbs could be derived from a comparison of the syntactic contexts in which they typically occur. More specifically, we wanted to know whether syntactic overlaps holding between *look* and *see* could serve to *unite* these verbs, whereas the spatial analysis had revealed significant differences between their contexts of use. And, we wanted to know whether syntactic distinctions could serve to *separate look* from the other verbs typically occurring in near-object contexts (*give, put, hold* and *play*). In principle, if such patterns existed they could provide Kelli with evidence about similarities in meaning between *look* and *see* and the differences in meaning between *look* and the other near-object verbs—differences that had not been provided through their spatial contexts of use.

We therefore performed an analysis of the syntactic contexts occurring in the mother's use of the verbs. The analysis presupposes that young learners like Kelli can parse incoming utterances in such a way as to yield their hierarchical (tree-structure) representations. That is, the child is assumed to be able to analyze heard utterances in terms of the major phrasal categories, noun phrase, verb phrase, prepositional phrase, etc., and each such category into lexical categories such as noun, verb, preposition, etc. (See Gleitman & Wanner, 1982, for evidence that these representational formats are available to and exploited by young children.) Such an analysis would allow the learner to ascertain the internal organization of a spoken utterance in such a way as to differentiate, say, a sentence containing a single object noun phrase ("let's see if Granny's home"), from one containing an object noun phrase followed by a prepositional phrase ("let's give a cookie to Barbara").

The analyses revealed two important facts. First, we discovered that the predictive power of the spatial analysis for *look* and *see* was greatly increased when one considered only the most common structures occurring in the mother's speech (simple sentences including deictic interjectives and declaratives containing one noun phrase). Considering only these formats, the near-object contexts for *look* rose to 1.00 from .73 (in the purely spatial analysis, see above) and for *see* they rose to .72 from .39 (as above). Apparently, the occasions for far and no-object contexts concerned talk of events and abstractions (e.g. "You look like a hunchback" or "Let's see whether granny's home"). Hence, if Kelli were so inclined, she could have collapsed together *look* and *see* based on their spatial contexts for simple sentences only. Of course, this does not solve the problem of either differentiating the two verbs from each other, or differentiating them from other verbs that occurred frequently in near-object contexts.

But second, the analysis revealed that there were distinct sets of structures associated with *look* and *see* as against the other verbs occurring in the near-object contexts. Three key examples follow. First, all of the near-object verbs except *play* occurred with locative prepositions freely (*play* occurred only with *with*). Second, *give, put,* and *hold* occurred in three-argument structures, while *look* and *see* never did. (The mother said "Daddy gave the doll to your sister" but never "Daddy saw the doll to your sister.") Finally, only *look* and *see* occurred with sentential complements and *how* free relatives ("Look how I do this"/ "Let's see if Granny's home"); and only *look* and *see* occurred as interjectives, with *look* as a deictic command ("Look, there's a boot!") and *see* as a query ("See? There's the frog").

In principle, such stable differential syntactic patterns could have provided Kelli with information about the meanings of the different verbs, if in fact these patterns reflect components of verb meanings (see Talmy, 1983; Jackendoff, 1983). It seems reasonable to suppose that this is so. To begin with, following Gruber's (1968) analysis, the verbs of perception behave syntactically much like verbs of physical motion, e.g. *come* and *go*. As one example, they all typically take locative prepositions freely (as they did in Kelli's mother's speech). Recall that *play* did not occur with locatives in this way, and so could have been ruled out of the motion category of verbs by considering this syntactic property. Second, a major group of verbs that occurred in the near-object contexts were verbs of motion that express alienable acts of motion—e.g. in "John gives Mary the ball," the agent causes movement of the object (ball) to the goal. This is true for the verbs *give, put, hold, get*; and is syntactically reflected in the fact that these verbs typically take three arguments (expressing agent/source, object, and goal). The visual verbs *look* and *see* express inalienable motion (of the gaze or hand), hence do not separately express the agent and object of motion. That is, they do not take three arguments (except in special usages such as "I looked him in the eye" or "Swann looked the ball into this hands"). The number of arguments taken by the perceptual as opposed to the non-perceptual motion verbs could have allowed Kelli to separate these two categories of verbs from each other. Third, only the perceptual verbs *look* and *see* take sentential complements and *how* relatives ("Look at how I do it"; "Let's see if Granny's home"; but *Put how I do it; *Let's give if the tree is pretty). Notionally, this is because one can perceive events, but not perform actions on them. Kelli's mother did use these structures with the visual verbs, but no others. Finally, the active/stative distinction (*look/see*) that Kelli mastered has its syntactic reflex in the mother's speech. *Look* but not *see* was used in interjective deictic commands; and *see* but not *look* was used in interjective deictic queries. These syntactic distinctions could have provided part of the basis for Kelli's inductions about the meanings of visual verbs.

Summary

By the age of three, the blind child begins to learn about the spatial properties of certain visual concepts, especially, their linguistic encoding as visual verbs. Our analysis of the ambient environment accompanying Kelli's learning of *look* and *see* suggests that an analysis of the spatial contexts accompanying utterances could have been an important contributor to this learning. However, while this spatial analysis might be necessary to help explain the child's accomplishments, it was not sufficient. Rather, a syntactically controlled analysis of the environment, combined with the information about spatial relationships holding among agents/sources, objects, and patients/goals seemed in principle to provide the information needed for a blind child to learn the meanings of visual verbs *look* and *see*. This evidence once again supports the notion that the blind child—like the sighted child—must be strongly disposed to organize the environment in highly specific ways relevant to the particular domain of learning.

FINAL THOUGHTS

In beginning, it was suggested that part of the reason for psychologists' interest in the spatial world of the blind is the strong intuition that vision is the supreme spatial sense. It seems undeniable that the blind must often have less information about space to rely on as they confront the world. But the force of the argument in this chapter has been that such differences need not impinge on the development of knowledge—spatial knowledge or other knowledge systems such as language, that depend in part on spatial knowledge. Quite to the contrary, the evidence reviewed here suggests that the young blind child can develop the knowledge that enables her to explore and recognize objects, navigate the world, interpret symbolic physical representations of space, and even learn the meanings of sighted verbs. And she seems to do so with as little effort as her sighted counterpart.

These facts suggest that some basic principles of children's developing knowledge systems arise independently of the nature or degree of particular experiential confrontations with the physical world. Whether the child confronts the environment mainly by hand or by eye, she is capable of using these principles to construct a spatial world populated by objects and events. This construction supports the many diverse accomplishments described in this chapter.

Viewed in this way, the problem of the blind child is just the same as that of the sighted child: developing knowledge using the limited information available in the world. And this development in the blind child, while awesome, is in principle no more of a feat than the same development in the sighted child. While this perspective may sit uncomfortably with our intuitions about vision and its role in the development of knowledge, perhaps this just shows how inadequate such simple intuitions can be.

REFERENCES

Abravanel, E. 1970. Choice for shape versus textural matching by young children. *Perceptual and Motor Skills.* 31:527-533.

Abravanel, E. 1968. The development of intersensory patterning with regards to selected spatial dimensions. *Monographs of the Society for Research in Child Development.* 33(2).

Andersen, E. S., Dunlea, A. and Kekelis, L. S. 1984. Blind children's language: Resolving some differences. *Journal of Child Language.* 11(3):645-664.

Berkeley, B. 1709. An essay towards a new theory of vision. In D. M. Armstrong (Ed.), *Berkeley's philosophical writings.* New York: Macmillan, 1965.

Berla, E. P. 1982. Haptic perception of tangible graphic displays. In W. Schiff and E. Foulke (Eds.), *Tactual perception: A source book.* New York: Cambridge University Press.

Bliss, J. C. 1978. Reading machines for the blind. In G. Gordon (Ed.), *Active touch: The mechanism of recognition of objects by manipulation.* New York: Pergamon Press.

Bloom, L. 1983. Tensions in psycholinguistics. *Science.* 220:843-844.

Bloom, L., Lightbown, P., & Hood, L. 1975. Structure and variation in child language. *Monographs of the Society for Research in Child Development.* 160.

Bower, T. G. R. 1977. *A Primer of infant development.* San Francisco: W. H. Freeman and Co.

Braine, M. D. S., & Hardy, J. A., 1982. On what case categories there are, why they are, and how they develop: An amalgam of "a priori" considerations, speculations, and evidence from children. In E. Wanner and L. R. Gleitman (Eds.), *Language acquisition: State of the art.* New York: Cambridge University Press.

Davidson, P. W. 1972. Haptic judgements of curvature by blind and sighted humans. *Journal of Experimental Psychology.* 93(1):43-45.

Descartes, R. 1637. *Discourse on method, optics, geometry, and meteorology.* P. J. Olscamp, (trans.), Indianapolis: Bobbs—Merrill, 1965.

Fraiberg, S. 1977. *Insights from the blind.* New York: Basic Books.

Gentner, D. 1982. Why nouns are learned before verbs: Linguistic relativity vs. natural partitioning. In S. Kuczaj (Ed.), *Language development: Language, culture, and cognition.* Hillsdale, NJ: Lawrence Erlbaum Associates.

Gibson, J. J. 1962. Observations on active touch. *Psychological Review.* 69(6):447-491.

Gibson, E. J. & Walker, A. S. 1984. Development of knowledge of visual-tactual affordances of substance. *Child Development.* 55:453-460.

Gibson, E. J. & Spelke, E. 1983. The development of perception. In J. H. Flavell and E. Markman (Eds.), *Cognitive development.* Vol. 3 of P. H. Mussen (Ed.), *Handbook of cognitive psychology.* New York: Wiley.

Gilson, E. Q., & Baddeley, A. D. 1969. Tactile short term memory. *Quarterly Journal of Experimental Psychology.* 21:180-184.

Gleitman, L. R., & Wanner, E. 1982. Language acquisition: The state of the art. In E. Wanner and L. R. Gleitman (Eds.), *Language acquisition: State of the art.* New York: Cambridge University Press.

Gliner, C. R., Pick, A. D., Pick, H. L., & Hales, J. J. 1969. A developmental investigation of visual and haptic preferences for shape and texture. *Monographs of the Society for Research in Child Development.* 34.

Gruber, J. 1968. Look and see. *Language.* 43(4):937-947.

Hochberg, J. 1978. *Perception.* Englewood Cliffs, NJ: Prentice-Hall.

Hochberg, J. 1968. In the mind's eye. In R. N. Haber (Ed.), *Contemporary theory and research in visual perception.* New York: Holt, Rinehart, and Winston.

Hochberg, J., & Brooks, V. 1962. Pictoral recognition as an unlearned ability: A study of one child's performance. *American Journal of Psychology.* 75:624-628.

Jackendoff, R. 1983. *Semantics and cognition.* Cambridge: MIT Press.

Jeannerod, M. 1983. How do we direct our actions in space? In A. Hein and M. Jeannerod (Eds.), *Spatially oriented behavior.* New York: Springer-Verlag.

Kellogg, W. 1962. Sonar system of the blind. *Science.* 137:399-404.

Kennedy, J. M. 1982. Haptic pictures. In W. Schiff and E. Foulke (Eds.), *Tactual perception: A source book.* New York: Cambridge University Press.

Kennedy, J. M. 1978. Haptics. In E. C. Carteiette and M. P. Friedman (Eds.), *Handbook of perception, Vol. 8.* New York: Academic Press.

Knapp, L., Gleitman, H., & Landau, B. 1984. Development of spatial knowledge with and without vision. Paper presented at E.P.A., Baltimore, MD.

Krueger, L. E. 1970. David Katz's der aufbau der tastwelt (The world of touch): A synopsis. *Perception and Psychophysics.* 7(6):337-341.

Landau, B. 1986. Early map use as an unlearned ability. *Cognition.* 22:201-223.

Landau, B., & Gleitman, L. R. 1985. *Language and experience: Evidence from the blind child.* Cambridge, Mass.: Harvard University Press.

Landau, B., & Spelke, E. 1985. Spatial knowledge and its manifestations. In H. M. Wellman (Ed.), *Children's searching: The development of search skill and spatial representation.* Hillsdale, NJ: Lawrence Erlbaum Associates.

Landau, B., Spelke, E. S., & Gleitman, H. 1984. Spatial knowledge in a young blind child. *Cognition.* 16:225-260.

Lederman, S. J. 1978. Heightening tactile impressions of surface texture. In G. Gordon (Ed.), *Active touch: The mechanism of recognition of objects by manipulation.* New York: Pergamon Press.

Leonard, J. A., & Newman, R. C. 1957. Spatial orientation in the blind. *Nature.* 215:1413-1414.

Locke, J. 1690. *An essay concerning human understanding.* (1964). A. D. Woozley (Ed.), Cleveland: Meridian Books.

Maratsos, M. 1983. Some current issues in the study of the acquisition of grammar. In J. H. Flavell and E. Markam (Eds.), *Cognitive development.* Volume 3 of P. H. Mussen (Ed.), *Handbook of cognitive psychology.* New York: Wiley.

Millar, S. 1978. Aspects of memory for information from touch and movement. In G. Gordon (Ed.), *Active touch: The mechanism of recognition of objects by manipulation.* New York: Pergamon Press.

Millar, S. 1975. Spatial memory by blind and sighted children. *British Journal of Psychology.* 66(4):449-459.

Millar, S. 1974. Tactile short—term memory by blind and sighted children. *British Journal of Psychology.* 65(2):253-263.

Mulford, R. 1985. First words of the blind child. In M. D. Smith and J. L. Locke (Eds.), *The emergent lexicon: The child's development of a linguistic vocabulary.* New York: Academic Press.

O'Keefe, J., & Nadel, L. 1978. *The hippocampus as a cognitive map.* Oxford: Oxford University Press.

Piaget, J., & Inhelder, B. 1948. *The child's conception of space.* New York: Norton, 1967.

Pinker, S. 1984. *Language learnability and language development.* Cambridge: Harvard University Press.

Rieser, J., Lockman, J. & Pick, H. 1980. The role of visual experience in knowledge of spatial layout. *Perception and Psychophysics.* 28:189-190.

Rose, S. A., Gottfried, A. W., & Bridger, W. 1981. Cross-modal transfer in 6 month-old infants. *Developmental Psychology.* 17(5):661-669.

Senden, M. von. 1932. *Space and sight: The perception of space and shape in the congenitally blind before and after operation.* Glencoe, Illinois: Free Press, 1960.

Strelow, E. R. 1985. What is needed for a theory of mobility: Direct perception and cognitive maps—Lessons from the blind. *Psychological Review.* 92(2):226-248.

Sullivan, E. V., & Turvey, M. T. 1972. Short term retention of tactile stimulation. *Quarterly Journal of Experimental Psychology.* 24:253-261.

Talmy, L. 1983. How language structures space. In H. Pick and L. Acredolo (Eds.), *Spatial orientation: Theory, research, and application.* New York: Plenum Press.

Warren, D. H. 1982. Development of haptic perception. In W. Schiff and E. Foulke (Eds.), *Tactual perception: A source book.* New York: Cambridge University Press.

Warren, D., Anooshian, L., & Bollinger, J. 1973. Early versus late blindness: The role of early vision in spatial behavior. *American Foundation for the Blind: Research Bulletin.* 26:151-170.

Werth, P. 1983. Meaning in language acquisition. In A. E. Mills (Ed.), *Language acquisition in the blind child.* London: Croom Helm.

Zaporozhets, A. V. 1965. The development of perception in the pre-school child. In P. H. Mussen (Ed.), European research in cognitive development. *Monographs of the Society for Research in Child Development.* 30:82-101.

NEUROPSYCHOLOGICAL STUDY OF THE DEVELOPMENT OF SPATIAL COGNITION

17

SANDRA F. WITELSON
McMaster University

JANICE A. SWALLOW
McMaster University

Neuropsychological study of various perceptual and mnemonic skills involved in spatial cognition may be useful in addressing two main issues. One concerns the functional organization of the brain in mediating spatial cognition—knowledge which is essential for understanding how the brain serves as the substrate which mediates spatial cognition. Another concerns how neuropsychological studies may be used to delineate the subcomponents of spatial cognition and their interrelationships.

This paper will focus on these two issues in relation to spatial cognition in children and thus its development and change over time. Special consideration will be given to the neurological aspect of brain organization reflected in specialization of the right hemisphere for spatial cognition. A brief discussion of precisely what is meant by the terms "spatial ability" and "spatial cognition" is warranted. This is done, not with the intention of providing a comprehensive definition, but merely to illustrate the complexity of the problem.

SPATIAL COGNITION

One of the most striking and perplexing features of the work on spatial skills is the diversity of the tasks and mental processes subsumed under the terms spatial ability and spatial cognition. Clearly spatial, like linguistic, ability includes a heterogeneous cluster of tasks, but which specific tasks are examples of spatial cognition and what the nature is of the cognitive processes involved in the performance of those tasks is certainly not clear. The adjective "spatial" is used, more often than not, as if its meaning were self-evident— which, at an intuitive level, it may be. However, at a more empirical level, the complexity of what exactly is spatial ability is highlighted. Does it simply refer to any task involving the perception of stimuli in the visual or somesthetic sensory modalities? Does it include only those tasks that involve the perception, or the physical or mental manipulation of objects in Euclidean space? Or, does it refer to any task that cannot be clearly categorized as linguistic? All of these descriptions have been used. An example of the last possibility is given in Linn and Petersen (1985) who state that "spatial ability generally refers to skill in representing, transforming, generating and recalling symbolic, nonlinguistic information" (p. 1482). Such definitions by exclusion abound in the current literature.

The issue of the definition of spatial ability becomes even more complex when functional asymmetry of the human brain and sex differences in spatial ability are taken into consideration. Relatively few authors have attempted a clear definition of spatial ability and those who have, in conjunction with considering spatial ability in respect to brain localization and individual differences, have often been seduced into speculating whether all tasks on which males outperform females, or which are processed predominantly by the right hemisphere, involve a spatial component. For example, one major attempt by Harris (1978) in a review of sex differences in spatial ability noted that there are no female chess players of grand master status. This observation led him to suggest: "One wonders whether chess involves a strong spatial component, therefore making it more difficult for females" (Harris, 1978, p. 409).

In general the term "spatial" appears to be used in a relatively global fashion and may be somewhat misleading. Spatial cognition is often used to refer to the type of mental processing involved in an apparently disparate group of tasks. Using a meta-analysis procedure to synthesize the literature between 1974 and 1982, Linn and Petersen (1985) identified three main categories of spatial ability— spatial perception, mental rotation, and spatial visualization. However, it is often unclear to which category a particular task belongs, especially if the task does not have a readily discernible spatial component. In some instances, spatial cognition is defined as those tests assumed to be primarily dependent on, or more efficiently processed by, the right cerebral hemisphere. A catalogue of such tasks would include many which clearly have a strong spatial component such as recognition of shapes, mental rotation of objects, face perception, and spatial orientation or a sense of direction. However, the same list would also include many tasks in which the spatial component is either absent or at least not readily discernible, for example, the perception of music, the prosodic aspects of speech, and the perception and expression of emotions. Several recent reviews concerning spatial functions, and right hemisphere functions in general, are available (e.g., Critchley & Henson, 1977; De Renzi, 1982; Heilman & Valenstein, 1985; Liben, Patterson & Newcombe, 1981; Perecman, 1983; Potegal, 1982; Young, 1983; see also Morrow & Ratcliff, this volume).

To further complicate the issue, some tasks which would seem to have a very strong spatial component have been found to be more dependent on the left than the right hemisphere. For example, some disorders involving personal, as opposed to extrapersonal, space are associated with left-hemisphere damage (Ratcliff, 1982). In contrast to the fact that seemingly similar tasks may be processed by different hemispheres, some tasks which superficially appear to be quite different, and might be predicted to involve different cognitive processes, prove to be mediated by the same hemisphere, as for example face perception and melodic perception. Such findings indicate that the stimulus characteristics of a given task are not the only predictors of the cognitive process necessary for its performance. Furthermore, the finding that very different tasks are processed by the right hemisphere suggests that they have some aspects of cognitive processing in common that are distinct from those involved in tasks which are dependent on the left hemisphere.

A neuropsychological approach which attempts to discover the functional organization of the brain as it relates to a variety of spatial skills may be a productive method of gaining information about the associations and distinctiveness of the cognitive processes used in such tasks. This paper will focus on neuropsychological studies of spatial cognition in children and will highlight individual studies which exemplify the role of neuropsychology in dissecting the nature of the cognitive process involved.

RIGHT HEMISPHERE SPECIALIZATION: STUDIES WITH BRAIN-DAMAGED CHILDREN

Historically, the study of the right hemisphere and its functions began later than that of the left hemisphere and, until relatively recently, has received considerably less attention. The right hemisphere has been found to be necessary in tasks involving the perception of two- and three-dimensional shapes, line orientation, faces, color, spatial position and orientation, tactile shapes, musical chords and melodies, timbre and intensity of musical stimuli, emotional tones and intonation patterns, the ability to dress oneself, sing, construct block models, and direct attention to both lateral sensory fields. Current thought is that functional asymmetry reflects the fact that the hemispheres are specialized for two different types or modes of information processing and that lateralization is determined by the type of processing required by the task or by the cognitive strategy selected by the subject and not by the sensory modality or stimulus characteristics of the task. One working hypothesis is that the right hemisphere is specialized for processing information such that stimuli are synthesized and sustained to form a unified configuration in which any temporal aspects of the stimuli are superseded. The perception of faces, melodies, and three-dimensional objects is thought to depend on this integrative type of cognitive processing.

Hemisphere specialization for linguistic and spatial functions exists within the first few postnatal months. The literature attesting to this conclusion has been reviewed elsewhere (Witelson, 1977a; 1985; 1987). In this chapter, studies of right-hemisphere representation of spatial cognition in children will be discussed within this given framework, not to address the issue of the existence of early right-hemisphere specialization for spatial skills, but to consider the more cognitive issues such as the specific spatial skills associated with specific brain regions during development and what such information might indicate about the nature of spatial cognition during development.

Information concerning the neurology of spatial cognition during development has come from two sources—initially from the study of the behavioral and cognitive deficits in brain-damaged children and later, with the development of tests of perceptual asymmetry and of measures of electrophysiological asymmetry, from the study of neurologically intact children.

Limitations of Studies with Brain-Damaged Children

The basic method in the study of brain-damaged individuals, whether children or adults, is to correlate the location of the neural lesion with any subsequent cognitive deficits. Compared to the wealth of knowledge available concerning the neural substrate of speech and language functions in children, there is a remarkable dearth of information regarding spatial abilities. Several factors likely contribute to this situation. First, any deficit in visual-spatial or constructional ability in the daily behavioral repertoire subsequent to brain damage is likely to be less dramatic than the loss or disruption of speech and language functions, and therefore less likely to be noticed, documented, or investigated. Second, the incidence of definable unilateral lesions, resulting from strokes or from neurosurgical procedures involving removal of precisely definable areas of cortical tissue, which has increased in adults in the last two decades, remains low in children. Such specific lesions provide the clearest information regarding brain-behavior relationships. They make possible the finding of a *double dissociation* effect. This refers to the situation in which Lesion A is associated with a deficit in Function X but less so or not at all in Function Y, while Lesion B is associated with a deficit in Function Y but less so in Function X. A double dissociation effect provides the most convincing evidence that a particular neural region is essential for a specific cognitive function and allows such general factors as level of intellect, attention, or motivation to be ruled out as the cause of the poor performance.

The relative rarity of therapeutic neurosurgery in children also precludes the possibility of obtaining information from the diagnostic procedures that may accompany such surgery. Speech lateralization as assessed by intracarotid Amytal testing (e.g., Blume, Grabow, Darley & Aronson, 1973) is rarely done in children, and when it is, testing for spatial ability is almost never included. Mapping of the location of different cognitive functions by electrical stimulation of the cortex (e.g., Ojemann, 1983) is rarely possible in children. One case of a 4-year-old has recently been studied in this respect but it was the left language-dominant hemisphere that was exposed and stimulated (Ojemann, 1986). Commissurotomy, which involves separating the fiber tracts connecting the two hemispheres (Gazzaniga, 1970) as a last resort in the treatment of intractable epilepsy, is not usually done until patients are in their late teens or early twenties.

In addition to the low incidence of appropriate cases for study, there are further difficulties in the nature and timing of the psychological testing. In order to provide unequivocal evidence of the existence of the localization of particular functions or hemisphere specialization at any particular point in development, certain minimal methodological requirements must be met. Not only must the brain damage be verifiably unilateral, but the age of onset must be known and cognitive assessments must be performed as soon as practicable after the initial shock of the cerebral trauma has subsided. Failure to meet these requirements is often associated with logical errors in interpreting the results. Only immediate assessment of the presence or absence of deficits following brain damage can unequivocally address the issue of hemisphere specialization at the time of the injury and thus at specific stages of development, and thereby provide a possible neurological probe as to the interrelationships of various spatial tasks. The results of psychological assessments done years after the injury attest to the extent of recovery of function and the underlying neuronal plasticity.

In the past it often has been difficult to know the exact site and extent of the brain damage. Recent technological developments such as computerized tomography (CT) and magnetic resonance imaging (MRI) have made more sophisticated imaging of the location of brain damage possible and have reduced some of the uncertainty in localizing lesions. However, in view of the fact that marked physical maturation of the brain occurs in the first few years of life and that early damage in one region has been demonstrated experimentally to alter anatomical connections (Goldman-Rakic, Isserhoff, Schwartz & Bugbee, 1983), it is impossible, even with clearly localized lesions, to know the full anatomical repercussions of brain damage in infancy or early childhood. Since age at the time of damage has an effect on subsequent brain development and the pattern of cognitive deficits, it is essential that the age at which the original lesion was sustained be known. For those clinical cases in which the first sign of neural damage is a behavioral syndrome, such as epilepsy, or lack of behavioral or cognitive development, pinpointing the onset of the damage is generally impossible.

Because the existence of neurological damage may not be suspected until months or years after its occurrence, and often because research subjects may only be recruited retrospectively from clinical records, cognitive assessment is often delayed. The results of such delayed assessment can provide information only about the status of hemisphere specialization at the time of testing. They reveal nothing about the situation that may have existed at the time of injury. When the assessment is delayed, recovery of function may have occurred and may obscure any immediate loss of function. The effects of recovery of function are often erroneously interpreted as a lack of, or as less severe, cognitive deficits associated with specific brain regions. Due to all of the factors described above the data available regarding children are limited in both quality and quantity. Most of the available studies are of this latter type, with assessment done in adolescence or young adulthood involving retrospective knowledge of brain damage sustained at an earlier age.

One further factor which contributes to the difficulty in interpreting the results of studies with brain-damaged individuals, particularly with spatial tasks in children, has been even less recognized than any of the issues mentioned so far. This is the issue of the *general* versus the *specific* effects of brain damage. The specific effects of brain damage are those in which particular functions are impaired following specific localized lesions. In contrast, the general effects of brain damage are thought to reflect an impairment in an individual's inherited intellectual power from which all of his learned perceptions and behaviors are derived. It then follows that early, as opposed to later, brain damage will result in a lower overall level of intellectual functioning as it disrupts learning ability and problem solving ability at an earlier stage of development. Thus, the degree of impairment associated with the general effects of brain damage is greater with damage sustained earlier and the phenomenon of greater plasticity of the immature brain is not applicable for these psychological characteristics. The specific effects of brain damage, on the other hand, tend to affect the level of ability on particular tasks, different skills being affected depending on the locus of the lesion, and in this case plasticity operates such that earlier lesions result in less severe impairment. The apparent inconsistency of different studies of the effects of early versus late brain damage with both humans and nonhumans is largely eliminated if the tasks measured are considered in terms of specific or general functions. In studying hemisphere specialization, it is crucial that the tasks used to assess the functions of the two hemispheres are not confounded with tasks reflecting the specific versus general factors. In studies of spatial cognition, this is particularly important as the nonverbal, problem-solving types of tasks often used as measures of right-hemisphere functions also appear to be the tasks most sensitive to reflecting the general effects of brain damage. (For a more detailed discussion of this issue see Witelson, 1985, p. 55-57; 1987.)

Neural Substrate of Spatial Functions
via Study of Brain-Damaged Children

Neuropsychological study of brain-damaged individuals may be conceptualized as falling into three main types of studies as outlined in Table 17.1. In Type IA studies, performance on various cognitive tests is assessed either by clinical observation or as part of a more formally planned psychological evaluation of cognitive deficits in

Table 17.1
Types of Neuropsychological Study with Brain-Damaged Individuals

Type	Aim	Known (Independent Variable)	Unknown (Dependent Variable)
IA	Clinical assessment of brain-damaged individuals	Localized lesion	Presence or absence of deficits on various cognitive tests
IB	Clinical assessment for diagnosis of brain damage	Clinically observed behavioral or cognitive deficits	Performance on specific neuropsychological tests used to infer presence and location of brain damage
II	Brain localization of specific cognitive functions	Localized lesion	Performance on specific cognitive tasks associated with lesions in other populations

brain-damaged patients. Most of the early studies are of this type, such as the study of the level of performance of right-hemisphere damaged children on Performance IQ tests and memory for visual designs. Type IB studies are those in which some clinically observed behavioral or cognitive deficit raises the suspicion of brain dysfunction not confirmable by neurological tests, and based on information garnered from Type IA studies, a test battery is selected to aid in determining the possible presence and location of some brain dysfunction. Such case studies would be examples of hypothetico-deductive clinical neuropsychological assessment. In Type II studies, existing knowledge of brain-behavior relationships is used to investigate the neural localization of cognitive tasks as yet unstudied in children. The study of whether right-hemisphere damage leads to visual field neglect in children, as it does in adults (e.g., Ferro, Martins & Tavora, 1984), is an example of this type of study.

The available research concerning spatial ability associated with right-hemisphere damage in children has been reviewed previously (Witelson, 1977a; 1985) and is still surprisingly limited. Table 17.2 provides a brief summary of the available studies (excluding cases with right hemispherectomy). A few other early studies are available but studies done in the 1960s tended to include primarily cases of diffuse brain damage with heterogeneous etiologies and many cases in which age of onset was unclear (e.g., Fitzhugh & Fitzhugh, 1964; Meier & French, 1966; Pennington, Galliani & Voegele, 1965; Reed & Fitzhugh, 1966; Reed & Reitan, 1969). The psychological assessments in these studies were delayed and usually consisted of

Studies of Spatial Ability in Children With Right-Hemisphere Damage

Study	N	Lesion Symptom	Age at Onset of Damage	Age at Testing	Spatial Tests Administered
McFie, 1961	13	Right hemisphere damage: frontal = 2, temporal = 6, parietal = 5	1–15 yr	5–15 yr	WISC Perf IQ, Memory for Designs
Fedio & Mirsky, 1969	15	Right temporal focal EEG abnormality	3–10 yr (seizure onset)	6–14 yr	WISC Perf IQ, Memory for visual designs, Rey-Osterrieth Figure Test
Rudel, Teuber & Twitchell, 1974	36	"Right" hemisphere encephalopathy based on history and neurological examination	Pre- or perinatal	7–18 yr	WISC Perf IQ, Visual route-finding, Body scheme
Kershner & King, 1974	7	Left hemiplegia	0–15 mo	6–9 yr	WISC Perf IQ, Reitan-Indiana Tests
Woods, 1980	23	Left hemiparesis	Pre- and perinatal (n = 10) 1–14 yr (n = 13)	9–17 yr 5–16 yr	WISC Perf IQ W-B II Perf IQ
Ferro, Martins & Tavora, 1984	3	Right hemisphere lesions (CT scans)	5–9 yr	Immediately after onset of lesion	Visual neglect testing, Visuoconstructional tests, Visual retention, spontaneous drawing
Stiles-Davis, Sugarman & Nass, 1985	4	Left hemiparesis	Prenatal—3 mo	2 and 3 yr	WPPSI Perf IQ, Manipulative classification tasks of spatial relations

IQ tests only. Lowered Verbal and Performance IQs were observed which may represent diffuse bilateral damage. Because these studies are subject to a variety of interpretational difficulties and because the information yielded is low for the current issues, they have not been included in Table 17.2.

In general, the results of the studies summarized in Table 17.2 indicate that children with right-hemisphere damage perform less well on a variety of measures of spatial ability compared to children with left-hemisphere damage or to other control groups. Since the testing was usually delayed following the damage, these results indicate that even with the operation of possible neuronal plasticity, there is not complete equipotentiality of other regions for some right-hemisphere regions in mediating some cognitive skills. The measures found to be most sensitive to right-hemisphere damage were tests of specific spatial skills. Overall Performance IQ scores in some cases were not depressed (e.g., Fedio & Mirsky, 1969; Stiles-Davis, Sugarman & Nass, 1985; Stiles-Davis, this volume).

All of these studies involved cognitive assessments done some years after the onset of the brain damage, with only one exception (Ferro et al., 1984) and thus cannot address the issue of hemisphere specialization at the time of the injury, which may have been in infancy or early childhood. In three of the studies, children with early right-hemisphere damage were tested at a relatively young age: in one case the children ranged in age from 6 to 9 years (Kershner & King, 1974), in another from 5 to 9 years (Ferro et al., 1984), and in the third, the children were tested twice, at 2 and again at 3 years of age (Stiles-Davis et al., 1985). The results of these studies indicate that at least by these test ages, some spatial functions are more dependent on right- than left-hemisphere regions.

In light of the progress made in cognitive psychology concerning the nature or at least the conceptualizations of spatial cognition, it is evident from the available literature that the psychological aspect of the neurocognitive analyses is still quite gross in most cases. The tests selected in the main are standardized tests and are not based on particular cognitive principles. The samples studied are so disparate as to age and locus and extent of lesion that results cannot be compared across studies in order to consider the possible interrelationships between different spatial tasks. There is much need for further study of the deficits associated with right-hemisphere damage in children. In the case of brain-damaged infants and young children, some of the new cognitive measures apparently related to spatial skill, such as the ability of infants as young as 3 months of age to discriminate various aspects of face stimuli (e.g., Maurer &

Barrera, 1981) and other complex tactual and visual spatial stimuli (e.g., Rose, Gottfried & Bridger, 1983) might be studied immediately following brain damage in young children.

Interhemispheric Transfer of Spatial Functions

Given the lack of studies with young brain-damaged children, very little information is available concerning the critical period during which spatial skills may be transferred to the left hemisphere in the event of right-hemisphere damage. The case of hemispherectomy provides the only relevant data and it is subject to all the limitations that exist in the studies with brain-damaged children. In right-hemispherectomy cases the right hemisphere is either totally or partially removed, usually as a result of very early and extensive damage, and only the left hemisphere remains. The results of such cases provide evidence for the marked plasticity of the human brain following early lesions. For example, Kohn and Dennis (1974) tested four right hemispherectomy patients in whom the onset of damage occurred in the first year of life. Their mean age at the time of surgery and testing was 12 and 20 years respectively. Their overall level of intellectual functioning and their performance on some spatial tasks did not differ from that of a comparable group of left hemispherectomies, although the IQ scores for both groups were low, which may reflect the general effects of brain damage. However, the right hemispherectomy group did perform less well than the left hemispherectomies on two maze tests, a road map test, and a map reading test—tests which Kohn and Dennis (1974) pointed out require later developing skills than those on which performance was normal. Findings such as these indicate that although a remarkable degree of plasticity is possible after early lesions, it is not without limits. In addition, the lower performance of the right compared to the left hemispherectomy group on some spatial tasks attests to the existence of right-hemisphere specialization for spatial functions at least at the time of testing.

The results of this study (Kohn & Dennis, 1974) clearly indicate that, within limits, the left hemisphere is capable of mediating spatial skills, but they provide little information regarding the possible critical period for the transfer of those skills since the onset of damage in all cases was within the first year of life. Interhemispheric transfer, therefore, could have occurred very early. Information relevant to this particular issue can only be obtained from cases in which the onset of the original lesion occurred later in life. Two such cases in the literature are relevant, but the interpretation of the conflicting findings is unclear. In one case, a severe closed-head injury was sustained by a 5-year-old girl and was followed by right hemispherectomy at age 20 and testing at age 34 (Damasio, Lima & Damasio, 1975). Prior to the head injury, development had been normal. The finding that this woman's performance at age 34 years was within normal limits on tests of three-dimensional construction, face discrimination, and route-finding tasks, suggests that the left hemisphere may be able to assume its nondominant function of spatial processing reasonably well up to at least 5 years of age. Unfortunately, hand preference was never reported and greater bihemispheric representation of functions than usual may have existed from the start. In another case, Day and Ulatowska (1979) tested a right-handed girl who underwent a subtotal right hemispherectomy at 4 years of age subsequent to seizure onset first documented at 3.6 years. Unlike the patient described by Damasio et al. (1975), she showed deficits on many spatial tasks when tested during the period from 4 to 6 years of age. In this latter case, occipital lobe tissue was spared which suggests that the original lesion was less extensive. Either factor, a less severe lesion or remaining right-hemisphere tissue, may have resulted in a lesser degree of transfer of spatial functions to the left hemisphere.

The transferability of spatial functions from the right to the left hemisphere may be influenced by a variety of factors which likely include age at onset of damage and extent of the lesion. The issue also remains as to the nature of the cognitive process or strategy used by individuals with only a left hemisphere in performing these functions. Furthermore, as discussed earlier, many tests of spatial ability may be more dependent on general problem-solving ability than on specific spatial skills, and thus the extent to which the observed deficits reflect specific spatial deficits or general learning deficits must be considered.

The issue of the relative timing of critical periods in the interhemispheric transfer of cognitive functions has relevance for an issue receiving much current interest. The issue is whether one hemisphere may mature earlier than the other. There are few data but there is much controversy. If the transfer of language functions can occur up to a later age than can the transfer of spatial functions, this might suggest that the right hemisphere matures later than the left, in other words, remains plastic for a longer period.

Corballis and Morgan (1978) and Liederman (1983), based on psychological data, and Yakovlev and Rakic (1966), based on the anatomical finding of left-hemisphere fibers crossing earlier in the pyramidal decussation, have suggested that the left hemisphere matures earlier. Based on the work of Taylor (1969), who studied the incidence of early left- and right-sided epilepsy, Geschwind and Galaburda (1985) suggested that the right hemisphere matures earlier. The apparent relative sparing of verbal ability compared to spatial ability following early left-sided lesions has led to the popular idea that language functions take precedence over spatial functions. In view of the above discussion, it is possible that the observation of sparing of verbal ability may be a result of the right hemisphere maturing later and therefore having greater plasticity to adopt other functions.

RIGHT HEMISPHERE SPECIALIZATION: STUDIES WITH NORMAL CHILDREN

Although early neuropsychological studies were, of necessity, based on the assessment of populations of brain-damaged individuals, there are now methods available which make it possible to study the neural substrate of spatial perception in normal children. These methods circumvent the methodological problems associated with studies of brain-damaged children although they entail their own limitations. Available methods include tests of perceptual asymmetry, lateral motoric tasks, concurrent interference of lateralized behavior, lateralized activation techniques, and electrophysiological measures of brain asymmetry. A detailed description of the methods, their limitations, and a review of the literature have been presented in earlier papers (Witelson, 1977a, Table 5; 1985, pp. 69-70).

Types of Neuropsychological Studies with Normal Children

Conceptually, these methods may be used in different ways depending on the aim of the study and the information already known, that is, depending on what are considered to be the dependent and independent variables. Table 17.3 presents an outline of different types of approaches that can be taken to the study of hemisphere specialization with neurologically normal individuals. This categorization is methodologically helpful in ensuring that a study does not involve two unknown variables. For example, before attempting to determine the lateralization of a new task in a new group, it is necessary first to ensure that either brain lateralization for the new group is known by means of other tasks of documented lateralization in normal individuals, or that the lateralization of the new task is known in individuals with known brain lateralization. If these

Table 17.3
Types of Experimental Studies of Hemisphere Specialization Involving Neurologically Normal Individuals

Type	Aim	Known (Independent Variable)	Unknown (Dependent Variable)
1	Determine lateralization of specific cognitive task	Brain lateralization pattern for known task (e.g., right lateralization for faces)	Brain lateralization for new task (e.g., lateralization for unfamiliar faces)
2	Determine lateralization of specific group	Brain lateralization for known task (e.g., right lateralization for faces in adults)	Brain lateralization for same task in specific group (e.g., lateralization for faces in 5-yr-olds)
3	Determine cognitive strategy for task in specific group	Brain lateralization for a specific task in a specific group (e.g., left lateralization for tactual letters in normal children)	Brain lateralization for same task in specific group with known lateralization, to determine cognitive strategy (e.g., lateralization for tactual letters in dyslexics)

requirements are not met, interpretation of results becomes quite problematic in that it is impossible to determine whether the subjects under study differ in their neural organization or whether they differ in the cognitive strategies used to do the task.

The most prevalent type of study, referred to here as Type 1, is that in which the lateralization of a specific, as yet unstudied, cognitive skill, for example the perception of some type of facial stimuli, is to be investigated. If it is known or can be assumed that the group to be studied shows right-hemisphere specialization for other stimuli previously documented to be dependent on the right hemisphere, and if this new task is also observed to be lateralized to the right hemisphere, then it is reasonable to suggest that the new task is processed mainly by the right hemisphere and thus may have some aspects of cognitive processing in common with other right-hemisphere dependent tasks.

Type 2 studies, in contrast, aim to investigate the pattern of functional asymmetry in a specific group by using a task of known lateralization in a different group. An example of a Type 2 study would be to study young children using a task known to be dependent on the right hemisphere in adults.

A third type of study (Type 3) is most relevant to the study of cognition and can provide information about the cognitive strategy used on a task by different groups of individuals. Such studies compare the pattern of lateralization in different groups when the lateralization and, by inference, the cognitive strategy, for the task being used is known for one of the groups. For example, right-hemisphere specialization has been documented for the perception of both familiar and unfamiliar faces in adults, but only for familiar faces in children (e.g., Levine, 1985). The observation of a different pattern of hemispheric lateralization in the two groups for unfamiliar faces suggests that a different cognitive strategy is being used for unfamiliar faces in children and that the age of the subject may be a factor. Type 3 studies may also use tasks or stimuli that involve *dual processing*, that is, processing of both spatial and linguistic components. If the lateralization of the two groups for more unitary verbal or spatial tasks is already known, differences in lateralization between the groups may then be interpreted as reflecting the use of different cognitive strategies. For example, the perception of pairs of tactually presented letters or words would appear to necessitate spatial imagery prior to naming. Different behavioral asymmetries were observed between normal boys and dyslexic boys (Witelson, 1977b) and between normal boys and girls (Cioffi & Kandel, 1979). These differences in asymmetry have been interpreted as reflecting different use of cognitive strategies, with greater dependence on spatial strategies shown by boys than girls and by dyslexic boys than normal boys. However, in studies using dual processing tasks, caution must be exercised in ensuring that the number of unknowns is not so great that the results are uninterpretable.

The study of the lateralization of American Sign Language (ASL) in congenitally deaf individuals provides a good case to illustrate these points. Information on the lateralization of ASL and on patterns of brain lateralization in congenitally deaf individuals is just beginning to be gathered. Because ASL may well involve both linguistic and spatial components and because congenitally deaf individuals may have atypical neuroanatomical development (cf. Innocenti, Frost & Illes, 1985) and appear to have atypical physiological brain development (e.g., Neville, Schmidt & Kutas, 1983) due to marked early auditory deprivation, any studies of lateralization of ASL in deaf individuals would require prior studies, each with only one unknown. For example, studies of perceptual asymmetry of tachistoscopically presented ASL in congenitally deaf individuals include too many unknowns. It has now been shown in current work with adult deaf ASL signers who have suffered brain damage that ASL, even though it may be conceptualized as a visual-spatial language system, is dependent on the left hemisphere. Additionally, the same individuals have been shown to have typical nonlinguistic visual-spatial functions such as block design dependent on the right hemisphere (Poizner, Kaplan, Bellugi & Padden, 1984).

Neural Substrate of Spatial Functions via Study of Normal Children

In general, the results of studies using mainly visual half-field and dichhaptic stimulation tasks indicate that right-hemisphere specialization for the perception of shapes, patterns, and faces exists in children as early as 5 years of age, the youngest age included in most studies. Studies using other behavioral and electrophysiological measures have demonstrated right-hemisphere specialization in infants. In almost all of the studies, stimuli presented to the left visual half-field or to the left hand were more accurately perceived than when they were presented to the right sensory field (see previous reviews, Witelson, 1977a; 1985). Left-visual field or left-hand superiority, by inference, suggests right-hemisphere specialization. The majority of the more recent studies which will be reviewed here have used tasks involving the perception of faces or dichhaptically presented forms. The results of these more recent studies are consistent in their support of right-hemisphere superiority for the perception of spatial stimuli and also allow for some consideration of the nature of spatial perception and how such cognition may change over development.

Tactual spatial perception. Using a dichhaptic stimulation technique which involves the simultaneous presentation of two different stimuli for perception by active (haptic) touch, form perception recently has been documented to be more dependent on right- than left-hemisphere processing in children as young as 4 years of age (Etaugh & Levy, 1981). In the years since a left-hand superiority was first found for the perception of dichhaptically presented nonsense shapes (Witelson, 1974; 1976), several other studies have used similar tasks with children. Many used the same shapes designed by Witelson (1974), while others used different but similar shapes. Although these studies vary somewhat in the size of the shapes used, the materials from which the shapes were constructed, presentation time, and hand of response, the majority have found a left-hand advantage and, by inference, right-hemisphere specialization for tactually perceived forms in the youngest age groups tested (Cioffi & Kandel, 1979; Dawson, 1981; Denes & Spinaci, 1981; Etaugh & Levy, 1981; Gibson & Bryden, 1983; Klein & Rosenfield, 1980). Flanery and Balling (1979) did not observe a left-hand advantage in their 7- and 9- year-old groups, although they did for their

11-year-old and adult groups. This last study, however, used computer-generated random angular shapes which were very similar to each other and may well have allowed or required different cognitive processing than the nonsense shapes used by Witelson and others. In addition, tactual rather than visual recognition was used, and both unimanual and dichhaptic presentations were given and the results were reported only for the two conditions combined. Cranney and Ashton (1980) also failed to observe a left-hand advantage in 7- and 11-year-old children. Their study, however, was unique in that the stimuli used, for no stated reason, were at least five times larger than those in other studies and may have required whole arm movements, and thus involvement of both ipsilateral and contralateral neural pathways rather than only the contralateral connections as when just finger movement is required (see Witelson, 1974). In studies of lateralization of deaf children (Vargha-Khadem, 1982), Klinefelter syndrome boys (Netley & Rovet, 1984), and children varying in musical ability (Hassler & Birbaumer, 1986), the control groups did not show left-hand superiority. The lack of behavioral asymmetry in some of these studies provides a cautionary note that factors other than hemispheric asymmetry in cognitive processing may be operating in this task. Cognitive strategy may be related to age since those studies failing to find a left-hand advantage are often the studies using the oldest subjects.

One further study warrants mention here for its use of a neuropsychological task to study the development of a cognitive function. Koenig and Hauert (1986) adapted the dichhaptic paradigm for use with geometric objects varying in several dimensions, such as shape, texture, and center of gravity, to examine some Piagetian concepts of the development of object perception. Hand superiority varied for different tasks at different ages. The test differed in several essential ways from other studies so that it is difficult to compare the results in terms of lateralization. The main result is one which suggested that at some ages, specifically 6 and 8 years, various object dimensions cannot be processed separately and result in poor shape perception.

A variation of the dichhaptic procedure was designed for use with very young children in which the child palpates a three-dimensional shape with either the right or left hand and is then presented visually with a pair of stimuli—the shape just palpated and a novel shape. Longer fixation on the novel shape is typically observed and is interpreted as reflecting recognition of the familiar shape. Rose (1984; 1985) found that in 2- to 5-year-old children, this effect was greater when familiarization of the stimulus was done with the left than with the right hand. This result was not observed in a group of 1-year-old infants. Using a competing task paradigm involving auditory input (musical stimulation) concurrent with tactual palpation, it was found that left-hand tactual perception on this task was disrupted among 4- and 5-year-olds. Such results support the idea of common lateralization to the right hemisphere of tactual perception and musical perception in young children (Rose, 1985).

The results of studies of form perception in dichhaptic presentation are presented in Table 17.4. In summary, the body of research evaluating right-hemisphere specialization for aspects of spatial perception in children has increased and supports the existence of cerebral asymmetry in children as young as 2 to 3 years of age and possibly in infants. There remains a major gap in the study of children up to age 3 years.

Visual spatial perception. Studies in the visual modality also indicate right-hemisphere specialization for aspects of spatial perception in children as in adults. In children as young as 6 years of age a left-visual field advantage, as measured by accuracy of recognition or reaction time, has been observed for patterns of dots (Young & Bion, 1979), for human figures (Witelson, 1977c), and for face perception in several studies (Broman, 1978; Levine, 1985; Marcel & Rajan, 1975; Young & Bion, 1980; 1981a; Young & Ellis, 1976). In one study using children as young as age 5 years, Levine and Levy (1986) used a task requiring a judgement of which face of a pair of chimeric faces presented in free vision looked happier. The pairs were constructed such that they were mirror images of each other— in one face the smile was to the viewer's left, in the other to the right. In all age groups, from kindergarten children to elderly adults, faces with the smile to the viewer's left were perceived to be happier. This finding supports the specialization of the right hemisphere for some aspects of face perception as early as 5 years of age.

Two studies in which the response involved the naming of non-linguistic stimuli have yielded a right-visual field advantage similar to that found in adults. Young and Bion (1981b) observed a right-visual field advantage for naming line drawings of common objects in 5- and 7-year-old children and Jones and Anuza (1982) for identifying the sex of faces tachistoscopically presented to the right- and left-visual fields in 3- and 4-year-old children. Results such as these highlight the fact that the stimulus characteristics per se do not dictate the cognitive process and the requirements of the task likely play a major role in determining the process, and therefore the predominant hemisphere, used. The right-field advantage observed in these tasks suggests that feature analysis and verbal processing are important components of these particular spatial tasks. These two studies, although not originally reported this way, could be good illustrations of the Type 3 study of lateralization.

Almost all of the earlier work in the area of visual-spatial perception was done exclusively with English speaking subjects and the left-field superiority for various nonlingustic stimuli might be related to a bias derived from directional scanning from left to right as one does when reading English. One study with children relevant to this hypothesis (Braine, 1968) involved groups of native readers of Hebrew using both unilateral and bilateral (extending across both visual fields) visual patterns as stimuli. It was found that the older subjects, who were university undergraduate students, showed greater accuracy for the left-visual field and tended to organize series of items from left to right. Students in grades 3 and 5, however, attended primarily to the right side while grade 7 students showed no visual field difference. These results indicate that reading habits do not solely account for the perceptual asymmetry since if scanning bias due to reading habits were responsible, it would be expected that with the experience of Hebrew reading from right to left, the right-sided bias observed in the younger children would increase with age rather than diminish and then reverse. Braine (1968) suggested that these findings reflect a left-field bias in attentiveness to visual patterns that emerges at about the age of 11 years, although the etiology of this biased attentiveness was not elaborated. However, given right-hemisphere dominance for the processing of nonlinguistic stimuli, an alternate explanation might be that brain lateralization is a relevant factor and interacts with the reading-related scanning bias differentially at different ages.

Neuropsychological analysis of face perception. The neuropsychological study of face perception has been particularly helpful in studying the development of face perception per se in children. In adults, it has been documented that unfamiliar as well as familiar faces are processed predominantly by the right hemisphere. In children, right-hemisphere processing is predominant for familiar faces, but it is not until approximately age 10 years that unfamiliar faces come to be mainly processed by the right hemisphere (Levine, 1985). Similarly, Reynolds and Jeeves (1978) observed no perceptual asymmetry for unfamiliar faces in 7-and 8-year-old children although a left-field advantage was present for adolescent and adult groups. The finding that unfamiliar faces are predominantly processed by the right hemisphere in adults and older children but not in younger children, cou-

Table 17.4

Summary of Studies of Dichhaptic Form Perception in Children

Study	Subjects	Stimuli	Exposure Time	Response and Score	Results
Witelson, 1974	7,10 & 13 yr N = 26 Boys	1) Nonsense shapes 1.5 × 1.5in[a]	10 sec	Visual recognition	SHAPES: significant left-hand advantage (LHA) for each group
		2) Pairs of 2 upper case letters presented consecutively 1 × 0.75in.	2 sec per pair	Naming accuracy per hand	LETTERS: no significant difference between hands
Witelson, 1976	6,8,10 & 12 yr N = 200 Boys (B) Girls (G)	Nonsense shapes (as in Witelson, 1974)	10 sec	Visual recognition accuracy per hand	BOYS: LHA for total group. Youngest group analyzed separately, also showed LHA GIRLS: no significant difference between hands
Cioffi & Kandel, 1979	6–14 yr N = 112 B & G	1) Nonsense shapes (as in Witelson, 1974)	10 sec	Visual recognition	SHAPES: LHA for B & for G
		2) 2-letter words	10 sec	accuracy per hand	WORDS: significant right-hand advantage (RHA) for B & for G
		3) 2-letter consonant bigrams	10 sec		BIGRAMS: LHA for B RHA for G

Table 17.4 (Cont'd)

Summary of Studies of Dichhaptic Form Perception in Children

Study	Subjects	Stimuli	Exposure Time	Response and Score	Results
Flanery & Balling, 1979	7, 9 & 11 yr N = 48 B & G	Randomly generated nonsense shapes presented unimanually and dichhaptically, 1.5 × 1.5in 24 subjects received unimanual & 24 dichhaptic stimulation	10 sec	Tactual same-different judgement one recognition form presented for 5 sec accuracy per hand & a laterality index	Unimanual and dichhaptic conditions combined for analysis: ACCURACY: LHA for oldest group LATERALITY: oldest group had significant LHA, but not the two youngest groups
Cranney & Ashton, 1980	7 & 11 yr N = 20 B & G	Nonsense shapes (as in Witelson, 1974) but larger 4 × 1.5in	10 sec	Visual recognition accuracy per hand	No significant difference between hands for any group
Klein & Rosenfield, 1980	9 yr N = 30 B & G	1) Nonsense shapes (as in Witelson, 1974) 2) Upper case letters, 1.5 × 1.5in	10 sec 10 sec	Visual recognition accuracy per hand	SHAPES: LHA for B & for G LETTERS: no significant difference between hands for B or G
Dawson, 1981	7 yr N = 40 12 yr N = 40 B & G	Nonsense shapes	10 sec	Visual recognition accuracy per hand	BOYS: LHA for 7-yr-olds and 12-yr-olds (latter: p = .056) GIRLS: no significant difference between hands for either age group

393

Table 17.4 (Cont'd)
Summary of Studies of Dichhaptic Form Perception in Children

Study	Subjects	Stimuli	Exposure Time	Response and Score	Results
Etaugh & Levy, 1981	4–5 yr N = 46 B & G	Nonsense shapes (as in Witelson, 1974)	10 sec	Visual recognition accuracy per hand	LHA for total group
Denes & Spinaci, 1981	6,8,10 & 13 yr N = 80 B & G	Nonsense shapes, 1.3 × 1.6in	10 sec	Visual recognition accuracy per hand	LHA for total group and for each age sub-group
Vargha-Khadem, 1982	13–16 yr N = 16 B & G	1) Nonsense shapes (as in Witelson, 1974) 2) 3-letter words presented in 2-letter pairs	10 sec 5 sec per letter pair	Visual recognition accuracy per hand	SHAPES: no significant difference between hands for total group LETTERS: RHA for total group
Gibson & Bryden, 1983	8,10,12 & 14 yr N = 80 B & G	1) Nonsense shapes 2) Upper case letters	2 sec 2 sec	Visual recognition accuracy per hand laterality index	ACCURACY & LATERAL-ITY: SHAPES: LHA for total group, and for 8-yr and 12-yr subgroups LETTERS: no significant difference between hands
Netley & Rovet, 1984	11–16 yr (inferred from report) N = 79 B	Nonsense shapes (as in Witelson, 1974)	10 sec	Visual recognition laterality index	No significant difference between hands

Table 17.4 (Cont'd)

Summary of Studies of Dichhaptic Form Perception in Children

Study	Subjects	Stimuli	Exposure Time	Response and Score	Results
Rose, 1984	1,2 & 3 yr N = 72 B & G	Nonsense shapes palpated unimanually, 1 × 1 × 0.6in	25 sec	Visual recognition length of fixation on familiar vs novel shape presented in pairs for 10 sec	In 2- and 3-yr-olds, significantly longer fixation on novel shapes when the paired familiar object was presented previously to the left hand compared to the right hand
Rose, 1985	2,3,4 & 5 yr N = 96 B & G	Nonsense shapes palpated unimanually, 1 × 1 × 0.6in (also concurrent music conditions)	25 sec	Visual recognition length of fixation on familiar vs novel shape presented in pairs for 10 sec	NONMUSIC CONDITION: LHA for each age group
Hassler & Birbaumer, 1986	9–14 yr N = 101 B & G	Nonsense shapes (as in Witelson, 1974) tested 3 times, 1 yr apart	10 sec	Visual recognition accuracy per hand	No significant difference between hands for B or for G at any testing

NOTES

a: Depth of stimulus is an invariant and irrelevant dimension in these tasks (except Rose 1984; 1985) and is not included here. Depth is about 0.25 inches in the few studies reporting it.

B: Boys

G: Girls

LHA: Left-hand advantage, refers only to a statistically significant difference.

RHA: Right-hand advantage, as above.

pled with the finding that right-hemisphere specialization exists for familiar faces in children of all ages, suggests that a different type of information processing or a different cognitive strategy may be used by young children for familiar versus unfamiliar faces. Such results do not indicate that hemisphere specialization itself changes over the course of development. Based on the different perceptual asymmetry for familiar and unfamiliar faces in children, Levine (1985) has suggested that young children process familiar faces configurationally, the type of processing inferred to be dependent on the right hemisphere, and that unfamiliar faces are processed by more specific feature or item analysis (Type 3 study). The finding of different physiological responses in electrodermal skin conductance in response to familiar and unfamiliar faces in brain-damaged adults with prosopagnosia, that is, patients who are unable to recognize visually familiar faces (e.g., Tranel & Damasio, 1985), further corroborates the dissociation of the perception of familiar and unfamiliar faces.

Given the difficulties involved in testing infants, very little work has been done regarding lateralization of face perception in this age group. However, one study of 3-month-old infants used lateral eye gaze as a measure of hemispheric activation (Barerra, Dalrymple & Witelson, 1978). Duplicate pairs of familiar faces, unfamiliar faces, or checkerboards were presented bilaterally. Duration of lateral eye gaze was greater to the left side for familiar faces and checkerboards but greater to the right side for unfamiliar faces. These results, in addition to indicating right-hemisphere specialization for some visual stimuli at a very early age, again reveal a dissociation between the neural processing of familiar versus unfamiliar faces. Since 3-month-old infants are known to be more readily able to discriminate familiar faces and checkerboards than unfamiliar faces, it was suggested that the former stimuli may be processed differently, specifically as configurations, and that leftward gaze reflected predominant engagement of the right hemisphere (Barerra et al., 1978). One other study, which reported asymmetric suppression of alpha rhythm during the processing of faces and scenes in children ranging in age from 6 months to 9 years, corroborates the existence of right-hemisphere specialization for visual processing in infancy (Nava & Butler, 1977).

Studies of face perception in free viewing situations show that recognition of faces improves up to approximately 10 years of age at which time it appears to change in some respects. For example, older children appear to process unfamiliar faces in the same holistic or configurational manner that they processed familiar faces at an earlier age (Carey & Diamond, 1977). In addition, adults are able to recognize faces more accurately when they are presented in an upright than in an inverted orientation (Carey & Diamond, 1977). Face inversion presented fewer difficulties for children under 10 years of age than for adults. Again there may be some relationship of this aspect of face perception to hemispheric lateralization, since a left-field advantage has been observed for upright but not inverted faces in adults and children (Young & Bion, 1981a).

Furthermore, there is a change in accuracy of face perception around age 10. The rate of accuracy of recognition of faces increases steadily from age 2 to 10 years (e.g., Diamond & Carey, 1977) after which there is generally a decline in accuracy around age 12 years followed by a further increase to adult levels of proficiency (Carey, Diamond & Woods, 1980). A recent study has shown that the timing of this disruption in the accuracy of face perception in early adolescence is more closely related to pubertal status than to chronological age (Diamond, Carey & Back, 1983). These differences have been interpreted as reflecting maturation of the right hemisphere which results in cognitive changes and makes possible the type of processing for which the right hemisphere is specialized. As a result, different aspects of face perception may become amenable to configurational encoding.

Interestingly the results of several studies of different skills in different populations converge to suggest that the developmental period around 10 years of age may mark an important point in the development of spatial cognition. In a study of interhemispheric functioning, children older, but not younger, than age 10 were found to benefit from separate input of different and conflicting stimulation to the two hemispheres (Merola & Liederman, 1985). In lateralization studies of other spatial tasks such as visual recognition of geometric patterns (Braine, 1968) and the naming and discrimination of tactile Braille stimuli (Rudel, Denckla & Spalten, 1974; Rudel, Denckla & Hirsch, 1977 respectively), children on either side of age 10 have shown different perceptual asymmetries. Left hemispherectomies tested at maturity show the greatest deficits for those spatial skills which normally develop after age 10 (Kohn & Dennis, 1974). In addition to suggesting that some spatial tasks may only come to be processed by the right hemisphere in later childhood, such results may also offer some support to the hypothesis that the right hemisphere matures later than the left as discussed in the previous section on brain-damaged children.

SPATIAL COGNITION AND ITS BIOLOGICAL BASIS
VIA THE STUDY OF NEUROBIOLOGICAL VARIATION

Marked variation in cognition exists not only between individuals but also between groups, as for example between the sexes. Although sex differences have often been conceptualized as mainly associated with environmental causes, sex clearly implies the possibility of biological factors, such as the effects of sex chromosomes and sex hormones. In the study of sex differences in behavior it is important to investigate their source as well as documenting their existence. Therefore, the sex differences observed in some spatial tasks in normal adults and children (e.g., Harris, 1978; Maccoby & Jacklin, 1974) may be helpful in studying how the variation in cognition, both within and between the sexes, may be dependent on the action of sex chromosomes or hormones. Consideration of the biological mechanisms underlying sex differences in behavior may be useful in elucidating the neurobiological substrate of spatial abilities and the nature of cognition per se.

The view that environmental factors play a major role in causing behavioral sex differences has not been experimentally tested. Definitive studies would be extremely difficult to implement. In many situations in which sex differences are found it is difficult to imagine how environmental factors could be the underlying cause of the observed behavior. For example, on Piaget's test of the horizontality of the level of liquids, males perform substantially more accurately than females even as early as the fourth grade level and this sex difference persists at least until early adulthood (Harris, 1981).

The magnitude of the differences found between males and females on tests of spatial ability is not large and the variation within each sex may be greater than that between the sexes. However, there is some evidence that the nature of the difference may include the manner in which the tasks are performed and not only the level of ability. For example, when computer-generated two-dimensional representations of three-dimensional block clusters were presented in pairs, with the degree of rotation differing within pairs from 0 to 180 degrees, it was found that response time for same-different judgements was correlated with the degree of rotation (Shepard & Metzler, 1971; see also Shepard, this volume). The correlation of response time and degree of rotation suggests that mental rotation is involved in this task. Tapley and Bryden (1977) studied the performance of each sex separately on such a task and found that not only were men more accurate than women, but more importantly in this context, that the slope of the linear function relating response time to accuracy was steeper in women. This finding suggests that even when women obtained the correct answer, it took them longer to perform mental rotation, particularly on some rotation conditions. Finally, response-time slope was correlated with other tests of imagery in men but not in women. These latter findings suggest a difference in the nature of the cognitive process used by men and women on the same task. It would seem unlikely that environmental factors could be the sole cause of such early or such orderly cognitive differences between the sexes.

Recent evidence derived from several diverse fields is converging to suggest a neurobiological basis for sex differences in behavior and cognition. A considerable body of literature now exists which indicates that the presence of sex hormones during fetal life or during a short postnatal period in several animal species has profound effects not only on sexual behavior but also on some nonreproductive behavior. Animal research involving various combinations and sequences of gonadectomy and hormone injections indicates that early levels of gonadal hormones permanently influence both sexual and nonreproductive behavior (e.g., Goy & McEwen, 1980) and the anatomy and function of the brain (e.g., Gorski & Jacobson, 1982; Nottebohm, 1980; Toran-Allerand, 1980). Given the evidence demonstrating the early effects of gonadal hormones on the brain and behavior in many species of animals, it is likely that some such mechanisms also exist in humans.

Research on the early effects of hormones in humans is possible by investigation of individuals with clinical disorders involving atypical prenatal hormonal environments due to genetic conditions or therapeutic exposure to hormones. For example, individuals with Turner's syndrome provide a clear control of the influences of social and biological sex factors in determining cognitive behavior and neural organization underlying cognition. These individuals who have a 45,XO karyotype, that is they are missing one X-chromosome, have a female phenotype and gender identity, yet they have reduced levels of both testosterone and estrogen compared to normal females from the time of conception (Money & Ehrhardt, 1972). Although they usually perform within the normal range on tests of linguistic aptitude, they frequently show lower than normal ability on tests of spatial ability (e.g., Rovet & Netley, 1980; 1982; Swallow, 1980; Waber, 1979).

Another informative syndrome is that of congenital adrenal hyperplasia (CAH). CAH is an autosomal recessive disorder clearly associated with elevated prenatal levels of adrenal androgen in chromosomally normal males and females. A recent study has found that CAH females show better performance on tests of spatial ability than normal females although CAH males and normal males did not differ (Resnick, Berenbaum, Gottesman & Bouchard, 1986).

Some of the studies not only reveal differences in level of performance but in the nature of the cognitive processes between the clinical and normal groups. For example, on a task involving mental rotation of geometric figures, the Turner syndrome group showed a more rapid increase in reaction time as the degree of rotation increased (Rovet & Netley, 1982). Such findings may provide clues to possible differences in the nature of cognitive processing both between and within the sexes.

Several reviews of work with chromosomally and hormonally aberrant groups are available (e.g., Hines, 1982; Nyborg, 1984; Pennington, Heaton, Karzmark, Pendleton, Lehman & Shucard, 1985). However, caution should be exercised in extrapolating the neural and behavioral effects of atypical levels of hormones to the possible role of hormonal variation in normal populations. Just as the long term sequelae of brain damage may reflect atypical reorganization of neural regions in subserving cognition, the subsequent effects of atypical perinatal hormonal levels may reflect some atypical development. Moreover, the cognitive variation associated with extreme hormonal environments may not reflect correlations of cognition to hormone levels within the normal range.

Within hormonally normal populations, some cognitive abilities have been shown to vary with the degree of development of secondary sex characteristics and, by inference, with the level of sex hormones. For example, Petersen (1976) found a negative correlation between degree of secondary sex characteristics and spatial ability within each sex. Because at least some sex differences in cognitive ability (e.g., on Piaget's test of liquid horizontality) occur before puberty, it would appear that prenatal or perinatal levels of hormones likely play some determining role, in addition to any activating effect that hormones may have during puberty.

The association of hormones and cognition has also been examined by studying the timing of the onset of puberty and variation in cognition. Waber (1977) suggested that since onset of sexual maturation is earlier in girls than boys, it may be age and maturation and not sex per se that is correlated with level of cognitive ability. The research in this area is still inconclusive. For example, some studies have reported an association between the timing of puberty and level of spatial ability (Newcombe & Bandura, 1983; Sanders &

Soares, 1986; Waber, 1977) and some have failed to find such a relationship (e.g., Petersen, 1976; Rierdan & Koff, 1984; Waber, Mann, Merola & Moylan, 1985). However, the findings such as those regarding the developmental changes that occur in face perception (Diamond, et al., 1983; Levine, 1985) suggest that there may very well be a relationship between physiological maturational events and the neural mechanisms underlying the development of spatial cognition, although it is unlikely to be a simple one.

With regard to the neural mechanisms underlying normal variation in cognition, patterns of hemisphere specialization may play some role. In one study Harshman, Hampson and Berenbaum (1983) found that in normal individuals, level of cognitive abilities is associated with both sex and handedness, with hand preference used as a rough indicator of brain lateralizaton (e.g., Bryden, 1982). The authors interpreted the data as possibly indicating that naturally occurring differences in brain organization are factors underlying differences in cognitive ability. It is interesting to note that the cognitive skills for which sex differences are observed are often the same skills that are differentially processed by the cerebral hemispheres. Moreover, there is evidence that the pattern of hemisphere specialization also varies with sex in both adults (e.g., Bryden, 1982 Inglis & Lawson, 1981;) and children (for reviews see Kinsbourne & Hiscock, 1983; Witelson, 1977a). In those studies that observe sex differences, males show a greater degree of lateralization than do females for both verbal and spatial functions. There is also the evidence that groups of individuals with aberrant levels of sex hormones may have atypical patterns of hemisphere specialization. For example, greater bilateral representation of linguistic functions has been found in individuals with Turner's syndrome compared to normal girls (Netley & Rovet, 1982; Swallow, 1980; Waber, 1979). Thus several converging lines of evidence suggest that hemisphere specialization may be part of the neural basis underlying individual differences in spatial cognition.

SUMMARY

In general, the results of studies of spatial perception and cognition with both brain-damaged and normal children provide evidence that the right hemisphere is specialized for these functions early in life, possibly even from birth. Furthermore, the lack of evidence that the degree of specialization changes over time suggests that it is invariant in normal development. However, this does not preclude the possibility that as the child's behavioral repertoire and level of cognitive ability increases, more skills become available for processing by the right hemisphere. Nor does it preclude the possibility of recovery of function via the operation of neural plasticity in the event of right-hemisphere damage. Hemisphere specialization and plasticity are separate neural characteristics. A more complete discussion of this hypothesis is presented in other papers (Witelson, 1985; 1987).

Clearly, many questions regarding spatial cognition and its neural basis remain to be answered. The sometimes inconsistent results in the existing literature indicate that stimulus and response characteristics of the tasks used to some extent influence or determine the cognitive strategy and thus the hemisphere predominantly engaged. In some respects the nature of spatial cognition may be delineated by neuropsychological study. It would likely be worthwhile to systematically investigate the impact of such variables. In addition there is a need for more neuropsychological work with young children and infants and the development of appropriate tasks for use with brain-damaged and normal young children.

The finding of sex differences in spatial ability and in the degree of hemisphere specialization and the correlation of level of sex hormones with behavior and cognition in several species and in normal and clinical human populations suggests that biological variables such as the sex hormones or chromosomes may play a role in determining brain organization and level of cognitive ability. There are many unanswered questions but the development of new technologies for observing both the activity and the anatomy of the living human brain, in conjunction with the design of new behavioral tasks which tap specific cognitive skills provide many possible avenues for future research. (Witelson, 1985; 1987).

ACKNOWLEDGMENTS

Preparation of this paper was supported in part by U.S. NIH-NINCDS grant R01-NS 18954 and by Ontario Mental Health Foundation research grant 803, awarded to SFW.

REFERENCES

Barrera, M.E., Dalrymple, A. & Witelson, S.F. 1978. Behavioral evidence of right hemisphere asymmetry in early infancy. Paper presented at the

39th Annual Meeting of the Canadian Psychological Association, Ottawa, Ontario, Canada.

Blume, W.T., Grabow, J.S., Darley, F.L. & Aronson, A.E. 1973. Intracarotid Amobarbital test of language and memory before temporal lobectomy for seizure control. *Neurology,* 23:812-819.

Braine, L. Ghent. 1968. Asymmetries of pattern perception observed in Israelis. *Neuropsychologia,* 6:73-88.

Broman, M. 1978. Reaction-time differences between the left and right hemispheres for face and letter discrimination in children and adults. *Cortex,* 14:578-591.

Bryden, M.P. 1982. *Laterality: Functional asymmetry in the intact brain.* New York: Academic Press.

Carey, S. & Diamond, R. 1977. From piecemeal to configurational representation of faces. *Science,* 195:312-314.

Carey, S., Diamond, R. & Woods, B. 1980. Development of face recognition—A maturational component? *Developmental Psychology,* 16:257-269.

Cioffi, J. & Kandel, G.L. 1979. Laterality of stereognostic accuracy of children for words, shapes and bigrams: A sex difference for bigrams. *Science,* 204:1432-1434.

Corballis, M.C. & Morgan, M.J. 1978. On the biological basis of human laterality: I. Evidence for a maturational left-right gradient. *Behavioral and Brain Sciences,* 2:261-336.

Cranney, J. & Ashton, R. 1980. Note. Witelson's dichhaptic task as a measure of hemispheric asymmetry in deaf and hearing populations. *Neuropsychologia,* 18:95-98.

Critchley, M. & Henson, R.A. (Eds.) 1977. *Music and the brain: Studies in the Neurology of music.* Southampton: Camelot Press.

Damasio, A.R., Lima, A. & Damasio, H. 1975. Nervous function after right hemispherectomy. *Neurology,* 25:89-93.

Dawson, G.L. 1981. Sex differences in dichhaptic processing. *Perceptual and Motor Skills,* 53:935-944.

Day, P.S. & Ulatowska, H.K. 1979. Perceptual, cognitive, and linguistic development after early hemispherectomy: Two case studies. *Brain and Language,* 7:17-33.

Denes, G. & Spinaci, M.P. 1981. Influence of association value in recognition of random shapes under dichhaptic presentation. *Cortex,* 17:597-602.

De Renzi, E. 1982. *Disorders of space exploration and cognition.* New York: Wiley.

Diamond, R. & Carey, S. 1977. Developmental changes in the representation of faces. *Journal of Experimental Child Psychology,* 23:1-22.

Diamond, R., Carey, S. & Back, K.J. 1983. Genetic influences on the development of spatial skills during early adolescence. *Cognition,* 13:167-185.

Etaugh, C. & Levy, R.B. 1981. Hemispheric specialization for tactile-spatial processing in preschool children. *Perceptual and Motor Skills,* 53:621-622.

Fedio, P. & Mirsky, A.F. 1969. Selective intellectual deficits in children with temporal lobe or centrencephalic epilepsy. *Neuropsychologia*, 7:287-300.

Ferro, J.M., Martins, I.P. & Tavora, L. 1984. Neglect in children. *Annals of Neurology*, 15:281-284.

Fitzhugh, L.C. & Fitzhugh, K.B. 1964. Relationships between Wechsler-Bellevue Form 1 and WAIS performances of subjects with longstanding cerebral dysfunction. *Perceptual and Motor Skills*, 19:539-543.

Flanery, R.C. & Balling, J.D. 1979. Development changes in hemisphere specialization for tactile spatial ability. *Developmental Psychology*, 15:364-372.

Gazzaniga, M.S. 1970. *The bisected brain.* New York: Appleton-Century-Crofts.

Geschwind, N. & Galaburda, A.M. 1985. Cerebral lateralization. Biological mechanisms, associations, and pathology: I. A hypothesis and a program for research. *Archives of Neurology*, 42:428-459.

Gibson, C. & Bryden, M.P. 1983. Dichhaptic recognition of shapes and letters in children. *Canadian Journal of Psychology*, 37:132-143.

Goldman-Rakic, P.S., Isseroff, A., Schwartz, M.L. & Bugbee, N.M. 1983. The neurobiology of cognitive development. In P.H. Mussen (Ed.) *Handbook of child psychology.* 4th Ed., Vol. II. New York: Wiley, 281-344.

Gorski, R.A. & Jacobson, C.D. 1982. Sexual differentiation of the brain. *Frontiers in Hormone Research*, 10:1-14.

Goy, R.W. & McEwen, B.S. 1980. *Sexual differentiation of the brain.* Cambridge, Mass.: MIT Press.

Harris, L.J. 1978. Sex differences in spatial ability: Possible environmental, genetic, and neurological factors. In M. Kinsbourne (Ed.) *Asymmetrical function of the brain.* New York: Cambridge University Press, 223-255.

Harris, L.J. 1981. Sex related variations in spatial skill. In L. S. Liben, A.H. Patterson and N. Newcombe (Eds.) *Spatial representation and behavior across the life span: Theory and application.* New York: Academic Press, 83-125.

Harshman, R.A., Hampson, E. & Berenbaum, S.A. 1983. Individual differences in cognitive abilities and brain organization, Part 1: Sex and handedness differences in ability. *Canadian Journal of Psychology*, 37:144-192.

Hassler, M. & Birbaumer, N. 1986. Witelson's dichhaptic stimulation test and children with different levels of musical talent. *Neuropsychologia*, 24:435-440.

Heilman, K.M. & Valenstein, E. (Eds.) 1985. *Clinical neuropsychology.* 2nd Edition. New York: Oxford University Press.

Hines, M. 1982. Prenatal gonadal hormones and sex differences in human behavior. *Psychological Bulletin*, 92:56-80.

Inglis, J. & Lawson, J.S. 1981. Sex differences in the effects of unilateral brain damage on intelligence. *Science*, 212:693-695.

Innocenti, G.M., Frost, D.O. & Illes, J. 1985. Maturation of visual callosal connections in visually deprived kittens: A challenging critical period. *Journal of Neuroscience*, 5:255-267.

Jones, B. & Anuza, T. 1982. Note: Sex differences in cerebral lateralization in 3- and 4-year old children. *Neuropsychologia*, 20:347-350.

Kershner, J.R. & King, A.J. 1974. Laterality of cognitive functions in achieving hemiplegic children. *Perceptual and Motor Skills*, 39:1238-1289.

Kinsbourne, M. & Hiscock, M. 1983. The normal and deviant development of functional lateralization of the brain. In P.H. Mussen (Ed.) *Handbook of child psychology*. 4th Ed., Vol. II. New York: Wiley, 157-280.

Klein, S.P. & Rosenfield, W.D. 1980. The hemispheric specialization for linguistic and non-linguistic tactile stimuli in third grade children. *Cortex*, 16:205-212.

Koenig, O. & Hauert, C. 1986. Construction de l'object chez l'enfant de 5 a 9 ans: Approche dichhaptique. *Cahiers de Psychologie Cognitive*, 6:21-39.

Kohn, B. & Dennis, M. 1974. Selective impairments of visuo-spatial abilities in infantile hemiplegics after right cerebral hemidecortication. *Neuropsychologia*, 12:505-512.

Levine, S.C. 1985. Developmental changes in right-hemisphere involvement in face recognition. In C. Best (Ed.) *Hemisphere function and collaboration in the child*. New York: Academic Press, 157-191.

Levine, S.C. & Levy, J. 1986. Perceptual asymmetry for chimeric faces across the life span. *Brain and Cognition*, 5:291-306.

Liben, L.S., Patterson, A.H. & Newcombe, N. (Eds.) 1981. *Spatial representation and behavior across the life span. Theory and application*. New York: Academic Press.

Liederman, J. 1983. Mechanisms underlying discontinuities in the development of handedness. In G. Young, C. Corter, S.J. Segalowitz and S. Trehub (Eds.) *Manual specialization and the developing brain*. New York: Academic Press, 71-92.

Linn, M.C. & Petersen, A.C. 1985. Emergence and characterization of sex differences in spatial ability: A meta-analysis. *Child Development*, 56:1479-1498.

Maccoby, E.E. & Jacklin, C.N. 1974. *The psychology of sex differences*. California: Stanford University Press.

Marcel, T. & Rajan, P. 1975. Lateral specialization for recognition of words and faces in good and poor readers. *Neuropsychologia*, 13:489-497.

Maurer, D. & Barrera, M. 1981. Infants' perception of natural and distorted arrangements of a schematic face. *Child Development*, 52:196-202.

McFie, J. 1961. Intellectual impairment in children with localized post-infantile cerebral lesions. *Journal of Neurology, Neurosurgery and Psychiatry*, 24:361-365.

Meier, M.J. & French, L.A. 1966. Longitudinal assessment of intellectual functioning following unilateral temporal lobectomy. *Journal of Clinical Psychology*, 22:22-27.

Merola, J.L. & Liederman, J. 1985. Developmental changes in hemispheric independence. *Child Development,* 56:1184-1194.

Money, J. & Ehrhardt, A.A. 1972. *Man and woman, boy and girl.* Baltimore: Johns Hopkins University Press.

Nàva, P.L. & Butler, S.R. 1977. Development of cerebral dominance monitored by asymmetries in the alpha rhythm. *Electroencephalography and Clinical Neurophysiology,* 43:582.

Netley, C. & Rovet, J. 1982. Atypical hemisphere lateralization in Turner syndrome subjects. *Cortex,* 18:377-384.

Netley, C. & Rovet, J. 1984. Hemispheric lateralization in 47,XXY Klinefelter's syndrome boys. *Brain and Cognition,* 3:10-18.

Neville, H.J., Schmidt, A. & Kutas, M. 1983. Altered visual-evoked potentials in congenitally deaf adults. *Brain Research,* 266:127-132.

Newcombe, N. & Bandura, M.M. 1983. Effect of age at puberty on spatial ability in girls: A question of mechanism. *Developmental Psychology,* 19:215-224.

Nottebohm, F. 1980. Testosterone triggers growth of brain vocal control nuclei in adult female canaries. *Brain Research,* 189:429-436.

Nyborg, H. 1984. Performance and intelligence in hormonally different groups. In G.J. De Vries, J.D.C. De Bruin, H.B.M. Uylings & M.A. Corner (Eds.) Sex differences in the brain. The relation between structure and function. *Progress in Brain Research,* 61:491-508.

Ojemann, G.A. 1983. The intrahemispheric organization of human language, derived with electrical stimulation techniques. *Trends in NeuroSciences,* 6:184-189.

Ojemann, G.A. 1986. Personal communication, May.

Pennington, H., Galliani, C. & Voegele, G. 1965. Unilateral electroencephalographic dysrhythmia and children's intelligence. *Child Development,* 36:539-546.

Pennington, B.F., Heaton, R.K., Karzmark, P., Pendleton, M.G., Lehman, R. & Shucard, D.W. 1985. The neuropsychological phenotype in Turner syndrome. *Cortex,* 21:391-404.

Perecman, E. (Ed.) 1983. *Cognitive processing in the right hemisphere.* New York: Academic Press.

Petersen, A.C. 1976. Physical androgeny and cognitive functioning in adolescence. *Developmental Psychology,* 12:524-533.

Poizner, H., Kaplan, E., Bellugi, U. & Padden, C.A. 1984. Visual-spatial processing in deaf brain-damaged signers. *Brain and Cognition,* 3:281-306.

Potegal, M. (Ed.) 1982. *Spatial abilities. Development and physiological foundations.* Toronto: Academic Press.

Ratcliff, G. 1982. Disturbances of spatial orientation associated with cerebral lesions. In M. Potegal (Ed.) *Spatial abilities. Development and physiological foundations.* Toronto: Academic Press, 301-331.

Reed, H.B.C. & Fitzhugh, K. 1966. Patterns of deficits in relation to severity of cerebral dysfunction in children and adults. *Journal of Consulting Psychology,* 30:98-102.

Reed, J.C. & Reitan, R.M. 1969. Verbal and performance differences among brain-injured children with lateralized motor deficits. *Perceptual and Motor Skills,* 29:747-752.

Resnick, S.M., Berenbaum, S.A., Gottesmann, I.I. & Bouchard, T.J. 1986. Early hormonal influences on cognitive functioning in congenital adrenal hyperplasia. *Developmental Psychology,* 22:191-198.

Reynolds, D.M. & Jeeves, M.A. 1978. A developmental study of hemisphere specialization for recognition of faces in normal subjects. *Cortex,* 14:511-520.

Rierdan, J. & Koff, E. 1984. Age at menarche and cognitive functioning. *Bulletin of the Psychonomic Society,* 22:174-176.

Rose, S.A. 1984. Developmental changes in hemisphere specialization for tactual processing in very young children: Evidence from cross-modal transfer. *Developmental Psychology,* 20:568-574.

Rose, S.A. 1985. Influence of concurrent auditory input on tactual processing in very young children: Developmental changes. *Developmental Psychology,* 21:168-175.

Rose, S.A., Gottfried, A.W. & Bridger, W.H. 1983. Infants cross-modal transfer from solid objects to their graphic representations. *Child Development,* 54:686-694.

Rovet, J. & Netley, C. 1980. The mental rotation task performance of Turner syndrome subjects. *Behavior Genetics,* 10:437-443.

Rovet, J. & Netley, C. 1982. Processing deficits in Turner's syndrome. *Developmental Psychology,* 18:77-94.

Rudel, R.G., Denckla, M.B. & Hirsch, S. 1977. The development of left-hand superiority for discriminating Braille configurations. *Neurology,* 27:160-164.

Rudel, R.G., Denckla, M. & Spalten, E. 1974. The functional asymmetry of Braille letter learning in normal sighted children. *Neurology,* 24:733-738.

Rudel, R.G., Teuber, H.L., & Twitchell, T.E. 1974. Levels of impairment of sensori-motor functions in children with early brain damage. *Neuropsychologia,* 12:95-108.

Sanders, B. & Soares, M.P. 1986. Sexual maturation and spatial ability in college students. *Developmental Psychology,* 22:199-203.

Shepard, R.N. & Metzler, J. 1971. Mental rotation of three-dimensional objects. *Science,* 171:701-703.

Stiles-Davis, J., Sugarman, S. & Nass, R. 1985. The development of spatial and class relations in four young children with right-cerebral-hemisphere damage: Evidence for an early spatial constructive deficit. *Brain and Cognition,* 4:388-412.

Swallow, J.A. 1980. The influence of biological sex on cognition and hemisphere specialization: a study of Turner syndrome. Master's thesis, McMaster University, Hamilton, Ont.,Canada.

Tapley, S.M. & Bryden, M.P. 1977. An investigation of sex differences in spatial ability: Mental rotation of three-dimensional objects. *Canadian Journal of Psychology,* 31:122-130.

Taylor, D.C. 1969. Differential rates of cerebral maturation between sexes and between hemispheres. *Lancet,* ii:140-142.

Toran-Allerand, C.D. 1980. Sex steroids and the development of the newborn mouse hypothalamus and preoptic area in vitro: II. Morphological correlates and hormonal specificity. *Brain Research,* 189:413-427.

Tranel, D. & Damasio, A.R. 1985. Knowledge without awareness: An autonomic index of facial recognition by prosopagnosics. *Science,* 228:1453-1454.

Vargha-Khadem, F. 1982. Hemispheric specialization for the processing of tactual stimuli in congenitally deaf and hearing children. *Cortex, 18:*277-286.

Waber, D.P. 1977. Sex differences in mental abilities, hemispheric lateralization, and rate of physical growth at adolescence. *Developmental Psychology,* 13:29-38.

Waber, D.P. 1979. Neuropsychological aspects of Turner's syndrome. *Developmental Medicine and Child Neurology,* 21:58-69.

Waber, D.P., Mann, M.B., Merola, J. & Moylan, P.M. 1985. Physical maturation rate and cognitive performance in early adolescence: A longitudinal examination. *Developmental Psychology,* 21:666-681.

Witelson, S.F. 1974. Hemispheric specialization for linguistic and non-linguistic tactual perception using a dichotomous stimulation technique. *Cortex,* 10:3-17.

Witelson, S.F. 1976. Sex and the single hemisphere: Right hemisphere specialization for spatial processing. *Science,* 193:425-427.

Witelson, S.F. 1977a. Early hemisphere specialization and interhemisphere plasticity: An empirical and theoretical review. In S.J. Segalowitz & F. Gruber (Eds.) *Language development and neurological theory.* New York: Academic Press, 213-287.

Witelson, S.F. 1977b. Developmental dyslexia: Two right hemispheres and none left. *Science,* 195:309-311.

Witelson, S.F. 1977c. Neural and cognitive correlates of developmental dyslexia: Age and sex differences. In C. Shagass, S. Gershon, & A.J. Friedhoff (Eds.) *Psychopathology and brain dysfunction.* New York: Raven Press, 15-49.

Witelson, S.F. 1985. On hemisphere specialization and cerebral plasticity from birth: Mark II. In C. Best (Ed.) *Hemispheric function and collaboration in the child.* New York: Academic Press, 33-85.

Witelson, S.F. 1987. Neurobiological aspects of language in children. *Child Development, 58:* 653-688.

Woods, B.T. 1980. The restricted effects of right-hemisphere lesions after age one. Wechsler test data. *Neuropsychologia,* 18:65-70.

Yakovlev, P.I. & Rakic, P. 1966. Patterns of decussation of bulbar pyramids and distribution of pyramidal tracts on two sides of the spinal cord. *Transactions of the American Neurological Association,* 91:366-367.

Young, A.W. (Ed.) 1983. *Functions of the Right Cerebral Hemisphere.* New York: Academic Press.

Young, A.W., & Bion, P.J. 1979. Hemispheric laterality effects in the enumeration of visually presented collections of dots by children. *Neuropsychologia,* 17:99-102.

Young, A.W. & Bion, P.J. 1980. Absence of any developmental trend in right hemisphere superiority for face recognition. *Cortex,* 16:213-221.

Young, A.W. & Bion, P.J. 1981a. Accuracy of naming laterally presented known faces by children and adults. *Cortex,* 17:97-106.

Young, A.W. & Bion, P.J. 1981b. Identification and storage of line drawings presented to the left and right cerebral hemispheres of adults and children. *Cortex,* 17:459-464.

Young, A.W. & Ellis, H.D. 1976. An experimental investigation of developmental differences in ability to recognize faces presented to the left and right cerebral hemispheres. *Neuropsychologia,* 14:495-498.

PART IV

DISCUSSION

We organized the Spatial Cognition conference and the book so that it represented three different sections comprising different disciplines, each bearing in a specific way on frontier research in the development of spatial cognition and its brain bases. Each group had a scribe and discussant, and they have worked together to present final summaries of the discussions and chapters in their section.

Section I: Zola-Morgan and Kritchevsky present a summary of the chapters in Spatial Cognition in Adults. They review the major points addressed, and discuss a framework for a theory of spatial cognition. Section II: Jean Mandler raises some central issues that were broached in The Development of Spatial Cognition. She provides a thoughtful essay on the representation of spatial cognition, stemming from the chapters in the section. Section III: Diane Lillo-Martin and Paula Tallal discuss the themes of the chapters on The Effects of Different Early Experiences on the Development of Spatial Cognition. They examine three major issues which are brought into focus from these studies: The principles which shape children's developing knowledge systems, the autonomy of specific cognitive functions, and brain organization and plasticity for spatial cognition. Thus the final section of the book raises issues for future directions and for theories of spatial cognition—its brain bases and development.

SPATIAL COGNITION IN ADULTS

18

STUART ZOLA-MORGAN
V.A. Medical Center and University of California, San Diego

MARK KRITCHEVSKY
V.A. Medical Center and University of California, San Diego

The five chapters in the first section of this volume cover a wide range of topic areas relating to spatial cognition in adults. Here we will focus on three major themes from these chapters: descriptions of the disorders of spatial cognition in brain damaged humans and animals; neuroanatomic bases of spatial function; and hypotheses and frameworks for theories that could explain spatial function. We will comment on how investigations and findings that relate to each of these themes have brought us closer to the goal of achieving a comprehensive theory of spatial cognition and to an understanding of how spatial cognition may be organized in the brain.

DISORDERS OF SPATIAL COGNITION: THEIR DESCRIPTION AND SIGNIFICANCE

A careful and complete characterization of behavioral dysfunction is often a first step in establishing the relation between a particular brain area and the role that area may normally play in behavior. Thus, over the years dysfunctions of spatial cognition have been well documented and described in some detail. In this regard, Morrow and Ratcliff, Andersen, and Kritchevsky (this volume) have pointed to disorders of object localization, the neglect syndrome, constructional apraxia, topographical amnesia, and amnesia for spatial material as the most frequent ways in which normal spatial abilities can break down. Morrow and Ratcliff, and Kritchevsky have discussed in addition impairments in mental rotation. Shepard (this volume) also discusses mental rotation as a spatial cognitive function, reviewing his studies in normal adults. Finally, Farah (this volume) discusses disorders of mental imagery. Mental image generation may reflect spatial cognitive processes.

A single patient may have one or more of these defects of spatial ability. For example, constructional apraxia can occur in isolation or in association with deficits of other spatial functions (see Kritchevsky, this volume). Moreover, spatial dysfunction can occur in patients in the absence of other cognitive deficits. Thus, spatial function can break down in selective ways, and spatial dysfunction can appear on the background of otherwise normal cognitive performance. These two facts mean that it should be possible to identify specific brain areas that are associated with specific spatial dysfunctions.

Characterizing normal spatial *function* may be more difficult than it would first appear, because the emphasis in neuropsychological research has been to study *dysfunction* of spatial ability. Correlations between spatial dysfunction and area of brain damage may not reveal the precise functional role played by these areas. Two examples from research in visual function are instructive. A lesion of the lateral geniculate on one side produces a contralateral visual field defect. This does not mean that the function of the lateral geniculate is to see in contralateral space. Likewise, the receptive field of a neuron in the lateral geniculate is, roughly, a spot of light. But the function of the lateral geniculate is neither to respond to nor sense spots of light (Ranck, 1979). The function of a part of the brain is the transformation which occurs within it, that is, the relation of inputs and outputs. Similarly, disruption of the right parietal lobe can cause inability to perform mental rotations. This indicates that the parietal lobe normally performs some spatial function which when disrupted, causes an inability to perform the mental rotation task. In this sense, the normal function of the parietal lobe must eventually be characterized in such a way that disruption of that function explains the observed behavioral deficits.

THE NEUROANATOMY OF SPATIAL FUNCTION

As described above, there is a consensus regarding the behavioral impairments of spatial function caused by brain damage. With regard to the neuroanatomic basis of spatial cognition, all authors agree on the predominant role of the right hemisphere for most spatial functions. This is consistent with current notions of hemispheric specialization.

There is a difference in emphasis in regard to the neuroanatomic correlates of specific spatial functions. Andersen discusses spatial dysfunction in humans and monkeys that is produced exclusively by parietal lobe damage. Morrow and Ratcliff, and Kritchevsky agree that the parietal lobes are of primary importance for most spatial functions. Kritchevsky also demonstrates that in humans, spatial abilities are disrupted by damage in many additional cortical and subcortical areas of the brain. Farah points to the predominant role of the left posterior hemisphere for the process of mental image generation.

There is a lack of consensus among the authors on the anatomic issue of where in the brain spatial memories are stored. Andersen states two possibilities: the parietal lobes either contain topological memory traces or they are necessary for the recall of such memory traces. Kritchevsky emphasizes that the right hippocampus and mediodorsal nucleus of the thalamus are involved in the process of storage of spatial memories, and states that the site of storage is unknown.

It is unlikely that information based only on human case studies will allow us to identify with certainty the brain regions which when damaged result in spatial dysfunction. This is because (1) brain damage can be precisely localized only at autopsy; (2) patients are rarely found with identically localized lesions; and (3) premorbid neurobehavioral status is generally unavailable for individual human cases.

Here it would seem that the use of animals, in particular nonhuman primates, might prove to be a powerful research strategy. Carefully placed lesions can be verified at postmortem examination. Behavioral testing can be done using tasks that are known to be sensitive to spatial dysfunction in humans. Groups of animals with known premorbid state and nearly identical lesions can be studied. For these reasons, the lesion technique has been a useful tool in the initial stages of identifying the neural structures involved in behavior (see Zola-Morgan, 1984, for a detailed discussion of this issue).

Mountcastle (1978) and more recently Andersen (this volume) have elegantly demonstrated the usefulness of a neurophysiologic technique using animals. Awake behaving monkeys can be studied with electrical recording from individual parietal lobe neurons. This methodology provides us with a way of correlating, in the absence of brain damage, neuronal activity with ongoing behavior. Using this technique, it has been shown that there are several different cortical fields within the inferior parietal lobule of the monkey. Each of these fields appears to be specialized for certain aspects of spatial analysis.

As we have described, there are two complementary ways of precisely studying spatial cognition in experimental nonhuman primates. Lesion and neurophysiologic recording techniques will help answer specific questions concerning spatial cognition by means of empirical observations. It must be mentioned that hemispheric specialization for spatial functions, to our knowledge, has not been demonstrated in animals. Thus, it is possible that the findings from humans and the findings from monkeys might not be entirely analagous. Nevertheless, as Andersen describes in this volume, the effects of parietal lobe lesions on spatial function are similar in monkeys and humans. For the reasons described in the last several paragraphs, continued work with animals will be important in the development of our understanding of the neuroanatomic bases of spatial cognition and in the development of a theoretical framework for understanding spatial behavior.

FRAMEWORK FOR A THEORY OF SPATIAL COGNITION

We believe that the development of our understanding about spatial cognition will follow a pattern that is common to science: from a series of related hypotheses to a theory, and from that theory to a better theory. Prior to the emergence and acceptance of a theory, scientific activity is characterized by the accumulation of large quantities of data and the proliferation of numerous hypotheses (Kuhn, 1970; Nadel & O'Keefe, 1974). Each hypothesis can account for part of the data, but none can account for all of it. Typically the hypothesis is only tied to the empirical world in one direction, usually to the behavioral domain.

A theory, on the other hand, can subsume data previously accounted for under different hypotheses, and typically relates at least two empirical domains (e.g., behavioral and neurobiological). A complete theory which will permit an understanding of spatial cognition will require explanation at all levels of analysis: behavioral, anatomic and neurobiological. In particular, this theory must include an explanation of how these levels interconnect.

Hypotheses about spatial cognition often describe a behavioral deficit (e.g., neglect) that follows damage to a specific brain region.

Kritchevsky analyzes deficits of spatial ability in terms of elementary spatial functions. These functions can be disrupted by brain damage in one or more cortical or subcortical brain structures. He does not propose that elementary spatial functions correspond to actual spatial cognitive functions, but notes that they have proved useful in the analysis of spatial behavior.

Kritchevsky's hypotheses about elementary spatial functions in humans are well described and are based on a commonly agreed upon group of symptoms. They provide a series of testable notions concerning the specific brain regions that mediate aspects of spatial cognition. Further work will determine whether the nervous system honors the behavioral distinctions proposed by Kritchevsky. It is possible that two or more of the behavioral dysfunctions may be shown to be consistently associated with each other and with damage to the same brain area. This would suggest the presence of a single spatial function, more elementary than previously described. More importantly, it needs to be understood how particular brain areas mediate their respective spatial functions.

Farah, and Morrow and Ratcliff each present a research strategy that is similar to that of Kritchevsky. However, they focus on a different level of behavioral analysis, making contact between a cognitive theory and neurologic information. Specifically, Farah implicates the posterior left hemisphere as critical for the image generation process. For her, images are rich in implicit spatial information.

Studies of image generation may provide us with insights about how the brain organizes space. Morrow and Ratcliff suggest that spatial deficits following right hemisphere lesions may be due to a deficiency of internal representation. Whether one takes a molar view as in the case of Farah, and Morrow and Ratcliff, or a reductionist view as in the case of Kritchevsky, the findings from both of these research strategies are likely to contribute significantly to our understanding of the neurologic foundation of spatial cognition.

Shepard provides a cognitive psychological framework for one aspect of spatial cognition. He describes his search for the psychological metric of the space in which mental operations such as rotational transformations are performed. Because his work is based on experiments in normal adults his approach necessarily focuses on characterizations of normal spatial function. Ultimately, the findings from studies of impaired spatial behavior will have to be mapped on to what we know about normal spatial function.

Andersen demonstrates how studies with animals may provide another level of explanation about spatial function. Using a neurobiological approach, he has delineated the areas of the brain in the monkey that appear to mediate components of spatial function. He and his coworkers have demonstrated that the inferior parietal lobule plays a central role in spatial perception and visual attention. Based on their own experiments and those of others, they have suggested that many of the cells in this area appear to encode, among other things, the position of visual objects in head- or ego-centered coordinates.

Andersen and his colleagues have developed a long-term research program to investigate the functions of the various cortical fields in the inferior parietal lobule and to clarify the interaction of these cortical fields. Their approach is well-grounded empirically, and they are in a position to simultaneously investigate behavioral, anatomic and neurophysiologic components of spatial behavior. In this sense, their work has the potential for approximating a complete theory of spatial function in the monkey. The ideas generated from this work would presumably apply to human spatial function as well.

As can be seen from this discussion, there is not yet a comprehensive theory of spatial cognition. There are, however, many hypotheses that relate to a variety of spatial behaviors. These hypotheses have been generated from a wide range of research disciplines. These include studies in adult humans, both brain damaged and normal. They also include studies in monkeys, using both lesion and neurophysiologic recording techniques. The continuation of such experimental and theoretical work, as exemplified by the authors in this section, will provide us with a framework by which we should be able to achieve a comprehensive theory of spatial cognition in humans and animals.

REFERENCES

Kuhn, T. 1970. The structure of scientific revolutions. In: *International encyclopedia of unified science*, vol. 2. Chicago: University of Chicago Press.

Mountcastle, V. 1978. Brain mechanisms for directed attention. *Journal of the Royal Society of Medicine.* 71:14-27.

Nadel, L., and O'Keefe, J. 1974. The hippocampus in pieces and patches: an essay on modes of explanation in physiological psychology. In R. Bellairs and E.G. Gray (Eds.) *Essays on the nervous system: a festschrift for J.Z. Young.* Oxford: Clarendon Press.

Ranck, J. B. 1979. On O'Keefe, Nadel, space and brain. *The Behavioral and Brain Sciences.* 2:513-514.

Zola-Morgan, S. 1984. Toward an animal model of human amnesia: some critical issues. In L.R. Squire and N. Butters (Eds.), *The neuropsychology of memory*. New York: Guilord Press.

THE DEVELOPMENT OF SPATIAL COGNITION: ON TOPOLOGICAL AND EUCLIDEAN REPRESENTATION

19

JEAN M. MANDLER
University of California, San Diego

Why should rubber sheets serve as a launch site for spatial cognition? I would like to consider this query of Judith Johnston's because the field of cognitive development seems to have widely accepted Piaget and Inhelder's (1956) topological analysis of the development of spatial representation. In this analysis young children begin the task of representing space solely in topological terms, then advance to an understanding of projective and Euclidean information, and finally achieve a mature representation of space that relies heavily on the use of coordinate axes and metric information. This ingenious hypothesis was seemingly well supported by Piaget and Inhelder's many experiments with children. Their theory was also a major step forward in our understanding that spatial representation might be a construction, rather than come predetermined by our sensory apparatus. The view that spatial knowledge is given by what we see still permeates our commonsense thinking, and as Barbara Landau describes, is evident in the theory that vision is required to form an accurate spatial representation.

In spite of the advance that Piaget and Inhelder's theory provided, however, its widespread acceptance has tended to preclude consideration of alternative hypotheses. There are many ways to explain the fact that spatial representation increases in accuracy with development and possibly changes qualitatively as well. I will mention only two. The first is that people are sensitive to both topological and Euclidean information from birth, but switch from primary reliance on topological information in the early years to primary reliance on Euclidean information with development. It is the switch to reliance on Euclidean information that accounts for the increases in accuracy of adult representations and for the appearance of qualitative change. The second hypothesis is that there is sensitivity to both types of information from birth, with primary reliance on topological information at all ages. In this view, no qualitative change takes place, but with development, there is increasing accuracy in the use of both types of information.

To evaluate these alternatives, we must examine more closely what we mean by topological information, in the psychological, rather than the mathematical, sense of the term. And as Lynn Liben and Herb Pick point out in their chapters, we must also be clear about what we mean by spatial representation, as opposed to spatial perception. I will begin with the representational issue, since it is important not only for developmental issues but for all the chapters of this book. Then I will return to a discussion of topological concepts and whether they can provide an adequate description of early spatial representation. I will end with a brief evaluation of the two hypotheses mentioned above.

SPATIAL REPRESENTATION

Although Liben expresses concern that developmental psychologists are not typically sensitive to the difference between perception and representation, I do not think that is the case. Anyone grounded in Piagetian theory (and what developmental psychologist these days is not?) must be aware of the distinction between knowing *how* to see and *how* to move through space (variously called sensorimotor, practical, or procedural knowledge), and knowing *that* certain spatial relationships obtain in a given situation (variously called conceptual, representational, or declarative knowledge). I have used the contrast between procedural and declarative knowledge (Mandler, 1983; 1984) and will do so here, although these terms have their own disadvantages (not the least of which is their tendency to act as a red flag in front of some psychological bulls). In addition, there is some danger in lumping perception and motor routines together under the rubric of procedural knowledge. Perception sometimes gets short shrift in this joint assignment, as it does in Piaget's theory of sensorimotor development. However, for present purposes this terminology will serve, as long as we bear in mind that by declarative knowledge we are talking about potentially accessible knowledge. This is the kind of knowledge that we can recall, can think about, can manipulate for purposes of problem-solving, and if we have language can talk about. Neither perceptual or motor routines are so privileged. True, we have naive theories about what we see and can talk about them, but this knowledge too is declarative knowledge. As for the kinds of information stored in our perceptual identification and motor procedures, they are inaccessible.

It would be helpful if we all used the same terminology, but I think that the differences are not a major source of confusion. Thus, Pick wishes to use the term perception to include some aspects of finding objects that are out of sight. He notes that this may seem mysterious to those who define (visual) perception as restricted to situations in which we can see and cognition to inferences about what we cannot see. But I have no difficulty with the point he is making. There indeed seem to be perceptual and motor routines that enable us to find hidden objects and to anticipate future positions of visible objects. The work he cites on infants' anticipatory reaching or on the ability of birds to intercept targets that move behind screens, are good cases in point. This is procedural knowledge that includes perception (and what many have called perceptual inferences) and is not accessible.

However, there is one aspect of the distinction between procedural and declarative knowledge that does seem to cause some confusion, and that is awareness. By definition, we can only be aware of accessible knowledge. So it may be incorrect to say, as Pick does, that "our awareness of the position of objects out of view does not necessarily have to be based on 'map-like' representations of spatial layout" (this volume). It may be true that to *find* objects out of view we do not always need map-like representations, but then we, like birds, are not aware of how we do it either. When we become aware of, or think about, the position of objects out of view we *do* need map-like representations, although these may be primitive and route-like in some cases rather than configurational maps.

When do such representations begin to be formed? Following Piaget, it has usually been thought that accessible representations evolve out of procedural ones, and thus represent a later, more advanced, stage of development. Furthermore, this progression is thought to be a protracted one, requiring a year and a half to be accomplished. I am not convinced that this is the case. Although there may be asynchrony in the onset of sensorimotor procedures and the ability to represent spatial information in an accessible fashion, there is increasing evidence for accessible spatial representations quite early in life. Mental life may well have a sensorimotor beginning, in which the perceptual foundations of spatial understanding and the development of simple motor routines involving manipulation of objects are laid down. But I believe that as early as six months a more conceptual, nonprocedural view of space begins to emerge.

Although various pieces of evidence might be cited, the most convincing seem to me to be demonstrations of recall of location in seven to nine month olds (e.g., Ashmead & Perlmutter, 1980). Piaget used the contrast between recognition and recall to differentiate the two kinds of spatial knowledge (sensorimotor procedures versus accessible spatial concepts). That is, he used recall as the hallmark of a conceptual, as opposed to a merely sensorimotor, system. However, he did not observe recall until later in development. If recall can occur as early as seven months, it suggests that accessible, conceptual representations may in general be parallel, rather than successive, accomplishments to recognitory and motor procedures.

Understanding the onset of these two forms of spatial representation, and also in what sorts of tasks they are used, is crucial for the interpretation not only of developmental data but for the neuropsychological studies described in other sections of this book. We all agree that the knowledge required for locomotion through space or for perception of space differs from the knowledge needed to imagine or think about space. But as Liben points out, we have often not engaged in the task analysis that is necessary to understand the kinds of processes that are required for a given task. We must also be sensitive to the possibility that younger children are using one sort of process and adults another, even if both types of process are in place and usable at both ages.

A simple example is the manipulation of a stacking toy. The year—old child may solve this problem in a purely procedural way. While engaging in the task the infant may also be carrying out the perceptual analysis that is required to form a bit of accessible knowledge about order relations. But even though the task *can* be solved in a purely procedural fashion, it seems unlikely that an adult engaged in the same task would typically rely solely on this form of knowledge. Indeed, it is amnesic adults' exclusive reliance on procedural knowledge to solve this type of problem that seems so startling to us (Cohen, 1984). In addition, as Pick points out, there are also likely to be differences in what children and adults attend to when solving such problems. Pick notes that children may expend a lot of attention on guidance of their behavior rather than acquiring new spatial concepts. Concentration on the execution of a procedure means that the child has less attention to expend of the sort that is required to store spatial information in an accessible form.

THE PRIMACY OF TOPOLOGICAL CONCEPTS

I return now to the issue with which I began. Once accessible representations are formed, what kinds of information do they contain? As far as perceptual and motor procedures are concerned, Euclidean information is obviously used from birth. The newborn distinguishes straight from curved lines (Fantz & Miranda, 1975) and the four-month-old reaches out accurately to intercept a moving object (von Hofsten, 1983). Awareness is not required for this kind of activity, just as we are not aware of the complexities of proportion, shading, and contour that we use when we recognize familiar faces. But what about the kinds of information that are accessible to us?

The concepts that Piaget and Inhelder (1956) used to describe early accessible representations of space were the topological notions of proximity or neighborhoods, continuity of lines, order of succession of points, and enclosure. Although Piaget and Inhelder imply that these topological relations can be given a strict mathematical interpretation, their definitions are not the same as those of mathematicians (see Mandler, 1983). There would be nothing wrong in such an adaptation, as long as the psychological definitions of topological concepts were clearly specified. But they have not been, and have been loosely used by many psychologists who have adopted the terminology. Thus, the topological concept of neighborhood has been widely used to mean proximity to a landmark. But neither in topology nor Euclidean geometry is one point designated as a landmark and another as secondary. Consequently, the use of a landmark by either child or adult implicates neither kind of representation. Similar comments can be made about representing something as in or on something else. As Johnston points out, "in" and "on" are two of the earliest spatial concepts the child acquires. Yet "in" is distinguished in topology, whereas "on" is not. Other early aspects of spatial reference, such as "up" and "down" are not topological concepts at all.

It seems that we would be better off specifying a list of the primitives used to construct any spatial representation, then to study how and when they are acquired *and* the extent to which both children and adults rely on them. It is sometimes assumed that topological relations must be more accessible to young children than metric ones merely because they are topological. Yet many topological concepts are highly sophisticated. A charming book by Sauvy and Sauvy (1974), apparently designed for teachers to use with elementary school children, is full of topological puzzles, some of which seem, at least to this reader wrestling with them, more suitable for adults than for children.

Johnston suggests one important determiner of the order in which spatial concepts are acquired, namely, the number of elements involved in the computation. She points out that "next to" requires a single decision about the relative proximity of two points, whereas a judgment of "in back of" requires the coordination of three elements (the observer and two points), and in addition requires a computation involving the order of the elements. Similar considerations apply to the concept of "between," except that an axis including the observer can for the most part be ignored. Liben makes a similar point when she notes that some developmental differences in the effects of barriers on spatial representations are observed because the methods of judgement required by the task exceed children's processing capacity. What at first glance appears to be a differential reliance on topological versus Euclidean encoding, upon further analysis appears to be confounded with the computational requirements of the methods used to elicit the judgments.

Whether or not we wish to call concepts such as "between" or "next to" topological, they are different from metric concepts. When might the latter be acquired? For example, when might the child's concept of a square include the notion of straight lines or four corners? I noted earlier that the perceptual apparatus provides at least some metric information from birth, and some simple numerical distinctions as well (Strauss & Curtis, 1984), so the information necessary to form the concept of a straight line or four corners is potentially available from an early age. Because of the paucity of experimental work on infant perception at the time that Piaget and Inhelder formulated their theory, they did not know that Euclidean perception was possible for the infant. They assumed that early perception was topological in nature and that one of the main accomplishments of the sensorimotor period was the acquisition of the ability to perceive straight lines and other Euclidean distinctions. Hence, their launch site for representation was based on the presumed characteristics of early perception.

The viability of their theory does not require that spatial representation be preceded by similar perceptual developments. Nevertheless, much of its plausibility derives from this presumed parallelism. Once it was discovered that infants perceive Euclidean information, it became reasonable to ask just why such distinctions should take four years or more to emerge in children's spatial thinking. In fact, the belief that preoperational children lack Euclidean representation has been disputed for a good many years. A number of investigators have found representational distinctions between curvilinear and rectilinear shapes, as well as between circular and elliptical forms, at a relatively early age (see Mandler, 1983). Even some of Piaget and Inhelder's (1956) own observations give evidence of Euclidean representation. For example, they reproduce a young child's drawing of a square as a closed form of indeterminate shape, but which includes four hatch marks that presumably were meant to represent the four angles. Piaget and Inhelder call this a "symbolic suggestion" of Euclidean information, but clearly it is difficult in translating this information to the page rather than lack of the information itself that is responsible for such a production. As has been frequently observed, drawing is not an appropriate way to assess the presence or absence of a given type of information in a representational system.

It seems to me that the work of Landau and her colleagues on the ability of a young blind child to construct a spatial representation of a room provides better evidence for the kinds of information that are accessible to young children. Liben is unhappy about the conclusions that I drew from this work (Mandler, 1983). However, I will reiterate those conclusions. Not all of Landau's work on which I based my opinion in 1983 was published at that time, but it has now been formally presented in a detailed publication (Landau, Spelke, & Gleitman, 1984; see also Landau's chapter in this volume).

Liben objects that the child could have solved the problems she was set solely on the basis of procedural knowledge. However, Landau et al. had ample evidence that they were studying representational activity. They used extensive controls to rule out contamination by potential perceptual cues in the environment, such as sound cues, experimenter cues, or echolocation. In a number of separate experiments they found that the child used angle information to locate objects via paths she had never traversed before. She was also able to use a tactile map to assess angular information, an activity usually considered to be representational in nature. Her distance estimation was less accurate, but on the other hand was not absent. Liben was unhappy because the child committed large distance errors (3.5 ft or 70%). However, the child made such a large error only once and was considerably more accurate on the other trials. Considering that she was estimating the distance of a spot she had never seen in a relatively unexplored space (and doing so without feedback), her performance seems quite remarkable. Landau et al. were probably being overly conservative when they concluded that the child's distance estimates were "moderate to poor." For one thing, in order to compute the correct angle to get from one location to another, distance information is required; that is, one must know how far one has travelled from the first point to the second in order to figure out the correct angle to reach the third.

In any case, Liben's discussion reminds me of the argument about being just a little bit pregnant. If all known perceptual cues to the solution of a spatial task are eliminated, the parsimonious conclusion should be that the child is operating on the basis of her representational capacity. Either the child represents some Euclidean information or she does not. Inferring angle information alone would suffice to reach the conclusion that she does.

HYPOTHESES ON SPATIAL COGNITIVE DEVELOPMENT

Concluding that Euclidean information is represented from an early age does not, however, tell us which of the alternative hypotheses I mentioned earlier may be correct. There does not appear to be enough experimental work at present to provide a complete evaluation. Nevertheless, there are a number of indications that the first hypothesis is incorrect. There is relatively little evidence to suggest a switch from primary reliance on topological information in the early years to primary reliance on Euclidean information in adulthood (see Mandler, 1983). The spatial primitives of landmarks, containment, support relations, and so forth seem to be basic at all ages, with metric information secondary. Certainly the many distortions shown in representational activity even in adulthood indicate the imprecision of our Euclidean encoding. Liben cites examples of adults' difficulties with the representation of horizontal and vertical lines. Stevens and Coupe (1978) provide evidence for the pervasiveness in adult spatial thought of the notion of regions that contain things, often with little metric information about the distance of one point to another when the points reside in different regions. Many adults' distance estimates are poor, even when perceptual cues are available. Landmarks play important and distorting roles in the formation of cognitive maps at all ages. Many other examples could be cited. In short, a number of non-Euclidean properties seem to be the most essential aspects of spatial knowledge at all ages. We code things as inside or outside of regions, nearby landmarks, on or under other things. Typically we do not process metric details because they are unnecessary for our usual commerce with the environment. And when we do not attend, we do not represent.

Nevertheless, there is a great deal of data showing that with increased experience metric relations become more accurately encoded and represented. At the same time, the increase in accuracy that accrues with experience occurs with spatial primitives as well (Mandler, 1983). The work described by Linda Acredolo in this volume shows that as children begin to locomote through space they pay better attention to where things are located. The increased attention alone means that their representations are more apt to contain accurate information, whether of primitives such as proximity relations or of metric ones such as the degree of proximity. In other words, increased accuracy by itself should not be taken to mean the onset of a new form of representation.

In summary, I believe that the second hypothesis will turn out to be correct. There is a basic superstructure of spatial representation that may take time to be constructed, but once it is in place it remains the same throughout life. Although many of the primitives of this superstructure can be characterized as topological in nature, others such as "up" and "down" cannot. We need to examine these properties thoroughly and also to examine just why our spatial representations, even as they become more accurate with experience, still tend to remain somewhat sketchy and distorted.

ACKNOWLEDGMENT

Preparation of this chapter was supported in part by National Science Foundation Grant BNS 81-09657.

REFERENCES

Ashmead, D. H., & Perlmutter, M. 1980. Infant memory in everyday life. In M. Perlmutter (Ed.), *New directions for child development: Children's memory* (Vol. 10). San Francisco: Jossey-Bass.

Cohen, N. J. 1984. Amnesia and the distinction between procedural and declarative knowledge. In N. Butters & L. R. Squire (Eds.), *The neuropsychology of memory*. New York: Guildford Press.

Fantz, R. L., & Miranda, S. B. 1975. Newborn infant attention to form of contour. *Child Development*. 46:224-228.

Hofsten, C. von. 1983. Catching skills in infancy. *Journal of Experimental Psychology: Human Perception and Performance*. 9:75-85.

Landau, B., Spelke, E., & Gleitman, H. 1984. Spatial knowledge in a young blind child. *Cognition.* 16:225-260.

Mandler, J. M. 1984. Representation and recall in infancy. In M. Moscovitch (Ed.), *Infant memory.* New York: Plenum.

Mandler, J. M. 1983. Representation. In J. H. Flavell & E. M. Markman (Eds). *Cognitive development.* Vol. 3 of P. Mussen (Ed.), *Manual of child psychology.* New York: Wiley.

Piaget, J., & Inhelder, B. 1956. *The child's conception of space.* London: Routledge & Kegan Paul.

Sauvy, J., & Sauvy, S. 1974. *The child's discovery of space: From hopscotch to mazes.* Baltimore: Penguin.

Stevens, A., & Coupe, P. 1978. Distortions in judged spatial relations. *Cognitive Psychology.* 10:422-437.

Strauss, M. E., & Curtis, L. E. 1984. Development of numerical concepts in infancy. In C. Sophian (Ed.), *Origins of cognitive skills.* Hillsdale, N.J.: Lawrence Erlbaum Associates.

EFFECTS OF DIFFERENT EARLY EXPERIENCES ON THE DEVELOPMENT OF SPATIAL COGNITION

20

DIANE LILLO-MARTIN
University of Connecticut

PAULA TALLAL
University of California, San Diego

The approaches to understanding the brain bases and development of spatial cognition in this book have taken many paths. When trying to discover how the normal human brain functions within any particular realm, one route to take is to examine functions in a related realm, or functions under different-than-normal circumstances. This is the approach taken by the authors in this final section. These chapters present information about how different circumstances—in this case, different early experiences—do and do not affect the normal course of development of spatial cognition. It is interesting that in many cases, these studies bring out the unexpected: examples of effects and lack of effects that to some extent are surprising. Yet, these results fit together in interesting ways, with common themes leading to a model of the development and representation of spatial cognition and other functions. There are caveats to keep in mind; cautions that inferences about the "normal" condition cannot be unequivocally derived from studies of individuals in some way different from the norm. There are also many implications for future study, ideas and new directions. By looking carefully at the methods, results, and discussions of a variety of studies using different populations, suggestions can be raised and theories synthesized which may add to our understanding of the development of spatial cognition. Perhaps this approach will provide unique information that would be difficult to obtain using other research approaches.

THEMES AND ISSUES

There are three main issues within the brain bases and development
of spatial cognition that the chapters in this section address: the
rationalist/empiricist question, autonomy, and brain organization.

Rationalism/Empiricism

The rationalist/empiricist question focuses on whether innate principles exist which shape the development of a particular domain of
cognition. Several of the chapters support the theory that such principles do exist, especially in the areas of language and spatial cognition. For example, in Barbara Landau's chapter, "Spatial
Knowledge in Blind and Sighted Children," it was shown that in
four domains (perception of objects, navigation by short-cuts, physical representations of space, and the language of space and vision),
blind children develop spatial cognitive abilities comparable to those
of sighted children. In related work, Landau and Gleitman (1985),
the development of blind children's linguistic abilities is also found
to be comparable to that for sighted children. Landau argues that
the development of these abilities, despite the vast differences in
environmental factors, supports the theory that both blind and
sighted children face the tasks of language and spatial cognitive
development with certain innate organizing principles. As Landau
says, "These facts suggest that some basic principles of children's
developing knowledge systems arise independently of the nature or
degree of particular experiential confrontations with the physical
world. Whether the child confronts the environment mainly by hand
or by eye, she is capable of using these principles to construct a spatial world populated by objects, and events" (this volume).

Joan Stiles-Davis' chapter, "Spatial Dysfunctions in Young Children with Right Cerebral Hemisphere Injury," reports on studies
with right- and left-hemisphere damaged infants on several manipulative classification tasks, which also support innate organizational
principles for spatial cognition. Her studies showed that the right-
hemisphere damaged infants could display normal ability to identify
class relations, as long as the expression of these relations did not
require spatial grouping. However, on spatial groupings and the
range of spatial relations expressed, the right-hemisphere damaged
infants were impaired compared to the left-hemisphere damaged
children who performed similarly to the normals on the spatial
tasks. These early localization findings also suggest that separate
principles, which generally show up in separate cerebral areas, guide

the development of spatial cognitive functions. Stiles-Davis thus suggests, "the developing brain is not, even very early in life, equipotential for all functions" (this volume).

If innate organizing principles do guide the development of spatial cognition, then findings of normal development of spatial cognition even with vast changes in the environment, such as those Landau discussed, are to be expected. In addition, Pettito and Bellugi's findings (discussed in more detail below) follow from a theory of separate principles guiding the development of spatial and linguistic functions. If language development is guided by specifically linguistic principles, then the influences that the spatial modality might otherwise afford on the acquisition of American Sign Language(ASL) should be negligible. Furthermore, early localization of cerebral dominance for these functions, as brought out in Stiles-Davis' chapter, and the chapter by Witelson and Swallow, would be predicted in a model of innate principles.

Autonomy

The second issue is that of modularity, or autonomy of various cognitive functions. Are all cognitive functions so related that they are tied and interweaved together, or are separations evident at some level?

In Ursula Bellugi, Helene Sabo, and Jyotsna Vaid's chapter, "Spatial Deficits in Children with Williams Syndrome," a group of children with a specific metabolic disorder known as Williams Syndrome were studied. These children are generally mentally retarded, but as this chapter shows, their profile is not even. Rather, some areas of cognition (such as Piagetian conservation tasks) are highly impaired, while language is much closer to chronological age level and sophisticated in many ways. In addition, there is an uneven profile even within spatial cognitive tasks: visuoperceptive skills are well within the normal range, while visuospatial skills are greatly impaired. It is known from studies of the aphasias that language can be selectively, and even differentially, impaired. Yet, this dissociation of spatial, linguistic, and other cognitive areas in children with Williams Syndrome shows that not only can language be selectively preserved, but even visuopatial abilities can be preserved over visuoperceptual ones, thus supporting an autonomous view of these various functions.

Laura· Petitto and Ursula Bellugi, in "Spatial Cognition and Brain Organization: Clues from the Acquisition of a Language in Space," discussed the acquisition by deaf children with deaf, signing parents of a language in which many grammatical constructs are expressed using spatial relations, American Sign Language. For example, in the acquisition of first- and second-person deixis ("me" and "you"), the spatial-gestural nature of the lexical items (actually pointing to the appropriate referent) might be predicted to facilitate deaf children's acquisition, despite the fact that young hearing children learning spoken languages often have particular problems learning the correct referents to first- and second-person terms. However, the deaf children, like the hearing children, do go through stages of not using first- and second-person terms, then using them incorrectly, and finally using them appropriately, at about the same ages as the hearing children's stages. These results indicate, perhaps surprisingly, that despite the obvious visual-spatial cues intrinsic to learning this aspect of ASL, the linguistic function appears to take precedence in acquisition. Petitto and Bellugi also report that similar results are found in studies of brain-damaged, deaf signers. Right-hemisphere damaged patients, although displaying severe spatial deficits, do not display linguistic deficits in their signing. Conversely, left-hemisphere damaged patients do have linguistic deficits, including the spatially represented syntax, without major spatial cognitive deficits. This implicates left hemisphere processing of ASL, consistent with its linguistic function, but not right hemisphere predominance, despite its spatial nature. These data provide further support for the separability of functions.

If linguistic and spatial components of behavior were not to some degree autonomous, then it would be expected that the spatial nature of ASL would influence its acquisition, and that a deficit in the spatial cognition of Williams children would result in an equivalent deficit in linguistic abilities. Furthermore, the visuospatial deficit alongside normal visuoperceptive skills indicates separable components even within spatial cognition. Thus, the findings reported by Petitto and Bellugi, and by Bellugi, Sabo, and Vaid, support an autonomy model. In addition, the separation of linguistic from spatial functions in early brain damaged infants discussed by Stiles-Davis, and separation of visual from spatial-cognitive abilities in blind children discussed by Landau, also support the theory that some degree of modularity or autonomy is present. In Stiles-Davis' words, "These children represent a kind of 'natural experiment' for observing the dissociation of cognitive functions during development" (this volume); yet as she notes, "it does not rule out the possibility that the functions may interact in a noncontingent way during the normal course of development" (this volume).

Brain Organization

The third issue is that of brain organization and plasticity for these various functions. The studies here support a moderate approach to this question; while the well-known left- and right-hemisphere distinctions are upheld, some degree of plasticity, transferability, and compensatory change are indicated.

Helen Neville's chapter, "Cerebral Organization for Spatial Attention," looked at deaf individuals who had acquired American Sign Language as their native language. Using event-related brain potentials, Neville explored the brain activity of deaf subjects, hearing subjects with no knowledge of ASL, and hearing subjects who had themselves had deaf, signing parents, so that they also acquired ASL as a native language (along with spoken English). She investigated brain activity on a task involving the perception of motion in peripheral visual areas. She found that auditory deprivation and early exposure to a visual language have strong and differing effects on the brain's processing of peripheral spatial tasks. The deaf subjects, unlike either hearing group, showed enhanced occipital activity in both hemispheres, displaying compensatory hypertrophy, a mechanism which has been found in previous animal studies. On the other hand, the deaf and hearing groups with early exposure to ASL both showed increased activity over the left temporal-parietal regions, compared to the hearing group with no knowledge of ASL, displaying functional reallocation, which also has been found in previous animal studies.

In a similar study by Poizner and Tallal (1985), deaf signers and normally hearing subjects who did not know sign language were found to perform equally well on a series of fine-grained, visually presented psychophysical tasks. That is, no compensatory performance was found. One of the differences between Poizner and Tallal and Neville's studies was the location of presentation of the visual stimuli to be processed; whereas Neville presented stimuli to the periphery, Poizner and Tallal presented them to the fovea. There were also differences in stimuli and methods between the two studies. Neville used perception of apparent movement of white squares, while Poizner and Tallal used critical flicker frequency and two-point thresholds signals with no verbal labels. Whereas Neville's task tapped the secondary, or "where" visual system, Poizner and Tallal's tasks tapped temporal and primary, or "what" visual systems. The different results for the two studies thus suggest the specificity of neurophysiological development. Rather than a general enhancement of overall visual processing skills resulting from learning language through the visual modality, specific compensations can be observed.

These results indicate that the left hemisphere lateralization of a language which crucially uses the perception of movement might cause some of the structures which mediate the perception of movement to also be more left lateralized than in normally hearing people without the knowledge of a spatial language. Thus this chapter supports left hemisphere specialization for language, even a visual-spatial language, although a moderate approach with regards to brain reorganization must be taken.

Sandra Witelson and Janice Swallow's chapter, "Developmental Neurocognitive Studies of Spatial Cognition" reviewed studies with normal and brain-damaged children which investigate whether right hemisphere specialization for spatial cognitive functions is present at all for young children, whether it is present but to a lesser degree than in adulthood, or whether it is strongly present even from infancy. This work indicates that (as with left hemisphere specialization for language), some right hemisphere specialization for spatial cognitive functions appears to be present from infancy. This specialization increases as general cognitive growth increases, with important maturational points at age 5 years and puberty. This somewhat weakened early localization approach is warranted by studies which show some limited plasticity and transferability of function after right hemisphere damage. Just as the right hemisphere alone cannot seem to handle some aspects of complex syntax even after early left hemisphere damage (or hemispherectomy) and transfer of function, so too the lone left hemisphere cannot perform spatially as well as the intact brain or even a lone right hemisphere.

Overall, then, it appears that *function* rather than *form* dictates cerebral organization, at least for language and spatial cognition. Linguistic material is left-lateralized in all of the studies cited. Furthermore, although the behavioral manifestations of the development of spatial cognition was found to be dissociated from linguistic abilities and environmental factors in the Williams children and the blind, cerebral lateralization for some spatial functions was found to be affected by congenital deafness and by the acquisition of a spatial language. It remains to be seen if some functional reallocation or compensatory hypertrophy is found in blind individuals, but their presence in the deaf and signing subjects indicate that some plasticity is available in the human brain. As Neville summarizes, "These results...suggest that the left hemisphere is innately predisposed to serve as the substrate for the acquisition of language, but that critical parameters of the language play a role in specifying other functions that the left hemisphere will mediate, and those which the right hemisphere subserve" (this volume).

MODEL FOR THE DEVELOPMENT OF SPATIAL COGNITION

The issues addressed and conclusions drawn in the above studies could lead to the following model of the development and representation of spatial cognition. In this model, some innate principles, or underlying structures, are proposed, which guide the growing child to organize various types of information in particular ways. These principles are specific to various domains of cognition, such as spatial cognition, language, etc., and are autonomous of one another; each is also predisposed to localize in certain areas of the brain. There are connections between these areas, and possible interactions during development. Disruptions in one modality do not necessarily cause disruptions in another, although compensatory increases are possible.

Should damage occur in an area which is predisposed to handle certain functions, then under some circumstances (such as early age) those functions can be subserved by other areas; however, such transferred abilities do not reach the same levels of complexity as when processed by the original areas. This is an approach of nativism and modularity, but with some moderation in recognition of the changes and limited plasticity seen. Perhaps Chomsky's (e.g. 1980) analogue of a mental organ is appropriate: like the growth of an organ such as the heart or kidneys, nourishment and the state of the environment can have an effect on the growth of the mental organs of language, visuoperceptual functions, classification skills, etc.; but only in severely aberrant cases will the heart not grow at all, or grow into something else.

CAVEATS AND COMMENTS

This discussion, while informed by many other studies with adults and normally developing children, takes into consideration much data from children and adults with "different" early experiences. As such, it should be kept in mind that studies of "different" do not unequivocally provide information pertaining to the norm; studies of children do not necessarily lead to conclusions about adults; studies of the *product* of behavior do not always tell us about the *process* of of behavior. This is not to deny the relevance of such studies. To the contrary, it emphasizes the importance of examining a variety of studies, taking several vantage points, to create a synthesized whole. The chapters in sections one and two of this book, focused on spatial cognition in adults and the development of spatial cognition, together with those in section three, pertaining to the effects of different early experiences, contribute to a more complete picture of the brain bases and development of spatial cognition.

Along another line, there is a different aspect of spatial cognition that has not yet been addressed directly, although many of the studies in this section and in others may actually relate to it. This is the notion of temporal perception, and the question of the relationship between the development of temporal and spatial perception. Many of the studies in this book (e.g. Anderson's, Shepard's, Neville's) have a critical temporal component in their tasks of apparent motion, or localization in space, which has not been factored out. Notice that in this context, temporal does not mean temporal order, but the extent to which temporal analysis enters into various aspects of spatial analysis. Some questions to consider include how rapidly spatial information must be perceived, and to what extent temporal components are critical for specific aspects of spatial perception. This consideration brings out the point that interactions of spatial processing with other, related areas, such as temporal processing, is an integral part of understanding spatial cognition.

FUTURE DIRECTIONS

Each of the chapters in this section has left some questions unanswered. Related studies are underway to address many of these questions. As future technologies and procedures open up, many new questions can be, and are being raised.

For example, Witelson and Swallow have suggested that more studies with brain-damaged infants be done, to assess spatial-cognitive deficits soon after damage, so that real deficits rather than recoverability factors are measured. Stiles-Davis is presently undertaking just this type of study. More studies of this kind are needed. Stiles-Davis, in her chapter, highlights the question of deficit versus delay. That is, will young brain damaged infants such as those in her study eventually achieve the same level of spatial cognition as normal children? Will the brain damage cause only a delay in the maturational timetable, or will it result in permanent deficit? Additional studies addressing these questions, and the related question of just how much knowledge, once lost, is recoverable, are indicated. Bellugi, Sabo, and Vaid's study of the Williams children also suggests that attention should be paid to the difference between visuospatial and visuoperceptual skills. Are there differences in the development of these areas which could be brought out in the studies of brain damaged infants?

Petitto and Bellugi's study on the development of American Sign Language brings to mind questions about the development of spatial cognition in the young deaf child. Will there be differences in the development of spatial cognition between deaf and hearing children? Neville's findings concerning the effects on adult spatial cognition of early lack of hearing and exposure to a visual languagu suggest that additional studies comparing deaf and hearing subjects are warranted. Neville's work also suggests that studies of neurophysiological compensation in other populations might be fruitful. For example, would the blind children that Landau studied display any cerebral localization differences?

As these and other questions are addressed, the understanding of spatial cognition, its development and brain bases is increased. Not all studies give the same results; not all authors agree on how to interpret those results. The collection of a variety of studies such as those in this book, however, gives each reader the opportunity to form their own interpretations and analyses, and to formulate new issues and questions.

REFERENCES

Chomsky, N. 1980. Rules and Representations. *Behavioral and Brain Sciences.* 3: 1-61.

Landau, B., and Gleitman, L. R. 1985. *Language and Experience: Evidence from the Blind Child.* Harvard University Press.

Poizner, H., and Tallal, P. 1985. Temporal Processing in Deaf Signers. Submitted to *Brain and Language.*

AUTHOR INDEX

Page numbers in *italics* indicate references; page numbers followed by n indicate footnotes.

SUBJECT INDEX

A

Adrenal hyperplasia, congenital, 399–400
Adults, spatial cognition in, 415–420
  model of, 111–134
  neurobiological basis of, 57–75
  neuropsychology of, 5–26
  role of transformation in, 81–101
Agnosia, visuospatial, 8–9
American Sign Language (ASL), see Sign
  language
Amnesia, see also Memory
  anterograde, 119, 120–121
  retrograde, 119
  topographical, 61–62, 113
Apraxia, Constructional, see Construc-
  tional apraxia
Arousal, mediation of, asymmetrical, 20
ASL (American Sign Language), see Sign
  language
Attention, 115, 121–124, 327–338
  parietal physiology and, 74
Attentional deficits, see Hemi-inattention
Attention-arousal hypothesis, neglect
  syndrome and, 19
Auditory localization, 117
Autotopagnosia, 11
Ayres Space Visualization Test, 291

B

Benton Line Orientation test, 117–118,
  290–291
Benton Test of Facial Recognition, 118–
  119, 293–294
Blindness, 148–150, 434
  attention and, 328–329
  spatial knowledge and, 174–177, 343–
  368, 429–430, see also Knowledge
Block Design Test, 288–289
Body image, 119
  spatial inattention and, 122
Boston Diagnostic Aphasia Examination,
  285–287
Brain lesions, see Cerebral lesions;
  specific type

Brodman Area 7A, intraparietal, 70–71
  representation of space in, 72–73
Brodman Area 7B, intraparietal, 71

C

Cerebral lesions, 5–26, 434–435, see also
  Left hemisphere lesions; Parietal
  lobe; Right hemisphere lesions
  cortial visual systems and, 9–10
  early work on visuospatial disorders
  and, 6–9
  mental imagery and, 35–46
  nature of spatial impairment and, 11–
  14
  representation deficit and, 23–25
  syntax breakdown with, 318–320
  topographical orientation disorders
  and, 14–17
  unilateral neglect and, 17–23
Charcot-Wilbrand syndrome, 62
Child(ren)
  blind and sighted, spatial knowledge
  in, 174–177, 343–368, 429–430
  brain-damaged, neurological and
  behavioral examinations for, 255
  deaf, see also Sign languages
  storytelling by, 313–316
  drawing in, 231–244, 261–262
  preschool
  logical and spatial operations in,
  210–226
  spatial activity versus spatial cognition in, 173–179
  spatial representation versus spatial
  knowledge in, 208–210
  right hemisphere specialization in, see
  Right hemisphere specialization
  spatial dysfunctions in, right hemisphere injury and, 251–269, see also
  Right hemisphere injury
  verbal representation of spatial location by, 195–202
Classification tasks, 253–259
Cognitive maps, 177–178